THE BATTLE OF LONDON

THE
BATTLE
OF LONDON

TRUDEAU, THATCHER, AND THE FIGHT FOR CANADA'S CONSTITUTION

FRÉDÉRIC BASTIEN

TRANSLATED BY JACOB HOMEL

DUNDURN
TORONTO

Editor: Allison Hirst
Design: Courtney Horner
Printer: Webcom
Cover design by Jesse Hooper

Library and Archives Canada Cataloguing in Publication

Bastien, Frédéric, 1969-

[Bataille de Londres. English]
    The battle of London : Trudeau, Thatcher, and the fight for Canada's Constitution / by Frédéric Bastien ; translated by Jacob Homel.

Translation of: La bataille de Londres.
Includes bibliographical references and index.
Issued in print and electronic formats.
ISBN 978-1-4597-2329-0

    1. Constitutional history--Canada. 2. Separation of powers--Canada.
3. Federal government--Canada. 4. Canada--Politics and government--
1980-1984. 5. Great Britain--Politics and government--1979-1997. I. Title.
II. Title: Bataille de Londres. English.

KE4199.B3713 2014   342.7102'9   C2014-904977-3
KF4482.B38 2014   C2014-904978-1

1   2   3   4   5   18   17   16   15   14

We acknowledge the support of the **Canada Council for the Arts** and the **Ontario Arts Council** for our publishing program. We also acknowledge the financial support of the **Government of Canada** through the **Canada Book Fund** and **Livres Canada Books**, and the **Government of Ontario** through the **Ontario Book Publishing Tax Credit** and the **Ontario Media Development Corporation**.

We acknowledge the financial support of the Government of Canada through the National Translation Program for Book Publishing, an initiative of the *Roadmap for Canada's Official Languages 2013-2018: Education, Immigration, Communities*, for our translation activities.

VISIT US AT
Dundurn.com | @dundurnpress
Facebook.com/dundurnpress | Pinterest.com/dundurnpress

Dundurn
3 Church Street, Suite 500
Toronto, Ontario, Canada
M5E 1M2

For my wife, Marie-Ève, and my children, Sacha, Rafaelle, and Mickaël

CONTENTS

INTRODUCTION

Let's begin with a now-familiar scene, one that made quite an impression at the time. Let's say it is April 17, 1982, a little after noon in Ottawa. On this historic day, the national capital has put on its finest in order to celebrate the patriation of Canada's constitution. With a crowd of thirty thousand beginning to gather around Parliament despite the grey skies, nine fighter planes screech through the air above the Hill. The main entry that leads to the Peace Tower is bedecked with a seemingly endless red carpet that is linked to a huge platform that had been set up in the middle of the esplanade.[1] A few minutes earlier, with staging worthy of a rock concert, Elizabeth II, Queen of Canada, officially signed the new constitution. That signature would be the symbol of this unique day.

For thousands of spectators, the day had started much earlier. The crowd came from St. John's and Victoria and everywhere in between. At seven in the morning, they were already beginning to arrive in great numbers in the hope of getting the best seats for the ceremony. Here and there, banners were unfurled, their slogans proclaiming "Proud to be Canadian" and "Thank you, *merci*, Pierre."

Some of these demonstrations of patriotism were sincere; others smelled of propaganda. Questioned by journalists, some standard-bearers candidly admitted that they were there under express orders of their employer: the Liberal Party of Canada.[2]

Whether spontaneous or fabricated, the fervour of the crowd attracted hawkers of merchandise. There were T-shirts and buttons for sale, sporting the slogan "Separation, no thanks!" For those who preferred light reading, copies of the new constitutional law were being sold for $2.75, while copies of the Canadian Charter of Rights and Freedoms were being peddled at the bargain price of one dollar.

Shoppers looking for legal erudition were few and far between among the spectators, who were tightly packed along the route taken by the Queen and Prince Philip. The royal couple arrived — following archaic pageantry — in a horse-drawn carriage flanked by officers of the Royal Canadian Mounted Police, clad in their legendary red tunics. The crowd roared as the sovereigns passed by — the prince wearing the uniform of the Royal Canadian Regiment, the Queen in a turquoise dress and a mink stole. All the while, spectators waved tiny Canadian flags, given out for free. Some were even moved to tears as they watched the Queen, who, when she reached the Hill, oversaw the lowering of the Canadian flag and the raising of the flag of the House of Windsor to the top of the Peace Tower.

At the time, no one mentioned this strange paradox: Canada was dusting off its old traditions for a ritual whose purpose was to sacrifice those selfsame traditions in order to build a new country, one that Trudeau wanted to see fundamentally restructured — a hara-kiri of sorts that would, symbolically, take place on the altar of the new nation.

Despite royal protocol and the presence of the Queen, there was no doubt that this fateful day would change Canada forever. The man responsible for that transformation was, of course, Pierre Elliot Trudeau, who, in the parade of dignitaries, came right behind the sovereign. As British High Commissioner John Ford would note, "Mr. Trudeau has bestridden the stage like a colossus. He not only conceived the plot, wrote the script, set the scenario, produced and directed the play and himself performed the leading role but also, through his Government's manipulation of the media, to some extent determined the reaction of the public."[3]

For the occasion, Trudeau was flanked by his three sons, all wearing navy blue suits and — in Sacha and Michel's case — sneakers. The prime minister took his seat on the dais with the other dignitaries, where he would soon be joined by nine of the ten provincial premiers. Like Trudeau, they were all wearing their Sunday best: top hats and tails all around — except for

Alberta's Peter Lougheed, who had put on his everyday suit and tie. "They don't understand that sort of thing in the West," an aide explained.[4]

This small incident did not keep Prime Minister Trudeau from savouring the moment. Congratulations poured in from around the globe. American president Ronald Reagan would write to "Her Majesty" to "give Canada and all Canadians the congratulations of the American people." From South Africa, still under apartheid, Prime Minister P.W. Botha would also send his best wishes, as would the president of the European Community, Gaston Thorn, and the Algerian prime minister, Mohamed Ben Ahmed Abdelghani.

The event would even be celebrated in Havana, where Fidel Castro, Trudeau's old friend, would attend a concert and soirée at the Canadian ambassador's residence to join in the historic moment.[5] The Cuban dictator and the rest of these world leaders were congratulating Trudeau for the patriation of the constitution, meaning that Canada could now unilaterally modify the document without Westminster's approval. The country had cut one of its last ties with the United Kingdom. This new situation attracted media attention from around the world, making front-page news. The *Los Angeles Times* would write: "Canada: Last Colonial Tie Broken."

In short, the world was rejoicing over this newfound independence. But in that short missive he sent out to the heads of state who wrote to him, the prime minister of Canada didn't insist on that particular aspect of the historic day. The man who once claimed that patriation was "a can of worms,"[6] now spoke to his counterparts of his pride at being the father of the Canadian Charter of Rights and Freedoms, which protected liberties and described our common values. In the words of Michael Kirby, who was a close adviser at the time, "the charter of rights was the critical piece … nobody gave a damn about patriation other than provincial premiers."[7]

He would thus make a speech on the sacrosanct Charter that April day, as well as on Quebec's absence from the ceremonies. After having insisted on these new rights that guaranteed francophones outside Quebec and Anglo-Québécois an education in their mother tongue, he claimed to take history as a witness: "Nothing essential to the originality of Quebec has been sacrificed. The Government of Quebec decided that it wasn't enough…. I know that many Quebeckers feel themselves pulled in two directions by that decision. But one needs look only at the results of the referendum in May 1980 to realize how strong is the attachment to Canada among the people of Quebec. By definition, the silent majority does not make a lot of noise; it is content to make history."[8]

As he spoke these words, a gust of wind blew what was left of the prime minister's hair hither and thither[9] — an unexpected cloud loomed on the horizon, blowing in from the Quebec side of the Ottawa River. Trudeau's voice was drowned out by the storm's growing thunder, the crackling of falling rain, the clicking of opening umbrellas, and the rustling of raincoats or large green bags being slipped on by the crowd. In Quebec's absence, Mother Nature's anger seemed indicative of destiny's wrath. A number of guests saw in this storm a sign. Even Trudeau would later wonder whether it wasn't an omen of events to come.[10]

The storm was particularly threatening for the MPs, ministers, provincial premiers, and other dignitaries who were seated on a stage devoid of any protection; only a few were wearing clothes that might protect them from the weather. Some brandished chairs abandoned by their seatmates and hoisted them over their heads. Others imitated Jeanne Sauvé, Speaker of the House of Commons, who stoically endured the rain falling on her suede jacket.

While the celebratory mood might have been dampened by the storm, nothing would prevent the official signing of the constitution, at the risk of droplets washing away the signature of minister André Ouellet, one of the three people who, with the Queen, would sign the document.[11] The other signatory, minister Jean Chrétien, blurted out a heartfelt *Merde!* when his pen refused to co-operate. The Queen couldn't help but smile at his interjection.

Next to Chrétien and Ouellet, Trudeau put his pen to paper, meaning that the three Canadian signatories of the Canadian constitution were from Quebec — perhaps to compensate for Quebec's absence. The Queen, the last to lay down her John Hancock, would refer to this situation in her speech. Her notes almost flew off the stage thanks to a great gust of wind; all the while, hail began to fall on the crowd in a Dantean display. The release of five hundred pigeons disguised as doves, supposed to be climax of the event, lost most of its effect. "At least it is not snowing," the Duke of Edinburgh remarked with very British phlegm. As for the Queen, she'd quip, during the evening's celebration, "I was dry!"[12]

AN EMERGENCY REWRITE

It wasn't only Mother Nature that took aim at the sovereign's speech on that historic day. Indeed, it was rewritten in a complete state of panic in order to find a way to not worsen the pains of a number of Quebeckers who disapproved of the way the constitution had been agreed upon. And so, the weekend preceding the ceremony, unsatisfied by the first draft written by his speechwriter, Jim Moore, Trudeau would summon his adviser André Burelle in order to polish the text, even if the latter's reservations about the constitutional operation had meant he'd been previously pulled off the file. With both men in attendance, the prime minister read aloud Moore's first draft:

> Today is indeed a day of joyous celebration for Canadians who yearn for ever stronger unity of spirit and purpose among all our people. From all parts of Canada they came … they came to speak for the dignity, the rights and the equality of women, helping those who make the laws to remove the hardy barnacles of discrimination which have marred the beauty and freedom of the Canadian ship of state … speaking the many tongues of our many cultures they came….[13]

With these words, Trudeau stopped reading and turned to Moore: "I wish you were describing what really happened, but let's face it, it was a mean process." He then turned to Burelle: "[Even if] I know your initial reticence to collaborate on these texts, I'm asking you to rewrite my weekend's speech as well as the queen's so that our words might not be so far from reality."[14]

Burelle felt that he couldn't recuse himself. He explained that the speeches needed to recognize the dissent and division of Quebeckers, and believed there was a need to evoke changes that would be coming for Quebec. He finished the rewrite the night before the ceremony and ran to 24 Sussex to present it. Examining the new text with satisfaction, the former editorialist for *Cité Libre* allowed himself a rare confidence: "Trudeau told me that when he read my notes strongly denouncing his post-referendum strategy he'd been troubled to the point of risking [finding] himself paralyzed by indecision. This is why he'd decided to push me to the side and surround himself with advisors favourable to the iron will that would be needed to break the impasse in which the country was stuck due to the impossible unanimity needed between the Provinces and Ottawa." [15]

After excusing the man who stopped him from turning in circles, the father of the patriation of the constitution decided it was time to calm things down. And so it would be for the Queen to carry most of the burden, which meant that she would mention "the regretted absence of the Prime Minister of Quebec," despite which "it's only right to associate all Quebeckers to this celebration of renewal, since without them, Canada wouldn't be what it is today." [16] When a journalist asks her to comment on Quebec's boycott, she replied simply and not without empathy: "It's sad." [17]

Indeed, April 17 was not a day of celebration in Quebec, especially in Montreal, where rain also began to fall on the demonstration led by René Lévesque to denounce the event. The contrast between Montreal and Ottawa, between Quebec and the rest of Canada, between Péquistes (members of the Parti Québécois) and federal Liberals, between Lévesque and Trudeau, had never been more striking. Some fifteen thousand demonstrators came to walk through the streets of the city, from Lafontaine Park all the way to Mount Royal, René Lévesque at the helm, wearing a T-shirt, grey vest, and a pair of jeans, flanked by his wife, Corinne, a number of his ministers, and the head of the Quebec Federation of Labour, Louis Laberge. A forest of fleurs-de-lis of all sizes rose from the crowd while a van outfitted with speakers blared out "Quebec for Quebeckers!" The crowd replied with colourful slogans: String up Trudeau! Elizabeth, *go home!*

A concert of honking horns accompanied the demonstrators, an ironic response to the federal government's invitation to honk to celebrate the day. [18]

Parti Québécois ministers were as angry as the rest of the crowd. "We've been royally fucked," Jacques-Yvan Morin claimed, while Bernard Landry raised the morale of the troops by declaring that one day Quebec's flag would fly at the United Nations. [19] As they spoke, a plane overflew the demonstration, dragging behind it a streamer accusing the PQ government of having lost Quebec's right to a veto and asking it to resign from power. The suggestion drew boos throughout the crowd.

This distraction, added to the torrential rain, didn't slow the demonstrators as they walked all the way to George-Étienne Cartier's statue in front of which René Lévesque made a speech. "This Constitution is an aberration built without us, against us and behind our backs. It's somebody else's country." [20]

Yet it wouldn't only be among Quebeckers that dissension was heard. Indeed, the National Indian Brotherhood made the celebration anathema by claiming that any aboriginal who participated in it would be guilty of treason. In fact, First Nations people were furious. They kept their children at home instead of sending them to school, wore black armbands, and flew flags at half-mast on reserves.[21] A number of groups voiced their discontent throughout the country. In Halifax, around fifty Micmac met in front of the lieutenant-governor's mansion, despite the latter being in Ottawa for the official ceremonies. His chauffeur received this unexpected delegation.[22] One spokesperson accused Great Britain, whose Parliament had voted in favour of the patriation of the constitution, of having reneged on a 1752 amity treaty between it and the Micmac Nation. In the new constitution, the spokesperson continued, the Micmac Nation was no longer recognized.

Having First Nations groups blaming Britain does indeed highlight how they perceived the importance of the role of British authorities in this story. In October 1980, when Pierre Trudeau proposed his unilateral measures to patriate the constitution, the provinces that opposed him immediately thought of waging their war on English soil. "Our objective is to have the U.K. Parliament defeat the resolution," a confidential memo prepared for Alberta premier Peter Lougheed explained.[23]

Other rebellious provinces also saw in the United Kingdom an opportunity to ensure their desired outcomes were reached. Trudeau's initial target was to modify the constitution unilaterally despite their opposition, with no one on the Canadian side of the Atlantic able to do anything about it. As Roy Romanow, then Saskatchewan's minister of intergovernmental affairs, wrote, "Only three institutions had the authority to stop the federal government's plan to have the constitution patriated through a unilateral request: the Supreme Court, the Parliament of Canada, and the Parliament of the United Kingdom." And of those three institutions, "Westminster posed the greatest threat. There was no question that it had the legal right to thwart the federal government's plans. The United Kingdom's constitutional position was that its parliament had the authority to enact, or refuse to enact, any provision which was put before it ..."[24]

For Romanow, the importance of the British in the patriation of the Canadian constitution is "one of the most interesting aspects of the story."[25] In fact, the disparity in outlooks was so divisive, the antagonism between both camps so strong, and their fight so all-encompassing that the Battle of London, which we'll be seeing throughout this book, remains the most important dimension of this entire saga. For many readers, it will be difficult to admit that the birth of the new constitutional regime was engineered in Great Britain. How can it be possible, indeed, that such changes could have been determined in Whitehall's corridors, behind the scenes in Westminster? And doesn't this fact cast a shadow on the sacrosanct Charter and highlight the fact that Canadians were at each other's throats with such virulence over this issue that they were compelled, in a way, to ask the British to help them out of the impasse they'd put themselves in?

THE THREE HEROINES OF PATRIATION

The story we're about to explore isn't the one that's been oft-repeated, despite the fact that Pierre Trudeau himself corroborated the interpretation found in these pages. "I always said that it was thanks to three women that we were eventually able to reform our Constitution,"[26] he wrote ten years after the event. Why is it that we owe the patriation to three female figures? How does the role of these women attest to the importance of Great Britain in the whole proceedings?

First off, two members of this trio were British. The first was a character whom we've already spoken of: Elizabeth II. From the get-go she was favourable to patriation. Her advisers kept her informed throughout the process. She was always available to Trudeau's government.

The second, less well-known, was Jean Wadds, the only Canadian among the three heroines. As High Commissioner of Canada to the United Kingdom, she was on the front lines of the Battle of London. A clever political operator, daughter of William Rowe, former leader of Ontario's Conservatives, with whom she'd sat in Parliament, she received the Order of Canada for her essential role in the patriation of the constitution.

It should be said that her task wasn't an easy one. For more than eighteen months she went from one crisis to another. Better than anyone else, Wadds was a prime witness to the extent to which relations between Britain and Canada suffered at the time. A month before the April 17 celebrations, she cabled the following message to Ottawa: "There is a strong feeling in London that Westminster should be invited and represented at the ceremony." The time was ripe to express thanks and to begin "some needed mending with Westminster and the British government. For better or worse only Westminster had the power to pass the Canadian act,"[27] Wadds concluded that it would be correct to invite the speaker of the House of Commons, that of the House of Lords and even a number of government ministers.

This recommendation wasn't received favourably in the federal capital. In the margin of Wadds's telegram, someone even scribbled a sarcastic "Wow!" — a comment on the attitude of British politicians throughout the patriation process. Many of these Britons didn't particularly appreciate Trudeau's methods. "He's played dirty tricks on us," Ian Gilmour said at the time — as he was then Lord Privy Seal, one of the ministers most involved in the patriation portfolio — while one of his colleagues added "Really only a cad would do this."[28] At the end of the Battle of London, Labour MP George Cunningham would summarize the events this way: "I think Mr. Trudeau was impudent in the extreme. But we have paid him back in spades. Our impudence has greatly exceeded his."[29]

The entire process left a sour taste in the mouths of a number of MPs and ministers, including prime minister Margaret Thatcher. She was the third woman who made patriation possible and, by far, Trudeau is most indebted to her. Even in the worst moments of this roiling battle, when she was facing down her cabinet's doubts and a revolt among her MPs, this unique politician kept Trudeau and his charter afloat. Immensely thankful, the latter wanted her to be present at the ceremonies to such an extent that he spared no effort in convincing her to come to Ottawa. But on April 2, 1982, she answered politely:

> Dear Pierre
> I am deeply grateful for your invitation to me to visit Canada on the occasion of the Proclamation of the Constitution Act, 1982, by Her Majesty the Queen. I would have much liked to be with you on this historic occasion, but greatly regret that my commitments here will not allow this. My thoughts will be with you and Canada at the time.[30]

In fact, the Iron Lady didn't seem particularly keen to attend the ceremony, as demonstrated by a note to her written by one of her advisers,

Michael Alexander: "Clive [Linklater] and I both feel that a visit to North America purely for this purpose would probably not be worthwhile, but it could provide the occasion for a quick visit to Washington if you wanted to discuss U.S. economic politics with President Reagan."[31]

Unfortunately for the federal government, Reagan wasn't able to host Thatcher, thus denying Canada her presence. The Lord Chancellor ended up making the trip to Ottawa. To explain the absence of the head of Her Majesty's government, he'd invoke the perfect excuse: the invasion of the Falklands by Argentina — a pious lie that none would question among the flights of dignitaries in the capital, all disappointed by the prime minister's absence.

What was the real reason behind Thatcher's absence? A chance encounter with James McKibben, agent general of Alberta in London, allows us to better understand her state of mind. Bumping into the prime minister at a cocktail reception after patriation, McKibben joked with her: "So I am off your back," referring to the period when Alberta led the charge in London against Trudeau's project. Thatcher, who was never known for her sense of humour, didn't find the joke quite so funny. "Your prime minister told me he would have the support of both houses, that it would not be a problem. He was wrong!"[32]

It should be said that, despite the eighteen requests previously made to Westminster to modify the constitution, the process had never faced such a deluge of criticism, led by a diplomatic offensive by eight dissident provinces. Former diplomat Daniel Gagnier, then at the High Commission of Canada in London, was at centre stage.

> Each Province would "come out swinging" from time to time: they might be for it, against it…. Each Minister, each MP had an opinion, some were very pro-Province because a written Constitution stood against British traditions; others, more conservative, didn't like the idea of the Charter, it was a question of ideology. Others still didn't like Mr. Trudeau, because they saw him as a socialist.[33]

At first, almost no one in London believed the process would be so diffi-cult. But over the months, the provincial rebellion gained in importance, its effects being felt as far as Germany, France, Australia, and throughout the Commonwealth. This caused unexpected, unbelievable, inextricable complications for the Thatcher government. Martin Berthoud, then responsible for North America at the Foreign Office, remembers this intense period: "I spent far more time on Canada than my other responsibilities…. I had to generate a lot of paper which went to Lord Carrington, the Foreign Secretary. One day … I asked the Private Secretary what the hottest issue was at the time. To my surprise (and my gratification), he said 'the Canadian Constitution.'"[34]

And when a diplomat from the British High Commission in Ottawa asked him, almost pleadingly, whether he might be overloading him with the number of summaries, notes, analyses, and press reviews on the constitution that he'd been asking for from the Canadian front, the response he received from Berthoud was unequivocal: "This is a moment of maximum activity on the Canadian constitutional front. Ministers and others seize hungrily on any new information or informed opinion about how things are going or likely to go."[35]

It's easy to understand his point: the battle that unfolded in London was of extreme intensity. A survey of archival sources in the British capital, as in Canada, allowed us to see that London was the location of the decisive episode of the patriation of the constitution: the opposition by the British Parliament was so important that it forced Pierre Trudeau to compromise on certain issues. A Canadian reader of this book will discover here a number of events that occurred on the British political scene, with leading men and women often unknown here. But let's remember that the main topic of this book is Canada, seen and understood through the eyes of our former motherland — involuntary referee of our internal conflicts, often the confidant of one or another camp, and guardian of some of the best-kept state secrets still hidden to this day.

CHAPTER 1

OPENING VOLLEYS

The Constitution Act of 1867 includes no mention of an amendment formula, likely in accordance with London's wishes. The Canadian provinces and the federal government, forced to work within these strictures, quickly adopted practices to exercise constitutional power. When a constitutional modification was necessary, Parliament, after a vote in both chambers, sent an amendment request to the British sovereign, which was then transmitted to the imperial government, introduced in the Parliament of Westminster, and eventually adopted by this last body.

From the very beginning, the provinces contested Ottawa's right to exercise this power without their consent, an objection that was respected by the federal government. Constitutional changes in Canada would only occur after Ottawa had obtained unanimous consent from the provinces (insofar as the changes touched upon their jurisdiction).[1]

At the turn of the 1930s, during the negotiations that eventually led to the Statute of Westminster, the time was ripe for Canada's complete independence. A functional amendment formula had to be found so that the country might "patriate" its constitution; that is, become the sole agent able to modify its own supreme laws. The catch was that the provinces and the federal government were unable to agree. At first glance, the issue seemed rather technical and unlikely to raise passions. But as the constitutionalist Barry Strayer aptly remarked, "The view which one takes of an amending procedure will largely depend on the concept he has of the nature and purpose of the constitution itself."[2]

In other words, agreeing on the number of consenting provinces needed to modify the supreme law of the land would confirm the interpretation of some — while denying that of others — of the nature of the country itself. For example, would the consent of the provinces need to be unanimous or would a simple majority suffice? Or perhaps the level of consent should vary according to circumstances? Would particular provinces have a veto? If so, which ones? And if a veto was given to some provinces and not others, under which principles would the equality between provinces be set aside: The idea of two foundational people? Acquired rights? Demographic weight? Historical communities? The concept of covenant? All of the above?

At the time, despite the abilities of Prime Minister Mackenzie King, a former expert labour mediator, Ottawa was unable to obtain unanimous consent from the provinces for an amendment procedure. As King believed that the federal government couldn't speak in the name of the entire country in constitutional matters, it was finally agreed that the British Parliament should conserve — temporarily — the power to modify Canada's constitution.[3] This was recognized according to Article 7(1) of the 1931 Statute of Westminster. With this law, every dominion became, *de jure*, fully independent — with a few nuances; that is, every dominion except Canada, in constitutional terms.

But as is often the case in politics, what was to be temporary became practically permanent. After Mackenzie King, neither Bennett or St-Laurent in the 1950s, nor Diefenbaker or Pearson in the 1960s, was able to obtain the approval of every province, which would have essentially solved the issue. It should be added that from that point on the rise of Quebec nationalism turned the Canadian political landscape on its head, endowing the constitutional issue with a new dimension. First under Jean Lesage, then doubly so under Daniel Johnson Sr., Quebec's government began affirming the idea that Quebeckers were one of the country's two founding peoples,[4] thus appealing to the new nationalist ideology that was beginning to take shape. According to this logic, the federal government had been insensitive — for decades — to the economically inferior position of French Canadians, a situation that in time would threaten the survival of the nation. The state had to intervene to correct the situation, and only the provincial government could act in an efficient way, being controlled by the francophone majority.[5] Quebec thus requested additional powers and, if need be, special constitutional status. Before Quebec would even consider approving a constitutional amendment formula, the matter in which powers were to be shared had to be revised in a satisfactory manner.

A HERO'S JOURNEY

In this context, the major protagonist of this tale appears: Pierre Elliott Trudeau. Having become minister of justice under Lester Pearson in 1967, he'd overseen the constitutional portfolio, and had kept ownership over it once he became prime minister, one year later. But who was this man considered by many as a sort of Canadian John F. Kennedy, a guarantor of renewal, fighting his way to the loftiest position on the political podium?

He was, above all, a man with a singular path. Born in 1919, he was the son of a dyed-in-the-wool nationalist named Charles Trudeau. Charles was one of a handful of francophones at the time who had made their fortunes in the business world — in the middle on the 1930s, no less. Pierre's mother, Grace Elliott, somewhat more self-effacing, came from anglophone high society and was of Scottish origin. It is she who taught him, from birth, the language of Shakespeare. After a golden childhood, Trudeau threw himself entirely into the nationalist cause, fighting conscription during the Second World War, flirting with far-right ideologies, and pulling provocative stunts like riding his motorcycle on country roads north of Montreal with a German soldier's helmet on his head. Despite his successive escapades, he was secretly cherishing a dream to become prime minister, although he also had hopes for an independent Quebec, which he believed might become reality in 1976.[6]

He was also a man who underwent a decisive break with his own past. As he turned thirty, coming back to Canada after years of study and travel, the man who once saw himself as a hard-line nationalist had become its bitter rival. And there would be no turning back. One after the other, the governments of Duplessis, Lesage, and Johnson Sr. would suffer the wrath of his pen to the extent that, in 1965, the *Cité Libre* polemicist decided to take the plunge into federal politics to better fight against an ideology he now considered odious.

Trudeau was also a character the likes of which Canada had never seen. At the worst of the Cold War, he attempted to reach Cuba from Florida. Minister, then prime minister, he never stopped surprising the public with his actions and words, which would, in time, give birth to "Trudeaumania": he was seen in the company of Barbara Streisand, performed a pirouette behind the Queen's back and a back flip off a diving board, and later roamed the streets of Ottawa at the wheel of his convertible Jaguar.

Trudeau was a politician doubling as an intellectual. He read, spoke, wrote, polemicized, and then abandoned the pen to take up the political sword, a new task he proved himself just as gifted at, facing down the separatists as the FLQ's bombs exploded and the country held its breath.

His favourite battlefield was the constitution. It was from this starting point that he opposed the granting of supplementary powers to Quebec on the basis that it constituted a nation. He was also opposed to a potential decentralization of powers to the provinces. His weapon: full bilingualism, which he sought to spread from coast to coast, so that French Canadians might feel at home across the country, and not only in Quebec. Over the generations, francophones developed a strong attachment to their province. Trudeau came with an abstract vision, at the antipodes of this historical attachment. And he intended to impose this vision, if only he might be given a chance.

And so, for Trudeau, this became the constitutional path to follow. He hit the ground running as soon as he came to power; the first years of his mandate were the scene of frenetic activity. In 1971, a meeting of provincial premiers in Victoria led the provinces to unanimously agree on constitutional patriation. The agreement provided for the integration of a charter of rights and freedoms in the constitution, albeit with limited scope when compared to the one that would become law ten years later. Language rights were limited to the reinforcement of the position of French and English at the federal level and in some provinces. There was no mention of language rights for Anglo-Quebeckers or for francophones outside of Quebec. The amendment formula provided for a veto for any province constituting or having constituted 25 percent of the population, meaning Quebec and Ontario. It would also be necessary to obtain the consent of two out of the four Maritime provinces as well as two of four Western provinces. Finally, the provinces were to be consulted when it came time to nominate judges to the Supreme Court.

The ink wasn't yet dry when Robert Bourassa, Quebec's premier, did an about-face. Quebec sought increased powers, and Trudeau refused to budge on the issue. Criticized from all sides, Bourassa withdrew his support. The agreement fell apart.

The federal prime minister had to wait for more favourable circumstances to emerge before reviving his project; his time would come five years later, May 6, 1976. Trudeau summoned the premiers to Ottawa for a two-day conference on the price of oil, since his government was seeking ways to control its variance. The evening before the discussion, he announced that he was ready to rekindle constitutional talks, but that he intended to sound out his provincial counterparts.[7] He gave them until September 15 to think about it.

Of course, the matter at hand was much too important to not get a rise from politicians and the media alike. The federal-provincial meeting was not yet over when *Le Journal de Montréal*, citing a British source, confirmed that Great Britain would not consent to constitutional patriation without the provinces' support — an approach that Trudeau had been considering, according to hearsay. The Parti Québécois picked up on the issue on the floor of Quebec's National Assembly, demanding an explanation from the British consulate.

In Ottawa, John Johnston, the British High Commissioner (a posting equivalent to that of ambassador in relationships among Commonwealth countries), was far from happy with this turn of events. It must be said that this former colonial administrator had become, by necessity, an expert in crisis management among former colonies. Notably, in 1965, he was the High Commissioner to Rhodesia, which was then controlled by the openly racist government of Prime Minister Ian Smith, who'd declared independence. Nothing to do with Canada, of course, but Johnston believed that the fact that a separatist party like the PQ used Great Britain for purposes of political propaganda was a bad sign indeed. "It seems far preferable to stop further speculation and set the record straight by making it clear by means of a statement or through an inspired parliamentary question,"[8] he sent a message to London. At the Foreign Office — following the lead of Gordon Robertson, the Clerk of the Privy Council in Ottawa whom Johnston regularly consulted — everyone agreed with this proposition. The only issue that remained was the manner in which to deliver this message. Her Majesty's government opted for a little stagecraft at the House of Commons in London. On June 10, 1976, MP John Cartwright asked Minister Roy Hattersley, responsible for the Canadian constitution dossier, whether the government had received a request for patriation and what its reaction would be if it did:

> I have received no proposals from the Canadian Government on this matter. The British North America Acts, which contain the constitution of Canada, can be amended in certain important respects only by act of the United Kingdom Parliament.… If a request to effect such a change were to be received from the Parliament of Canada it would be in accordance with precedent for the United Kingdom Government to introduce in Parliament, and for Parliament to enact, appropriate legislation in compliance with the request.[9]

This comment was sent to the PQ, while the media amply covered it, describing it as a green light given to Ottawa for unilateral patriation. However, this wasn't exactly the case: all the while giving the lion's share of powers to the federal government, the declaration was also written in a way to not explicitly engage the British government and Parliament.[10]

In the days following these events, another federal-provincial summit took place. If they seemed to agree that it was time to take another look at patriation, a number of provinces wanted a little more time. Trudeau replied that he'd be willing to wait until the end of that summer for their proposals.

Bourassa, on his end, did not wait that long. He immediately offered his conditions, demanding that Quebec receive authority over telecommunications, culture, and immigration. These requests would be echoed by the rest of the provinces a few weeks later, in addition to others related to the Supreme Court and powers over spending.[11]

PIERRE TRUDEAU AND THE SCAPEGOAT

By the end of the summer the situation was at an impasse. But Trudeau was determined to act without the provinces, if necessary. What would be the reaction from across the pond? As luck would have it, the British prime minister, James Callaghan, was travelling through Canada for a week. After having arrived in Alberta, where he met with, among other people,

Premier Peter Lougheed, the chief of the British government would then go to Montreal to watch a hockey game between Canada and Czechoslovakia with Trudeau (a game that would end in a 4-4 tie).

The two men then returned to Ottawa together, where the hushed ambiance better suited international meetings. Trudeau underlined the extent to which the current constitutional situation was seen by Canadians as a colonial relic, something he sought to put a term to. This clarification made, he continued with a suggestion that, to say the least, left Callaghan perplexed: "Mr. Trudeau suggested that it would help the Canadians if we were to display some reticence on the subject, since the Canadians would then unite in favour of it. The prime minister thanked Mr. Trudeau for this suggestion, but said that we had no intention of playing the part of whipping boy."[12] Certainly, Pierre Elliott Trudeau had been known for his schoolboy pranks when he attended the Collège Jean-de-Brébeuf; but forty years later, such a suggestion was quite surprising coming from a man who'd become the prime minister of the country.

Despite rejecting this idea out of hand, Callaghan was apparently not insulted, and would continue on his trip, arriving in Quebec City, where he'd spend seven hours with Robert Bourassa. For this visit from a British prime minister in Quebec's capital, the first such event since the famous Churchill-Roosevelt meeting in 1943–44, Quebec's government clearly didn't skimp on trying to impress its visitor. After a visit to Old Quebec, Callaghan was brought to Lac à l'Épaule, a pastoral site ideally positioned to allow visitors to admire the fall colours and enjoy a gastronomic experience. It would be the moment Bourassa chose to reveal his position. Essentially, the premier wanted to know: could Callaghan promise not to patriate the constitution without the unanimous consent of the provinces?[13]

Callaghan, who was by then at his fourth meeting with a provincial premier, was not particularly surprised by this question. His visit to Quebec had been preceded by meetings in Saskatchewan, Ontario, and Alberta; and here again the conversation took the same turn, just as it had in Banff a few days earlier with Peter Lougheed, a conversation that was summarized thusly by one of Callaghan's advisers:

> The Prime Minister took the line which has been taken
> in Parliament on the subject (i.e. the constitution), and

emphasised that we had no wish to intervene in a subject which it was for the Federal Government and the Provincial Premiers to sort out between themselves. Premier Lougheed expressed concern that the Federal Government might try to push the question through without first obtaining Provincial agreement … he saw real problems ahead. The Prime Minister said that, if that situation arose, we might have to take legal advice. But he emphasised that our dealings on the matter would have to be with the Federal Government.[14]

Bourassa, who received the same response as Lougheed, wasn't taken aback. He even began considering triggering elections over the issue of patriation; he would present himself as a bulwark against possible over-extension by Ottawa. The fact that he was even considering this scenario illustrates the deterioration of his relationship with his federal counterpart; the refusal of the Victoria agreement was only the first in a long line of misunderstandings between both men. A new low in their relationship was reached in 1974–75 with the enacting of Bill 22.[15] The Quebec government declared that French would be Quebec's only official language, it imposed "francization" measures on companies and restricted access to English schools through the enactment of language competency tests. These measures provoked all sorts of controversy in Quebec, as well as being in flagrant opposition with the vision of bilingualism Ottawa was attempting to impose on a national scale.

Trudeau obviously didn't appreciate the gesture, and 1976 would not be the year of reconciliation. On March 5, as he was travelling through Quebec, Trudeau took advantage of the opportunity to visit the bunker, the government's headquarters. Bourassa was at that time grappling with an Olympic construction site paralyzed by strikes, sabotage, and corruption, which had made the project's costs explode. A journalist who'd been waiting for the federal prime minister to arrive asked him whether he'd brought a gift, by which he meant some sort of financial contribution, to help pay for the Olympics. "No, but I've brought my lunch," Trudeau replied. "I hear this one only eats all-dressed hot dogs,"[16] referring to *Maclean's* front page showing the premier of Quebec eating a hot dog with the title "The New Bourassa."

A few months later, in early October, this battle of wry remarks continued at a meeting at the Hilton Hotel in Quebec City where, ironically, both men were meeting each other in an attempt at reconciliation. "You're not going to speak to me about the Constitution?" a sardonic Trudeau asked Bourassa. Bourassa answered that he'd prefer receiving $200 million to pay off a portion of Quebec's Olympic debt. I don't have a penny, Trudeau answered, continuing on to say that he could patriate the constitution without Quebec — a comment he would repeat, swaggering, in front of the journalists waiting outside the meeting, claiming that he needed neither Bourassa, nor the Pope, nor Callaghan to modify the supreme law of the land.[17]

Even if half his cabinet was opposed to the idea, Quebec's premier was more decided than ever: he'd ask his people to help stop Ottawa in its tracks. On October 18, he'd trigger elections for the following November 15, confident in his ability to rally undecided voters.[18] However, polls were telling a different story, and, since the last election, the PQ had adopted a more complete political platform that included both better government as well as the idea of *étapisme*, meaning that the question of sovereignty would be answered through a referendum.

As if to add to his government's misfortune, the leader of the Liberal Party led a terrible campaign. Bourassa isolated himself, travelling through Quebec surrounded only by bodyguards, and speaking to journalists solely through pre-recorded messages, a habit that would lead him to earn the new nickname of "Bourassa the cassette tape."[19] *La Presse*, a major newspaper, withdrew its support, and the public didn't seem to understand why elections had been called early despite his government having one hundred MNAs in the National Assembly.

Meanwhile, the PQ's campaign radiated confidence. Lévesque was in great form, and the headlines of the past few years gave him quite enough ammo to mount attacks against the Liberals. There was the question of language with Bill 22, as well as the fight francophone pilots and air traffic controllers were leading to gain the right to speak their language amongst themselves in Quebec, while their opponents banned French for security reasons. Lévesque wasn't shy about denouncing the corruption of the Liberal government, tarnished by a number of scandals since 1974. Finally, the PQ chief accused his rival of kowtowing to Pierre Trudeau.

Two weeks before E-day, the Liberals attempted to agitate fear of separatism in order to regain lost ground. Finance Minister Raymond Garneau spoke of the potential loss of old age pensions, while Jean Marchand, a star candidate in a riding near Quebec City, compared René Lévesque to Stalin and Castro.[20] On his end, Charles Bronfman, the famous anglophone Jewish businessman, declared that PQ supporters were "a bunch of bastards who are trying to kill us,"[21] likening the PQ to the heirs of Nazi Germany.

The Liberals no longer knew which saint to turn to for salvation. Bourassa even announced that he would amend Bill 22 and remove the infamous language tests. Despite everything, by November 15 the die was cast. The initial results immediately foreshadowed a majority PQ victory. From his riding of Taillon, on the South Shore of Montreal, where he began the evening, René Lévesque rode into Montreal via the Jacques Cartier Bridge where the traffic was bumper-to-bumper with spontaneous victory parades. Some climbed on the roofs of their cars, waving flags. A concert of horns accompanied the scene, and the enthusiasm took off when some people recognized René Lévesque, whose cortege was trying to find its way through the crowd.[22] Electoral fever was stronger than hockey fever: in the middle of a game between the Canadiens and the Blues, a cry rang out in the Forum when the PQ victory was announced.

Enthusiasm reached its apex as René Lévesque arrived at Centre Paul-Sauvé. The future premier could barely calm the raving of the crowd, cheering for long minutes as he stood on the stage. If he wore a solemn air, the words he spoke seemed to come to him naturally: "We are not a small people, we might be something of a great people. I never thought I could as proud of being a Quebecker as I am tonight."[23]

Trudeau addressed the nation after Lévesque. For the head of the federal Liberal Party, who had declared the previous summer that separatism was dead, the PQ's victory was a slap in the face. From the federal capital, the atmosphere seemed more hushed than usual, and he reminded everyone, his face static and his eyes cold, that the election didn't mean the advent of an independent Quebec, an option that would be rejected by the majority, he predicted.[24]

A few days later, the sworn enemy of nationalists performed an about-face. He, who had been threatening a month earlier to patriate the constitution unilaterally, suddenly declared himself open to the provinces' demands, affirming that he had in the past negotiated from the perspective of a functional federalism — an interesting project that had been aborted much too early "because it was decided to attempt to patriate the Constitution and agree to an amending formula first, but they could be resumed if and when the provinces wanted to discuss the separation of powers." He concluded by saying that Quebec independence is akin "to sin against the spirit, to sin against humanity.[25]

IN THE SPIRIT OF LORD DURHAM

Be it a sin against humanity or not, it wasn't just in Ottawa that the PQ victory had caused surprise. The news spread like wildfire around the world, including in Great Britain. It was on the front page of British newspapers the next day, with articles being written about it for days afterward. The turn of events caught the attention of Simon Dawbarn, the new British consul in Montreal. He shared with London his point of view on the eventuality of Quebec's independence:

> This is surely a vain hope. Quebec is simply too small, and too much exposed to North American influences, to preserve its chastity. So far as native culture is concerned, it is no good looking for a renaissance because, to put it brutally, the arts do not flourish in Quebec. In the last few weeks alone the Montreal Symphony Orchestra (whose best musicians are American) has chased out the director, the internal blood-letting, and a political pamphleteer has been awarded the prix David. It is not so long since the Quebec Opera folded. Nor does learning flourish all that vigorously. Two of the three French-speaking universities have been closed for several months…. The policies of the PQ can only intensify and perpetuate this parochialism.
>
> At least I am less pessimistic than Bougainville, who (quite a long time ago) wrote: "Woe to this land! It will perish the victim of its prejudices, of its blind confidence, of the stupidity or crookedness of its chiefs. This oracle is more certain than that of Calchas."[26]

If Dawbarn's colleagues were not particularly knowledgeable about Admiral Louis Antoine de Bougainville, they seemed to share his thoughts on the small-mindedness of Quebeckers in general, and Pequistes in particular. This was certainly the case of Terry Empson who, from his seat at the British High Commission in Ottawa, added his own words to the mix: "It seems to me an excellent description of the state of Quebec 'culture,' which, apart from a few *chansonniers*, does not amount to a row of beans. The introspection and parochialism that Simon detects are, if anything, even more noticeable from outside the province."[27]

You'd think you were re-reading the Durham Report, whose ideas seemed to still pervade the ranks of Her Majesty's representatives in Canada. But the fact that the people of Quebec were seen as without history and literature did not change the fact that its potential independence, unimaginable in 1839, would not be without consequence. An analysis was prepared for Anthony Crosland, the Foreign Secretary, in order to explore this theme. Its author, Bertram Anthony Flack, political counsellor at the British High Commission in Ottawa, was not only surprised by the PQ victory, but also by the magnitude of its margins. However, he did point out that the PQ had nothing to do with the Quebec Liberation Front (FLQ), that its team was experienced, and that it wasn't elected with a mandate to proclaim independence. There was no need to be alarmed, at least for now:

> The battle between Quebec and the federal government has not yet been seriously joined and it is impossible to make any precise forecast of the way in which it will be fought, let alone its eventual outcome. Canada faces a worrying and testing period of uncertainty. Canada's friends can only watch with anxiety — particularly to be felt by her allies in NATO, for the PQ's programme includes the withdrawal of an independent (and republican) Quebec from that alliance. For the United States Government a new and uncertain neighbour on its northern frontier pledged also to withdraw from the North American Air Defence Agreement must be disturbing. The argument is, however, an internal Canadian matter and there is no way HMG in the United Kingdom can or should seek to influence it. If

an independent Quebec became an imminent reality, we
should need at that time to consult with our partners in
both NATO and the EEC on the consequences.[28]

The chosen strategy was a simple one: wait and see. But passivity wasn't
the rule if we are to believe the director of the North American Bureau at the
Foreign Office, Ramsay Melhuish, who commented that "if Mr. Lévesque's
drive for independence looks like picking up speed, we would have to consider very carefully whether there might be anything we could do to help
preserve the unity of Canada."[29] What exactly was he thinking of? Impossible
to know. However, apparently whatever Melhuish was talking about was
not carried any farther.

Meanwhile, a first federal-provincial meeting was held in Ottawa, two
weeks after the election. Trudeau wasn't as morose as before, and hoped
to force Lévesque onto the defensive, while the latter intended to present his intentions to his Canadian counterparts. Peter Lougheed gave him
the opportunity over dinner: "What does Quebec want?" Immediately,
the leader of the PQ firmly and calmly answered that he intended to take
Quebec out of Canada, period.[30]

This conversation was recounted to High Commissioner John Johnston,
who wrote: "At the dinner party at 24 Sussex Drive during the December
meeting with the provincial premiers, several of them had sought to sound out
the resolution of Mr. Lévesque over separation.… Lévesque had been absolutely
forthright in stating his determination to take Quebec out of the Federation."[31]

The plans of Quebec's new premier certainly didn't help in advancing the
constitutional issue, an objective that Trudeau hadn't given up on. On January
10, 1977, Johnston took stock of recent events with the Clerk of the Privy
Council, Gordon Robertson. Through Peter Lougheed, the provinces asked
once again for new powers. Trudeau, Robertson explained, reiterated "his belief
that the best course would be to complete patriation *tout court*, and deal with
the distribution of powers thereafter."[32] Thoughtful, Johnston replied that, from
the British point of view, "it seemed very important that patriation should be
effected before any constitutional changes were made, especially if such changes
affect Quebec: the debate should take place in the Canadian Parliament and
not at Westminster."[33] Robertson reassured him: he was entirely in agreement
and had no doubt the federal prime minister shared his point of view.

The High Commissioner seemed satisfied with this answer. The situation might not be as inextricable as it seemed. After all, he noted in a message around the holidays, René Lévesque had publicly declared himself favourable to the patriation of the constitution under certain conditions, one of them being that the right to self-determination of Quebeckers be recognized. A few days later, a new meeting with Robertson reinforced the satisfaction of the British:

> Mr. Robertson made it clear that Mr. Trudeau would not now be proceeding with unilateral patriation. I said I presumed that the overriding consideration in this decision … was a desire to avoid giving Lévesque anything he could exploit. Mr. Robertson confirmed this was so, for two reasons.
>
> Mr. Lévesque would attack unilateral patriation as further evidence of the arrogance of the Federal Government and its preparedness to ride roughshod over the Provinces. He could also argue that this was a move to impose further obstacles in the PQ's path, since patriation on the basis currently proposed would mean that any amendments to the constitution relating to Quebec thereafter could be vetoed by other Provinces. In theory (though this would be against all precedent) the constitutional status quo (in the absence of an amending formula) would leave it open to the Federal Parliament to request an amendment to the constitution related only to Quebec on their own authority.[34]

No major actions would be undertaken any time soon, and Trudeau himself explained this to Callaghan on March 12, 1977. Back in Washington, the British prime minister did a quick hop over to visit his Canadian counterpart, the latter receiving him in his official residence at Harrington Lake, in the Gatineau Park. While journalists were interested only in the matrimonial debacle between Trudeau and his wife, Margaret, the constitution was at the centre of discussions between the two men. Trudeau explained that while patriation was consensual among anglophones, the PQ coming into power complicated the situation. He'd prefer to wait for his Quebec counterpart to compromise himself a bit more.[35]

So whether it was in Ottawa or London, the narrative of the day was patience. But the idea of independence continued to provoke fears among the British, who noted with satisfaction, however, that Lévesque had begun leading a charge against leftists and other dreamers in his party, resolutely distancing himself from some elements of the PQ platform, like withdrawal from the North American Aerospace Defence Command (NORAD) and the North Atlantic Treaty Alliance (NATO), as well as the nationalization of large portions of the industrial sector. However, these guarantees didn't carry much weight on the geopolitical balance, and the hostility of Her Majesty's government didn't seem to abate, as explained by John Johnston in a confidential note in March 1977:

> The fragmentation of Canada would unquestionably be detrimental to the interests of HMG … and the Western world. A small independent power on the North American continent, preoccupied by its own internal concerns and difficulties, neutralist by inclination, and indifferent to the wider interests of the West, would be a matter of concern for the Americans and ourselves, and for the whole of NATO. There is therefore a specific British and a specific Western interest in the circumvention of Mr. Lévesque's designs.[36]

Johnston went on to say that the British couldn't do much to stop the breakup of Canada, except perhaps keep their distance toward the PQ government. He was convinced, moreover, that Trudeau himself didn't wish for foreign intervention, supposing that such an intervention could have a positive effect on the federalist cause in Quebec, which Johnston doubted.

Whatever the case may be, the situation would remain quiet for a time, since the PQ hadn't yet announced the date of the referendum. No worries on the short term on the constitutional front either. The only element that could cause surprise in the immediate future, the diplomat wrote, was the language laws proposed by the PQ. They were a priority, an issue that both the federal government and the anglophone community in Quebec were watching with concern.

CHAPTER 2

ALL HANDS ON DECK

In early 1977, a political fight loomed on the horizon. As Denis Symington, British consul in Quebec City, wrote: "The battle lines have barely yet been drawn, the jostling for manoeuvre is only in its initial stages."[1]

And what was this subject that was raising passions? Language.

When the Parti Québécois was the Official Opposition, René Lévesque had been slow to condemn Bill 22.[2] During the previous electoral campaign, he'd nonetheless promised to abolish language tests that would determine which children would be allowed to go to English schools. He'd also promised that Quebec would be as French as Ontario was English.

However, the PQ leader was not so much leading as following his party on this issue. Language issues would later constitute the principal point of discord with Trudeau. The conflict was primed though not yet at the surface as Lévesque came to power. As Lévesque once told Bourassa, "Laws and languages don't mix."[3] The new premier was aware of the language issue all the same, a problem which, if nothing was done, would make Quebec a "second Louisiana."[4] What's more, a number of his ministers, his entourage, and his supporters hoped that the issue would be treated energetically. Lévesque thus decided to entrust senior cabinet minister Camille Laurin with the task of reviewing Bill 22 (ironically, the latter was an old friend of Pierre Trudeau).

Above all, Lévesque sought to eliminate language tests; he wasn't aware at first that his minister was aiming for a round of electroshock therapy on Quebec society whose objective would be to eradicate the progression of English in the province. It should be said that Laurin, the future father of Bill 101, kept his cards close to his chest, moving carefully, garnering support, anticipating reactions. Only in February 1977 did he share his vision with the rest of the Cabinet. Among the measures he proposed were that French would become the only language of the court system, large corporations would be compelled to obtain certificates of French competence (called *francization*), and, as his pièce de résistance, access to schooling in English would be reserved for children who'd studied in the language in Quebec in either elementary or high school.

TOWARD A COLONIAL EXODUS?

While reservations about the language project were expressed within the government, it quickly became clear that a majority supported Laurin. He publicly announced his intentions on April 1, during the tabling of a white paper in the National Assembly. Hostile reactions soon followed, including from the business community. Bernard Finestone, the CEO of the Montreal Chamber of Commerce, predicted the collapse of Quebec's economy, stating that it would "only take the 13 largest companies leaving Quebec for there to be 13,000 jobs lost." As for Earle McLaughlin, head of the Royal Bank, he threatened to leave altogether.[5]

These sensational comments did nothing to reassure the British, who were worried, among other things, about the impact of Bill 101 on their economic interests in the province, where they were the second most important foreign investor after the United States. In Montreal, their consulate was taken by storm by both British citizens as well Canadians whose parents or grandparents were British. An exodus seemed to be in the works, of the sort seen when European colonists fled colonial countries being granted their independence. It seemed like everyone and his cousin were preparing to flee back to Great Britain. As a British diplomat in Montreal noted, "These reactions have been strong and in some cases very emotional, based on a belief that the bill aims to extinguish the Anglophone community in Quebec. There is a great deal of bitterness and a fear that there could be violent incidents."[6]

The statement by Trudeau in which he claimed that Bill 101 would throw Quebec back into the Middle Ages didn't help lower the stakes, as can be imagined. It was the sort of comment that angered Lévesque, though he had become used to Trudeau's approach. Take, for example, the conversation they'd had in the cafeteria of Radio-Canada's offices in Montreal in the 1950s, when Gérard Pelletier had first introduced them to each other. Faced with the television star that Lévesque was at the time, the *Cité Libre* polemicist immediately set the tone of the exchange:

> You're René Lévesque. You speak very well, you know. But do you know how to write?

> Why would you ask?

> You were asked to write for *Cité Libre*, and you never followed up on it.

> Listen, it would take a lot of time.

> Of course, as well as ideas, naturally, I can understand that. But if you tried, perhaps you'd be able to anyway.[7]

As time would tell, this sort of exchange would become typical of the relationship between the two men. And despite the fact that they made common cause against Duplessis, and that Lévesque admired Trudeau's intelligence, he'd still call him a "show-off of a champagne socialist," damning him for his months of travel abroad to Beijing, Paris, or Timbuktu, only to return to stand in a picket line before leaving again for a few months.[8]

For Lévesque, Duplessis was the incarnation of tyranny; for Trudeau, he lacked culture. Lack of culture — that was what Bill 101 was all about for Trudeau, who raged against the bill with all his might.

But Trudeau's condemnation of the law didn't prevent the British from recognizing that the project for a charter of the French language was supported by the francophone majority. And while Trudeau couldn't find words strong enough to attack what was occurring, he didn't go as far as to use his powers of disallowance, which gave him the right to invalidate a provincial law. On Elgin Street, the following observation was made: "Mr. Trudeau probably realizes that the PQ would only be too happy to fight their referendum on the issue of language policy, an issue for which he is likely to have the solid backing of most francophone Quebeckers."[9]

No, Trudeau wouldn't go after Bill 101 with a head-on assault. He instead looked for a way to establish a single language regime across Canada, a topic under discussion by the provincial premiers at their yearly meeting, which took place in St. Andrews, New Brunswick, in July 1977. Lévesque took advantage of the situation to make an offer to his provincial counterparts — a "reciprocity clause," as he called it. He proposed that the citizens of the anglophone provinces where francophones were allowed to study in French be given the right to study in English in Quebec. Citizens of other provinces would have to study in French.

Trudeau immediately reacted by maintaining that language rights constituted the foundation of Confederation. They were not open to any sort of haggling among the provinces, which he compared to a "prisoner exchange."[10] Moreover, such agreements would officially recognize the asymmetry of language rights that *de facto* existed in Canada at a time when the prime minister dreamed of a uniformly bilingual country, from Yukon to Nova Scotia. The federal government hoped to impose new language rights in education, dispositions that would finally be included in the Charter of Rights, in 1982. Later, Ottawa would state that it was an identical clause to Lévesque's 1977 reciprocity clause.

Nothing could be further from the truth. During the conference in St. Andrews, Quebec's premier claimed he wouldn't abandon Quebec's jurisdiction over education by permitting the Supreme Court to decide who would be allowed to go to school in English in Quebec, an exercise the Canadian magistrates would perform by interpreting language rights in a charter. Such a situation would be "unthinkable," Lévesque claimed at the time[11]; he highlighted the fact that in matters related to language, the Supreme Court's injunctions had often remained unheeded in English Canada, as demonstrated, notably, by Manitoba's history. With the reciprocity system he was proposing, the government of Quebec would remain master of its own rights and be able to react convincingly to other provinces that might break their promise.[12] Faced with anglophone provinces that wouldn't allow francophones to study in their language, Quebec could simply close the doors of its English schools to citizens of those provinces.

For Trudeau, this proposal was a slap in the face; all the more since Quebec was making a valid point. As was noted on Elgin Street, "the proposal is curious, but it is flying, that is, taken seriously."[13] And so, the federation of francophone communities outside Quebec supported Lévesque, and the reciprocity clause even interested some of his provincial counterparts. However, as New Brunswicker Richard Hatfield would explain a year later, "some premiers were ready to accept reciprocity, but Trudeau called us to threaten us with a reduction in transfer payments."[14] Faced with such pressure, anglophone provinces backed off. They ended up agreeing on a declaration of principles that stated, without any form of guarantee, that they would do everything they could to offer French-language education when and where the numbers made sense.

René Lévesque decided to impose the "Quebec clause": citizens of other provinces wouldn't be allowed to go to English schools in Quebec. On August 26, Bill 1, having become Bill 101, was adopted by the National Assembly.

A TIME FOR ACTION

Through all of this, fears inspired by the PQ victory rallied support to Trudeau's government from 29 percent to 50 percent.[15] The prime minister presented himself as being ready to open up the conversation on a full revision of the constitution, including a sharing of powers. He also hoped to offer an alternative path to Quebeckers during the referendum, and believed that a constitutional agreement would be his wild card.

Trudeau delegated his lieutenant Marc Lalonde to study the issue. The man had a reputation for being cold, and wasn't known for his sensitivity to the provinces' desires; his nomination did nothing to reassure them. What's more, the situation was complicated by Ottawa's new energy policy. It raised significant opposition, especially in Saskatchewan and Alberta, both producers of gas and oil, natural resources whose ownership was guaranteed to the provinces by the constitution.

Despite this, Trudeau's government voted through the Petroleum Administration Act, whose avowed goal was to fix the price of oil under the global price. Motorists and truckers could fill up their tanks for less.

Of course, such an approach couldn't work without a strong dose of state control in the form of a series of strict measures aimed at subsuming both the producer provinces as well as the petroleum industry, measures imposed by the federal government. First, an export tax was instituted, preventing Canadian producers from selling their oil for a higher price on the international market, leading to losses of billions of dollars. Ottawa disallowed the practice by petroleum companies of deducting their provincial licence fees from their federal tax burden. How did the Trudeau government justify such interventionism? "Because a provincial resource is also a national resource."[16]

This centralizing vision underpins the constitutional proposal that Marc Lalonde presented in 1978 in a document entitled *A Time for Action*. Unexpectedly, he suggested that the discussion be separated into two stages. First, talks would focus on a charter that would contain language rights, described in more detail than those presented in Victoria. Provinces would be free to adhere to these clauses. In parallel to this, Ottawa would keep its power to modify central institutions like the Supreme Court and the Senate. To reach this objective, Trudeau didn't wait for the opinion of the provinces and presented a draft bill to the House — C-60 — that, notably, proposed to transform the upper house into a House of the Federation, which would eliminate the regional legitimacy of provinces to the advantage of Parliament and the federal government. Then Ottawa gave itself the right to go over the authority of the provinces by taking questions directly to the people through referenda.[17]

This would be the content of the initial negotiations, set to end on July 1, 1979, at the end of the Liberal government's mandate. None of the subjects seen as having priority by the provinces — sharing of powers, for example — would have been discussed at this stage. Only in the second portion of the negotiations, which would take place between July 1979 and July 1981, would such discussions occur. Obviously, no one knew whether Trudeau would still be there or even whether his eventual successor would feel tied to the engagements made by him, which gave the entire proposal an eminently unpredictable character.

Unsurprisingly, the months that followed the tabling of the draft law led to a flow of recriminations. First, the transformation of the Senate into a House of the Federation didn't please the provinces. They instead sought better guarantees of their authority over natural resources, a greater consultation on the nomination of Supreme Court judges, as well as limits to the federal government's ability to sign treaties.[18]

Disapproval didn't stop there. To Lougheed and Lévesque, one could now add Brian Peckford of Newfoundland to the premiers openly hostile to

Trudeau. The last British colony to become part of Confederation demanded jurisdiction over the submarine resources off its coast, rich in petroleum, which Ottawa refused. Sterling Lyon would be next. The premier of Manitoba, an avowed supporter of traditional Canada, criticized Trudeau for scuttling parliamentary democracy with his Charter of Rights and Freedoms, and also accused him of republicanism, since the federal proposals didn't contain, according to him, clear enough engagements toward the monarchy.

Lyon didn't know it at the time, but the diplomats on Elgin Street certainly shared his point of view. Moreover, they weren't at all impressed by Ottawa's strategy:

> The present situation is a mess, and a worrying mess.... By publishing their proposals in the form of a bill, the federal government did what they had said all along they would avoid, i.e., they have pinned themselves down to a series of specific proposals for their opponents to attack. The fact that the government have emphasised that they are still open to discussion does not alter this ... publication of the Bill C-60 ... conceived as acknowledging the current situation sparked an emotional debate.
>
> Trudeau's dilemma is a real one.... He considers it essential that the Quebec voters should have a clear promise of revised federalism before they vote in their referendum. In practice, however, there are no indications that these proposals have attracted the interest of Quebec voters.
>
> Even if they had, the opposition they have aroused in the rest of Canada would take the gilt off the gingerbread pretty comprehensively. (The truth is that they are largely irrelevant to the real constitutional issue, the division of powers between the provinces and Ottawa). Meanwhile, Mr. Lévesque's position is, if anything, strengthened by the way in which he can find common cause with the other Provincial Premiers against the Federal Government.... It seems unlikely that Mr. Trudeau's meetings with the Provincial Premiers will result in anything approaching consensus....[19]

Terry Empson didn't know how right he was. He'd barely had time to cable his message to London, and already Trudeau was inviting the premiers to a conference on October 30, 1978. His renewed popularity that followed the PQ victory had by then all but evaporated. He was at the end of his term, weakened and desperately attempting to realize his great dream of constitutional patriation. On the first day of the meeting, he proposed seven subjects for discussion: transfer payments, regional disparities, family law, spending powers, ownership over resources, communications, and declaratory power. This was deemed insufficient by his counterparts. "We can add other issues," Trudeau went on to say, suggesting talks on an amendment formula and the Supreme Court, as well as the Charter of Rights and Freedoms, monarchy, fisheries and offshore resources, as well as the Senate. Understanding the dangers of dealing with an unpopular prime minister, the provinces preferred not to commit, especially since the charter project was stirring up opposition. All this despite the fact that, in the words of John Ford, recently appointed British High Commissioner, "Trudeau showed a surprising degree of flexibility."[20]

The conference ended in failure, but that didn't stop things from going forward on other fronts. On January 25, 1979, the Pépin-Robarts Commission, set up by Trudeau after the PQ victory to find solutions to the problem of national unity, published its report. The commission's co-chairs were quite respected: Jean-Luc Pépin was a minister under Pearson and then Trudeau; John Robarts was a former premier of Ontario. Both men favoured more decentralization and a form of asymmetry that would favour Quebec, including recognizing the right to self-determination. No charter would be inserted into the supreme law, while language would become a provincial jurisdiction.

Trudeau was furious. When he was handed the report, he threw it directly into the trash, to the surprise of his advisers.[21] He could wish all he wanted for the report never to have been written, but its publication a few days before a new federal-provincial conference set the tone for the discussions. Lévesque feared that Trudeau would have used the report to demonstrate that sovereignty was useless. But since the head of the federal government attempted to bury the document, his Quebec counterpart did everything to champion it.[22]

The talks that opened on February 5, 1979, were once again difficult. Trudeau believed he'd made sufficient compromises to the provinces, proposing, notably, that family law become a provincial jurisdiction. However, he refused to budge in terms of communications, which led him to be accused by Lévesque of barely offering anything to the provinces. Angered, the former exclaimed, "We've almost given up the shop to you people."[23]

This comment did nothing to reduce tensions. It should be said that it wasn't only the sharing of powers that raised controversy. Peter Lougheed waged battle on a new front against Ottawa, which he accused of wanting to keep an iron fist over natural resources in the name of "authoritarian national interest," an argument that Lévesque would quickly pursue as well.[24] Trudeau would reply that the federal government was responsible for international and interprovincial commerce, and it had to have some authority over the way a province disposed of its resources outside its territory.

PIERRE ELLIOTT TRUDEAU STAKES HIS ALL

The issue of fisheries wasn't much riper for resolution, with Newfoundland still opposing Ottawa. As for the reform of the Supreme Court, it was going nowhere fast. All the provinces wanted to be consulted before nominations. Ottawa didn't oppose the principle, but application was where things got tricky. Not to mention the Charter of Rights and Freedoms, which was met with the same opposition. The conference ended in general cacophony.

Frustrated, Trudeau drew his own conclusions from this failed meeting. He now believed that it was his duty to oppose any concessions to the provinces; agreeing to any one concession would mean having to face down more.[25] The country was sliding down a slippery slope, and what was important was to stop this nosedive before the federal government's powers were categorically amputated.

High Commissioner John Ford reported on developments to London in the following way:

> Trudeau sees in himself the exemplar of the true Canadian
> — bilingual and bi-cultural … a strong believer in cen-
> tralised and firm government. It has always been our hope
> that the Westminster Parliament would be able to perform
> its constitutional duty without facing a chorus of criticism
> from dissenting provinces. It is thus a matter for relief that
> it looks unlikely that Mr. Trudeau will now attempt to

rush a Patriation Bill through Parliament. Yet it remains very much in the cards that if he is returned to power and resumes constitutional negotiation he may wish at some stage to proceed with patriation before full agreement has been reached on all of the other issues or even on an Amending Formula…. Quebec at least will protest.[26]

In the British capital, Ford's message was heard loud and clear. His cable was copied and distributed throughout the Foreign Office. A few weeks later, Trudeau decided to stake his all and triggered elections for May 22. He returned to his favourite topic, the eternal constitutional question, ignoring the counsel of his advisers, who pleaded with him to not raise the issue again. Determined, the former polemicist asked his organizers to fill Maple Leaf Gardens in Toronto so that he might announce his intentions to the country.

The Liberal electoral machine was in full steam for this operation that would be held on May 9. One hundred thousand tickets were printed and distributed, while the Gardens could only hold sixteen thousand spectators. On the day of the event, some three thousand faithful had to stand outside to listen to their idol. Trudeau was greeted with the delirious enthusiasm of the good old days of Trudeaumania. Thousands of supporters waved and chanted "Tru-deau! Tru-deau! Tru-deau!"

The climax of this bacchanalia was, of course, Trudeau's speech. On stage, he began describing, one by one, the particulars of his charter: language rights, fundamental rights, democratic rights, the amendment formula, et cetera.[27] Even for Liberal supporters, this was too much. The exaltation that had welcomed their leader was now replaced by silence. Boredom overtook the crowd, soon yawns erupted throughout. Fortunately for him, Trudeau managed to pepper his speech with a few titillating passages: for example, when he threatened the provinces that he would act without them by going directly to the people through a referendum. Despite the sweat that broke out on his skin and dripped onto his brown corduroy suit, this fifty-nine-year-old man's passion was still intact. And he still knew how to communicate to his troops: with anti-provincial slogans, haranguing them to — alongside him — face down an enemy that refused to endorse the new order he was attempting to establish throughout the country.[28]

The Liberal leader didn't stop at this one speech. He began the next day in a Montreal hotel. In front of a crowd of 1,500, he insisted on language rights that would allow Canadians to live in their native tongue anywhere in the country, from Vancouver to Newfoundland.

For Manitoba's premier, these declarations were entirely unacceptable. Sterling Lyon roared his disapproval at the threat of a referendum held up like a bogeyman by Ottawa, which to him constituted "the most inappropriate way to decide anything as complicated as a Constitution," adding that Trudeau was speaking nonsense. The constitution, he concluded, was a balanced, flexible document that had served the country well.[29]

The idea of starting a new Canada from scratch led to a lot of gnashing of teeth in Quebec, especially for Claude Ryan, who succeeded Robert Bourassa as leader of the Liberal Party of Quebec. If Canadians had not patriated the constitution, he declared, it wasn't due to indifference or lack of will, but because they hadn't "been able to agree on more fundamental questions. To think that unilateral patriation will overcome these profound difficulties is quite simply to delude oneself."[30]

Whatever the case may be, on May 22, 1979, Trudeau lost the election, paying the price for high unemployment, the energy crisis, deficits, and especially the voting system. Despite the fact that he'd managed to earn 40 percent of popular vote compared to 36 percent for Joe Clark, the latter obtained more seats. He would head a minority government. Trudeau found himself in the opposition, and decided he needed a vacation. After a canoe trip in northern Canada, he returned to Ottawa, announcing he was leaving the political life. He would say his tearful goodbyes to his colleagues in the House of Commons — a departure with all the grandeur of tragedy to echo Bonaparte's expression.

THE HONOURABLE LADY

The constitution would remain in Great Britain. But the problem it represented returned to the surface in May 1979. A historic event had occurred: Margaret Thatcher was elected to the head of the British government. The first woman to lead a major Western country, she was about to put her mark on both people and events from Great Britain to Argentina, as well as in Europe and the Soviet Union ... and Canada. Nothing had prepared the second wife of Denis Thatcher, born Roberts, the daughter of a Grantham grocer and conservative activist, to such a destiny.

Her career was explosive. After receiving a diploma in chemistry from Oxford University, she studied law while working, all of this after having twins. Elected to Parliament in 1959, she became parliamentary under-secretary only two years later, then education minister in 1970 in Edward Heath's government.

At the time, very few people understood "the honourable lady's" ambition, and rarer still were the colleagues who took her seriously. It should be said that the future prime minister hid her intentions behind her always impeccable blonde hair, her feminine allure, and her good manners.[31] And when asked whether a woman could become prime minister, she always answered — without truly believing it — that prejudices were too strong for that to happen. She wouldn't see the first female prime minister in her lifetime, she said.

Having become a middleweight in the Conservative team, she surprised everyone in 1974 when, after her party's loss in the previous elections, she challenged her leader Edward Heath for the leadership. Against all odds, she succeeded. After a difficult stay in opposition, it would be her turn to shine five years later. The "Iron Lady" — an expression a Soviet newspaper first used in an attempt to discredit her — took advantage of the discontent that was growing in the United Kingdom. The country had been paralyzed by a series of strikes that the Labour government had been unable to control.

Coming to 10 Downing Street, the hard-working Thatcher had done her homework, including on Canada. She'd visited the country as leader of the Opposition and met Canadian personalities in London, including Peter Lougheed in 1977.[32] She had mentioned to him that Canada, in her opinion, was a very decentralized country, which hadn't stopped her visitor from implying that it could be even further.

Whatever the case may be, foreign policy wasn't one of the priorities of the new prime minister. Her ministers weren't necessarily experts in the domain, with the notable exception of Lord Carrington, the foreign secretary. Pointed nose, thick glasses, thinning grey hair, this veteran of the Second World War and former minister under Macmillan was no doubt one of the big names in Cabinet. But as soon as the topic strayed from Europe or the United States, international issues bored him to death.[33]

In the prime minister's inner circle, there was no inkling that the Canadian constitution might poison Thatcher's life. Only Nicholas Ridley, a long-term supporter whom she had appointed minister of state at the

Foreign Office, saw the writing on the wall. Ridley was one of the few people who believed a woman who represented the right wing of the Conservative Party could lead it and, from there, head the government. He was part of her inner circle,[34] and his work consisted of warning her of various obstacles, traps, and ambushes that always await high-ranking politicians. He was familiar with the programs and controversial reforms the Iron Lady hoped to pass. He also knew that she was determined not be distracted by foreign affairs.[35] However, among the documents Ridley examined when he came to the Foreign Office was a summary of cables by the British High Commissioner in Ottawa, John Ford. This is how he discovered the existence of the Canadian constitutional issue — just the sort of thing he dreaded, and one which led him to ask his civil servants a very simple question: "Could we not pre-empt a new British North America Act introducing a Bill disclaiming any further responsibility for Canadian Constitutional matters, and putting the legal responsibility onto Ottawa?"[36]

The Foreign Office immediately began brainstorming on the matter. But the exercise had barely started when events forced the issue once more. In 1979, the National Indian Brotherhood (NIB), an organization representing First Nations people who felt excluded from constitutional discussions, decided to call on the British government, sending a delegation to London of some three hundred chiefs, a visit put together by Labour MP Bruce George. The First Nations members asked that certain specific rights be recognized and that they be accepted as equal partners in Confederation.

It should be said that aboriginals had very good reason to be suspicious of Ottawa's motives. A few years earlier, in 1969, Trudeau had proposed to put an end to the special status of Canada's aboriginals and abolish reservations and the Department of Indian Affairs. Ignoring their territorial demands, as well as their demands for more autonomy and recognition as founding people, he offered them theoretical equality in Canadian society, similar to Quebec's position in Canada.[37] These proposals led to a general outcry among aboriginal communities, forcing Trudeau to retreat two years later. In the words of the prime minister himself at the time, "The government was very naïve ... too theoretical ... too abstract ... not pragmatic or understanding enough."[38]

Some First Nations organizations were happy about Trudeau's 1979 loss and that the constitutional project had been set aside for the moment.

However, First Nations groups had decided to maintain the same level of mobilization, notably with a visit by leading chiefs to London. Apparently, Thatcher knew nothing of the situation. From Canada, the group's spokesperson wrote to 10 Downing Street in the hopes of meeting her: "The British Parliament has residual responsibilities for Indian people in Canada by virtue of the BNA Act. It is these responsibilities of the British Governments that we wish to discuss with you. I look forward to a positive response."[39]

Needless to say, the announcement of a visit of more than three hundred aboriginal chiefs didn't arouse much enthusiasm among the British government. The door needed to be slammed shut as quickly as possible to these untimely visitors. Quickly, the chiefs were informed that the prime minister would be unable to meet them; her schedule was unfortunately already full. By pure coincidence, the head of the Foreign Office, Lord Carrington, sent them the same answer. It was absolutely out of the question for the aboriginal visitors to enter Buckingham Palace to hand their petition to the Queen.

Every door seemed locked, but never mind that. The delegation landed in London on July 2, 1979, to great fanfare, but not dressed in traditional garb as they sometimes did for Her Majesty in respect for ceremony in times of peace. Instead, they donned suits and ties, ready for a political fight.

The mission started on a bad note. Five of the three hundred chiefs disappeared on the first day, to the great dismay of the organizers. They were soon found in their hotel rooms, completely drunk and unfit to be seen. The temptations of the British capital would be too much for them, and they wouldn't sober up before leaving London.[40] Fortunately, the rest of the aboriginal leaders remained professional and the incident didn't compromise the mission.

The First Nations leaders enjoyed the support of the NGO Survival International, whose mandate was to aid aboriginal peoples across the globe. Meetings were organized with Amnesty International, the Catholic Institute for International Relations, as well as with the United Nations Associations. Against all odds, the Archbishop of Canterbury, Donald Coggan, gave them an audience, following an intervention by the bishop of Saskatchewan. The visitors were also able to meet former prime minister James Callaghan, who agreed to a last-minute meeting. The latter would turn out to be "surprisingly knowledgeable and keenly interested."[41]

As for Archbishop Donald Coggan, he promised to study their issues and intervene on their behalf with the Foreign Office and the Queen. He followed up on his promise a few weeks later by writing to Lord Carrington to tell him of his sympathy for their cause and how impressed he was by "their very real loyalty to the British Crown."[42] Carrington politely replied that the aboriginals need only turn to their own government, adding that Prime Minister Joe Clark had promised to study the question.

None of this satisfied the chiefs or their allies in the British capital, most notably Labour MP Bruce George, a member of the Marxist wing of the party, who contacted Nicholas Ridley, enjoining him to meet with the visitors. Tired of arguing, and out of pure politeness, the latter accepted that three chiefs be received by an equivalent number of civil servants, all seat fillers. It would be in this agitated atmosphere that the Foreign Office's experts began examining scenarios that would allow the British to get rid of this damned Canadian constitution. Would it be possible to vote in a law that would unilaterally put an end to Great Britain's role, as Ridley hoped? If so, how, and what would Canada's reaction be? These serious questions would require four more months of work, studying the pros and cons and examining the judicial, historical, and political implications. The recommendations were finally ready in October 1979, under the guise of a confidential report. The new person responsible for the North America bureau, Martin Berthoud, wrote:

> The United Kingdom Parliament has the power in constitutional law unilaterally to patriate the Canadian constitution … there are, however, strong political reasons for not patriating the constitution unilaterally. These are supported by our High Commission in Ottawa … the provinces believe, some of them very strongly, that the best safeguard for their rights vis-à-vis Ottawa lies in the continued retention of the Canadian constitution in Westminster.… If, therefore, by taking unilateral action we were to put the entire legal responsibility on to Ottawa, we should in effect be taking sides with the Federal Government against the interests of those Provinces which are withholding agreement.[43]

Obviously, this wasn't the answer Ridley was hoping for: "We shouldn't have this power, it is nothing but an embarrassment. We should tell Prime Minister Clark in due course," he insisted.[44]

CHAPTER 3

THE REFERENDUM FIGHT

Joe Clark became prime minister of Canada in May 1979, but by that fall his government had already begun to experience failure. Clark was not able to reach an agreement with Alberta regarding energy issues, relations with Bill Davis's Ontario went from bad to worse, and all this at a time when the Conservatives lacked sufficient revenue to fulfill some of their electoral promises.[1] The minister of finance, John Crosbie, sought to enact a new tax on gasoline despite the fact that a number of his colleagues were opposed to this measure. He would end up winning that fight, and gas prices would go up by eighteen cents a gallon.

This new measure was part of a budget that, as Ottawa had expected, wouldn't be particularly popular. But Crosbie remained optimistic. Trudeau had announced his resignation a few weeks earlier, and without a leader, the Liberals wouldn't likely overthrow Clark's minority government. A carefree Conservative team presented its budget on December 11, despite the fact that the document not only contained a tax hike on gasoline, but on tobacco and alcohol as well.

These last two products were certainly bountiful on the menu the following day on the Hill, as the Liberals got together for their Christmas party. Trudeau made a quick appearance and took the opportunity to address his former caucus. He recommended that the Liberals vote against the budget, adding that he wouldn't jump back into the political arena if elections were triggered.

Despite his words, some believed that he'd let himself be tempted anyway. They hoped he'd jump back into the fray, especially since two separate polls confirmed the Liberals' advantage in voting intentions. Jim Coutts, one of the Liberal Party strategists, did the rounds with speeches and confabulations. He encouraged his members to join the New Democratic Party, who'd already announced they'd be voting against the budget.

On December 13, the day of the vote, Coutts rallied his troops. The Liberals were waiting in ambush. There was uncertainty, however, about what Fabien Roy's five Social Credit members were going to do: they often voted with the Conservatives, even though the latter had a tendency to take them for granted. If Social Credit did support the Conservatives, then the Liberals and New Democrats would be down a vote. This was enough to reassure the Conservatives, who now made their way to the floor like sheep for the slaughter, forgetting that two of their ministers were away on travel and one of their MPs was sick in bed. Fortunately for them, quite a few Liberal seats were empty a few minutes before the vote as well.

The Speaker then began counting votes, calling on each MP in turn, first counting those who were for the motion, then those against. Right at the beginning of this second act, a number of Liberals suddenly materialized and made their way to their side of the aisle, including some MPs believed to be on their deathbeds.[2] Then, in a second dramatic turn, the Social Credit members abstained, depriving the government of their necessary votes. At 10:20 p.m., the verdict was handed down: 139 to 133 votes against the Conservative budget. The government had fallen.

RESURRECTION

A few days later, there was a new development as Trudeau announced his return to the political fold. His political exile had given him time to read the numerous comments in newspapers across the country that spoke of him, most of them underlining his failure to achieve all the main objectives he'd set for himself.[3] But here was his opportunity for resurrection. What's more, it coincided with the looming referendum in Quebec.

This electoral fight was entirely different than in 1979. The Conservatives were ready to campaign on the issues, but the Liberal leader simply dodged conversations of substance and concentrated entirely on style, wearing the most fashionable suits and ice-skating on the Rideau Canal as the camera looked on. Trudeau went on the radio, discussing an excerpt from a poem that an announcer had challenged him to identify. He refused to participate in a debate against Clark, as he'd done in 1979, or to hold press conferences. He skirted the issues to such an extent that journalists ended up sending him a petition, which would convince him to finally hold a press conference ... one time only.[4] More than anything, Trudeau censored himself and didn't speak of the constitution a single time, settling for attacks on the Conservatives' record.

On February 18, 1980, the day of the vote, the strategy proved effective. Early in the election coverage, the Liberals seemed to have wide margins in the Atlantic provinces. Then they captured every seat in Quebec except one, and went on to obtain fifty-two of the ninety-five ridings in Ontario. Though the results from the rest of the country weren't yet in, the Liberals had already won a majority — fortunate for them, since they only managed to get two MPs elected in the Prairies and British Columbia. With this imbalance, the West's alienation had reached new levels.

Clark soon admitted defeat, and Trudeau made an appearance at the Château Laurier, where he was greeted by a jubilant crowd. "Welcome to the 1980s," he began, before continuing with a speech in which he reminded his compatriots that Canada "is more than the sum of its parts."[5] He then added that the decade would be filled with challenges and opportunities.

While the Liberals were all in the mood for a party, some observers weren't so happy. John Ford, the British High Commissioner, felt that "Trudeau's re-election has not improved the atmosphere. He could take strong action if he felt himself cornered and personality conflict will not help resolve the crisis."[6]

Naturally, Ford didn't publicly air his doubts. For the time being, all eyes were on the referendum, which Lévesque had finally decided to set for the spring of 1980, despite unfavourable polls. The weeks following the Liberals' win coincided with an acceleration of preparations for the decisive battle.

The PQ government attempted by any means to win over undecided voters to their cause, up to and including a dose of ambiguity. For example, the white paper tabled in October 1979 was called *Québec-Canada: A New Deal*. The word *sovereignty* no longer appeared by itself. *Sovereignty-association* was the flavour of the day, representing an independent Quebec within a larger Quebec-Canada framework.

Federalists accused the PQ government of intellectual dishonesty. This, however, didn't stop the latter from putting on a good show in the parliamentary debates that preceded the referendum in March. Claude Ryan wasn't properly prepared. He'd spent too much time on his constitutional policy, explained in his "beige book." The document was severely criticized by the PQ, which accused Ryan of aiming for the status quo, as well as being coldly received by Trudeau.[7]

In a message sent to Lord Carrington, John Ford seemed worried. "Though 1979 was not a good year for the Quebec separatist, things seem to be going their way again. The latest opinion poll suggests that the 'yes' vote may win in the coming referendum."[8] Faced with this situation, the diplomats of Elgin Street expected a forceful intervention by Ottawa. The federal government certainly didn't disappoint.

Their polls indicated that economic uncertainty greatly worried Quebeckers.[9] Federal authorities jumped on the issue. First, Trudeau's government distributed throughout Quebec thousands of copies of a brochure that demonstrated the beneficial effects of federalism. Second, every minister in the federal government of Québécois origin was put to use. Minister of justice Jean Chrétien was tasked with overseeing the daily activities of the federal government. He described the PQ as "gangrene, rot that's reached the thumb, if it keeps going we'll have to cut the arm off."[10] He was seconded by Marc Lalonde, the minister of energy, who predicted a catastrophic future for an independent Quebec. "The separatists' dreams can only lead to a sombre and sinister reality,"[11] he said, basing himself on the idea that, thanks to federal energy policies, Quebec benefited from cheap oil, a resource that would cost it much more if it had to pay true market price.[12]

Even if the Parti Québécois claimed that an independent Quebec would continue using the Canadian dollar, the "No" vote supporters called phone-in radio shows to say that after Mexico with its peso, Quebec would have its "parizo,"[13] a play on the minister of finance's surname, Parizeau. A sovereign Quebec, Jean Chrétien claimed, was a passport for poverty.[14] As for Marc Lalonde, he repeated ad nauseam that Quebeckers would lose their old age pensions entirely.

For British diplomats closely watching the situation, the federal Liberals' tactics seemed surprising. As John Rich, consul in Montreal, wrote, "It is disquieting that both the senior ministers appointed to deal with the Provinces,

Messrs Chrétien and Lalonde, have track records of strongly centralizing attitudes and abrasive manners towards the provinces."[15]

Not everyone shared this opinion at the Foreign Office, where Trudeau could count on a number of admirers. But the priority was still to figure out the ideal course to follow in regards to the now-imminent referendum. In March 1980, a meeting of all mission chiefs posted to Canada was organized in Ottawa by Martin Berthoud. All working north of the forty-ninth parallel were present, including the High Commissioner and his deputies. They came to the following conclusions:

> (a) A united Canada would likely be a much stronger and better ally than bits of a Canada fragmented into two or more parts.

> (b) Even though an independent Quebec would likely stay within the Alliance, there was at least the possibility that Quebec could go in a different direction, or at least use the threat of it as a lever to obtain undesirable concessions from Canada/the U.S.A.

> (c) The process of secession would inevitably be a very painful one. This would not only damage the fabric of Canada/Quebec, but might involve the U.K. because of our constitutional position.[16]

AN INDEPENDENT AND VIABLE QUEBEC

Since the risks of being pulled into the fray were becoming greater every day, it became essential for the British to prepare a contingency plan. In the case of separation, it would be necessary to immediately implement constitutional changes in Canada. Obviously, the British were sincerely hoping for a victory for federal Canada, but what would their attitude have been if the sovereignists had won? In March 1980, while the Yes camp was gaining in the polls, the consul in Montreal, John Rich, began the thought exercise. He started with the anglophone community.

Most of the incorrigible exponents of "Herrenvolk" attitudes have moved to Ontario and elsewhere (where they
continue to do damage to the image of [the] Province and
of the city of Montreal). A few remain, and the British
Consul-General in Montreal sometimes finds himself
cornered by them on social occasions. Until 1979 their
attitudes were still reflected in the pages of the "Montreal
Gazette," but under a new publisher that newspaper
appears now to take a more forward-looking view.[17]

Besides the behaviour of anglophones, it was also important to consider
a newly independent Quebec's economy. Should one prepare for a return
to the Stone Age, as some federal government big names implied? With or
without an economic association, the British weren't worried.

Britain has sizable interests in Quebec Province, and vice-
versa. While the ideal is that Canada should remain strong
and united we have to treat French Canada as a distinct
entity, even within Confederation. If Quebec becomes
independent it would be a viable state; the PQ envisages
remaining in the Commonwealth and NATO. We must
have regard to the future of our relations in the contingency of independence....
　　　Clearly it is important for Britain that Canada, our
Commonwealth and NATO Partner, should remain strong
and united. Conversely, it is not in our interest that the
"Quebec Problem" should be a running sore which becomes
worse rather than better and consequently weakens the
Atlantic Community to a degree disproportionate to its
intrinsic importance. After initial troubles adjusting its
economy, if the economic union with the rest of Canada
were dissolved, I believe that an independent Quebec would
be a viable state on the scale of the Scandinavian countries
and play a responsible role in the international community.
　　　Quebec as a separate country would come about the
30th on the value table of Britain's export markets. Taking

1978 figures she was ahead of Venezuela and Malaysia, a little behind Egypt, Greece and Iraq, and not very far behind Brazil.[18]

The consul ended his report by maintaining that, despite the now favourable polls, the PQ would lose the referendum. The reason? "The instinctive caution and common sense of the French Canadian in the street, which counter-balances nationalist enthusiasm, provided his indignation is not over-provoked."[19] Rich's report was sent to London by John Ford, who also made his own recommendation to Lord Carrington:

> My Lord, it is too soon to see how the Quebec drama will unfold. If Quebec does secede that need not be a disaster for Quebec or our interests, though it would be a traumatic experience for anglophone Canada....
>
> It is arguable that the Trudeau era has shown a steady decline in the power of Canada as a centralised Federation; and there is at present little sign of any national will to make the sacrifices necessary to re-equip Canada to play a full part in NATO or a really positive role through more active participation UN peace-keeping or in aid-giving activities. Mr. Trudeau's credibility as world statesman, if it ever was more than an ephemeral feature of the early 70s, is now unlikely to be capable of restoration by him on the basis of Canada's present financial or military strength. It is not inconceivable that a strong and independent Quebec could be comparable as an ally within NATO to, for example, Norway or Denmark ...
>
> More dangerous would be the results to the rest of Canada. The federation originally achieved by Sir John Macdonald and carried forward by his successors is a delicately poised balance of provincial and federal interests which might well be fatally upset by the secession of any of its component parts and by the geographical separation which would result from the secession of Quebec.... Whatever the political changes, our underlying trading relationships seem likely to continue; and, as I have fre-

quently urged, the increasing balkanisation of Canada is a fact which British businessmen must face up to in their dealings with this country....

Seen from Ottawa the U.S.A. has the same interest as the United Kingdom in a strong and unified Canada. But, like the British businessmen, U.S. traders have learnt to adapt to Canada's balkanisation provincialism.[20]

Quebec was another point of convergence between London and Washington, in addition to a number of other points that constituted the "special relationship" between both countries. If we are to believe testimony by Ken Curtis, former governor of Maine and ambassador of the United States to Ottawa in 1980, the American position would have been almost identical to that of the British. "This was a matter for Canadians to settle and I would have preferred to see Canada remain as a fully unified country. But the relationship with Canada would require the U.S. to adapt to whatever decision was reached."[21]

To be adaptive also meant diplomatically recognizing an independent Quebec. In London, Ford and Rich's recommendations were well received by their colleagues. As Martin Berthoud wrote: "As seen from here, this gets the balance about right."[22] The reactions from the Foreign Office diplomats leave no room for doubt. "We did think at the time that we would accept a separate Quebec," Berthoud explained years later. "Such acceptance would have been in line with our policy of non-interference in the internal politics of members of the Commonwealth."[23]

However, one can certainly wonder if this approach would have been accepted in the political sphere. Questioned thirty years later, Lord Carrington didn't have any specific memories of the episode surrounding the referendum. Malcolm Rifkind, former minister under Thatcher, on the other hand, did have a few thoughts to share. He'd also been secretary of the Foreign Office under John Major during the 1995 referendum. Questioned on the attitude that his country would have taken following a narrow victory for the Yes camp, Rifkind answered that

in British diplomatic tradition, recognition of a Government has never been intended to imply approval or support for that Government. Rather it has been intended to recognise that the Government has de facto power and that the international status of the country in question is not in dispute. For these reasons the United Kingdom was one of the first countries to recognise the Soviet Union in the 1920s, and the People's Republic of China at a time when the United States was unwilling to afford such recognition.[24]

Compared to Mao's China or Stalin's Russia, recognizing an independent Quebec didn't seem to pose much problem to Her Majesty's government. But preparing for an eventuality didn't mean announcing one's intentions. On the contrary, it was essential to not release details on what remained for the time being a contingency plan, as John Ford explained three weeks before the vote:

> I should perhaps add that given our involvement in the BNA Act there may be questions to us about our attitude to the referendum and its results. I have thought about this but can see no valid alternative to taking a rather unhelpful "no comment" line. It seems to me that there is nothing we can say which would not offend either the Federal Government or the Province of Quebec. It is not in our interests to do either. If asked, about our attitude to the possible separation of Quebec, I have indicated that the Canadian Federation has played a constructive role in the world and still has an important part to play not only on the world stage but also in the defence of parliamentary democracy. We hope that a united Canada will go on playing her part in the Free world but we recognise that the decision is for the Canadians to make and that it would not be right for us to intervene.[25]

This prudence is perfectly understandable. The federal government hammered home the idea that sovereignty would lead to economic disaster. Had London publicly contradicted Ottawa, it would have constituted a severe blow to their cause, and undoubtedly buoyed the PQ government. The situation was the same in the case of eventual diplomatic recognition: implying that Quebec would be recognized without much effort would have given important munitions to René Lévesque's troops.

Publicly, the British remained neutrally benevolent toward Ottawa. But when compared to their seeming shock and horror at the PQ's electoral victory in 1976, their vision had considerably evolved. It should be mentioned that Lévesque's government worked hard to project an image both responsible and respectable, as Robert Normand, then deputy minister at intergovernmental affairs, recounted:

> We'd invited Peter Thorneycroft, the President of the British Conservative Party. We'd brought him out hunting on Anticosti Island. We'd gotten him to kill a couple deer, he came with his wife; we made sure that his deer meat got back home safe to Great Britain. When you're talking with a guy up at the lodge in Saint-Geneviève, there, you sort of untie the tie, you let go of diplomatic decorum, and you roll up your sleeves. So, we'd really rattled him.[26]

All of this would be for naught, however, if the PQ didn't win the referendum. Their campaign was flagging, especially since Minister Lise Payette attacked Claude Ryan's wife, accusing her of being submissive and traditionalist.

MUM'S THE WORD

Apart from the mistakes committed by his own camp, René Lévesque could count on Pierre Trudeau to put him on the defensive. Over the course of his first three speeches, the head of the federal government essentially returned to his main arguments: the central government must speak for all of Canada; sovereignty-association would lead to an impasse; the referendum question is dishonest; Quebeckers play an important role in Canada. Those who were expecting a bit of substance in the speeches, like High Commissioner John Ford, were disappointed:

> Trudeau continues to keep mum about his ideas. He made it clear that he regarded a "yes" vote as a vote for a cul-de-sac, which could prevent any negotiations; but he has not indicated what he would do about constitutional change

in the event of a "no" vote. Moreover, he shows no sign of recognising the pressure for change out West. In general I find his continuing insensitivity to public and parliamentary opinion disquieting.[27]

For Ford, Trudeau's silence was that much more striking since it put him in an awkward position in regards to the anglophone provinces. The latter were hammering home their own message that a Yes vote would lead to an impasse or economic catastrophe. Yet a number of the provinces were also pointing out that the status quo was unacceptable and they, too, had demands they wanted to be heard.[28] Saskatchewan declared itself in favour of an asymmetric distribution of powers,[29] while Bill Davis of Ontario travelled to Montreal to make a speech. For the first time, he even risked reading a few paragraphs in French.[30]

The No camp hadn't yet won the referendum, and the discussion was already moving toward constitutional patriation, notably through a vote in the House of Commons. Even Trudeau began adopting a more conciliatory tone toward the provinces.[31] It now seemed out of the question to ignore the provinces during an eventual constitutional renewal.

At the Foreign Office, many doubted the sincerity of the Canadian prime minister. That was the case with Brian Perry, who worked at the North American office. In the margins of a report sent by the British High Commission in Ottawa, he wrote: "This suggests that although Mr. Trudeau went out of his way to play down the suggestion that he wanted to act unilaterally he certainly has not ruled out this possibility if agreement with the provinces continues to elude him. Many of my contacts who have watched Mr. Trudeau closely over the years are convinced that he is determined to bring the constitution 'home' before he stands down."[32]

On May 14, six days before the vote, a federalist rally at the Paul-Sauvé Centre represented Trudeau's ultimate opportunity to have his voice heard. Wearing a sombre three-piece suit with a boutonniere, the prime minister walked on stage with great ceremony, flanked by his main allies in the No camp, including Claude Ryan, who would be totally eclipsed that night. Trudeau's eyes were sharp, he was greeted with elation. His speech was clear, his voice solemn, his logic implacable:

The government of Canada and the government of every
province in Canada have already expressed themselves
clearly. If the answer given to the referendum's question is
no, then we have all said that this No will be interpreted
as mandate to change the Constitution, to renew federalism…. A no means change.

I'm addressing myself solemnly to all Canadians of
other provinces. We're putting ourselves at stake, we MPs
from Quebec, because we're asking Quebeckers to vote
no. And we tell you all, in the other provinces, that, later,
we won't tolerate this No to be interpreted by you as an
indication that all is well and that everything can remain
as it was before. We want change, we're putting our seats
on the line for change![33]

Trudeau went on to add that a majority Yes vote would lead to an impasse.
Sovereignty-association couldn't work, since the rest of Canada didn't relish
simply being associated, and the democratic will of Quebeckers couldn't
force it to accept a new reality. Moreover, since the PQ government hadn't
asked for a mandate for sovereignty without association, it couldn't follow
this path, even after a majority Yes vote.

The prime minister's intervention was soon felt across the province, like a
wave wiping out all objections in its path. Even supporters of the Yes camp
seemed rattled. Claude Morin, then minister for intergovernmental affairs,
was so impressed that he had to consider whether Trudeau had managed
to convince him.[34]

Trudeau hammered the last nail into the Yes camp's coffin. He'd also
sown an important controversy as to the exact nature of his promise. For
years, notably during discussions leading up to the Meech Lake Accord,
many politicians and commentators, federalist and sovereignist, accused
him of having lied to Quebeckers. Trudeau always denied the accusations.
"I promised Quebec change, and I gave Quebec change," he would later
write, "I gave Quebec, and all the rest of Canada, a new made-in-Canada
constitution, with a new amending formula and a new charter of rights."[35]
As Mark MacGuigan, then federal minister of external affairs, said, "One did
not have to know him very well to divine that this renewal would include a

charter or bill of rights, which he had first suggested in 1955, and which in his mind always included guarantees of linguistic rights."[36]

Perhaps. But we can at least blame Trudeau for having been deliberately vague; playing with the meaning of words in the same way the PQ had done with the referendum question. That night, if Trudeau had criticized decentralization and attacked Ryan's "beige book," the crowd might not have shown its support in the same way. It wouldn't have had tears in its eyes if the head of the federal government had proposed a charter with language rights, with the objective of transforming Canada into a truly bilingual country, where each and all could live in French from Vancouver to Newfoundland.[37] Even Trudeau's official biographer, John English, a former Liberal MP, admitted that the accusation of having played on ambiguity was founded.[38]

To better understand the nature of the criticism cast on the prime minister, it's essential to consider the words he chose that night. First, he used the phrase "We MPs from Quebec," speaking of a collective Quebec *We*, and not only as prime minister of Canada. And that *we* that he suddenly used was addressed to *them* — the citizens of English Canada — who Trudeau described as "you all, in the other provinces."

This distinction brought to mind a very precise vision of the country to which Quebeckers were deeply attached: a Canada made up of two nations. And Trudeau didn't stop there, with his belonging to the Canadian duality: he threw out a warning. The Quebecker *we* would no longer accept that the English-Canadian *you* kept standing in the way of its aspirations, a promise on which the seventy-five Quebecker MPs in Ottawa staked their seats. To the ears of Quebeckers, this was the only possible meaning of the change that was announced; a meaning reinforced by the messages of some anglophone provinces that implied they'd follow through on this change.

There's an additional fundamental element in this whole affair. This interpretation was shared by André Burelle, the same Burelle who'd written the May 14 speech.

"I indeed lent my words to Mr. Trudeau during the May 1980 referendum to sell to Quebeckers the idea of a Canada 'of many nations' under the guidance of a larger one, to echo Mounier's thoughts," he'd write thirteen years later — in reference to French personalist and political thinker Emmanuel Mounier — to Gérard Pelletier, a good friend of Trudeau. "But after having seemed to buy into my ideas (shared by many other federalists) in order to placate Quebec, Mr. Trudeau immediately threw them out as soon as the referendum was over."[39]

Burelle and millions of other Quebeckers interpreted Trudeau's words differently than the man himself. And they weren't the only ones. The British at the High Commission also thought they'd perceived a new Trudeau, as exemplified by a number of cables. For example, on May 27 diplomat Alan Montgomery wrote, "There is clear recognition that unless Quebec's sensibilities can be satisfied inside the framework of Confederation, the referendum victory may prove no more than a brief respite in the separatist struggle. Mr. Trudeau, the leaders of the other federal parties, and most of the provincial premiers have expressed the will to execute the necessary changes."[40]

However, others didn't believe Trudeau. On May 15, René Lévesque denounced his opponent's speech. "His are empty promises," he said, "more to add to the list of things he hasn't done in twelve years in power."[41] The PQ leader also reminded Quebeckers that his federal counterpart had promised, in 1974, to not freeze prices and salaries … only to do the exact opposite once he'd been elected. None of this would make a difference, and on the evening of May 20, the No camp won the referendum with a 60 percent majority.

At the Paul-Sauvé Arena in Montreal, where PQ supporters had rallied, the results were like a cold shower. Lévesque appeared on stage, accompanied by his wife, Corinne, and Minister Lise Payette, both dressed in black. Even if he'd never really believed in his chances of winning,[42] the man was in a state of shock. Tears in his eyes, his voice breaking, he stumbled through his speech. For the PQ, their leader's dejection only added to the drama of defeat.

Ryan spoke after Lévesque, to a half-empty room, with the bitter tone of a preacher. As for Trudeau, in his living room at 24 Sussex, where he'd been following the referendum on television, he certainly didn't like what he'd heard from Ryan. Like Churchill, he seemed to think that "in victory, magnanimity." At a press conference right after Ryan's speech, he presented himself as a rallying point. "If we count up broken friendships, broken hearts, injured pride, there isn't a single one among us who doesn't have some bruise on the soul that will need to heal in the days and weeks to come."[43] His tone was dignified, his speech soothing. But the federal leader didn't feel much sympathy for Lévesque, who, he would maintain in private, "never had the courage to clearly ask his question."[44]

Whatever the case may be, Trudeau intended to quickly move on the constitutional front. On Elgin Street, no one underestimated the new challenges that would soon be faced. Emery Davies, second-in-command at the British High Commission, summarized the situation to London in the following way.

> The chances of speedy progress over constitutional change look slim … the immediate future will require even greater efforts on our part to ensure that we understand political and constitutional developments as they occur and that in their pre-occupation with things … the federal and provincial governments do not lose sight of the fact that when they turn to HMG for action they must do so with politically and constitutionally reasonable proposals.[45]

But in London, almost no one took this warning seriously …

CHAPTER 4

THATCHER'S GREEN LIGHT

Quebec, Tuesday, May 21, 1980. In the aftermath of the referendum, Minister Claude Morin decided to stay home to absorb the shock of a defeat whose breadth was even clearer than the previous evening. Around noon, the phone rang. It was undersecretary Robert Normand, who told him that Jean Chrétien was in Quebec City and wanted to meet Morin with all due haste. The federal minister of justice would be available early in the evening.[1] He was beginning a tour of the country to prepare provincial premiers for the topic of the constitution.

Surprised, Morin claimed that it was too early for such a meeting. The Cabinet was to meet on Thursday to decide what the next steps were to be. The following Friday or Monday would be a better time to meet. Morin even mentioned that he'd be ready to travel to Ottawa, if need be. Five minutes after hanging up, Normand called again: Chrétien was about to leave on vacation and said he couldn't wait.[2] In the end, the two men would not meet.

Claude Morin didn't know at the time that Chrétien was touring under the express orders of Trudeau. Despite the fact that his lieutenant was exhausted following the referendum campaign (during which he'd lost fifteen pounds!), the prime minister demanded that he immediately visit every province to speak about the constitution. Chrétien, who was supposed to leave with his wife for Florida, was forced to postpone his trip a few days, to Aline's great displeasure. She herself was threatening to demand sovereignty-association.[3]

After having met with Bill Davis in Ontario, Chrétien travelled to Manitoba on May 22. There he met Sterling Lyon over breakfast, before flying to Saskatoon, where he lunched with Premier Allan Blakeney, leaving immediately for Edmonton to have tea with Peter Lougheed. He then ended his day over supper with Bill Bennett — British Columbia's premier — in Victoria. After a quick stop to spend a few hours with his wife, he left once again, this time for Halifax, where he spent the night. Awake at five in the morning, he had breakfast with Premier John Buchanan, before visiting Angus MacLean on Prince Edward Island, then Brian Peckford in Newfoundland.[4] He finally returned to Ottawa, where he packed his bags and took another plane, this time for Florida with his wife. Arriving in Boca Raton late in the night, Chrétien and Aline finally made their way to the house they'd rented for a week. But as misfortune would have it, their car broke down, and they were forced to hitchhike in the middle of the night on some Floridian road. As the protagonist himself would say of those eventful days, it was a "long, long, trip."[5]

Following his minister's groundwork, Trudeau summoned the premiers for a meeting on June 9. Back in Quebec City, the Cabinet met to decide whether the provincial government should participate in the constitutional negotiations. Lévesque explained that "the government needs to accept the [referendum's] verdict without hostility, all the while defending the traditional interests of Quebeckers and ensuring negotiations for political equality." With this in mind, the PQ leader indicated that he would publicly announce that "the government [would] participate in the negotiations in good faith, despite the fact that it considered renewed federalism to not be the true solution to Quebeckers' problems."[6]

A resigned Lévesque arrived to negotiate in good faith at the prime minister's summer residence on Harrington Lake on June 9. Defeated, he walked absent-mindedly past Trudeau:

> You're not shaking my hand, René?
>   Ah! You're here. You'll end up holding it against me;
> it's the second time I've done that.[7]

If the exchanges between the premiers and prime minister were polite at the formality stage, as soon as the constitution was discussed, voices were raised. Generally speaking, a number of provinces wished to resume discussions on the basis of Trudeau's 1979 proposal, which got them a firm refusal from the latter. More precisely, Lévesque raised the point of a new sharing of powers, recognition of Quebec's unique status, and a right to self-determination. Alberta and Saskatchewan revived the issue of natural resources, Newfoundland followed with the subject of its coastal resources, issues that set these three provinces against Ontario's Bill Davis, who urged the federal government not to make any concessions to the provinces on these topics.[8] On their end, Nova Scotia, New Brunswick, and Prince Edward Island insisted on obtaining guarantees for transfer payments. As for the Charter of Rights, it still irked a number of participants.

THE PEOPLE'S PACKAGE

Despite it all, the provinces agreed on one point: they had to be united on these issues before asking the British to vote on patriation. Only Ontario, once again, backed Ottawa's position.

It should be said that the process surrounding the constitutional talks had become a source of tension perhaps as important as the substance of the negotiations themselves. For Trudeau, the path was clear. There were themes like the charter, the preamble, the amendment formula, and regional disparities that transcended politics and truly raised passions among Canadians. All these subjects had been brought together with care under the heading of "the people's package" and, for the federal government, they had to be treated as a priority. If there was time left, once all had agreed on these primordial points, the participants would move on to the next step, that is, the "government's package," meaning sharing of powers, an essential issue for the provinces. On this topic, the federal government hoped to obtain greater economic powers to, so it said, increase commercial exchange and promote the circulation of workers within the country. However, none of the participants was blind to the fact that the proposed hierarchy of the talks prioritized all the matters the federal government held dear, while the question of power-sharing, if the provinces truly wanted to discuss it, was framed in a way that could lead to greater centralization.

These considerations aside, Trudeau maintained he was resolute in his desire to fight to ensure that Canadians finally obtained their rights — rights they'd never, it followed, truly benefited from. This constitutional populism raised the ire of the premiers. They raised a common front, demanding he give up this approach, which he eventually consented to, although certainly against his will.[9]

It would be his only concession, however. Coming into the talks in a position of strength, he wasted no time with his counterparts' lamentations. He said he wouldn't accept their demands for decentralization, since he claimed it would lead to the end of Canada as a country. Then, mirroring Theodore Roosevelt's motto of "speak softly and carry a big stick,"[10] he stated that "if you aren't happy, I'll go to England alone." Around the table, all knew that the prime minister was serious. Under this threat, the parties agreed to set up a new federal-provincial ministerial committee, which was to hand in a report at the end of the summer.

Each premier considered his options, counted up his supporters, and prepared his game plan. All knew that the situation in Great Britain was one of the more important variables. Since the month of May, Saskatchewan's agent general in London, Merv Johnson, had been reporting to Premier Allan Blakeney. The former believed that it would be possible to convince some MPs and Lords to oppose unilateral patriation.[11] However, one thing was certain: the British government "would deal with this as if it were a matter of international relations, not imperial matters, so it is going to deal with it by talking only to Ottawa."[12]

The same interpretation held sway in Ottawa as in Regina. Trudeau had every reason to believe that Her Majesty's government would get behind him. As his former adviser Michael Kirby explains, "If you did not make that assumption, then you would have been conceding that the provinces had an absolute veto on any type of constitutional reform. Given the situation with Quebec, that would have guaranteed that no constitutional reform would have been possible. And we were not prepared to concede that. That was the case because otherwise you would have been conceding that the British had authority over the Constitution."[13]

Trudeau's view of patriation was revealed here. In private and in public, the federal government's message was the same: Westminster had an obligation to approve any constitutional request sent by Ottawa. This is the position that was explained by the assistant deputy minister with external affairs,

De Montigny Marchand, in a note sent to Trudeau. It was all about ensuring that "the U.K. Government's compliance with the position that the Federal Government, with the Canadian Parliament, is solely responsible for the substance of the resolution and bill (except on purely technical matters)."[14]

In short, the role of the British was honorary and automatic. Trudeau himself, like a hypnotist with his pendulum, repeated this formula ad nauseam. However, not everyone agreed, and the prime minister knew this better than anyone. Barry Strayer, one of the most important constitutionalists in the country, then working at the Department of Justice, had prepared a confidential legal opinion on the matter. He explained that the role of the British Parliament was simply primordial, both in judicial terms as well as political ones. Why? First, because "the body generally recognized by our courts as having the legal authority to amend areas of our constitution is the U.K. parliament." If Ottawa decided to bypass Westminster, "this discontinuity in the constitution-making process amounts to a revolution in law … this could contribute seriously to undermining the political legitimacy of the revised constitution, particularly in those areas of the country where the political legitimacy of the federal system is already seriously questioned."[15] London thus remained essential. But no matter, Trudeau was convinced that the British would support him without reservations.

On June 17, 1980, Nicholas Ridley, the British minister delegated to the Foreign Office, was in the country for a few days. The subject of his visit was obvious. As he noted with amusement, "Everybody I meet is interested in the constitution."[16] Obviously, Jean Chrétien was among these people, since Trudeau asked him to lead the talks with the visiting official. The federal justice minister began by explaining that, even if it wouldn't be possible for federal and provincial governments to agree on everything, the pressure was strong on the latter, and he would likely be able to rally up to eight of them.[17] This demonstrated the federal government's openness, since "the provinces accuse the federal government of being unreasonable yet it is they who demand everything while we make all the concessions." In fact, the federal government "is not asking the provinces to give up any power, except with regard to personal liberties, e.g. language rights, where the issue was the protection of linguistic minorities."[18] On the subject of the PQ in particular, Chrétien, despite everything, believed that it was "not inconceivable that they would compromise on the constitutional question in order to cut the ground from under Mr. Ryan's feet and win the election."[19] Whatever the case may be, he concluded that if by September an agreement hadn't been reached, Ottawa would proceed without the provinces.

Ridley answered that it was important to keep the British government informed on the situation. "The parliamentary timetable is a choc-a-bloc and unless we have adequate notice the U.K. parliament might be unable to deliver the goods at the right time."[20] He also threw out a warning: "We do not wish to become embroiled in Canadian domestic affairs," citing as evidence the visit of the three hundred aboriginal chiefs the previous year, an event that he hadn't appreciated at all. "Our position is that if the Canadians ask us to patriate the constitution we will do so but we hope to avoid becoming middle-man in a row between the provinces and the federal government."[21]

The situation might become "very messy," Chrétien admitted. But the best way for the British to avoid this problem was to do what the Canadian Parliament asked of them, and get rid of this "thorn in the side."[22]

PIERRE AND MARGARET

The two men left each other on that note. Ridley had just enough time to get back to Great Britain and report to Margaret Thatcher; Pierre Trudeau landed in London on June 25 to meet with her. It was their first official meeting. From the outset, they got along quite well. Trudeau was a brilliant man, a smooth talker, and the British prime minister appreciated his easygoing attitude. When they spoke in private, they called each other by their first names. Between them, there was what de Gaulle called the muted respect of the strong for the strong. In other words, they both appreciated the political stature of the other.[23]

As for their respective conceptions of the world, it was an entirely different story. Margaret Thatcher was the daughter of a Methodist grocer from Grantham; married to a Second World War veteran, and deeply patriotic, she reached the summit of power through her strong hand. Faced with the Outremont millionaire, a socialist and a pacifist, it was a head-on collision. Their rows during the G7 summits became proverbial. In 1981, for example, in Montebello, the British prime minister began an interminable lesson aimed at denouncing Trudeau for his perceived indulgence toward the Soviets. Her matronly style was such that Reagan would later say that he thought she'd send Trudeau to stand in a corner.[24] Contrary to others, Trudeau wasn't at all impressed by the fact that she was a woman, and defended himself firmly, going a bit too far sometimes and bogging down the proceedings. In her memoirs, the Iron Lady characterized the Canadian as a "liberal leftist" incapable of understanding the brutality of Communism.[25]

In any case, June 25, 1980, marked the beginning of a relationship that would often be marked by ideological antagonism, though it didn't prevent Thatcher from supporting Trudeau from beginning to end on the constitutional issue. Simply put, the Conservative politician was following her instinct, which persuaded her to keep good relations with Canada … despite Pierre Trudeau. After all, this woman, who'd cut her political teeth at the time of the rise of European totalitarianism in the 1930s, always placed the defence of her country and the Atlantic Alliance at the centre of her preoccupations.[26]

If this perspective included the Americans first and foremost, it did not exclude Canada. Thatcher hadn't forgotten the sacrifices at Vimy, Passchendaele, Hong Kong, Dieppe, and Normandy, battles in which thousands of Canadians gave their lives for King, Empire, and British freedoms. She also didn't overlook Canada's role in NATO. These were things that mattered to her, and they came under federal jurisdiction. No matter the legitimacy of arguments presented by the provinces, Thatcher wanted to dance with Trudeau, and not Lougheed, Lévesque, or Peckford, who were of no use to her.

Well-informed about the problem, Thatcher had chosen sides before her first meeting with her Canadian counterpart. A woman of convictions to some, obstinate and stubborn to others, her opinions changed only under great duress, and the constitutional affair would be no exception.

The first Trudeau-Thatcher summit occurred in this context. It would last two hours, with a number of advisers on both sides of the table. Thatcher quickly went to the heart of the matter: "Are we going to be asked to pass any legislation?"[27]

The question was direct; but curiously, the answer wasn't as direct, as if Trudeau wasn't sure of the path to follow. "I cannot predict, at this moment, any course of action, but it is not inconceivable that Canadians will be taking steps towards patriation," he said, reiterating the promise he'd made to Quebeckers during the referendum. "I am determined on movement and sooner or later the British North America Act will have to be amended. I cannot give a time as this would depend on work throughout the summer and the results of the conference scheduled for September."

The Canadian prime minister stated that unanimous consent of the provinces was unlikely. This might lead to further delays, especially due to René Lévesque, whose interest lay in slowing down the process. Trudeau was hoping to move quickly enough to avoid giving Lévesque another opportunity to submit his option to the people. "I mean to unite Canadians if possible. But I recognize that I might in fact make things worse. In the best case I would not have to approach the U.K. parliament until spring 1981. However, in the worst case, we might want to move quickly to take a step towards patriation even if we have the support of only some provinces." In any case, "there would never be unanimity and the dissenting provinces would expect to be heard and one or more of them would say they were not getting what they wanted."

"I really do not think I should see provincial representatives," Thatcher replied. "If, for example, queues of Indians knock on the door of no. 10, the answer will be that it is for Canada to decide her future and not Her Majesty's Government, but we do not want to be accused of interfering in any way and I hope that I will not have masses of people lobbying in front of no. 10."

Trudeau agreed that it wasn't a good idea to speak with the provinces; their jurisdictions did not include addressing themselves directly to the British government. He then warned his counterpart: "You will be accused of interfering whichever way things go: as for unanimity, it can be forgotten but I will choose a course of action that will cause both governments the least trouble." London should also avoid all speculation. "If there are any questions," Thatcher claimed, "the answer will be that HMG had not been approached and it is a matter for the elected Government of Canada."

Then Nicholas Ridley intervened:

Ridley: "If asked, we would have no choice but to enact the required legislation."

Trudeau: "Are you hinting that this is what you would like to do?"

Thatcher: "It will be a government measure and the whips will be on. We will be as helpful as possible and will try to do anything we can without reneging on any pledges or obligations."

Trudeau: "The U.K. government does not really have a choice."

Thatcher: "If you ask us to act we will have to do so."

The meeting ended in agreement. With a few qualifiers, Trudeau had received the green light he was hoping for. The provinces could rebel however much they wanted, the constitutional train was on the rails.

It was a happy man who took the time to speak to the numerous journalists wanting to question him as he left 10 Downing Street. "We spoke of the G7 summit in Venice," he began, first putting the emphasis on the part of the discussion that wasn't linked to the constitution. But the journalists insisted. One of them asked him whether Thatcher had promised unconditional support. "I did not ask for it. I told her I was a Liberal and therefore an optimist and felt everything would come up roses in September."[28]

"But did you discuss the possibility of provincial opposition?" asked another. "I didn't bring up that hypothesis and I do not believe Mrs. Thatcher brought it up either."[29] The prime minister jaunted off just before his nose grew a few sizes bigger. He caught up with his son Justin, and together they made their way to Buckingham Palace. The Queen was expecting them.

This impromptu press conference had the desired effect. The *Globe and Mail* wrote the next day that "the two leaders … avoided the thorny issue of how the British Government would react to any move by the federal Government that did not have the unanimous support of the provinces."[30] By maintaining that he and Thatcher hadn't spoken of the provinces, Trudeau was sending a message: the provinces could expect no help from the British government. Ottawa was in a position of strength, and the provinces best co-operate. The prime minister might have been lying, but he knew full well that Thatcher wouldn't publicly contradict him. On the British side, however, a number of commentators weren't too pleased by this little number. High Commissioner John Ford, notably, wanted to retaliate, but in the end the slight was simply ignored.

It is legitimate to wonder why Trudeau felt the need to push the envelope with his comments. Thatcher's support was sufficiently clear and strong for there to be no need to tell an untruth, with the risks associated with such an act. By simply recounting his counterpart's words, he could have confirmed to the provinces what they already suspected, which is that the resident of 10 Downing Street intended to ignore them.

TRUDEAU: NEUROTIC AND PARANOID

Trudeau's attitude might seem irrational, and this indeed was Thatcher's impression. If she kept these thoughts to herself during their meeting, her instincts told her that the whole affair might become a lot more complicated before it got simpler — for example, if there was a revolt of the more Conservative provinces.

After the meeting with Trudeau, Thatcher met with Jean Wadds, Canada's High Commissioner in London. A dyed-in-the-wool Conservative whom Trudeau had decided to keep, Wadds was the perfect person to carry a very precise message back across the Atlantic. Using her status as an international star of the Conservative movement, Thatcher delivered simple instructions to Jean Wadds: the Conservative provinces were to remain calm. These words were immediately reported back to Herb Pickering, the agent general from Alberta, who sent a message to Edmonton without delay:

> Mrs. Wadds has asked that Dr. Meekison (i.e., deputy-minister of intergovernmental affairs) and Premier Lougheed to be informed of the issues raised during Mr. Trudeau's working luncheon with Mrs. Thatcher. Mrs. Wadds indicated that Mrs. Thatcher found Mr. Trudeau to be neurotic and paranoid regarding patriation. Mrs. Thatcher thought that Mr. Trudeau's paranoia was based on his fear that the provinces, especially those with Conservative governments, were opposed to the patriation of the constitution....
>
> Mrs. Thatcher perceives the provinces, especially those with Tory administrations, as the big bad ogre; Mr. Trudeau would likely have been influential in shaping this perception.

> It was perceived that other provinces and not Quebec were
> now the problem. Mrs. Thatcher was concerned about possible public embarrassment for her government should a federal-provincial dispute in this matter be carried into London.[31]

In other words, Thatcher believed that between Ottawa and the provinces, the latter were likelier to give way. She also imagined that the Canadian Tories, in particular Peter Lougheed, would be more inclined to back off following the admonitions of their British big brother, a party led by a Conservative superstar. However, this entire episode demonstrated one thing more than any other: the British prime minister hadn't properly measured, at this stage, the state of mind of the Western provinces' populations.

Two weeks after Trudeau's visit, the attitude of provinces was once again the subject of discussions between the British Foreign Secretary, Lord Carrington, and the Canadian minister of external affairs, Mark MacGuigan. They met at the United Nations in New York, and immediately seemed to get along. The Brit was an intelligent, devoted man, and one of only two ministers, with parliamentary leader Norman St. John-Stevas, able to make his boss laugh. Carrington even allowed himself a few not unkind jabs at his boss, often telling his interlocutors that he'd report their words to "My Mistress." The meeting confirmed Thatcher's fear: according to MacGuigan, Alberta's opposition was now a certainty, thanks to disagreements on energy policy. This opposition didn't change anything for the British government, Carrington replied, adding, "once the request is made there is bound to be a good deal of Canadian lobbying which could lead to a debate in the U.K. which you might find unseemly."[32]

This type of commentary wasn't the sort of thing that might change Pierre Trudeau's mind, especially after his meeting with Thatcher. For Emery Davies, an Elgin Street diplomat, "there seems little doubt that Mr. Trudeau was encouraged by this encounter. Certainly since his return he has appeared to take an even more vigorous line on patriation."[33] The accuracy of this statement was soon confirmed by Trudeau himself, who, over the summer, wrote to his counterpart to express the extent to which he was "gratified to receive your assurances of support."[34]

It should be said that among federalists, a sense of euphoria dominated. Many weeks after the referendum, the inebriating feeling of victory still hadn't dissipated. By beating Lévesque's government, Ottawa had not only ensured its pre-eminence over the PQ, but also over every province. In the capital, the federal government was congratulating itself with pats on the back and some even predicted that patriation would be signed, sealed, and delivered before the first snow. As journalists Robert Sheppard and Michael Valpy observed at the time, "They were almost drunk with a new sense of power and accomplishment."[35]

Within this context, negotiations began in the summer of 1980. On Elgin Street, there was both worry and skepticism: "It was clear that Trudeau was going to ignore the provinces," High Commissioner John Ford explained years later. "He was going to force the patriation bill through the Federal Parliament, including his contentious bill of rights. He would then send it to London to be rubberstamped by the British Parliament even if it was unconstitutional in spirit."[36]

Ford was convinced that the provinces would call on British MPs' spirit of fair play and the clear path to patriation would turn into a minefield. He used his time off back in Britain to warn his colleagues, but, as he himself said, "My fears were brushed away by the Foreign Office."[37]

While authorities in London were divesting themselves of the issue at hand, the summer of 1980 was a season of constitutional meetings in Canada. Led by Jean Chrétien, the exercise, which began in Montreal, brought together all the ministers responsible for the constitution for what was beginning to look more and more like an intense and interminable dentist's appointment. Besides the idea of bringing back the constitution to Canada, every other subject bred its own controversy, with every position unyielding. The margin of error was small.

This was the case for natural and coastal resources, over which many provinces demanded greater authority. Jean Chrétien immediately announced that this point should be discussed along with a renegotiation of the Canadian economic union. It was essential, he claimed, "to re-establish a proper balance of power between the two governments," adding, "We believe that Canadians would be better served if the federal government expanded some of its powers in the area of economic management."[38]

Around the table, a number of provincial ministers couldn't believe their ears. They were dismayed by Trudeau's about-face; after all, this was the same man who'd claimed, a year earlier, that he was willing to decentralize some powers to the provinces' benefit. This now seemed eons ago and ages away.

Chrétien had a number of documents prepared that all came to the same conclusion: in each of the important economic and commercial questions, it was essential to centralize.[39] The friendly words from 1979 about shared responsibilities in fisheries, coastal resources, international trade, and tele-communications were nowhere to be heard.[40]

After Montreal, the discussions moved to Toronto, where they took the shape of a boxing match. In the blue corner: Alberta, Newfoundland, British Columbia, Prince Edward Island, Quebec, and Manitoba. In the red: Ottawa and Ontario. And right in the middle: New Brunswick, Nova Scotia, and Saskatchewan — all at their wits' end.

The federal government proposed to take another look at the Victoria formula, which provided for a veto for any province constituting or having constituted 25 percent of the population, meaning Ontario and Quebec. This approach also required the support of two of the four Maritime provinces and two of the four Western provinces. In the latter case, the two provinces had to amount to 50 percent of the region's population.

All of this seemed engineered to displease Alberta, whose government saw in it a break with the traditional equality of provinces. Quebec was also opposed to the proposal. It saw no reason to adopt an amendment formula without first being heard on the sharing of powers. If the latter question remained unanswered and the constitution was repatriated nonetheless, there would be no more reason to listen to Quebec's demands. As for the amendment formula itself, the PQ preferred the Victoria formula (which would give it veto power), or, better yet, a right of withdrawal with financial compensation.[41] This last option was particularly unacceptable to Trudeau, who declared it to be one step removed from separation.

THE BIRTH OF MULTICULTURALISM

Another bone of contention was the preamble that Trudeau hoped might crown the constitution, the goal being to underline common Canadian values. The document referred to the people of Canada and underlined, among other things, the cultural pluralism of Canadian society. This line was a clear attempt to eradicate any reference to Canadian dualism in the constitution, an attempt that Trudeau had always been forthright about. Back when his government had voted in a law on multiculturalism in the early 1970s, the prime minister had declared to whomever might listen that "sometimes the word 'biculturalism' is used, but I don't think that it accurately describes this country. I prefer 'multiculturalism.'"[42] This approach was denounced at the time by Claude Ryan, then director of *Le Devoir*, as well as by René Lévesque, leader of the PQ, and then-premier Robert Bourassa.[43]

Ten years later, in 1980, the situation hadn't changed. The preamble project created an immediate controversy in Quebec. Columnist Marcel Adam rebelled in the pages of *La Presse*, asking whether Quebeckers had been hoodwinked when Trudeau claimed that a state could contain many nations. "On that topic, we perhaps should have voted Yes to show that Quebeckers formed a distinct people that possessed all the attributes of a nation."[44]

Criticism was immediate and overwhelming. Intellectual Gérard Bergeron all but lit his hair on fire over what he considered to be a "fine mess." Solange Chaput-Rolland, one of the Liberal Party of Quebec's big names, vigorously protested Trudeau's approach: "By voting for one country, Quebec didn't choose the concept of a single people."[45] As for Claude Ryan, he railed against the situation. Everything needed to be re-evaluated, according to him.[46]

Faced with this hue and cry, Trudeau called on André Burelle. An urgent facelift was needed to avoid a nationalist alliance in Quebec between sovereignists and federalists. The solution took the shape of an open letter to the people of Quebec, published in the dailies on July 11.

To quiet the uproar, Trudeau raised the idea of the "two principal linguistic and cultural communities that were the foundational peoples of Canada," along with aboriginal peoples. But he also spoke of the "will of Canadians to be the first to overcome the old concept of Nation-States." He discussed his reference to the "Canadian people" in the preamble project:

> The Swiss speak of the Swiss Nation, even if there exists among their Confederation four linguistic and cultural communities. Russians speak of the Soviet People, even if the 259 million citizens of the country are separated in 109 nationalities, including the Russians, Byelorussians, Ukrainians, Baltic people, Armenians, Georgians, Azerbaijani Turks, and many others.[47]

For High Commissioner John Ford, this sort of clarification wasn't convincing at all. Trudeau seemed to him more determined than ever to go forward, no matter what might happen in Quebec, the West, or the other provinces. This disregard for the provinces' demands would inevitably have repercussions in England. He took advantage of a meeting with Michael Kirby over the summer to warn the federal government. In the hypothetical situation of strong opposition from the provinces, he told the Canadian prime minister's adviser, Thatcher would firmly support Trudeau. She wouldn't be influenced by a provincial lobbying campaign, but he asserted that the situation was entirely different for other MPs and Lords, who would ultimately be the ones voting in favour of patriation. It would be enough to attract attention to this subject, as the party of aboriginal chiefs had demonstrated the previous year.

> I commented that the more contentious the governments' proposals, the greater perhaps the opportunity for Quebec to make trouble. Kirby said that he himself was unsufficiently [*sic*] acquainted with Quebec thinking and that it was difficult to discuss that subject with Trudeau, who had his own circle of advisers. He left me with the impression that he thought that Mr. Trudeau was emotional beyond reason on the subject and that this was something which had to be taken into account. I was left with the impression that Kirby, while sympathising in many ways with those urging caution, felt that the hawks were in the ascendant and that it was exhilarating to be bold and decisive and take risks … the chances of a relatively uncontentious proposal are slight and Kirby sees the hawks with the bit between the teeth.…[48]

Summer would decidedly not be a time for vacationing for the ministers responsible for the constitutional dossier. There was meeting after meeting, often starting over breakfast, as well as discussions with committees and subcommittees, most often under the artificial lights of windowless conference rooms. There were also the private conversations next to the water cooler. Sometimes, discussions kept going along a jogging path or on the racquetball court or even over a beer, at night, in jam-packed, smoky dance clubs where Roy Romanow, Jean Chrétien, Richard Hatfield, Dick Johnston, Tom Wells, and others went for a bit of R and R with the most recent disco hits as soundtrack. The only consolation for this improbable learned assembly was that they weren't missing much in the weather department: it rained cats and dogs throughout the summer, the highest levels of precipitations since statistics began to be compiled.[49]

Rain or shine, Chrétien always presented himself in the best light, as a reasonable interlocutor, disposed to confession — in stark opposition to Trudeau.[50] The two men formed a strange tandem in a well-synchronized good cop, bad cop routine. The minister of justice played the part of pacifier, with Trudeau sporadically appearing behind him, always ready to threaten the provinces with the greatest ills.

In order to reinforce this message, the Federal-Provincial Relations Office (FPRO) ordered three polls during the summer, disbursing $300,000 in all.[51] These tended to show — surprise, surprise — that the overwhelming majority of Canadians favoured Ottawa's proposals, particularly when it came to the Charter of Rights. Years later, Michael Kirby, who led the polling operation, proudly recalled the way the strategy was engineered. A smile playing on his lips, he told his story: "Were Canadians demanding a charter? No. But once the issue, as we painted it, was portrayed as a 'we the federal government' want to give you a certain set of rights that will prevent governments from taking those rights away from you, that was a very compelling political argument."[52] And again: "We also wanted to be able to say to the people, the provinces will not give you your rights unless we give them more powers. From there it was very easy to break it into a people's package, which had the right ring, and a powers package, which was offensive in the communications lingo."[53]

In other words, the question came down to: Do you want us to protect your rights? The answer was preordained; being for virtue is no sweat off a man's brow. Besides, another question in the poll asked whether respondents would like the federal government to keep them apprised of the situation. No surprise: an overwhelming majority answered in the affirmative. Ottawa decided to spend $6 million for a series of advertisements in which one could see awe-inspiring scenery underscored by a powerful soundtrack, with the Maple Leaf well in evidence.[54] The provinces were outraged. Quebec, notably, answered with its own ad campaign, at the more modest cost of $1 million.

The propaganda campaign was in full swing, and it certainly fed the discussions led by Chrétien and his provincial counterparts. Day after day, heady closed-door negotiations were taking place, with arguments hammered home by the weight of fists pounding on tables. At the end of the day, each minister repeated for the cameras what he had said earlier behind closed doors, polishing his message, burnishing his image, and moderating his words.[55] Wise, moderate, or abrupt, the ministers of the constitution had become in some way captives of their own exercise, "perhaps more than was good for us psychologically," as one participant would later say, likening his experience to Stockholm Syndrome.[56] Despite it all, by the end of the summer they hadn't been able to smooth out the differences. They would turn to their premiers and the prime minister to cut the Gordian Knot.

CHAPTER 5

JUSTICE VS. THE PROVINCES

While almost every aspect of patriation was mired in controversy, the inclusion of a charter of rights within the constitution was the single most divisive issue. The provinces were opposed to the project and Ottawa supported it.[1]

First there were the new legal guarantees that the charter would bestow on defendants, following the preliminary drafts that Chrétien periodically submitted to his counterparts over the summer. These guarantees would limit police powers during arrests and searches, evidence collection, and so on. The provinces believed this would radically transform criminal justice and give defendants such a range of mechanisms to defend themselves that criminals would eventually be able to get off scot-free.

There were the so-called "antidiscrimination" provisions. A number of provinces asserted that these would allow anyone in any circumstance to make a claim before the tribunals that they had been the object of discrimination by the government, a company, or another individual, and then demand reparations.

Then there was property law. Once again, the provinces contested the measures, claiming that expropriation would become practically impossible.

Ottawa also proposed a right to education in a minority language. Quebec saw in this a direct assault on Bill 101. Anglophone provinces, meanwhile, wondered how they'd find the means to set up French schools whenever a court ruling required it.

Another disposition sought to protect rights that weren't enumerated in the charter, per se. Here was a golden opportunity for the courts to invent wholly new rights, the provinces grumbled. The judicial branch would gain in pre-eminence.

Finally, there were the reasons that could be invoked by a government to act against the charter's dispositions — the future Article 1 of the Charter of Rights and Freedoms. Rights protected by the charter could evidently not be absolute; they could be restrained in certain circumstances in the name of certain principles, be they the maintenance of order, national security, or public health. However, the provinces claimed that all these criteria favoured Ottawa. The federal government would be empowered to not only promote but also elude the rights and constraints of the future charter. The provinces saw in this a clear indication of the partiality of the document: a double standard. The charter would subject them to the will of the courts, while the federal government would always have the means to shirk it.[2]

THE LEGALIZATION OF POLITICS

These objections didn't particularly impress Jean Chrétien, who saw in them a charge against society's most disadvantaged groups: "You come out against the rights of Indians and women and the handicapped and I'm going to cut you in little pieces,"[3] he said, presenting himself as the defender of the defenceless. With a different vocabulary but similar in spirit, Trudeau stated that no negotiation was possible: "We have drawn a distinction between the issues which are negotiable, that is the powers, the politician's quarrels over who will exercise that power and what authority ... and the other constitutional reforms which we consider essential for Canadians. The latter are the fundamental rights, including language rights."[4]

This declaration, made on July 4, completely contradicted what had been agreed on with the premiers on June 9, when Trudeau had accepted to put aside his people's package vs. government's package dichotomy. Clearly, he hadn't given up on that approach. Here was a dynamic at the heart of Trudeau's project: the legalization of politics. This approach consisted of conceiving of and formulating political debates using judicial vocabulary, as if respect for justice were involved in every aspect of the management of the State. For Ottawa, it came down to never mentioning that constitutional modifications are motivated by political objectives. It was essential instead to present the government as a protector of fundamental rights — so sacrosanct and immanent that it would be pure folly to leave them in the hands of mere mortals (like provincial politicians).

The proceedings of the summer of 1980 testify to the entrenchment of each side, with discussions having become impossible. This discord notably led to Sterling Lyon and Pierre Elliott Trudeau speaking at cross purposes, during which the premier of Manitoba raised the spectre that, if the charter were inserted in the constitution, there would be a clear risk of limiting rights and freedoms.

What did the Manitoban mean? First, there would no doubt be rights that wouldn't be described in the constitution, which would create a dangerous legal hierarchy. Could one seriously consider, for example, that the right to be informed without unreasonable delay of charges against an arrested individual — a right that Ottawa sought to inscribed in the charter — was more important than the disposition in the Criminal Code that proscribed murder? [5]

Moreover, attributing a definition of rights in the charter could fix their definitions in time, preventing them from evolving as society itself evolved. But when Lyon expressed these reservations in front of Trudeau, the latter ridiculed him:

> Maybe I will tell you tomorrow or the next day why, but right now my conclusion is that we have heard nothing else when it comes to powers of the provinces or powers of the federal government but put it in the constitution. Suddenly, we get to protect fundamental rights and freedoms of the citizen and you say, "don't put it in the constitution, the words are too hard to find." [6]

If the prime minister's rhetoric was, as was often the case, very efficient, Lyon was nonetheless raising a fundamental question, alluded to for the first time by Alexander Hamilton in the *Federalist Papers* in 1788. For this framer of the American Constitution, the enumeration of rights in a constitution was dangerous to the sanctity of democratic government.[7] In order to have a functioning government, the latter receives powers that are delegated to it by the people. Everything that isn't explicitly attributed to the government remains in the domain of rights and freedoms exercised by the people. Thus, it becomes unnecessary, for example, to specify in a charter that the freedom of the press is guaranteed by the constitution: this goes without saying, since this freedom has never been bestowed by the sovereign people to the government so that it might exercise this right in its place. Consequently, if this freedom is protected by an article of the constitution, a government could mount a charge against any form of freedom of the press that strayed from the definition described in the supreme law. As Hamilton reminds us:

> What is the liberty of the press? Who can give it any defini-
> tion which would not leave the utmost latitude for evasion?
> I hold it to be impracticable; and from this I infer that
> its security, whatever fine declarations may be inserted in
> any constitution respecting it, must altogether depend on
> public opinion, and on the general spirit of the people and
> the government.[8]

The usefulness of describing a right depends directly on our capacity to define it in a clear and precise manner. In other words, to engage in the definition of a right to freedom of the press or freedom of speech does not constitute the best guarantee for these rights to be protected to the advantage of the people.

In reality, the true question that needs to be asked is what can be considered reasonable when it comes to rights and freedoms. To use the example first described by the American judge Oliver Wendell Holmes, Jr., one cannot cry fire in a crowded theatre, thereby causing a panic, and then invoke freedom of speech to defend one's act. If we accept that rights are not absolute, we must determine where their limits lie. To set them in a charter simply passes the responsibility on to the hands of judges and lawyers, instead of keeping the debate in the hands of the elected representatives of the people. The political debates thus become legalized, in the sense that decision-making is handed to judges, with parliamentarians deferring to them one of their key functions, one which should have remained in the domain of popular sovereignty.[9]

Over the course of negotiations in the summer of 1980, Manitoba would stand its ground against this dynamic of legalized politics, swiftly followed by Alberta, Quebec, British Columbia, Newfoundland, and Prince Edward Island. Just like Sterling Lyon, the premiers of these provinces simply did not believe that rights were threatened in Canada.

THE SOVEREIGNTY OF PARLIAMENT AS A GUARANTOR OF RIGHTS

Obviously, Trudeau saw all this from the opposite angle. To support his thesis, he cited the internment of Japanese citizens during the Second World War, attacks against freedom of the press under William Aberhart in Alberta in the 1930s, and did not leave out reference to Duplessis and the Jehovah's Witnesses. Trudeau maintained that the fundamental rights of anglophones had been violated in Quebec since Bill 101 had been adopted, and the same situation had been true for francophones outside Quebec for longer still.[10]

According to Trudeau, this situation required urgent action — a claim which would raise a few eyebrows, including that of political scientist Peter Russell:

> Do you feel menaced by the prospect of the great Canadian majority, acting through its elected representatives in Ottawa, steamrolling over your basic rights and liberties in pursuit of its own interests? Are you comforted by entrenched rights that enable our judiciary to veto these strident majoritarian demands and secure your liberty? If you ask yourself these questions and answer them in the affirmative, what you surely need is a psychiatrist not a bill of rights.[11]

This paradigm held sway when it came time to debate the charter between 1980 and 1982, a paradigm in which Parliament and its majority were forever tempted to violate the rights of minorities. This concept was, however, antipodal to the classic theory of the British parliamentary regime, illustrated by the famous British constitutionalist Albert Venn Dicey. According to him, there exists no contradiction between the sovereign power of Parliament and the rights of men. In fact, rights are guaranteed because of the fact of absolute parliamentary sovereignty.

How did Dicey come to such a conclusion? A first component of the answer is found in the nature of parliamentary sovereignty, which is founded on two elements. First, no institution or person has a right to overstep or annul Parliament's laws. Second, Parliament, and only it, can make and annul all laws.

It is easy enough to explain how the maintenance of this second condition is essential to the protection of rights. If Parliament weren't the only body that could make and annul laws, then society would tear itself apart among many centres of power. It would become impossible to ensure social peace, without which it is equally impossible for a number of fundamental rights, including security, liberty, and property, to be exercised.

That said, order and security can also exist in a dictatorship and thus cannot be considered a sufficient condition to protect other rights. But there exists, according to Dicey, at least another right to which a sovereign Parliament is particularly protective of: freedom of speech. In 1938, just before reading out a famous opinion on this question in Alberta, the chief justice of the Supreme Court, Lyman Duff, noted that it was in the nature itself of parliamentary assembly to desire freedom of speech. "There can be no controversy that the institutions of parliament derive their efficacy from the free public discussion of affairs, from criticism and answer and counter-criticism, from attack upon policy and administration and defence and counterattack, from the freest and fullest examination from every point of view of political proposals."[12]

In short, if Parliament decided to stop defending freedom of speech, it would cease to be a parliament. Of course, one can offer up an objection: what would prevent this institution from turning against its nature, ceasing to be what it should be? Dicey answered that the nature of Parliament itself, and the sectarian debates that occur in it, constitute important protections in matters of rights and freedoms. First, it is not a monolithic arena. There is an upper chamber, a lower one, a party in power, and parties in opposition. Even when the government is in the majority, Parliament remains an institution that is distinct from the executive branch and never speaks in one voice. Admittedly, members of the government sit in Parliament. Party discipline sometimes allows the majority party to impose its views. But it's just this situation that allows the opposition freedom to object, to criticize and denounce the government's policies.[13] As much as the opposition has an interest in being very critical of any attacks on the freedoms of the people, there is an equal impulse for those who govern to prove their credentials in this regard, out of fear of seeing public opinion turn against them.

And so, it is almost impossible to conclude that the British parliamentary system, as it existed in Canada in 1980, was particularly susceptible to infringement on human rights. Does this mean that Trudeau was wrong to say they had been infringed on in the past? No. It is undeniable that violations occurred and the opposition sometimes made common cause with the government to bully a minority. If Dicey claimed that the British parliamentary system promotes the protection of rights, he did not maintain that this system is perfect. As Hamilton wrote, "It is the lot of all human institutions, even those of the most perfect kind, to have defects as well as excellencies, ill as well as good propensities. This results from the imperfection of the Institutor — Man."[14] Allan Blakeney, Saskatchewan's premier, would say during patriation, "Only citizens, and vigilant citizens, protect freedoms."[15]

Nothing would lead one to believe, at the time, that judges basing themselves on a charter of rights would reach better results than parliamentarians when it came time to protect rights. One need only think of the Dred Scott decision, in the middle of the nineteenth century, when the American Supreme Court decided that slavery was constitutional, despite the American Bill of Rights[16] and the fact that the practice had been abolished in the British Empire.

The defence of fundamental freedoms in a judicial context poses another problem: the invocation of these freedoms often leads to a reinterpretation of rights in order to advance political objectives. This then generates arguments in favour of the creation of new rights. The distinction between a judicial and a political process then begins to blur — which leads to the redefinition of rights becoming as normal as a revision of policy.[17] As noted by political scientist Janet Ajzenstat, this dynamic "attacks the idea that rights have a foundation in natural law, or in a lasting understanding of human nature ... it encourages dissatisfaction with the constitution and with the existing rights tradition."[18]

The dynamic present in the judicial sphere is completely different in Parliament, where the mention and defence of rights doesn't imply that they can be constantly redefined or reinterpreted. No one asks for new rights. The legislator has every interest in establishing a clear distinction between rights and policies. He must reassure citizens that the policies he puts forward respect their freedoms, understood here in their traditional sense; otherwise, the opposition will attack him with fists flying. This way of operating protects the distinction between the judicial and the political, and reinforces not only the idea that rights are founded in the state of nature, but also the legitimacy of the constitution.[19]

The battle that raged in 1980 surrounding the charter perfectly illustrated this dynamic. It also posed a fundamental question: what is a right? For centuries, rights were perceived as a natural and inalienable guarantee, which accrued to individuals so that they might protect themselves from others or from the government. This is the case, for example, of the right to life, liberty, and security, as well as freedom of speech.[20] Understood in this way, rights have as their only requirement non-interference in the life of others: to not assault them, to let them speak, et cetera.

In the 1970s and 1980s, this conception was questioned by the idea of positive rights, such as the right to education or housing.[21] To be respected, positive rights require more than passive non-interference. These rights also require the obligation to offer a service: someone must supply a house, pay a teacher, et cetera, which naturally leads to a violation of individual equality. Some must furnish resources so that others might benefit from their right to housing or education. Giving such demands, the label of "rights" is in fact motivated by a desire to attribute legitimacy to political demands, as well as making them unassailable, despite the fact that they remain political objectives that do not fall under the responsibility of courts.

This was exactly what Trudeau was doing, without — it should be said — offering up an explanation as to the source of the new rights he was proposing to integrate in the charter.[22] Are they natural rights? Rights created by man? Do these rights possess legitimacy other than what is conferred on them by the legislator? Or do their merits come from the support of certain groups, be it the bar, feminist organizations, or any other organization defending specific interests?

BIRTHING A NEW NATION

This question is of great relevance, especially in relation to the right to education in one's minority language, which Trudeau was particularly committed to seeing in the charter. The idea behind this measure was to prevent the creation of linguistic ghettos: each would be able to live in any place in Canada while speaking French or English, which, according to the prime minister, would contribute to national unity.

Here, we cannot speak of a natural right like freedom of speech or physical integrity. The right to send one's children to an English or French public school does not exist in nature. Moreover, a Mexican immigrant, for example, does not possess the right to have his children educated in Spanish. The legitimacy of the right to education in English or French directly stems from the project of national unity as conceived of by Trudeau: the only other source of legitimacy could be found in the concept of founding peoples,[23] which Trudeau had always opposed. This concept, with its roots in nationalism, was perceived as a danger to national cohesion. However, the granting of an official status to French and English — and only those two languages — cannot be entirely alien from the notion of historical communities that founded the country. This contradiction is explained when we understand that the bilingualism contained in the charter project sets its foundations on the idea of making Canada a bilingual nation from coast to coast, which was notably incompatible with Bill 101.[24] For Trudeau, the purpose of this enforced bilingualism was the creation of a new country, as he himself wrote before ever having begun his political career:

> History of civilization is a chronicle of the subordination of tribal nationalism to wider interests…. The die is cast in Canada: there are two main ethnic and linguistic groups; each is too strong and too deeply rooted in the past, too firmly bound to a mother-culture, to be able to engulf the other. But if the two will collaborate at the hub of a truly pluralistic state, Canada could become the envied seat of a form of federalism that belongs to tomorrow's world. Better than the American melting-pot,

> Canada could offer an example to all those new Asian and
> African states … a brilliant prototype for the moulding of
> tomorrow's civilization[25]

This quote perfectly summarizes Trudeau's project. But areas of provincial jurisdiction, education in particular, evaded his control. To make the country bilingual and multicultural despite the opposition of a large portion of the population, he needed to give power to the courts, to the detriment of the people's elected representatives.[26] This led to the necessity of including these rights in the charter.

During the negotiations in 1980–81, Saskatchewan's Premier Blakeney asked Trudeau why he held so dearly to integrating linguistic rights in the charter. "It is no more a human right to speak English than, say, Spanish," he said, adding that he knew of no place on earth where linguistic rights were included in a founding document. Why then this approach? Blakeney asked, before going on to offer up the answer himself: "I suggested that he was embedding them in the charter because it was easier to argue for a charter than it was to argue for freestanding language rights. He readily agreed. Since he clearly wanted the language rights provisions, he had decided to wrap them in a charter."[27]

CHAPTER 6

UNILATERALLY

It was August 20, 1980, and the ten provincial premiers were in Winnipeg holding their annual meeting, when a feeling of apprehension descended like a veil over the proceedings. The fateful federal-provincial meeting was quickly approaching — it was to occur in September — and the constitutional negotiations were still at an impasse.

On the last day of the meeting, the *Ottawa Citizen* published a confidential memorandum by Clerk of the Privy Council Michael Pitfield addressed to the prime minister.

In it, Pitfield told Trudeau the ways in which he might accomplish unilateral — that is, without the provinces — constitutional patriation. Ottawa should wait a few weeks after the federal-provincial conference to present its unilateral project so it would not give the appearance of having sabotaged the so-called "last-ditch meeting." This delay would make it possible to defend the idea that the federal government had negotiated in good faith.

Pitfield also referred to discussions about energy policy with Alberta, which had been dragging its feet despite a recent meeting with Lougheed. At this meeting, Trudeau had informed the Alberta premier of his intention to set up new price control measures for gasoline. However, as Pitfield explained, the time for talk was over. The federal government had to impose its decision on the petroleum-producing provinces. Lougheed couldn't believe what he read in the *Citizen*. Furious, he decreed a few days later a unilateral increase in the price of a barrel of oil.[1]

During a subsequent meeting with his provincial colleagues, Chrétien declared that the Pitfield memorandum was no more than a contingency plan.[2] Yet, even as the justice minister was attempting to calm everyone's nerves, Ottawa was secretly preparing to dispatch a team of jurists to the Foreign Office to deliver a unilateral patriation request. Only a few people were aware of this operation. It was so sensitive that the federal government didn't even inform the Canadian High Commission in London, fearing new leaks. And if ever the affair came to be discovered, it would once again be presented as a contingency plan.

Informed by John Ford of the federal government's intentions,[3] Lord Carrington refused to partake in such a game. The visit of a group of Canadian jurists to London would inevitably come to light eventually, he told Ford. The fact that the High Commission was being kept out of the loop would cause trouble between it and the Foreign Office if the truth were to come out. Jean Wadds and her team would be furious at having been bypassed in such a way and would lose their trust in their British counter- parts. This approach should be proscribed.[4]

THE GHOST AND MR. FORD

Secret manoeuvres, leaks, sensational declarations, threats of unilateral patriation: for John Ford, this was all too much. Years after the events, he would declare that "in such circumstances, I intuitively suspected that British backbenchers and the public sense of fair play might create parliamentary difficulty in London and a dangerous clash between the British and the federal Canadian Parliament."[5] For this enthusiast of open spaces, a lover of John Colombo's poetry and Robert William Service, admirer of the Group of Seven, a real Canadaphile at heart whose brother and one sister had chosen the country as their adoptive home, the situation was harrowing.

Not since Lord Byng had a representative of Her Majesty been so in touch with a sense of history pressing in around him; this was doubly so in Ford's case since he lived in Earnscliffe, the former residence of John A.

Macdonald. The latter's bust decorated the house's entrance, from time to time serving as the diplomat's hat stand. And despite the fact that the house's strange creaks and shivers had given it the reputation of being haunted, Ford didn't believe it for a second:

> It is not true. Earnscliffe is not haunted. The radiators are responsible for the nocturnal gurgling where Canada's first Prime Minister died: not the ghost of John A. Macdonald drowning in drink his misery over Canada's failure to fulfill his dreams. Yet I have sensed the spirit of Macdonald brooding over the old house; and daily his bust by the front door has regarded me with an amusedly quizzical look, as if to say: "I know, it always was a battle and it always will be; but my Canada has not done badly and her paradoxes are such fun."[6]

As Ford dialogued with Macdonald's bust, the ten premiers and the prime minister were in the national capital for the last-ditch meeting that was to start on September 8 and last several days. On September 7, the heads of government, each accompanied by his minister of constitutional affairs, were invited to dinner with governor general Edward Schreyer. The meal took place on a terrace on the ninth floor of the Department of External Affairs, on a warm night. A gourmet menu, great wine, an enchanting setting: nothing was spared to lighten the mood, promote good cheer in all, and ultimately facilitate negotiations.[7]

However, just as the second service was being savoured — crab, Creole-style — the storm clouds burst. Lougheed (Alberta), Blakeney (Saskatchewan), and Bennett (British Columbia) demanded that Lyon (Manitoba) be named co-chairman — alongside Trudeau — of the conference set to start the following day. The Manitoban saw himself as a positive force in such a role, since he'd been presiding over the conference of premiers for the past year. The purpose of this bold manoeuvre was to signify to Trudeau that Ottawa didn't speak in the name of all of Canada on the constitution, biting the thumb to Trudeau's famous credo "Who speaks for Canada?" The provinces were answering in unison with Lougheed's oft-heard response, "We all speak for Canada."[8]

Pierre Trudeau could fulminate all he wanted; the West's representatives didn't back off. Bennett gave as an example the summer's constitutional negotiations, during which Roy Romanow, Saskatchewan's minister of intergovernmental affairs, had served as Chrétien's co-chairman. "You mean like *deux nations*," Trudeau replied, as if the West had suddenly become separatist.[9]

Some proposed to touch base the next day in front of the television cameras, while others, such as Bill Davis of Ontario, sucking on his pipe, attempted to chuck the proposition out entirely. Brian Peckford (Newfoundland) railed against Trudeau's refusal, the latter mocking the alliance between the conservative Newfoundlander and the socialist Blakeney. The only socialist around the table is you, Peckford replied angrily.

After having heard from each around the table a first time, the next day's schedule had to be considered. Trudeau wanted to return to what had been decided by Chrétien and his provincial counterparts over the summer, namely that the charter would be the last subject to be discussed. Accusations of negotiating in bad faith immediately poured down on Trudeau. Even Richard Hatfield (New Brunswick), often in agreement with the prime minister, thought he was exaggerating.[10] The governor general then intervened in the hopes of leading the conversation in a more productive direction. "Hurry up," was Trudeau's only reply, cutting him off — rudeness that left John Buchanan (Nova Scotia) speechless.[11] "The princeling is certainly in high dudgeon tonight," Lévesque told Roy McMurtry, Ontario's attorney general, in a stage whisper, ensuring all around the table would hear him.[12] McMurtry was so shocked by the turn the dinner took that he called his wife to share his alarm. The conference seemed to be about to founder like the *Titanic*.

Faced with this appalling atmosphere, Hatfield desperately attempted to accelerate the dinner service. With great gestures and facial expressions, the former theatre student informed the servers to bring coffee. They immediately complied, presenting the coffee accompanied by a cake made in honour of Allan Blakeney's fifty-fifth birthday, a moment meant to be the night's crowning event. As Blakeney himself remembers, "It was the only festive note of the evening."[13]

This moment of light-heartedness lasted but a few seconds: Trudeau decided to lay his head on his arms on the table. Instead of the prescribed

Happy Birthday, dear Allan, voices one by one went mute, followed by whispers and dumbstruck looks. Suddenly, Trudeau got up, hands flat on the table, and, just before turning around and walking out, declared, "Well, this is going to be an interesting meeting." As he reached the door and saw his bodyguard following him, he left with a parting note to the man meant to protect him: "Fuck off and don't follow me home."[14]

These words would surprisingly not be the evening's most startling moment. Claude Morin and René Lévesque took advantage of the prime minister's theatrical exit to send an important message. "Where will you be tonight?" they asked the other ministers. "We have a confidential document to share with you."

AN EMBARRASSING LEAK

What document was he speaking of? For the past few days, the Quebec government had been in possession of a sixty-four-page memorandum written by Michael Kirby, an adviser to Trudeau. Originally, only a few numbered copies of the precious document were allowed to circulate. One of them was to be delivered to the deputy minister of Canadian external affairs, Allan Gotlieb. When one of his assistants secretly learned of it, he was bowled over by Ottawa's attitude toward Quebec and the other provinces.[15] He decided to photocopy the document and send it to Claude Morin, who received it like a gift from heaven.

After having established its authenticity, Morin and Lévesque, not without hesitation, decided to share it with their counterparts. The idea was to orchestrate a leak to the media without Quebec being singled out as having tried to sabotage the conference. Quebec's delegation rented a photocopier and produced ten new copies of this explosive memorandum. As for the original copy, it was destroyed.

These documents were sent to the other premiers on Sunday, September 7, at 11:00 p.m. The papers exposed the entire federal strategy. Within, one could find the following:

> The Premiers who are opposed should be put on the
> defensive very quickly and should be made to appear

that they prefer to trust politicians rather than impartial and non-partisan courts in the protection of the basic rights of citizens in a democratic society. It is evident that the Canadian people prefer their rights protected by judges rather than by politicians. As far as patriation is concerned, the issue can very easily be developed to make those provinces who oppose it look as though they believe that they are happy with Canada's problems being debated in the Parliament of another country....

In private, the provinces must be told that there is absolutely no question but that the federal government will proceed very quickly with at least all the elements of the People's Package and that it would therefore be to their advantage to bargain in good faith on the other issues so that they too will be relatively satisfied after the Conference. It should be made abundantly clear that on Powers and Institutions, the federal government expects give from the provinces as well as take.... The probability of an agreement is not high. Unilateral action is therefore a distinct possibility.... The challenge now lies with the federal government ... to show that disagreement leading to unilateral action is the result of ... the intransigence of the provincial governments and not the fault of the federal government....[16]

The document confirmed the worst fears of most premiers.[17] However, curiously, this piece of evidence wasn't even mentioned at the opening of the following day's proceedings. Not surprisingly, the conference soon turned to chaos, as much in public as behind closed doors. Entrenched in the moral values of his charter, Trudeau fired the first salvo: "There are some powers that shouldn't be touched by government, that should belong to the people, and that is why we call it the people's package because it isn't a quarrel or a quibbling of who can exercise what jurisdiction. It is a question of what basic fundamental rights of the people are so sacred that none of us should have jurisdiction in order to infringe those rights."[18]

"I understand your view on why you want a charter, but why impose it on us?" Lougheed railed, immediately followed by a volley of criticism aimed at

Ottawa's proposed amendment formula.[19] Blakeney added that British common law already protected rights. Then it was Lyon's turn to add to the mix. An admirer of Reagan and Thatcher, he was the most conservative of Trudeau's opponents, and he saw the prime minister as a socialist dreaming of transforming the country into a republic. Despite their opposing views, Lévesque and he joined forces in their visceral opposition to the charter. Lyon spoke this way: "Prime Minister, you have described the entrenchment of a charter of rights as a mechanism that would give more power to the people. In fact, sir, it takes power from the people and places it in the hands of men, albeit men learned in law, but not necessarily aware of the everyday concerns of Canadians."[20]

Not at all rattled, Trudeau stood firm in his positions when the discussions moved to the fifth floor to continue in private. This time, Lévesque attacked. First there was the issue of the preamble project. The federal leader wished to have it reference a union of the Canadian people. Lévesque preferred the expression "union of the provinces." There was also the issue of language education rights. The prime minister maintained that the referendum gave him a mandate to include these in a charter, an interpretation contested by Quebec's premier.[21]

Cantankerous, inflexible, Trudeau increased his attacks against Lévesque in the discussion that followed, so much so that the latter appeared a moderate in the eyes of many of his provincial colleagues. The PQ leader was negotiating in good faith, Lyon declared. You've transformed the constitutional debate into a vendetta against Lévesque, Bennett added. Between René Lévesque's vision of Canada and yours, Brian Peckford continued, I prefer his. "Have you got a bag, I think I want to vomit,"[22] Chrétien whispered into Trudeau's ear.

Angus MacLean, premier of PEI, explains:

> During that time my respect for Quebec premier René Lévesque increased and my regard for Trudeau shrank. I found Lévesque a reasonable person, not at all stiff-necked or rigid. I had an impression that if the federal politicians had had the kind of relationship with him that I did, we would have reached some sort of compromise on the constitution. Trudeau was particularly antagonistic.[23]

As John Ford would note in a message to London, "Buoyed by public polls which reveal across the country support for constitutional change, Mr. Trudeau's aim is to portray provincial premiers as unrepresentative and selfish power-grabbers with little view of a united Canada and to set [the] stage for unilateral action."[24]

And while the battle raged on, members of Quebec's delegation were surprised to observe that Kirby's confidential memorandum still hadn't leaked. "We looked at the papers, and nothing," Deputy Minister Robert Normand recounted. "We were expecting a leak, since men in politics, with such a hot document in their hands … I've never known one able to resist. So we started taking measures to orchestrate our own leak; just then, the *Globe and Mail* got the document, thanks to Hatfield."[25]

A good sport, the latter phoned Claude Morin on Monday night to bear some "bad news." Casually, he told him that someone had given a document to journalists, and that it would make the front pages on the following day. Quebec would be identified as the delegation having obtained the document, but it would also be mentioned that the leak wasn't its fault. Morin then informed Lévesque, who immediately expressed satisfaction. The provinces are pins that Trudeau wants to bowl, he said, and the public will at last know "where the ball is coming from."[26]

The Kirby memorandum affair erupted on Tuesday, September 9. But there is none so deaf as he who will not hear. Trudeau acted as if he hadn't heard the formidable thunderclap that reverberated through the conference centre. He presided over the discussions as if nothing had changed; all the while the RCMP went hunting for the mole, who'd soon be caught and lose his job. Meanwhile, the sixty-four pages of the confidential memorandum were dissected by one delegation after the other, each being called on to comment by the press. If Newfoundland, Alberta, and Quebec seemed outraged, other provinces attempted to avoid throwing oil on the fire. Far from the cameras, the leak was the stage for some unexpected scenes. Robert Normand, a good sport and truly impressed by the document, would tell Kirby, "What professionalism!"[27]

In the hope of minimizing the whole affair, the concerned party played the fool before the press. "If we were half as good as you guys think we are, we wouldn't be in this shit,"[28] Kirby threw out, half in earnest, half in jest. As for Trudeau, he claimed to whoever might listen that he'd never read the memorandum. These denials intrigued the British. Emery Davies, number two at the British High Commission in Ottawa, had the opportunity to shed light on the affair during a meeting with the now famous writer of the report. As he'd later report to the Foreign Office:

> We have been intrigued by Mr. Trudeau's repeated statements that he has not read the Kirby memorandum of last September. For our own information, Kirby assured me that this was correct, in a very technical sense! Mr. Trudeau had read all the separate position papers on various aspects of the constitutional issue which has [sic] been used as material for the memorandum which has been designed for Ministers not directly involved, but he had indeed not read the memorandum.[29]

As the Kirby report makes clear, the British feared that unilateral patriation might be contested before the courts. "A challenge in the court to the legality of a resolution under discussion by the Canadian parliament would place the U.K. parliament in a most embarrassing position," the diplomat Emery Davies noted. If Ottawa sent a unilateral request despite everything, "there would seem good justification in the parliament's refusing to consider the matter so long as it was *sub judice* in Canada; at the very least, it would provide plenty of grist for back bench lawyers in the commons and lords who were harnessed by dissenting provinces to obstruct."[30]

In the middle of the September talks, a preoccupied John Ford discussed this aspect of patriation during a meeting with Canadian deputy prime minister Allan MacEachen. The latter answered that "the issue would be political not legal," adding that "it's not for the British parliament to take account of any litigation in Canada. The Canadian public's reaction would be vigorous if it did!"[31]

TO HELL WITH CONSEQUENCES

On Friday, September 12, after five consecutive days of negotiations, and with the impasse still holding, the prime minister lost patience with his counterparts.

Trudeau: "You guys are laughing at me … but I am telling you, gentlemen, I have been warning you since 1976 that we could introduce a resolution in the House of Commons patriating the constitution, and if necessary unilaterally … we will go to London and we won't even bother asking a premier to come with us."

Lyon: "You are going to tear the country apart."

Trudeau: "If the country is going to be torn apart because we bring back from Britain our own constitution after 115 years … and because we have asked for a Canadian charter of rights, when most of you have provincial charters, then the country deserves to be torn apart."[32]

The failure of this last-ditch conference was assessed the following day by Trudeau. As he was closing the session, he expressed himself in a mysterious fashion. "It's the beginning of the end or the end of the beginning," he stated, adding that he'd learned a number of lessons from the exercise.[33] As Roy Romanow would later recall, "Undoubtedly, one of the most important factors in the failure was the reversal by the federal government of its 1980 policy towards constitutional reform from the 1978–79 period.… Ottawa wiped the slate clean and proceeded in an entirely different directions."[34] As for John Ford, he described the failure in the following way:

Trudeau's hope of a constitution where the definition of human rights would make the courts the main protector of the individual and power would be more centralized than hitherto, and the determination of the provinces to obtain a more effective voice in the federal institutions and to keep the elected provincial assemblies and the federal parliament as the main and more flexible guarantors of individual's rights.[35]

In London, many understood the situation along these lines, notably in Buckingham Palace. The Queen, who supported the prime minister without reserve, had already promised him — secretly — to travel to Canada with Prince Philip, constitution in hand. This promise, combined with the fact that the situation was getting bogged down, worried Philip Moore, her political counsellor. The latter believed that Her Majesty might find herself in the middle of a delicate situation. On September 12, he phoned Martin Berthoud, director for North America at the Foreign Office. Sir Philip emphasized that "when Mr. Michael Pitfield had been here with Mr. Trudeau in June, he had stressed the latter's determination to go ahead with patriation and (more or less) damn the consequences. The so far rather unfortunate results of Mr. Trudeau's attitude have been reflected in developments at the current constitution conference at Ottawa."[36]

Over the course of their meeting, the diplomats of Elgin Street understood one element that was becoming increasingly clear: no reticence or hesitation on London's part would be tolerated by Ottawa. As Emery Davies reported to the Foreign Office,

> All this would be perhaps little more than exasperating but for the fact that we have had a hint from one, particularly well-placed source, that should HMG not produce the goods promptly when required, Anglo-Canadian relations generally will suffer and that indeed the Canadians were even now considering what retaliatory measures they might undertake. Needless to say we shall attempt to discover what the Canadians have in mind by way of retaliation![37]

The British had every reason to be worried. Colonial issues were poisoning the Thatcher government's work. Lord Carrington was well placed to speak to this. For months he had been locked behind the doors of Lancaster House, in London, with the protagonists of the delicate Rhodesian issue, in which Ian Smith's white minority had declared independence a few years earlier, while simultaneously confiscating power from the black majority. This issue had just been solved with the independence of Zimbabwe when three other colonial problems appeared, designated at the Foreign Office under the acronym ABC, for Antigua, Belize, and Canada.

Antigua was an autonomous Caribbean colony that sought full independence. Its neighbour, the territory of Barbuda, objected to this scenario and sought to secede. Long and difficult negotiations took place in London to find a peaceful solution to the affair.

Then there was Belize, a Central American colony that had obtained its independence in 1981. Guatemala refused to recognize its existence, brandishing the threat of invasion. British troops had to be stationed there permanently to avoid the situation falling apart.

Finally, Canada represented the most Kafkaesque problem of all three. The challenges it posed to the Iron Lady would only be surpassed by the Falklands War two years later. Carrington sent a warning to his High Commissioner in Ottawa: "You should avoid giving any impression that we are seeking to intervene in this highly sensitive domestic issue."[38] Increasingly exasperated by Trudeau's attitude, and a few months away from retirement, Ford was — despite Carrington's warning — hatching a plan.

THE AUSTRALIAN CHANNEL

Meanwhile, the Canadian High Commission in London reminded Ottawa that the situation was constantly shifting in the British capital. The constitutional brouhaha was beginning to attract attention outside of the political sphere, as witnessed by an article in the *Times* (London) that referenced a quite interesting precedent between Australia and Great Britain. The affair, which was new reason to worry for the federal government, occurred in the first half of the 1970s. Progressive and centralizing, the Australian Labour prime minister Gough Whitlam had attempted to create a charter of rights, a project that had been torn to pieces by his country's states. He'd also attempted to cut the remaining links between Australia and Great Britain. Despite independence, the states had the possibility to appeal directly to the Privy Council in London in some judicial matters. Similarly, it was the sovereign (the Queen of the United Kingdom) who conferred royal assent on some laws, and named the lieutenant-governors without consulting Canberra, the federal capital. As the *Times* reported, "When the Whitlam government tried to end the States' reliance on British legislation, including the appeal to the Privy Council ... it was easily defeated by State representatives in London; the keys of parts of the Australian Constitution are thus retained in London by some States."[39]

A humiliation for Whitlam, this episode was followed in 1975 by a constructional crisis that led to the destitution of the Labour government by the governor general, opening the way to the election of Liberal Malcolm Fraser — the term "liberal" being attributable only to the name of the party he led. As the former defence minister, he made his name notably during the participation of his country in the Vietnam War, when he imposed conscription. He was one of the most right-wing federal prime ministers in Australia's history.

In short, if Whitlam was an Australian Trudeau, then Fraser was his antithesis incarnated. But they shared something else: in 1980, both were in command of their respective countries. Any issue involving Australia and having an incidence on the constitutional debate was potentially delicate. The day the *Times* article was published, Martin Berthoud received a call from Christian Hardy, the Deputy High Commissioner in London, who asked for clarification. As Berthoud reported, "It is clearly a sensitive issue, the Canadians did not want to make enquiries in Canberra. In helping the Canadians we would perhaps be giving them ammunition to use against their provinces, but I do not think that we could possibly refuse to cooperate over a request of this kind."[40]

Some of Berthoud's colleagues thought this was too risky. It might lead to complications with some Canadian provinces, as well as — and here lay the actual problem — with Canberra, since they'd be sharing with Canada the behind-the-scenes details of a situation that concerned only Australia and Great Britain. Finally, it was decided that the answer to Hardy should contain only information already published in the media.[41]

While Canadian diplomats were following crash courses in Australian constitutional law, Pierre Trudeau was whipping up the troops. He met with his caucus on September 17. Should they push for a minimalist constitutional reform, he asked, or attempt the "Cadillac" option that would include everything the federal government hoped for; that is, a strong charter and new economic powers for Ottawa? "We might end up in 4 years with a magnificent constitution but a defeated government," he warned, raising protests from his assembly. Trudeau thus continued more forcefully: "I understand that this caucus wants us to go with the full package, to be liberal, not temper our convictions with political expediency. If that is your will, I am delighted to follow it!"[42]

These words were music to the ears of Liberal MPs. Rested and refreshed over the summer, still intoxicated by their victories in the election and the referendum, they were like sharks smelling blood in the water. "Let's go for the Cadillac," one of them cried out, a credo immediately taken up by the rest of the caucus: "Cadillac! Cadillac! Cadillac!"[43]

This atmosphere still reigned during a cabinet meeting on September 18. One after the other, Jean Chrétien, Allan MacEachen, and Marc Lalonde exhorted their already convinced colleagues to keep the hard line. All the ministers were filled with fervour without precedent, aware that a page of history was being written. Only the general's orders were missing. Determined to crush the provinces' resistance, Pierre Trudeau threw himself into the battle of a lifetime. *Alea jacta est!* "We could tear up the goddamn country by this action," he said, "but we're going to do it anyway."[44]

CHAPTER 7

THATCHER DISCOVERS THE CHARTER

Thursday, October 2, 1980, eight o'clock in the evening. The prime minister is addressing the nation over the airwaves. Announced that same morning, his televised declarations take everyone by surprise. Solemn, measured, the head of government's natural authority was practically palpable. He explains the motivations for his unprecedented decision: unilateral patriation of the constitution:

> If the first ministers failed it is because they tried to reach perfection in a very human world and because of unanimity.... But we were led further still, towards a radically new concept of Canada, one in which the national good was merely the sum total of provincial demands.... We were led to bargain freedom against fish, fundamental rights against oil, the independence of our country against long distance telephone rates.... Rights belong to all the people.... Canadians must find a way to get away from 53 years of constitutional paralysis.[1]

Contrary to what Trudeau was claiming, the fifty-three previous years hadn't been characterized by paralysis. The constitution had been amended fourteen times, more often than in Australia or the United States during the same period. As the course of events would eventually prove, only after patriation would the Supreme Law become practically un-amendable.

But let's not put the cart before the horse. For now, let's return to the proposal that Trudeau presented in October 1980, and that he intended to send to London after having it voted on in the House and the Senate.

It came down to three things: first, the adoption of the charter; then, the constitutionalization of the principle of transfer payments, meaning federal financial compensation for poorer provinces; finally, the adoption, following a series of steps, of an amendment formula. In the two years following patriation, unanimity would be necessary for any constitutional change. After this probationary period, if an agreement on an amendment formula hadn't been reached, a decision would need to be made between three options. Behind door number one, Ottawa would impose the Victoria formula, with its veto for every province representing or having represented 25 percent of Canada's population (meaning Quebec and Ontario). This option also provided for approval of two of the four Western provinces and the same for the Maritimes. Behind door number two, the central government would propose a new, alternative amendment formula. And behind door number three, if seven provinces counting for 80 percent of the population agreed on a common solution, then all Canadians would be asked, by referendum, to choose between the federal proposal (described in the second scenario) and that of the provinces.[2]

As Canadians were learning the details of Trudeau's proposals, British diplomats had been dissecting it for a few days already. They'd been secretly allowed to learn of it in the last week of September. The fact that the request included a charter of rights, instead of simple patriation, led to some apprehension. On September 23, the secretary of state for external affairs, Mark MacGuigan, noted this unease when he met his counterpart, Lord Carrington, at the United Nations.[3]

> Carrington: "There will be no problem with the amend-
> ing formula but I have serious reservations about the
> Bill of Rights. Would it be possible to leave it outside of
> the package?"

MacGuigan: "It is at the heart of the proposed initiative. The charter alone, with its recognition of fundamental and linguistic rights, represents a response to the confidence in Canada expressed by the majority of Quebeckers in the Quebec referendum.

Carrington: "Of course. And it would be highly improper for the British government not to follow exactly any request for the Canadian Parliament in this area. But we are concerned about the possible effect of provincial lobbying on members of Parliament. There might be delays and harm to British-Canadian relations."

MacGuigan: "The federal government would not facilitate representation by the provinces to either the British government or the British Parliament."

Despite this warning, the head of the Foreign Office wholeheartedly supported Ottawa in this affair, unlike some of his colleagues. In government circles, many shared Carrington's apprehensions, including Robert Armstrong, the cabinet secretary, the most senior civil servant in the country. He was one of Thatcher's closest advisers. On September 29, he had the opportunity to broach the topic with his counterpart, Clerk of the Privy Council Michael Pitfield, during a meeting meant to prepare for the G7 meeting in Montebello. The two men enjoyed each other's company and had forged over time a relationship based on trust. It was completely natural for Pitfield to ask Armstrong to share his boss's gratitude with Thatcher "for her understanding approach on the questions of the patriation of the Canadian constitution." Of course, the Brit answered immediately adding that Thatcher wouldn't do anything to compromise the promise she'd made in June. However, things might get more complicated before they got simpler. As Armstrong reported:

I added that a unilateral request for patriation would present the prime minister with some political difficulties. The breakdown of Mr. Trudeau's talks with the provincial prime ministers had been reported in the British press ... the prime minister might encounter some objections to unilateral patriation from backbenchers in the House of Commons, particularly if provincial prime ministers sought to stir up opinion in Britain. Mr. Pitfield acknowledged this difficulty, but said that a poll had recently been conducted in Canada which showed an overwhelming majority in favour of patriation of the constitution, even in the western provinces.[4]

This polling data hadn't convinced the Brits entirely. Pitfield thus presented other polling information, which showed substantial support for the charter, reinforcing the federal position against the rebellious provinces. The poll had been conducted by Gallup over the month of August. To the question, "Should the constitution guarantee basic human rights to all Canadian citizens?" 91 percent answered Yes, including 83 percent in Quebec, with only 2 percent answering in the negative. By the time Pitfield had mentioned this to Armstrong, the data had already been analyzed by the Foreign Office. John Ford had shared the results with his colleagues a few days earlier, accompanied by the following note: "I doubt whether much significance should be attached to the figures. I believe that very different answers would have been obtained had the questions been worded differently."[5]

A few months later, another similar poll was analyzed by Whitehall, the centre of Her Majesty's government. It revealed that 86 percent of Canadians interrogated supported the idea of a charter, with positive responses equally distributed across the country, including in the West and Quebec. And to ensure that respondents understood the context, the questions included a preamble explaining the function of a charter in the constitution — that its purpose was "to provide individual Canadians with protection against unfair treatment by any level of government in Canada."[6] Martin Berthoud wasn't impressed. "This is a very flimsy basis for Mr. Trudeau's claim that 80 % of Canadians back his bill of rights. Is there another poll with a less leading question?"[7]

If the Foreign Office's diplomats were sometimes skeptical when it came to Ottawa's claims, they nevertheless attempted to keep their distance from the provinces, which had begun to accelerate their own activities. The ball got rolling in Quebec City, with British consul Robert de Burlet, not too long after the tabling of federal proposals. He was privy to deputy minister of intergovernmental affairs Robert Normand's reactions. Over lunch, Normand explained that Ottawa was attempting to go over the heads of the provinces and mount a charge against Quebec's jurisdiction over linguistic matters, a situation that would lead to a backlash of anti-British sentiment. The provinces hostile to Trudeau were organizing; they'd be throwing "the biggest media campaign they could put together to press the British government not to adopt an imperialistic role in altering the fundamental balance of the federation. They would also consider measures of economic retaliation should we do so."[8] De Burlet swallowed the comment without flinching: "I am very interested to receive all this information, including the threats, but … I have no reason to suppose that the British government would act in any way."

This remark didn't calm the deputy minister, who kept pressing his adversary. Quebec would turn to the U.N., he threatened, and "the issue would probably be raised there in the context of a neo-colonialist intention on the part of the British government." Stoic, De Burlet answered that "all this provincial activity is tantamount to spitting into the wind … if a refusal on our part to act on the objections of some of the provincial governments is to be construed as a neo-imperialist act, then a refusal to accede to the legal request of the federal parliament could certainly be seen in the same light and more strongly …"

As the Brit reported, "There was a lot more in this vein, with Normand sketching a doom-laden future if we persisted in our intentions while I stonewalled behind the entrenched position of our guidance lines." The atmosphere only lightened toward the end of the conversation. De Burlet told Normand that travelling to Westminster would be a waste of time, all the while specifying that the meal had been delicious and that Quebec's threats would cause him no indigestion. Normand found the quip quite funny and ended the discussion by proposing a meeting between René Lévesque and John Ford.

As the diplomat Emery Davies would note in a subsequent cable, "It is clear … that Bob has been and will undoubtedly continue to be under considerable pressure from the Quebec government. It is of course the reverse side of the advantage of having a man on the spot who is well dug into the local political scene …" These precisions made, it was still necessary to determine whether John Ford should travel to Quebec or not. According to Davies, such a delicate visit would certainly lead to Ford having "his head scrubbed by Lévesque and no doubt subsequently by the federal government at this end on his return."[9]

For now, Quebeckers were addressing themselves to Thatcher, by way of Agent General Gilles Loiselle, to remind her that Quebec's government "will oppose with every means at its command any attempt by the federal government of Canada to patriate the constitution unilaterally," an act that would be "wrong and most divisive since it strikes at the very basis of the federation and threatens the already fragile balance of power which exists in Canada."[10] In lieu of answer, the agent general received nothing more than a polite acknowledgement of receipt by the minister of state at the Foreign Office, Nicholas Ridley, assuring him that his letter had been noted.

Noted is a euphemism here. In reality, patriation had attracted Whitehall's attention to such an extent that Thatcher and her ministers discussed it the same day that Trudeau informed Canadians of his intentions. The committee that piloted the government's legislative program examined potential repercussions. The British Home Secretary began his analysis by claiming that the operation was so complex considering current circumstances that it might take an entire year to stumble through the process. While Canadians had been warned, they certainly wouldn't take the news lying down, he said, before adding that it was thus primordial that no firm promises be made to the federal government.[11] As for the Lord Chancellor, he was truly unhappy that the British would be forced to vote on a charter. It would be far more preferable to simply send back the constitution to Canada with an amendment formula, he believed. The brainstorming continued, and eventually Thatcher summarized the discussion:

> A bill incorporating a Charter of Rights and Freedoms would be complex and highly controversial and would take up a good deal of both Houses … there is little doubt that the Federal Government would greatly resent a refusal by HMG to enact legislation which contained this element and had been approved by the Federal Government. The Canadian Proposals in their present form will need further careful consideration.[12]

A ROYAL AUDIENCE

A new opportunity to consider the situation presented itself a few days later. The federal government dispatched ministers Mark MacGuigan and John Roberts to London to explain the federal thought process. They were perceived as being the Cabinet's hawks. Even before meeting members of the British government, they were received at Buckingham Palace by the Queen's adviser, Philip Moore. The following day, Sunday, October 4, the sovereign invited them to Balmoral Castle, in Scotland. As John Ford explained, this wasn't simple chance: "They cleverly showed the proposal to the Queen, in her capacity of Queen of Canada, before they even showed it to the government. She had the right to know but I think they hoped that she would put pressure on the government. I noted the fact."[13]

The royal audience began with lunch in a large, plainly decorated dining room. The conversation flowed easily on a variety of uncontroversial subjects while half a dozen small corgis sniffed and snuffled on the floor in the hopes of scrounging some of the crumbs the Queen threw on the carpet for them. The animals constantly zigged and zagged through the legs of the guests, to the great displeasure of the Canadians.[14]

Elizabeth than moved on to more serious considerations. Inviting the two emissaries to a drawing room, she immediately demonstrated her interest — and great understanding — of the constitutional dossier. MacGuigan was convinced that she would speak to Thatcher on the subject during their weekly conversation, despite the fact that he noted the relationship between the two women who held the highest positions in the British State was not particularly warm. The Queen was nonetheless won over to the federal cause; that's all that mattered. The last words of the conversation had barely settled into the lush carpets when the door to the drawing room swung open and the blasted pride of corgis was at their ankles again.

The next day, the emissaries met with the British prime minister for an hour. Despite the fact that her primary objective was to help Trudeau, the conversation wasn't as easy as it had been with the Queen. The Foreign Office's civil servants believed it was essential to act with circumspection, as explained by a confidential memorandum they'd prepared for Thatcher:

> The British Government, under both Labour and Conservative administrations, have consistently taken the general line that patriation would go through in this country if requested by the federal Government. There is no precedent for the U.K. purporting to question a Canadian request for amendment to the BNAA, although we have

made technical adjustments to Canadian proposals ... nevertheless, the assumption has been that the Address from the Canadian Parliament would be against a background of broad provincial agreement.... There now seems considerable provincial opposition to the constitutional proposals. Controversy in Canada is likely to be mirrored in this country. This could lead to difficult debate in Parliament and attempts at amendment; thus delay. Legislative programme already overfull ... MPs might be lobbied and ask why the Canadians wanted, in effect, to pass far-reaching constitutional measures, such as the Charter of Rights and Freedoms, through the British Parliament instead of sorting them out first in Canada and then simply coming to the U.K. for patriation along with an amending formula ...[15]

As was her habit, the Iron Lady had carefully studied beforehand, as witnessed by the proceedings, which occurred in the presence of her loyal minister Nicholas Ridley and John Ford, who had been asked to attend.[16] Thatcher didn't hide her surprise at the outset of the conversation; she'd been expecting a patriation request, nothing more. "But now you want the Westminster Parliament to pass a Bill of Rights," she declared. "Someone is certain to ask why the Canadian Parliament could not pass the Bill of Rights for themselves once the constitution has been patriated. The issue will become more controversial in this country, and ... as a consequence, its passage would be more prolonged."

MacGuigan replied that the measure was "necessary for the survival of Canada in its present form. Commitments had been entered vis-à-vis Quebec which had to be honoured."

The prime minister carried on: "Why can't you get the constitution and then pass the bill of rights yourselves? Put yourself in my position and imagine how I can answer my backbenchers."

The problem stemmed from the amendment formula, Roberts explained. It would have to be "somewhat rigid in order to protect the position of the provincial governments. Once it is in place it would be very difficult to secure the adoption of a Bill of Rights." In any case, he continued, the constitutional resolution had been presented in the House of Commons, and it was too late to remove the charter. The British government would need only claim that they acted following a request by the Canadian Parliament.

MacGuigan then announced that Ottawa would like the whole process to be signed and sealed by July 1, 1981, date of the fiftieth anniversary of the Statute of Westminster. "This will not be easy to observe," Thatcher remarked, before asking a question: "How likely is it that there would be an appeal in the Canadian Courts against the legality of what the British Government is going to do?"

"This is not in the cards," Roberts reassured her.

"Nonetheless, it would be very awkward," Nicholas Ridley objected, "if the British Parliament were to patriate a constitution that the Canadian courts might subsequently find illegal."

"Certainly," Roberts continued, "but a failure on the part of the British Government to respond to a request from the Canadian Government would involve [the] British Government more deeply than an agreement to a request." Thatcher then maintained that there was no question of refusing anything. She'd instead do her best to accommodate the Canadians. The discussion ended on that note.

A few comments should be made here. We should first note the extent to which both Canadian ministers were solicitous toward the provinces. They both preferred a rigid amendment formula that would protect them from eventual arbitrary modifications to the constitution coming from Ottawa. This interesting openness would only materialize after the adoption — without the provinces' consent — of a charter, thanks to Westminster. This measure was supposedly necessary following the promise Trudeau made to Quebec. Not only was the operation not hostile to the provinces, but there seemed to be no doubt across Canada on the legality of the process. This is what explains John Roberts's conviction that the courts would not be asked to consider the case — a claim he'd repeat a few hours later at a press conference.

THE GERMAN INTERVENTION

Apparently, Margaret Thatcher wasn't suckered in by this discourse, as attested to by a conversation she'd have not long after with German chancellor Helmut Schmidt. He was a good friend of Trudeau, and had once invited the Canadian PM to sail with him on his sailboat on the Baltic Sea. He took advantage of this meeting with the British prime minister to ask whether she had news of their Canadian counterpart. She told him of her thoughts on the patriation of the Canadian constitution:

> Chancellor Schmidt asked the prime minster for her assessment of the likely outcome of the present discussions on the patriation of the Canadian constitution. The prime minister said that it would be easy if the only question at issue was patriation. Unfortunately the Canadian government also wanted a bill of rights. They were seeking this at Westminster because they would not be able to secure agreement for it in Canada. The British government would have to respond positively to the Canadian request.... Chancellor Schmidt said that he followed Canadian problems closely but had begun to wonder whether Mr. Trudeau could steer Canada out of her present difficulties. In the Western provinces Ottawa was talked of in the same terms as Europeans talked of the New Hebrides. In British Columbia, the Maritimes were out of sight. Ontario was at odds with the rest of Canada, so was Quebec. They had the problems of OPEC versus non OPEC states in one country. Canada was a country with great troubles and great potential.
>
> Lord Carrington commented that ... Trudeau had done well so far and needed to be supported. It was a pity that he was making things difficult for the British government by asking them to do something which he could not do himself.[17]

Naturally, Thatcher never shared such reflections with Trudeau or Roberts and MacGuigan. But all this activity attracted media attention, notably from the prestigious weekly *The Economist*, which announced this incredible news item to its readers: "You can expect to see a charter of rights enacted by the British parliament within the next few months. This will, among other things, entrench certain minority language rights (Welsh papers please copy) ... but the British need not to get worked up with it, it will affect only Canada."[18]

Who knows whether British readers found this news item disguised as a joke funny, but it does remind us of the extent to which a charter, as opposed to parliamentary sovereignty, was controversial in Great Britain at the time. As Mark MacGuigan himself would note, "It must be remembered that the Thatcher government was strongly opposed to a bill of rights for the United Kingdom."[19] A true patriot, the Iron Lady was proud of her country's history, the first major nation to have elected a woman, and she was ready to stand up to defend the freedoms of the people. This was a sacred good that only the sovereign Parliament had agency over, and which, following the Whig tradition and the ideas of the constitutionalist Albert Venn Dicey, remained the supreme guarantor of human rights. This was the heart of Thatcher's political project, one she tirelessly repeated on every platform, driven by unshakable faith. As such, during her first official visit to Washington in 1979, she was already declaring that "we are determined to return to the first principles which have traditionally governed our political and economic life, namely the responsibility of the individual rather than the state for his own welfare, and the paramountcy of parliament for the protection of fundamental rights."[20]

Trudeau's charter thus made its way to Great Britain just as the Tories had declared war against the concepts that underpinned the charter. A debate was raging following the ratification by Westminster of the European Convention on Human Rights, whose dispositions had not yet been incorporated into English law. Many put forward the idea that, in order to approve the treaty, the adoption of a charter of rights was absolutely necessary. Some authors depicted a sombre portrait of the situation in the United Kingdom, a place apparently governed by tyrants. Their books, which had nothing to envy Orwell's *1984*, carried titles meant to instill fear: *The History and Practice of Political Police in Britain*, *Police Against Black People*, and *The Technology of Political Control*.[21] Exactly the sort of remarks that the Conservatives, and Margaret Thatcher in particular, viscerally hated.

However, opposition to a charter was also found outside the Conservative ranks. A number of important figures in the Labour party were also opposed, including Neil Kinnock, who'd become the party's leader.[22] As in Canada, the main criticism regarded the power of judges. This idea was defended in 1979 by the House of Lords, when a project for a charter of rights was presented to parliamentarians in order to help the country respect its engagements toward the European Convention on Human Rights. Lord Diplock, one of the Law Lords (the equivalent of Supreme Court judges in Canada), warned his colleagues that judges sometimes have the propensity to enter the political arena and that this phenomenon would become more prevalent if the country equipped itself with a charter:

> It seems to me that those who represent the people have been elected democratically in representative Parliament know better and are better judges than appointed judges, who have been appointed not for their social philosophies or their politics but because of their qualification in the law. If this bill becomes law in its present form, it will be open to every fanatic, every crackpot, to challenge any law they disagree with ...[23]

One year after this debate, the Canadian High Commission would ask Lord Diplock to write a judicial opinion on constitutional patriation. Unsurprisingly, the latter recommended foregoing the charter of rights entirely.[24]

This debate in Great Britain didn't make Jean Wadds's task, or that of her colleagues, any easier. As in Canada, Trudeau's associates in London first presented the charter as a measure for the people, aiming to give them rights to ward off government oppression — an argument that seemed straight out of the mouths of British supporters of a charter of rights. Ottawa soon understood that this approach created interference in England's debates.

This situation first manifested itself in impromptu leaks to the press: "Government faces Logjam in Parliament over Canadian Constitution," the British daily the *Guardian* ran on October 27, 1980, explaining that the federal request was going to sow chaos. The article clarified that "there is little doubt that constitutional experts in both houses of parliament would have major reservations about giving a swift endorsement to such a proposal which has constitutional implications for Britain."

After reading the *Guardian*, Mark MacGuigan would confess to "an awakening perception of the dimensions of the U.K. problem," especially since the article wasn't the only clue to complications on the horizon. He decided to warn Trudeau: "I sent a memorandum to the prime minister saying that my department was now a good deal less certain than it had been that the U.K. government was prepared to co-operate in expediting our bill through their parliament."[25]

THE CHARTER OF DISCORD

From London, Jean Wadds had developed the same impression, and she proposed that the Canadian charter of rights be accompanied by different arguments: "These might include justification on grounds of pledges made during Quebec referendum campaign and purely structural argument that [a] charter is [an] essential part of [a] constitution of a federal state (to make distinction with U.K. situation)."[26]

In Ottawa, some were astounded by the turn of events. "Why do the Tories consider the charter such an embarrassment," wrote assistant deputy minister of external affairs De Montigny Marchand. "Have there been genuine legal arguments that it in some way creates a precedent bearing on the U.K.?"[27] Whatever the case might be, Marchand also concluded that it was necessary to reorient discussion. He'd suggest the same to MacGuigan:

> We recognize that there are those in the U.K. who have reservations about a Charter of Rights in that country, but the situation in our two countries [is] different. We would not dream of judging the requirements of the U.K. and trust our British friends accept that the need for a Charter of Rights is a matter for Canadians to decide. Canada is a federation, and there are special arguments for a Charter of Rights in a federation. The Charter would ensure that all Canadians, regardless of their province of residence, enjoy the same basic rights. This is important for the unity of the country.[28]

MacGuigan agreed. He would propose a similar strategy to Trudeau. The latter would give the green light, indicating that the task to take toward London "should emphasize that we are entrenching bilingualism at the federal level and minority education rights at the provincial level."[29] As he himself would say soon after to British minister Ian Gilmour over supper, "The provinces' opposition to my proposal will be to break up Canada, whereas I am fighting to keep it together."[30]

In short, it was time to refocus the issue of the charter with an argument that had rarely been used by the federal government in Canada: that of national unity. To understand what this implied, we need to distinguish between constitutional patriation on one end and the charter of rights on the other. Patriation represents Canada's independence; it thus constituted an important potential source of pride. In this sense, the constitutional question was no doubt tied to national unity. However, this wasn't the case with the charter, at least in principle. Contrary to the government's package, the people's package — as we saw earlier — was presented as a supposedly disinterested proposition on Ottawa's part to benefit its citizens. According to Ottawa, the charter sought to protect the rights of citizens, and not to consolidate national unity. However, the political line that was employed overseas contradicted this. To prevent British political currents from affecting the debates on the Canadian charter in Westminster, the charter had to be very concretely tied to Canadian national unity. This shift in meaning revealed the ultimate goal of the constitutional project: to impose on the provinces, Quebec in particular, what Trudeau called minority language education rights, which would stand in stark opposition to Bill 101 in Lévesque's province.

Did Ottawa find it had more success with this approach? "Canadian ministers argued that the charter was necessary for Canada's unity," Daniel Gagnier, then working for Canada's High Commission, explained. "The British politely listened to this argument, but they never really bought it. Even those who supported our cause never really had any emotional reaction to this new logic."[31]

"It was a silly argument," Jonathan Aitken, a Conservative MP at the time, added. "For a long time the charter was demonstrably creating disunity."[32]

The problems caused by the charter weren't limited to political philosophy. The Canadian charter also gave ammunition to dissidents within Her Majesty's government. This was the case of the minister of arts and parliamentary leader Norman St. John-Stevas. He was considered part of a group called the "wets," more centrist members of the British Cabinet who, by their political beliefs, were hostile to Thatcher's right-wing governmental program. The presence of St. John-Stevas in the constitutional dossier didn't bode well for the federal government. The wets were constantly attempting to sabotage what they perceived as a cavalier attitude by their boss, which included, to a certain extent, her support for Trudeau on the constitutional issue.

In St. John-Stevas's case, it should be added that he saw himself as an untouchable. In the early 1970s, he served as minister of state under Thatcher at the time she was heading the Department of Education. Having become her protégé, he had an excellent relationship with her. Let's not forget that among Cabinet members, in addition to Carrington, he was the only one capable of making her laugh. He believed himself so immune to her wrath that, over time, he multiplied his pleasantries, even calling her, behind her back, Leaderene, Attila the Hen, and even The Blessed Margaret.[33] However, since her arrival at 10 Downing Street, Thatcher had become less and less inclined to appreciate these sorts of jokes.

St. John-Stevas saw none of it coming. Without consulting her, he took the initiative of getting the Canadians to understand that they couldn't just go about it willy-nilly. His manoeuvre took the form of a phone call to his counterpart, Yvon Pinard, Liberal parliamentary leader, to ask when the constitutional resolution would be adopted in Ottawa and sent to the Queen. Pinard told him that it would be ready before the end of January.[34] In that case, St. John-Stevas replied in a polite but firm tone, the Canadians could forget about the First of July. "If the package is without a Bill of Rights it should then be completed by the spring of 1982," he told Pinard. "With a Bill of Rights, it would take longer, perhaps August 1982, because of pressure on the backbenchers from the provinces and other groups."

> Pinard: "The reference to the provinces indicates a concern in our internal affairs."

> Stevas: "If the package were to include a Bill of Rights then it becomes our problem also."

> Pinard: "This is very disappointing and I cannot undertake to deliver by a certain date."

If things weren't going so roundly within the Conservative government, they seemed no better on Labour's end. At the end of October, the outgoing leader, James Callaghan, called Jean Wadds, who, as soon as the conversation ended, prepared a report for MacGuigan:

> The BNA question now appeared to him to be much more difficult than he had anticipated when he saw you and John Roberts earlier this month. He had not, at that time, understood all of the implications of the measures we were

putting before the British Parliament and the capacity for
trouble thereby made available to the rabble-rousers of all
parties. He highlighted three areas likely to be the focus of
back bench interest: the Bill of Rights; the Indian rights;
the federal/provincial relationship. In any event, Callaghan
wanted us to know that the difficulties, which he considers
are considerable, are at the level of back benchers.[35]

Callaghan even declared that he was ready to travel to Canada for a
non-official visit to discuss the situation and help out the federal government.
The offer was secretly transmitted to Trudeau, who did not follow up on it.
The latter decided instead to send MacGuigan back to London in an attempt
to put out these new fires.

Faced with these difficulties, Ottawa also decided to send a new man
to lend a hand to Jean Wadds's team at the Canadian High Commission.
Reeves Haggan, of British origin and former producer of the successful
show *This Hour Has Seven Days*, had recycled himself as a public servant and
become a veteran of constitutional conferences. Within the federal political
apparatus, he was one of the few people who had, from the start, predicted
that constitutional problems would arise with Great Britain. In London,
many expected his arrival to give renewed strength to the federal team.
While Wadds continued to cajole and charm, Haggan, a large, physically
impressive specimen, would make the perfect bad cop. As he said himself,
his task consisted of "working out who matters in the House of Lords and
Commons and putting myself in the way of meeting them.[36]

The need for reinforcements illustrates the extent to which the situation had evolved since the tabling of the constitutional request. Since then,
despite official denials, one thing was now certain for Mark MacGuigan:
Thatcher was struggling to control the situation. With a small majority in
the House, she'd recently suffered "two embarrassing defeats in the House of
Lords on two important domestic political issues."[37] It was now impossible
to assert that the constitutional resolution would not suffer the same fate.
In a secret memorandum stamped with the mention "Canadian eyes only,"
MacGuigan summarized the situation for Trudeau: "We face real problems
in the United Kingdom … with the government, with parliamentarians
more generally and with the press."[38]

CHAPTER 8

THE BATTLE BEGINS

Toronto, October 14, 1980. The provinces met at the Harbour Castle Hotel in Toronto at the initiative of Sterling Lyon, Manitoba's premier, who would act as chairman of the provincial premiers' conference. Constitutional patriation was now shaping up to be a political battle without precedent, pitching the provinces against the federal government. It was essential to coordinate the efforts of each and all. All of the premiers were present except for New Brunswick's Richard Hatfield, who would arrive hours late.[1] He wasn't comfortable with the front being organized. He'd come to warn his colleagues that he'd be siding with Trudeau, as Bill Davis of Ontario would, declaring that he agreed with the prime minister. Like the latter, Davis was convinced that language education rights were necessary to maintain national unity[2] — which didn't stop him from refusing bilingualism for his province when the time came.

TRUDEAU'S ODIUM

In addition to the two provinces that had decided to side with Trudeau, two others would remain neutral: John Buchanan's Nova Scotia and Allan Blakeney's Saskatchewan. While the latter rejected the federal government's unilateral approach, he still believed it was possible to come to an agreement with Trudeau. As for Buchanan, he didn't have strong feelings either way about the constitution, but preferred agreement over conflict. He was Peckford's (Newfoundland) rival in a contest to be champion of the Maritimes; both men had different views on coastal resources and fisheries management.[3] Buchanan was present at the meeting, remaining for the group photo, but called Lyon a week later to warn him he wouldn't be joining the rebellious provinces.

The final tally was this: Newfoundland, PEI, British Columbia, Manitoba, Alberta, and Quebec would be called the Group of Six. The kernel of this group would be the last three provinces, led by three men who respected and appreciated one another, while remaining somewhat wary of their colleagues' intentions. Lougheed would notably say of Lévesque, a few years later: "He was shrewd, affable, and naturally friendly. He saw me as an ally and we worked closely together … but dealing with a separatist who had just tried to take Quebec out of Canada was always front and center in my mind. It made me uneasy about where we were and where we would end up."[4] At the time, however, Lougheed had far fewer reservations than these words might lead us to believe, describing Lévesque as a man in his own image, "a strong provincialist."[5] As for Lévesque, he'd forgiven his Albertan counterpart for having supported the No camp during the referendum — especially after Lougheed had publicly accused Trudeau of not fulfilling the promise he'd made to Quebeckers. As for Lyon, he presented himself as a defender of a traditional Canada, meaning British Canada, and stood opposed to Trudeau, whom he saw as the gravedigger of the nation.[6] This was the cement that held together this improbable alliance: a visceral hostility toward Trudeau, whose name but proffered was enough to arouse anger from his opponents.

Of all of Trudeau's adversaries, the Albertan was certainly the most dangerous. As Jean Chrétien would later say, "I tended to see Lougheed as the leading Western voice. He was strong and articulate…. Often his silence was as eloquent as his words. And I could see others studying his look to read his mind. Even Allan Blakeney, the brainy socialist, seemed afraid to cross Lougheed."[7]

Indeed, the Albertan would fire the first shot. On October 20, his minister of intergovernmental affairs, Dick Johnston, presented a draft bill allowing for referenda in his province, something that was "extremely important for this government" since it would allow him to consult all Albertans "on matters of significant importance." On his end, Lougheed explained that the bill would aim to oppose the dispositions relating to referenda that Trudeau had included in his own constitutional proposal. If the latter had given himself the possibility of consulting Canadians without going through the provinces, then Alberta should be able to hold its own referenda as well. He'd also tell Ottawa — which had smelled a whiff of separatism in that gesture — that "we are not talking about separation and we never have been. We want to be a part of Canada."[8]

And while the Albertan premier swore he wasn't aiming for independence, those who dreamed of it not too long before were fighting Trudeau tooth and nail. The PQ was rising again. The failed referendum had crushed the party, sown doubt in its ranks, shaken its leader. It had robbed it of a mission, without which partisan life is nothing more than clientelism and politicking. But the constitutional question breathed new life into the party and endowed it with a renewed purpose.

This rebirth occurred over the course of that autumn, as the Lévesque government decided to push elections back to the next spring. In the interval, a motion aimed at denouncing Ottawa's unilateral action was presented in the National Assembly. The PQ leader hoped the Opposition would support the motion. As he himself wrote, "The Liberals couldn't ignore that unanimous support for the motion would have a strong impact on the British."[9] He believed he could convince Claude Ryan, knowing that the latter opposed Trudeau.

The text of the motion simply denounced unilateral patriation, avoiding the many contentious issues that lay like a minefield in the PQ's relationship with the Liberal Party. However, Ryan, who already saw himself as the next premier, didn't see the motion in the same light. He required that it be accompanied by a resolution underlining the attachment of Quebeckers to Canada, the advantages of a larger country, and the importance of rejecting sovereignty in a referendum. In short, he aimed to force Lévesque to publicly self-flagellate. Lévesque attempted to change Ryan's mind: "I begged him to try to see things from my point of view," Lévesque would write. "I was practically on my knees. As he spoke soothing words and tried to bridge the gap, the Liberal leader was happy to let me roast over an open flame. Under his air of saintly innocence there was a hint of something like sadistic delight. It's at that moment that I made myself a promise to only think of the next election and lead, if possible, the best campaign of my life."[10]

Lévesque's renewed strength was soon felt among his troops. The Pequistes lifted their chins and marched through the last months of 1980 on mission. Just like the federal side, they launched an ad campaign, distributing flyers to every home.[11] They described how the charter project had a double objective: to remove some of Quebec's powers and to create a melting pot in which its identity would be swallowed.[12] The campaign also had a televised chapter, with advertisements showing a priest criticizing Trudeau, a production that angered Jean Chrétien. Ironically, this ad campaign was rolled out at the same time as the latter was immersed in controversy on the relevance of mentioning "God" in the constitution's preamble.[13]

This end-of-year mobilization reached its apex in early December. A call to arms by the Coalition Quebec-Solidarity led to fourteen thousand nationalist activists cramming into the Montreal Forum. The rally was officially non-partisan, which explains Roch La Salle's presence — he was the only Conservative Party member elected in Quebec — as well as that of Michel Le Moignan, leader of the Union Nationale, and Denis Hardy, a former minister under Robert Bourassa. Despite the fact they denounced Ottawa, all three were showered with boos every time they made the mistake of speaking the words *Canada* or *renewed federalism*."[14] Of course, the booing stopped when René Lévesque climbed on stage. The hero of the hour had renewed his flamboyant eloquence. His attacks galvanized the crowd, resounding through the Forum. Trudeau was preparing a "coup d'état," and we must stop him, he cried. On their feet, the crowd applauded wildly, waving a forest of fleur-de-lis flags. Every attendee proudly wore a pin emblazoned with the words *J'ai signé*, in reference to a petition demanding that the constitution not be amended without Quebec's consent.

The conflict wasn't only taking shape in public, before crowds of adoring supporters. On October 23, the Group of Six decided to bring a case to court. It was agreed that Newfoundland, Quebec, and Manitoba would ask for a judicial opinion from their respective appellate courts. The three provinces asked three identical questions. First, would the federal proposal affect the federal-provincial relationship? Second, was it in accordance with constitutional convention for Ottawa to send a patriation request to London without the provinces' consent? Finally, was provincial consent required in the present case? As Claude Morin explained, "Recourse to the courts was less a question of attempting to solve a judicial problem than making a point to the British government and Parliament that the federal process was causing serious disturbances in Canada. "This strategy seemed potentially quite useful to us: it would postpone the process, bother Ottawa and make the British ill at ease."[15]

It was also resolved that the provinces would make a case for the idea that Ottawa was violating constitutional conventions, instead of trying to highlight the more formal aspects of law — an attempt to underline the political rather than legal dimensions of the exercise. Any actor, individual, or institutional can give an opinion of the existence of a convention whose possible violation can't lead to sanction by a judge. By agreeing to give their opinion on the matter, magistrates didn't really enforce law, judicially speaking. They simply joined their voices to the growing concert of protest that Trudeau's project sparked off. The prime minister was perfectly entitled to denounce a political operation prepared by the provinces, to which the courts were lending a hand. The only problem: he himself, through his charter project, had touched off the legalization of Canadian politics.

No matter, Trudeau still went forward. His maxim was that of Admiral W.F. Haisley — "Hit hard, hit fast, hit often." — and the key to his victory, Westminster. As Michael Pitfield (Clerk of the Privy Council) noted in his August memo, "There would be a strong strategic advantage in having the joint resolution passed and the U.K. legislation enacted before a Canadian court had occasion to pronounce on the validity of the measure and the procedure employed to achieve it."[16] In short, the objective was to use Great Britain to force Canada to accept a *fait accompli*. This haste provoked the anger of the Official Opposition in the House of Commons, which, through a speech by MP Perrin Beatty, demanded that the Supreme Court decide on the case. The idea left Trudeau cold:

> Many times since I have been in this house the opposition has demanded that this or that bill be referred to the supreme court. My answer generally has been that the courts should be brought into the subject when some citizen refers the matter to the courts, and this is what the minister of justice answered earlier. Let us patriate the constitution and have a bill of rights, and if some citizen or province feels aggrieved by that action and feels that

it is, to use the words of the honourable member, tainted with illegality, the place to plead that would be in front of the courts.[17]

In short, Pitfield's strategy making the front page of the newspapers and known to everyone under the sun would not make the federal government change course. But that certainly doesn't mean everyone in Great Britain appreciated this lack of finesse.

MARK MACGUIGAN'S NIGHTMARE

Mark MacGuigan was well placed to observe the beginnings of British discontent when he landed in London on November 10, after being once again dispatched by Trudeau. The mission of the secretary of state nonetheless began on a positive note following a discussion with Secretary-General of the Commonwealth Sonny Ramphal, whose sister lived in Toronto. Trudeau and MacGuigan had briefly met with him a few weeks prior and quickly come to the conclusion that he knew the country well. A great supporter of the equality of Commonwealth nations and independence, Ramphal was firmly on Ottawa's side in the whole affair.[18] Moreover, he seemed to have quite a lot of free time and hoped to be able to offer a helping hand in a dossier that he perceived as having great importance for his organization. He certainly didn't bide his time before beginning to lobby Her Majesty's government, enjoining the British to send the constitution back to Canada, no questions asked. Thatcher, however, was viscerally hostile to international organizations and didn't like the Commonwealth group, which often criticized her. Ramphal's attitude in the constitutional dossier was just the sort of interference she detested.

But let's not put the cart before the horse. First, MacGuigan was to speak with Lord Carrington. He met him in the company of Lord Privy Seal Ian Gilmour, a minister without a portfolio who worked, among other things, on patriation. Just like St. John-Stevas, Gilmour was a "wet."[19] He would eventually come to denounce Thatcher's governance, claiming she was "steering full speed ahead for the rocks"[20]; Thatcher would later toss him overboard — perhaps to save him the indignity of being shipwrecked ...

In any case, MacGuigan discovered that the guarantees the Iron Lady had given Trudeau weren't seen positively by the wets, especially since the provinces that opposed Trudeau had begun judicial action. Escorting the visitor to his meeting with Lord Carrington, Gilmour got to the heart of the issue: "It would cause us great difficulty if the patriation of the Canadian constitution were still *sub judice* in the Canadian courts when the request is made."[21] According to MacGuigan, cases such as these could last two or three years. "Couldn't you ask the Supreme Court to deal with it at once?" Gilmour asked.

"Our government would prefer not to do this. It would lend too much dignity to the proceedings. Moreover this is a political, rather than a legal question," was MacGuigan's reply.

Gilmour didn't care to reply, but as an adviser wrote, "The Lord Privy Seal interpreted what Mark MacGuigan had said as meaning that the Canadian government thought they would lose if they took the matter to the Supreme Court; and the Canadians were not going to help Her Majesty's Government out of its dilemma by doing so."[22]

In front of Carrington, the visitor repeated that patriation was a political issue and not a judicial one.[23] As for the charter: "This issue is more important to us than patriation.

"The Canadians seem to want us to do their dirty work for them," Carrington opined, adding that this whole business might lead to an intense lobbying effort aimed at British parliamentarians.

This meeting was followed by a second one, this time with St. John-Stevas, the parliamentary leader. After reiterating the importance of sending the constitutional request to London as quickly as possible, the Brit also wished to know whether including the charter was opening the door to judicial contestation.[24] MacGuigan repeated that the charter, with its minority language rights, was absolutely essential and that the provinces could always asked provincial courts to consider the question, though only the federal government could refer the whole thing to the Supreme Court. This last claim surprised St. John-Stevas. He insisted that the necessary verifications be made.

MacGuigan left the meeting convinced that St. John-Stevas was trouble just waiting to happen. He went on with his busy schedule by meeting, among others, a man who'd reveal himself as one of Trudeau's most consistent allies, James Callaghan. He wasn't opposed to the idea of a charter, but was convinced that the federal government was "buying trouble by laying it before the British house. It will be controversial for domestic British reasons and open for attack by pro-native lobby and any pro-provincial lobbies."[25] He wondered whether it would be possible to recognize First Nations rights in the charter. MacGuigan claimed that these rights were impossible to define and it was out of the question, adding that, except for Quebec, the provinces wouldn't be lobbying London. There'd be no problem in that case, the former premier replied. Quebec alone wouldn't have much of an impact.

MacGuigan greatly underestimated the capacity of the provinces to mobilize in London. He also made a second mistake in his perception of the way the Supreme Court worked, a somewhat more embarrassing one for a constitutionalist. As we have just seen, he told St. John-Stevas that the British need not worry about the provinces, since they couldn't bring a case before the country's highest court. Not long after MacGuigan had left London, Ottawa realized that this information had been incorrect. A somewhat embarrassed Jean Wadds was dispatched to explain that the provinces, except for Quebec, could, in certain circumstances, bring a case before the Supreme Court.

This was a quite serious problem, since it became clear that the judicial battle would be drawn out. If the provinces were to lose before their own courts, they'd likely appeal to the Supreme Court; if they won there, the federal government would go for its own appeal. Whatever happened, the affair would likely still be making its way through the court system by the time Westminster would be asked to choose. The Foreign Office's jurists were sounding the alarm. As one wrote, "Both government and parliament could reasonably be accused of showing disrespect to the Canadian courts and to legal process in Canada, in effect to the rule of law itself ... the government might also reasonably be accused of disrespect to parliament if it urges the enactment of the bill in those circumstances and it would be contrary to legal policy and arguably constitutionally improper to act on the request while the matter was *sub judice*."[26]

This was a major pitfall, and the affair was much too important to be left at that. The Cabinet needed to consider these new developments. A message was sent by the Foreign Office's jurists to Solicitor General Michael Havers: "Your advice is urgently needed."[27]

The provinces weren't entirely aware of it, but their judicial actions were provoking a reaction greater than they could have hoped for in London. Many in the provinces remained skeptical, however, that it would be possible to prevent the federal government's unilateral patriation by applying pressure on London. This wasn't the opinion of Gilles Loiselle, Quebec's agent general, who was attending a meeting of dissident provinces in Winnipeg. During a discussion in the Cabinet meeting room of the Legislative Assembly, he was asked to explain his views in front of a crowd of ministers and high-level civil servants. British parliamentarians don't want to be taken for rubber-stampers, he claimed. In constitutional matters, they see themselves as free thinkers and don't appreciate Ottawa's attitude.[28]

Attendees listened to him politely. Some were hoping to be convinced; others, like Bill Bennett, British Columbia's premier, were entirely hostile to the idea of leading an anti-Ottawa campaign in a foreign capital.[29] The operation might be perceived as anti-Canadian and would certainly be presented in this light by Trudeau. Only Brian Peckford from Newfoundland shared the enthusiasm of the Quebec delegation for bringing the battle to foreign shores.

This wasn't enough to dispirit Loiselle, who'd been hard at work for weeks. As Martin Berthoud explained to his colleagues at the Foreign Office, "He is an impressive performer."[30] It should be said that Loiselle wasn't at his first go-round. After working in various positions in Africa (he had even worked with the Emperor of Ethiopia in 1951) and Canada, including time spent in the media, he'd turned to public service. In 1976, he was part of small group of civil servants and elected officials responsible for piloting the Olympic portfolio, which had given him the opportunity to become familiar with constitutional issues: "I noticed that Bourassa, who I saw a lot, was quite preoccupied with complete failure of the Olympic Games. If we failed, it would give a terrible image of Quebec, and he was persuaded that Trudeau would take advantage of this by proceeding unilaterally with constitutional patriation."[31] As chance would have it, Loiselle was named agent general in Great Britain in 1977.

GILLES AND LORRAINE'S FABULOUS *SOUFFLÉ*

When the Battle of London began three years later, Loiselle was simultaneously convinced of the rightness of his cause and aware of the Herculean task before him: "We hadn't even managed to convince a majority of MPs in Ottawa to reject patriation," he'd later explain. "So how could we succeed in London?"[32]

But no matter the scale of the task before him, Loiselle had launched his offensive anyway. In mid-September, when Trudeau hadn't yet officially shown his true colours, Loiselle invited Martin Berthoud over. Following a tactic that he was only beginning to polish, he first sat him down for a thirty-minute tête-à-tête in his office before then having him over for lunch in a much less formal atmosphere.

In this second part of the meeting, his wife, Lorraine, oversaw operations. Assisted by the delegation staff, she would lead the kitchen; each morning, she'd wake at five to go purchase fresh fish and flowers to better impress her audience. As the *Times* then noted, "Gilles Loiselle has a kitchen in his London house which has now become famous throughout the city." A British MP, referring to the invitations being sent out in ever-increasing numbers by the provincial delegations or the Canadian High Commission, claimed he'd never seen "the booze flow with such abandon. If there isn't blood on the floor of the House, then there is sure to be claret."[33]

Martin Berthoud was one of the first to enjoy Lorraine Loiselle's exquisite cuisine, served to a backdrop of political conversation. The Brits, the agent general commented, have a duty to protect the federal nature of Canada, a country born out of a pact between the provinces. This is the meaning of the Statute of Westminster and, contrary to what Trudeau claimed, there was no earthly reason to precipitate affairs. Moreover, in the hypothetical situation where Her Majesty's government supported the centralizing project of the Canadian prime minister, Loiselle added a warning: "I would lobby unmercifully with some of the other Agents General."[34]

As he left his host's home, Berthoud realized that the Foreign Office hadn't prepared a counter-argument for this line of thinking. "Though it is probably far better to use general arguments rather than attempt to beat the Canadians on historical background, we must not be insufficiently armed on this front," he warned. As for Loiselle, Berthoud commented in his thank-you note that "the chocolate soufflé was fabulous!"[35]

Civil servants were not, however, the main targets of Quebec's diplomat. Since the parliamentarians would have final say on Trudeau's project, they were the ones who needed to be convinced. The first problem: Parliament wasn't in session in early autumn of that year. When the parliamentarians returned to work, Loiselle would need to find a way of attracting their attention to the constitution, competing against other major events of the day, including the Iranian revolution, with Ayatollah Khomeini's hostage-taking of American ambassadorial personnel, as well as the Polish Communist government preparing to crack down on the trade union Solidarity.

Once their attention was captured, they would need a class — *Canadian Constitution 101* — since most MPs and Lords knew nothing of the question, including that they were the only ones able to amend the supreme law of Canada: "Right away, they didn't fully understand what it meant for Canada to be a federal state," Gilles Loiselle explained. "And if they understood this already, they also knew that Quebec had secessionist ideas. Now, Great Britain had its own regional issues with Scotland and Wales. So, our story annoyed them. It was like blowing the opening whistle with no goalie in net. We were starting with absolutely nothing!"[36]

The cause seemed so far from won that some agents general simply lost faith. This was the case of Merv Johnson of Saskatchewan, who examined the situation with Loiselle in the middle of September. Despite the Quebecker claiming that it would be possible to convince Westminster of the anti-federal nature of Ottawa's approach, Johnson remained pessimistic. The Battle of London was lost in advance. Only Scottish and Welsh nationalists would be on the provinces' side.[37] And Johnson seemed to believe that their support would do more harm than good. However, in the eyes of a number of PQ ministers and their advisers, an alliance with Welsh and Scottish independence supporters would be a great start. Some among them didn't hesitate to offer their suggestions to Loiselle, who had difficulty getting them to understand that the support of sovereignists would alienate the great majority of Conservative and Labour MPs, who'd immediately refuse to give any credibility to the Canadian provinces: "The Ministers from Quebec who came to London wanted to convince the British that they had a right to forge independence. I would tell them: whoa, let's take it easy now. We haven't even convinced Quebeckers, we're not going to convince the British! We had a specific objective: block patriation."[38]

Like Talleyrand in Vienna in 1815, Loiselle didn't hesitate to mix it up a bit, presenting the PQ government as eminently reasonable, protecting British shores against a barbarian invasion. Not long after the provincial meeting in Winnipeg, he summarized for Martin Berthoud the discussion that had occurred at the provincial conference. "I have been shocked by the extreme attitude of Alberta and British Columbia in particular," he claimed, as serious as can be. "I found myself exerting a restraining influence on them and urging them to contribute to a well-balanced case."[39] So, in other words, the British should count their lucky stars to be able to depend upon, among the rebellious provinces, such deliberate and moderate individuals as the Quebeckers, chief among them Gilles Loiselle; surely they would calm the Western provinces' overreaching.

A magician at heart, Loiselle repeated his sleight of hand for every audience, almost managing to get his counterparts to forget that his province had attempted to secede only six months before.

And he still had a few other cards up his sleeve. It was crucial to begin influencing British MPs, even if they hadn't yet returned from vacation. Loiselle kindly offered to send to the Library of Parliament various analyses and judicial opinions that he'd asked a number of previously identified British constitutionalists to write. When the MPs and Lords would begin to seek out information on the constitution on their own, they would naturally turn to their own library, where they'd find, unbeknownst to them, information from the provinces' point of view.

Not only did Loiselle show remarkable skill, he was also lucky: a dangerous combination. One night, he invited over for dinner Peter Molloy, president of the Commonwealth Parliamentary Association — exactly the sort of man who needed to be convinced. Molloy's face felt familiar to the Quebecker, an impression that became a certainty when Mr. Molloy arrived. The agent general recalled a trip to Sudan in 1953. A young Loiselle had left by plane for this British colony with the objective of sailing down the Nile. Climbing out of the plane and onto the sandy track that served as an airport in Juba, he discovered the Nile dry. So there he stood, practically alone, in the middle of the desert. Suddenly, a jeep clanged over the potholed road toward him. The district commissioner was a certain Peter Molloy, who picked Loiselle up. Molloy would put him up on the residence's veranda for a few days, until the next plane flew in to pick up Loiselle. Both men literally hugged each other at this unexpected reunion thirty years later. "Let's just say that it got a bit easier to get a meeting in Parliament after that," Loiselle recalled.[40]

THE CONSTITUTIONAL EXPRESS

It wasn't only Quebec giving the British government headaches: aboriginal peoples led a new charge. Ottawa's unilateral resolution almost entirely ignored them. A single disposition of the charter mentions First Nations, specifying that the document "shall not be construed as denying the existence of any other rights or freedoms that exist in Canada, including any rights or freedoms that pertain to the native peoples of Canada."[41]

In October, an aboriginal delegation invited Labour MP Bruce George to visit Canada, so that he might better defend them in London. A few days later, the Native Council of Canada received an audience in Amsterdam with the Bertrand Russell Peace Foundation, which immediately condemned the "ethnocide"[42] committed by Canada. At the same time, the Union of British Columbia Indian Chiefs chartered a train, christened the "Constitutional Express," to go to Ottawa and then on to the U.N. headquarters.[43]

On November 7, the Express arrived in New York City, and the Foreign Office received a cable from the British mission to the United Nations: "Representatives of the World Council of Indigenous Peoples have asked to meet the permanent representative to express their distress at the Canadian Government's intention to patriate the British North America Act, to the detriment, in their view, of Indian rights in Canada."[44]

Lord Carrington's answer was clear: "You should not receive the Indians!"[45] From London, that was an easy thing to say. But in the Big Apple, the aboriginals were leading a true guerrilla propaganda campaign aimed at Her Majesty's diplomats. The latter were becoming exasperated by all the commotion. Throwing in the towel, one of them disregarded his instructions and received the representatives of the World Council of Indigenous Peoples.

Despite its impact in the media, this episode didn't change anything for the situation of the First Nations. The U.N. was powerless to help. With nowhere to turn to in Canada, they'd join the provinces in London.

CHAPTER 9

THE WRATH OF THE WEST

On the evening of October 29, 1980, Albertans were glued to their television sets. In a speech reminiscent of a State of the Union, premier Peter Lougheed was addressing all Albertans with great solemnity:

> Fellow Albertans, we face a serious situation in this province, as I'm sure you're aware, as a result of the federal budget and energy measures announced two days ago. They're an outright attempt to take over the resources of this province owned by each of you as Albertans ... the Ottawa Government has simply walked into our home and occupied the living room. Every single Albertan is involved in this whole issue and what is at stake in our province, for these resources do not belong to the Government of Alberta. They belong to individual Albertans, all two million of us ... but we are not prepared to surrender ... we are going to have a storm in this province.[1]

Lougheed announced a spectacular measure to counteract Ottawa. The province intended to gradually reduce its oil production by 180,000 barrels over the following nine months.

Lougheed's announcement reverberated across the country; a clarion call announcing Alberta's charge against the federal government and its blasted National Energy Program (NEP). Buoyed by impressive support in various polls,[2] Lougheed declared his opposition to Pierre Trudeau's desire to push the country toward what he called "energy independence." Over the next ten years, this policy of economic nationalism was to wean the country off foreign sources of energy. The head of the federal government hoped to build a wall behind which Canadians could live in a bubble, unfettered by the constraints of the world economy. By realizing this autarkic ideal, the country would be protected against oil shocks like the one in 1973, and Trudeau would be one step further in achieving his dream of a just society.

Ottawa's plan was bolstered by an already existing oil price control measure that dated from 1974. That year, Edmonton and Ottawa had negotiated a "Canadian price" for gasoline, well below the global price — probably the lowest price in the industrialized world, including the United States.

FORD AND THE WAR OVER OIL

Alberta was unhappy with the "Canadian price" agreement struck with the federal government in 1974, which was due to expire on June 30, 1980. It decided it would unilaterally determine its own price after this date. Trudeau answered during the federal budget presentation, partially nationalizing gas and oil production. First, the federal government imposed its own price for oil and gas over the next four years, which only it would be able to change, and added to this a series of new taxes, notably on the sale of both products in and out of the country. These measures substantially increased revenues coming from the petroleum industry, while ensuring the government's dominance over the sector, despite the fact that natural resources were exclusively of provincial jurisdiction. This approach was reinforced by a modification to the incentive structure for oil exploration and production. Companies that undertook such activities had previously been allowed certain fiscal advantages. Now, Ottawa would be handing them grants directly, which would naturally increase its influence over these companies. The predictable result of these measures would be billions of dollars of increased revenue for the central government's treasury. The only hiccup: the federal government would be like desperados plundering the Western part of the country. It was decided that the Western Fund should be created, an organization whose mission was to invest and spend out West a portion (and only a portion) of monies obtained thanks to the National Energy Program, so as not to seem too greedy.[3]

Unsurprisingly, relations between the West and Ottawa reached new heights of hostility. Roy Romanow noted: "The energy dispute added vigour and new dimensions to the constitutional conflict. The two disputes were inextricably linked, and everyone understood that the resolution of one depended on the other."[4] For people from Western Canada, the constitutional question became the catalyzer for years of frustration and feelings of injustice toward the central government in general — and Pierre Trudeau in particular.

On his end, High Commissioner John Ford was quite preoccupied by the NEP months before the budget was actually submitted. His sources informed him of the federal government's intentions, which convinced him to warn the Foreign Office of "an authoritarian energy policy ... which will take powers over energy sources which would conflict with the present division of powers."[5] On the day the budget was submitted, he added that "it is however in keeping with Mr. Trudeau's character when he believes he is on top to grind his opponent unmercifully ... should there be serious parliamentary difficulties or obstruction at Westminster, I believe he would have no compunction about attempting to generate an anti-British uproar here and to rush through some sort of unilateral declaration of independence on the basis of a referendum."[6]

Ford wasn't the only member of the diplomatic corps to think ill of the prime minister. His aversion was shared by French ambassador Pierre Maillard, a former collaborator of General de Gaulle. Both men regularly touched base with each other and in mid-November met to do just that. In the eyes of the European community, Ford said, Trudeau's economic nationalism was unfavourable. Trudeau was to travel to Paris soon. Would it be possible for the French president and prime minister to express this point of view? Maillard found the idea intriguing; he passed the message along. But he himself had a suggestion: perhaps France and Great Britain should keep each other in the loop in the constitutional dossier. Ford agreed and reported the idea back to London. He suggested that the French prime minister, Raymond Barre, before receiving Trudeau, call Thatcher to game out the situation.[7]

In London, Berthoud replied that it was indeed possible for the French to raise the constitutional question, as Helmut Schmidt had previously done with Thatcher. He doubted, however, that Barre would find the affair important enough to call the British prime minister. Whatever the case, care should be taken to not overextend: Trudeau would surely fly off the handle.

The Franco-British approach apparently went no further. This wasn't enough to prevent John Ford, taking advantage of a trip to Windsor, Ontario, from speaking about the Liberal government's economic policies. "There is a popular misconception that ambassadors and High Commissioners, and indeed all diplomatists are nothing but party goers and cookie-pushers," he said by way of introduction. However, he went on, he himself didn't adhere to this conception: "I hope that some of my remarks may be regarded as Aunt Sallies to evoke a reaction from some of you …"[8] Ford first underlined the extent to which British investors, scared off by the National Energy Program and the filtering of foreign investments, were tempted to turn to the United States and abandon Canada. He then continued on with his magisterial lesson:

> We in Britain … charge ourselves the full market prices for oil … you in Canada have chosen to keep your prices down; to give your industry a softer option; to encourage by low prices your people to remain the largest per capital users among major industrialised countries; and to pay your own producers about half what you pay your foreign suppliers.… It also gives Canadian industry what amounts to big subsidies for energy use and thus raises among industrialists in Europe pressure for protective measures against what they regard as damagingly unfair competition.

Ford may have received a few congratulatory comments after his intervention, but Mark MacGuigan, for one, was furious, doubly so because the High Commissioner had made his speech in MacGuigan's own riding. He reacted by accusing Ford of having "grossly misinterpreted our policy." Contrary to his claims, Ottawa's policy favoured energy savings. These savings wouldn't be dependent on a price hike to match global prices. Paying more, MacGuigan explained, wouldn't reduce consumption, at least not as much as the various energy conservation programs created by Ottawa and managed by its army of civil servants. Moreover, paying the true price for oil would surely create inequalities.

In private, the secretary of state was incensed, and he would still blame himself, years later, for not having been more careful around that blasted Englishman.[9] Ottawa prepared its reaction. Not long after the speech in Windsor, a scheduled lunch between the British diplomat and Michael Pitfield, with the participation of Jim Coutts, Trudeau's principal secretary, was cancelled just two hours in advance, without a whiff of explanation or apology. As Ford noted: "These actions contrasted strangely with the attitude … of the Deputy Under-Secretary De Montigny Marchand, who felt able to invite the Soviet Ambassador to a small intimate dinner within four months of the invasion of Afghanistan!"[10]

Two days after his intervention, Her Majesty's envoy nonetheless met with Allan Gotlieb to clarify a few things with the deputy minister of external affairs. The latter declared that the federal government had, of course, no intention of muzzling a foreign representative expressing an opinion on an affair affecting his country. The problem came from the fact that Ford had misunderstood and misinterpreted the fundamental question. All this confusion was quite unfortunate, Gotlieb continued, since the two countries were engaging in delicate discussions on the constitution. Consequently, "it would be helpful if British hicom would, as other foreign reps have occasionally, send an advance copy of his to the under-secretary of state, on a very informal and personal basis, so that he could, if he wished, be made aware in advance of any misinformation or possible misunderstandings."[11] Ford, who saw in this nothing extreme, had no problem with the request. Which didn't mean he had the intention of censoring himself, as Ottawa was about to discover.

Meanwhile, the question of Western Canada continued to make waves in Great Britain. Even before the constitutional talks had failed, hundreds of citizens of that region had taken the initiative to write to the British government to complain. As Berthoud wrote to Ford in late September:

> If Trudeau and his henchmen have taken for granted the
> British Parliament's acquiescence in whatever is requested
> of it, our Canadian correspondents certainly think oth-

erwise. Since mid-June, 163 members of the Canadian public have taken the trouble to write to Mrs. Thatcher, mainly (about 80%) criticising Trudeau as not being representative of voters in Western Canada.... Sue also tells us that she has received three paperbacks virulently attacking the Canadian Prime Minister.[12]

And this was only the start. Over the course of the fall, the epistolary assault would grow in size. In two months, the Foreign Office received 1,200 letters, including three hundred in the third week of November, while the Queen received another hundred or so over the course of the same period.[13] As Richard Berry of the Foreign Office reported to his colleague Emery Davies in Ottawa, "We have been sending periodically to Sue Bamforth small batches of letters from Canadians addressed to the prime minister, which contain dire warnings about unilateral patriation and/or the evils of Pierre Trudeau. As these are now amounting to a steady dribble, I should be grateful for your views on how we should deal with them."[14]

Thatcher wasn't the only one receiving missives from Canada. Ordinary MPs in the British Parliament were in the same situation. Labour member Bruce George, for example, received five hundred letters, including 450, he claimed, supporting his campaign in support of aboriginals.[15]

Who were these citizens who, pen in hand, wrote to complain about their government? And what exactly were they saying?

They were people like Joan Cherry from Vancouver, who wrote to John Osborne, the MP of her former riding in the United Kingdom.

As a former resident in the Hallam constituency before taking up residence in British Columbia, I am taking the liberty to presume on the ties I have with you as representing this former association. My family still resides in this constituency so I do feel I still have some small claim to your interest. I would be pleased if you would study seriously the proposal in respect of the patriation of the Canadian Constitution ... with the question uppermost in your mind as to whether these proposals should be automatically approved when so many of the provinces, and

the people of those provinces are diametrically opposed to
the content of same.[16]

Or another letter, this time from N. Downs, of Stockport, Cheshire.
Her sister married a Canadian aviator during the war and had adopted the
country of her spouse. Ms. Downs had received a message from her sister,
who'd asked her to forward a missive in which she asked her former local MP
to say no to Trudeau. Ms. Downs decided instead to send the whole letter
to Thatcher, adding a comment to the effect that she was "disturbed by the
tone of my sister's letters and the fact she had actually written … which is
not very often. She is the least politically motivated person … I know and
we were all most surprised to hear that for the first time in her 58 years she
had gone on the knockers.…[17]

The sheer volume of incoming mail was so large that parliamentarians,
not knowing what to do, were turning to the Foreign Office. Nicholas Ridley,
the minister of state, counselled them to address their questions to the
Canadian government and not comment on the topic. Despite that advice,
these innumerable letters, the great majority of them coming from Western
Canada, attracted the attention of a number of MPs who hadn't previously
heard about the request for patriation.

That was the case with Jonathan Aitken, a young Conservative MP of
advantageous physique with a promising career before him, which would
end dramatically in 1999 after he was sentenced to fifteen months in prison
for perjury. At the time of patriation, Aitken presented two particularities.
The first was his link with Canada: his father was an aviator originally from
Nova Scotia, and his great-uncle, Lord Beaverbrook, an Anglo-Canadian
businessman and politician who had a career on both sides of the Atlantic,
notably as a member of Winston Churchill's war cabinet.

Everything to do with Canada held quite some importance for Aitken,
whom Thatcher had decided not to name minister. The reason? The MP, and
here is his second characteristic, was the former lover of Carol Thatcher, the
prime minister's daughter. He'd left his fiancée, and the matriarch Thatcher
never forgave him for breaking her daughter's heart. I'll be damned before I give
work to a man "who made Carol cry," she was claimed to have said at the time.[18]

The result of this situation was that, not being a minister, Aitken had a
lot of time on his hands and, especially, nothing to lose. As long as Thatcher

was at the reins, he had no chance of making it onto Cabinet. This was the context in which he learned that Quebec was mounting an operation to convince Westminster to reject Trudeau's resolution. His first reaction was anger at what he perceived as an affront to the country of his father. He immediately made his way to Gilles Loiselle's office to share his fury. Gilles Loiselle described the meeting this way:

> I let him express himself. He was saying: we're being asked to patriate the Constitution, well what business of ours is it to keep it? I told him: have you also seen that you're being asked to vote us a charter of rights? Then, he began looking deeper in the whole thing, and then more or less began heading a movement allied to the provinces. There are no Labour or Conservative MPs in Great Britain that like the Charter. For them, it's all about the sovereign power of Parliament, and with a Charter, we'll be given that to the judges.[19]

The meeting with Loiselle sowed doubt in Aitken's mind, which was soon reinforced by the barrage of mail received by the MP. The more he read, the more he became hostile to the federal proposal. As he wrote in the *Times*, "British MPs will rub their eyes with astonishment … this goes far beyond a mere patriation … it is substantive new legislation, not only redefining the potential relationships between federal and provincial governments in a manner inimical to most of the latter, but also creating a new bill of rights for Canada."[20] The MP then developed the idea of creating an ad hoc parliamentary committee to examine the question in more detail, a topic he broached with his Conservative colleagues. As Aitken recalls:

> I remember addressing the 1922 committee, which is a very powerful committee of conservative backbenchers. I said look, I know you are all getting letters just as I am getting letters from Canada and I hope you will support my idea of just looking into the constitutional proposal. This was a minor announcement but instead of passing with a nod or a wink and no objections I got thunderous applause because everybody was getting letters and did not know

how to reply to them. They were slightly irritated by it
because Margaret Thatcher had sort of said to Mr. Trudeau
if you want that we will deliver it ... suddenly people were
saying maybe we should not deliver it.[21]

A few days later, he asked Labour MP Georges Foulkes if he'd agree to
co-preside over this committee with him, in order to make the operation
bipartisan. The latter accepted, and the committee was soon on its feet.

This new development certainly pleased James McKibben, the new agent
general for Alberta, who was also quite active in the British capital. At first
skeptical as to the provinces' ability to influence the course of events, he was
impressed by Loiselle's effort: "Quebec was doing a pretty good job ... but
on their own it was limited. Some British MPs were asking why is Quebec
into this? Because of language? It was not as strong as several provinces."[22]
Indeed, the Albertan delegate joining the dance certainly reinforced the
credibility of the rebellious provinces in London, especially after McKibben
developed the idea of a common front of agents general under his direction.
Loiselle was quite happy to let his colleague take the reins: this change
would certainly help the British forget the PQ's secessionist positions of a
few months before.

McKibben quickly scored a few points, or so he believed. In October,
he had the opportunity to speak with Thatcher over the course of a lunch
in which the prime minister was accompanied by her husband, Denis.
McKibben spoke at length with him and, as the Albertan deputy minister Peter Meekison reported to his boss, Dick Johnston, "He found
Mr. Thatcher particularly interested in the Canadian situation and eager
to hear our side."[23] However, as John Campbell, Thatcher's biographer,
noted, "Denis was infinitely skilful at supporting and protecting Margaret,
talking to those she could not (or did not want to) speak to and deflecting
people who tried to monopolize her."[24] McKibben had most likely been
a victim of this stratagem.

Meanwhile, Western media fed the controversy further. On November
25, the *Edmonton Journal* ran a headline that surprised everyone: "Pierre
threatening to quit commonwealth say U.K. MPs."[25] The daily notably
quoted Georges Foulkes, the co-president of the parliamentary committee
created by Aitken to study patriation. He was quoted as saying that the feds

warned him that his committee shouldn't hear provincial testimony: "The whole set-up is beginning to look a bit like blackmail," he declared. "That can sometimes get our backs up." The following day, a journalist for the *Edmonton Journal* called the Foreign Office. He wanted to know whether it was true that Canada had threatened to leave the Commonwealth or retaliate if the British refused to follow up on the constitutional resolution. A certain Myles Wickstead claimed there was never a question of such a thing. The journalist hung up, apparently not convinced by this denial.[26]

Whatever the case may be, the *Edmonton Journal*'s headline didn't fail to rouse reactions. The first one of these came, in fact, in the newspaper's editorial pages. If such rumours were founded, one could read, "they could be only the work of an autocratic government." After ruining relations with the provinces, Trudeau was now destroying those that Canada had with Great Britain, "one of Canada's oldest and closest friends."[27] On his end, Peter Lougheed declared that this story was "disturbing and incredible," adding that Western people were quite attached to the Commonwealth. If all of it was true, he added, this story was the proof that Pierre Trudeau wanted to destroy the country. The same sorts of comments were also heard from Allan Blakeney, who declared that this affair was "utter nonsense" and that it would put Saskatchewan first in line among Trudeau's opponents if it revealed itself to be true.[28]

In Ottawa, one of Mark MacGuigan's advisers tried to minimize the scandal. "The allegations have no foundation," he claimed, a refrain repeated by the Prime Minister's Office. One of Trudeau's assistants added that "such threats would be utterly alien to Trudeau's nature."[29] As for the Opposition, it picked up on the affair during question period. Forced to answer by MP Flora MacDonald, the prime minister declared that, contrary to the provinces, no one in the government's employ had put pressure on the British, adding that the latter couldn't reject the federal request since it would be construed as "pure colonialism."[30]

The federal government could issue denials until it was blue in the face; in reality, the government was actually devising a plan for retaliatory action against the British. Trudeau himself was considering pulling the country out of the Commonwealth following a referendum. Ford suspected the prime minister of such designs, and had warned London on the subject. However, there was no reason to go too far too fast. For now, it was simply better to put pressure on by implying a few things and letting imagination and interpretation do all the work. Who better to play this role than Sonny Ramphal, the Secretary-General of the Commonwealth, who had nothing better to do than join in on the fun?

On November 10, Ramphal decided to speak on the subject during a meeting with Lord Carrington, the head of the Foreign Office. Ramphal opened by saying that Trudeau had "intense concerns" in regards to patriation and that it would inevitably affect the Commonwealth. "Why should it be so?" Carrington replied, indicating that this affair concerned no one but Canada and Great Britain.[31] Ramphal replied that he was simply echoing Trudeau, who had sworn that the affair would have repercussions on the Commonwealth. Perhaps, Carrington declared, but Great Britain is a parliamentary democracy and, in such a system, the government cannot prevent Parliament from voting on the legislative measures presented to it. He added that "the Canadians, in asking us to pass the bill of rights with the constitution, are asking us to do something they are loath to do, or could not do themselves: some might see this as verging on sharp practice."

The meeting ended on that note, but Ramphal was visibly unsatisfied with this answer. He asked to meet Thatcher to bring up the issue. The summary of that meeting on December 4 isn't available, but considering that the Iron Lady had no love lost for the Commonwealth and that her husband spoke of "Sonny bloody Ramphal" when speaking of the Secretary-General,[32] one can imagine that she didn't much appreciate his intervention.

No matter. A few days later, Ramphal added more fuel to the fire, publicly this time, in a speech to the Royal Commonwealth Society. "There are no residual colonial responsibilities that interpose Britain between the Government of Canada and its people or between the Governments of Canada and of its Provinces," he said, disavowing the provinces. He expected British parliamentarians to follow up on the federal request without complaint and before the July 1 date fixed by Trudeau. He ended his comment with a warning: "I would not expect the Parliament at Westminster to imply in any way that there is less to celebrate in 1981 than the Commonwealth believes."[33]

The Commonwealth, Western provinces, and backbenchers were up in arms: it was with all this in mind that Lord Carrington had to consider the next steps. He presented to the Cabinet a confidential memorandum analyzing the situation. He'd done this under orders from Thatcher, who knew Carrington. They saw eye to eye on this issue.

> We have a major interest in maintaining good relations with Canada, an important Commonwealth country with a significant role to play in the Western alliance and on the international scene generally. To go back now on what the Canadians will regard as our undertakings over patriation would be to invite a major row. As annex A makes clear, the legal arguments justifying our acceding to a federal request for patriation are not unassailable; but we cannot please both the federal government and the provinces. It is with the federal government that we deal. Mr. Trudeau is in full control of the majority party and wedded to the ideal of patriation with a bill of rights. It is thus in my view inconceivable that we should fail to meet this request as quickly as possible if and when it comes. This is of course provided that the question of … the Canadian courts is resolved.[34]

Carrington continued by destroying the argument according to which the British had the responsibility to protect the federal nature of the country. He claimed that nothing in the Statute of Westminster spoke to that effect. Moreover, he added, London had in the past modified the constitution against the express will of some provinces, be it British Columbia in 1907 or Quebec in 1943. In the latter case, Ottawa wanted to put off a redistribution of seats in the House of Commons that had been outlined in the constitution, and which would give more weight to the francophone province following data from the census: "On this view, it is wrong to treat the Statute of Westminster as involving a preservation of the status quo as between the federal authorities and the provinces of which the U.K. was to be the stake-holder."

That being said, a last argument did present problems: the one according to which, by voting for a charter of rights, the British were involving themselves in the internal affairs of Canadians, and it would only be by abstaining that they would demonstrate their belief in non-interference. As Carrington noted, "The interference arguments in favour of Ottawa have some cogency."

But for this reasoning to be valid, a very specific logic had to be followed, one that posed a new set of problems. The British would need to either accept a unanimous patriation request or a simple patriation request with an amendment formula, leaving the charter by the wayside. "Arguably, readiness to act on a request confined to patriation with an amending formula was the maximum extent of the undertakings which have so far been given to Canadian ministers," Carrington continued. "But there could be great risks for our relations with the federal governments for appearing even to contemplate an alternative course of this kind." [35]

This was why a positive attitude toward the provinces wasn't possible, even if, in reality, the non-interference argument played in their favour. The provinces didn't count for much, and it seemed unthinkable, at this stage, that they might create serious headaches for the Conservative government. The potential problems caused by the provinces would never be as important as those that would come to pass if the relationship with Ottawa suffered a serious blow.

This is where Thatcher was wrong. As she would soon find out, the Canadian provinces were able to transform a constitutional question into an incredibly complex issue, and even slow the progress of the most determined leaders.

André Burelle with his boss, the prime minister. After composing Trudeau's speech, he would eventually tender his resignation following the exclusion of Quebec from the constitutional agreement.

Gilles Loiselle and his wife, Lorraine. Quebec's agent general in London was seen as a key player for the provinces opposed to Trudeau by the Foreign Office in the British capital.

Lord Carrington was a heavyweight in the Thatcher government; he believed that Ottawa was getting its dirty work done by London.

Denis Thatcher, accompanied here by two of the three women that made the patriation of the Canadian constitution possible: his wife, and Jean Wadds, Canada's representative in London. The third woman was, of course, Queen Elizabeth II, who doesn't appear in this picture.

Martin Berthoud was responsible for the North America Bureau; his superiors at the Foreign Office told him that his most important dossier was the patriation of the Canadian constitution.

John Ford, High Commissioner of Great Britain in Ottawa. His opposition to Pierre Trudeau's approach to patriation would be met with a recall back to London in the spring of 1981.

Lord Moran, John Ford's successor as British High Commissioner, stated that "the most difficult, prickly and unforthcoming [Canadians] are undoubtedly some of those who work for the federal government in Ottawa."

Francis Pym, a parliamentary leader and Conservative British minister, criticized Thatcher's political orientations. He believed that the she was threatening the survival of the Conservative government by helping Pierre Trudeau.

Sonny Ramphal, the secretary-general of the Commonwealth (first from the left), put pressure on London so that the British might produce an answer to Trudeau's patriation request. He's seen here with the prime minister of Australia, Malcolm Fraser, and General Obasanjo of Nigeria.

Anthony Kershaw, as president of the British parliamentary committee on foreign affairs, decided to have his committee consider the issue of constitutional patriation, raising Ottawa's ire.

Jonathan Aitken, a British MP of Canadian descent, led a faction of Conservatives against Trudeau's project.

Bora Laskin was an ardent supporter of the Charter of Rights. As the chief justice of the Supreme Court, he helped the Canadian and British governments in bringing to term the patriation project.

The Honourable Willard Zebedee Estey, a Supreme Court judge, gave legal advice to the federal government on the patriation issue.

Constitutional Conference. The first ministers and their senior advisers in the Centennial Room. Four Quebeckers who were drawn apart by the patriation project: (left to right) Jean Chrétien, Pierre Trudeau, Claude Morin, and René Lévesque (Michael Kirby in the background).

Ontario premier Bill Davis, loyal ally of Pierre Trudeau, is here shown in conversation with Peter Lougheed, premier of Alberta, at the Constitutional Conference.

Mark MacGuigan, secretary of state at External Affairs Canada. In the autumn of 1980, MacGuigan was convinced that the co-operation of the British government with Ottawa was no longer a given.

René Lévesque (right) and Peter Lougheed. The Western Conservative and the nationalistic Quebecker found themselves unlikely allies against a common enemy, Pierre Trudeau.

Three members of the Gang of Eight: (left to right) Sterling Lyon of Manitoba, Peter Lougheed of Alberta, and Brian Peckford of Newfoundland.

Bruce George (left), a British Labour Party MP who put himself at the service of the aboriginal cause. Here he's accompanied by George Erasmus (first from the right), Max Gros-Louis (second from the right), Earl Grey (centre), and an unidentified First Nations chief.

Pierre Trudeau and the Queen on the Hill in Ottawa for the official patriation ceremony. On the left, minister of labour Gerald Regan, and on the right, Michael Pitfield and Michael Kirby.

James McKibben, agent general of Alberta, and his wife. The Albertan had a source in Thatcher's entourage whom he referred to as "deep throat."

CHAPTER 10

THATCHER LOSES CONTROL

"*Labour isn't working.*" It was in part thanks to this slogan, accompanied by a picture of a queue at an unemployment office, that the Conservatives won the 1979 election. They'd promised to reduce inflation, get the country back to work, battle the unions' influence, and restore the grandeur of Albion. A year later, inflation had reached 22 percent, and some three million people were out of work. To face this crisis, the government had doubled the sales tax and increased interest rates to a record high.[1] This last measure had a doping effect on the pound, whose spectacular increase had directly affected British exports. Thanks to these measures, the Thatcher government obtained the unenviable title of the most unpopular government since the beginning of polls. This situation had repercussions on a number of levels. The Cabinet had never been more divided between partisans of austerity, called *dries* — Thatcher and a few key ministers — and those who opposed it, called *wets*. The situation was quite tense among MPs. As Ian Gow, the prime minister's parliamentary secretary, told the Iron Lady at the time, there was "serious deterioration in the morale of our backbenchers."[2]

This deterioration sapped the leadership of the woman who hadn't yet become the hero of the Falklands War and who didn't have an overwhelming majority in the House. The situation was worrying because, since the

1970s, backbenchers had been demonstrating greater independence from the party line, except on confidence votes. From 1970 to 1974, Edward Heath's Conservative government had lost six votes due to revolt among its ranks on important law projects, despite repeated attempts by whips to impose the party line. In the minority Labour government of James Callaghan, the same situation occurred seventeen times.[3] And this is without counting the numerous times the government had backed away from a project or compromised to avoid losing face. In the period that concerns us, the Thatcher government had been in power for a year and a half, and had faced down a number of such events. Her record unpopularity only added fuel to the fire.

For MPs hostile to Trudeau's project, it was an ideal moment to defy the prime minister. As Jonathan Aitken recalls, "The government did not want to start another fight, or quite a big fight. It was a good moment to make trouble, even if it was not our objective."[4]

A FOX IN THE HENHOUSE

Aware of this situation, Gilles Loiselle approached Sir Anthony Kershaw, president of the Parliamentary Commission on Foreign Affairs. The commission was part of a series of new Select House Committees with discretionary budgets for research and support personnel, created when the Conservatives took power. The parliamentary leader, St. John-Stevas, had launched this project without consulting Thatcher.[5] Occupied by a number of issues when she landed in 10 Downing Street, she only became aware of this initiative too late to prevent it. These official parliamentary forums that supervised the government's work certainly didn't inspire in her any sort of positive emotion. The course of events would show her the value of her instinct.

Contrary to Thatcher, Anthony Kershaw was a moderate Conservative, a junior minister under Edward Heath. Not very influential, he was aware he had little chance to return to the Cabinet. He owed nothing to his boss, and expected nothing back. A lawyer, veteran of the Second World War, having served with the hussars, always perfectly dressed and often monocled,[6] Sir Anthony was the incarnation of the perfect British gentleman, with a famous sense of fair play that might lead him to suffer from sympathies for the provincial cause. This was exactly what occurred. Gilles Loiselle was certainly inspired when he informed him that patriation just might be under the mandate of the committee he himself presided over. And, surprise, surprise, the commission had a bit of free time. It was supposed to study the Cypriot situation, but Lord Carrington had discreetly indicated that it was a sensitive subject that might embarrass the British. No one in the upper echelons of the party had thought that Kershaw would instead set his heart on the Canadian constitution. Now this seemed a distinct possibility. Martin Berthoud expressed just this thought to Nicholas Ridley, minister of state with the Foreign Office:

> To elaborate, some (even much) of the evidence submitted to the Foreign Affairs Committee (by others at least) would be likely to be critical of the federal government's case … the Canadian provinces could be expected instantly to present evidence (against patriation now) and to lobby members of the committee. Mr. Loiselle, the Quebec Agent General, is a much more persuasive spokesman than anyone the Canadian High Commission can produce. Perhaps more important, however, is the likelihood that the very existence of such Foreign Affairs Committee (FAC) proceedings would suggest to the federal government that the U.K. was in some measure reneging on successive undertakings (by the prime minister and others) that we would patriate the constitution if so requested by the government of Canada. I doubt if they would be mollified by a response from us that we have no control over the FAC.
>
> I fear there is little chance of keeping these proposed proceedings out of the political arena. The constitutional/legal aspects of the issue are inextricably entwined in Canadian politics. The Canadian government would probably, from these proceedings, conclude that the British were meddling in their internal affairs. North American Department's view is that the FAC should, if possible, be written off entirely.[7]

However, Berthoud was contradicted by the assistant deputy minister, Gordon Lennox, who made his own recommendations to his political masters:

> Although the timing of the enquiry obviously presents difficulties, I am doubtful of the wisdom of trying to persuade the committee not to hold it. Having already persuaded them to defer, and possibly drop, their enquiry on Cyprus, they might well regard our attitude as obstructive and decide to go ahead with the enquiry anyway. We should then merely have a weakened hand in trying to ride them off enquiries into delicate matters in the future. In my view, the most we could do is to tell the committee that we will of course cooperate with them over the enquiry but make quite clear what the risks and pitfalls are.[8]

This is the option that would eventually be chosen. The government simply wouldn't put pressure on the committee, and chose to live with the consequences, come what may. Carrington immediately informed John Ford that he was about to let a fox into the henhouse. He specified: "It is essential there should be no leaks about this matter."[9] But this is the constitution we're talking about, after all, so no leaks was just too much to ask. Two days after this warning, the *Times* announced that Kershaw's committee would study the issue, adding that "some ministers believe it would be helpful for the committee to examine the important constitutional questions that will arise if the Canadian government puts forward for approval by parliaments its wide ranging measures, which include a bill of rights."[10] The leaks provoked a chain reaction. First the Montreal daily the *Gazette* reached out to Kershaw for an interview. The latter couldn't ask for a better opportunity to lose himself in conjecture over an inquiry that hadn't even begun. It would be ideal, he declared, that unanimity, or close to it, be obtained: "If only one province opposed the move, his panel, and likely the British government, would be prepared to overlook it. But if the provinces are lined up against Ottawa, then I dare say we'd do nothing."[11]

This comment provoked anger from the federal government, whom the British hadn't forewarned. That an official House committee would study the request for patriation constituted in itself a denial of the idea that parliamentarians in Westminster would approve it virtually automatically.

In Ottawa, De Montigny Marchand hurried to John Ford's office. As the latter noted, "he reacted very badly saying that this was an unfriendly act and incompatible with what Mrs. Thatcher had told the Canadian prime minister and ministers. As the chairman of the committee was a conservative, the Canadians would have thought that Mr. Kershaw and the committee could be called to order."[12] Ford replied that Thatcher had warned Trudeau in June that if the request caused controversy in Canada, it would do so in Great Britain, as well. He had repeated the warning over and over again. As for permanent parliamentary commissions, he explained, they were new creations. Their members sought to be noticed, that's all, and sometimes didn't act with the government's best interest in mind. While these words pacified Marchand somewhat, he muttered about something being "unfriendly" as he took leave of Ford.

The Canadian High Commission was also informed of this meeting in London. An adviser at the commission, Henry Richardson, was sent to the Foreign Office with a clear mission. Barging into Martin Berthoud's office, he didn't beat around the bush. "My government will be most upset and will simply not understand," he said, adding that he didn't see in what way the committee's work could be useful.[13] Berthoud then risked showing his hand by adding that if the affair was still *sub judice* when the constitutional request arrived in London, the situation might become that much more complicated. "Mr. Richardson, who was already irritated because of the Foreign Affairs Committee investigation, reacted with some asperity to this idea."[14]

This is the internal affairs of Canada, the federal diplomat exclaimed, falling under the central government's purview, on every level, judicial or otherwise. The British should trust the Canadian government's word, he went on; every angle of the dossier had been examined. What the various tribunals and the Supreme Court might say, he added, would be tantamount to opinion, and "as such it would be likely to be ignored by the Canadian government." On that note, Berthoud risked contradicting his visitor a second time:

> People in the U.K. would be liable to question British patriation of the constitution if the Canadian courts were likely, after we had gone ahead, to declare the Canadian proposals unconstitutional or illegal. Mr. Richardson

incidentally objected to my use of the phrase *sub judice*.
He seemed to consider that the Canadian courts had, in
fact, no jurisdiction in a matter of this kind and there
was therefore no way in which they could be thought to
be taking a judicial view of the matter.[15]

It was on this discordant note that the representative took leave of
his host. The Canadian promised that he'd attempt to dissuade Kershaw,
whom he would be meeting a few days later. He would eventually
warn Kershaw that "people in Canada might regard the Foreign Affairs
Committee's activities as smacking of colonialism."[16] Kershaw didn't back
off: as president of a commission, he wasn't under governmental orders. At
least, Richardson continued, the committee might not hear testimony or
accept reports from Canada. The Brit promised nothing; he was starting
to think he had seen enough of this Richardson. He confided this not
long after to Nicholas Ridley, who was attempting — with somewhat
more subtlety — to influence him. The minister raised the fact that if the
commission decided to meet with Canadian provinces, or even aboriginals, Ottawa would be angry.[17] But refusing to hear the point of view of
Trudeau's opponents, Kershaw replied, would place him in an impossible
situation with his own colleagues. However, in order to help the government, it might be possible to listen to testimony by the federal government's opponents first, so as to be able to contradict it with later testimony.
Ridley agreed. Trying to make the best out of a bad situation, he believed
that the parliamentary commission might just serve as a pressure valve,
giving troublemakers a platform on which to vent some of their frustration. Once steam had been released, the debate in the House might be a
bit more serene. Moreover, Ridley believed, "there is also the additional
advantage that Canadian anger will be drawn on to Mr. Kershaw and not
on to [the] Ministers."[18]

Indeed, it would be difficult to find a better lightning rod than Kershaw.
The latter seemed overjoyed at the political and media interest he was sud-
denly arousing, and took advantage of it by multiplying public declarations
in front of the microphones that followed him wherever he went. All this led
Jean Wadds to cable a secret message to Ottawa, stamped with the mention
"Canadian Eyes Only":

We have reviewed latest developments and <u>are very seriously concerned with their implications</u>. Believe that we can no longer afford to ignore activities of committee and time has come to take notice and communicate, at least to Foreign secretary (i.e. Carrington), our concerns.... The proposed action of standing committee on Foreign affairs is in danger of becoming unacceptable intervention in affairs of Canada susceptible of damaging relations between two countries.[19]

But Pierre Elliott Trudeau had other ideas entirely: to publicly enjoin the British to keep their promise. On November 6, all the while defending himself against allegations that he was putting too much pressure on the British, he stated during a debate in the House that "the natural thing to do would be for the British government and parliament not to meddle in any way in Canadian affairs."[20]

A short time after, journalists cornered him. Are you frustrated by the situation? they asked.

Kershaw's committee, he answered, "is a committee of backbenchers ... it is not the British Government seizing it with any policy, but the committee itself examining the relations of the British Parliament with the BNA Act, one of their own laws, I can't take great offence to that."[21]

However, it seems that Trudeau took the affair quite seriously. The same week, he declared in Regina that Thatcher had promised him that his project would be adopted with a "three-line whip" — the term for an instruction written down and underlined three times, given to MPs by the prefects of discipline who are the whips. In such a case, parliamentarians must vote with the party line. The invocation of this guarantee became the new argument of the federal government. George Anderson, Western Europe's director at External Affairs, repeated the same argument to Emery Davies of the British High Commission. The latter was dubious: the summary of the Trudeau-Thatcher meeting made no mention of the "three-line whip."[22]

Parallel to this misunderstanding that seemed to be taking on a life of its own, Newfoundland premier Brian Peckford visited London at the end of November. He wished to speak before Kershaw's committee, but his request had been refused. The committee members ended up deciding to hear only British witnesses, while accepting written reports from any source. Newfoundland forwarded one. The provincial premier used his visit to the British capital to make a few public declarations. A November 26 speech in front of the British Canadian Chamber of Commerce was the highlight of his trip.

Peckford fired his first shot even before leaving his hotel that morning: "Trudeau has little understanding of Newfoundland," he said to the assembled journalists. "When he visits, he only stays about an hour and a half. I don't think he's ever slept overnight on our soil." The rebel provinces will flood the British with documents explaining their position, and, Peckford added, "Once Newfoundlanders start talking, they don't stop."[23]

That first point having been made, Peckford continued in the same vein in his speech later that day. He accused Trudeau of leading a "subtle but real demolition of the federal system. There exists a constitutional convention between your country and mine, that the Parliament of the United Kingdom will not act to repeal, amend or alter the BNA Act without receiving a proper constitutional request to do so from Canada."

He concluded by commenting that while revenues from oil might finally give Newfoundland the leeway to escape economic dependence, Trudeau's position would prevent this from ever happening by threatening the property rights of the province over its resources.[24]

A WALTZ FOR TWO ... OR MORE

Meanwhile, back in Canada, Joe Clark's Conservatives were attempting to slow down the federal Liberals. They forced Trudeau to set up a joint parliamentary committee in the House and Senate, whose mandate was to study the constitutional project by receiving written comments from groups or citizens, as well as inviting them to speak before the television cameras. Some provinces considered this just another manoeuvre by Ottawa. As Roy Romanow recalled, after participating in the exercise, "there was no doubt that the nature of the testimony which the committee heard was orchestrated by the government in order to isolate provincial opposition and to create a movement for an even more extensive charter."[25]

This sort of exercise renewed the legitimacy of various professional militants and pressure groups commonly known as "civil society," as if the Canadian

Congress for Learning Opportunities for Women, the Church of Jesus Christ of Latter-Day Saints, the Positive Action Committee, the German-Canadian Committee on the Constitution, the Indian Rights for Indian Women, and the World Federalists, to name but a few, were as legitimate stakeholders as the provinces, with their universal suffrage and recognized constitutional jurisdictions.

Whatever the case, activists from across the country congregated at the West Block, where this colourful procession would take place. And what were the demands of all these people? More rights. If a group from British Columbia demanded the right to use hallucinogenic mushrooms,[26] others asked for constitutionally mandated lower taxes; the fundamental right to live in a country free of nuclear weapons; the end of the death penalty; the rights of physically or mentally handicapped people, as well as those of the blind, the deaf, women, aboriginals, West Coast Chinese, Jews, homosexuals, transgendered people; the fundamental right to study in English in Quebec or in French in Newfoundland, et cetera.

Others, however, feared the advent of the charter — the Canadian Association of Police Chiefs, for example. Jack Ackroyd, chief of Toronto's police, warned the committee against an exaggerated emphasis on procedural rights during arrests. Referring to the American example, he wondered: "When murderers are set free because a police officer has made a minor mistake in the procedures he is required to follow, does society really benefit?" A similar opinion came from the Canadian Association of Crown Counsels, which claimed it was both illogical and "self-defeating" to attempt to control the behaviour of police by acquitting criminals.[27]

Over the course of the 270 hours of presentations, during which 814 individuals and 294 groups spoke, this sort of opposition to the charter was in the minority.[28] Indeed, the enthusiasm by pressure groups for a more exhaustive charter was so important that it even had an effect in London. The National Action Committee on the Status of Women (NAC) hired a representative in the British capital, Michael Butler. The latter attempted to warn British parliamentarians as well as Lord Carrington: "The charter of rights," he wrote, "as presently worded, would not provide equality for women in the law, and could actually make women worse off than they are now without entrenchment, and native women are at greatest risk. The provision for affirmative action in the Charter section is vaguely worded, and women are not specified as a disadvantaged group."[29]

Here we need to briefly consider the concept of liberty as presented during the audiences of the parliamentary committee. For a philosopher like Plato, this concept was linked to a transcendent good that all could enjoy. For Locke and Hobbes, the idea was tied to the state of nature.[30] However, for the activists who paraded before Parliament in 1980, the common good and natural rights were completely ignored in the conversation. Instead, everything was reduced to mobilization, pressure, and satisfying the interests of whatever group one belonged to. Meanwhile, the fact that the role of a constitution is to allow for impartial rules to structure and limit the power of the State, not to serve as a foundation for social reforms, completely disappeared. The idea that underpinned this activism is that constitutional order isn't founded on a shared vision of reason. Instead, it is the result of arbitrary preferences, reflecting power relations linked to race, gender, and class; hence, the importance for the self-proclaimed representatives of each minority group, each and all attempting to impose their own values. As Roy Romanow notes, "They all wanted a charter, and they all wanted a charter which protected the interests of their members."[31]

This race for new rights in the name of equality reveals another shift in meaning that was beginning to occur. In traditional liberal theory, liberties precede the creation of the State. When citizens constitute themselves into a society, they voluntarily relinquish a certain number of rights — for example, security — giving them to a government, so that the exercise of these rights by the State might allow them to better enjoy and exercise the rights they keep for themselves. Activists who spoke before the joint committee in 1980–81 didn't see things in that light. For them, rights existed only once they were enshrined in law. There was no concept of private freedoms here, those not granted to political power through a social contract. The State no longer protected these private freedoms, meaning that it no longer exercised solely the limited rights granted to it at its creation, allowing the people to enjoy the rights they kept for themselves. In the logic of the charter, the state instead becomes responsible for the exercise of all a citizen's rights, since rights only existed if they were recognized by law. Moreover, if these rights were inscribed in a charter, activists would be able to use the courts to invoke fundamental rights and compel the state to grant advantages that they could not previously obtain through political means. This approach also necessarily represented the end of a great understanding that prevailed since the Enlightenment — the equality of all before the Law — by granting different rights to different groups, following cultural, sexual, or other criteria. As Rosalie Abella, who would later become a Supreme Court judge, explained, the issue was treating us "differently to redress abuses our differences have attracted."[32]

MULTICULTURALISM: THE FLAVOUR OF THE DAY

Those who have since been called the "patriots of the charter" won their battle in the winter of 1981 — partially, at least. Following the consultations led by the parliamentary committee, Trudeau reinforced his charter project, notably through adding a clause that noted that the rights it contained were guaranteed as much to men as to women, and one that added physical and mental handicaps to the list of proscribed discrimination.[33] But the great victors in the exercise were the partisans of multiculturalism. In October 1980, they had been disappointed by the absence of the concept that had existed in the original preamble project. The president of the Ukrainian Canadian Congress had written to the prime minister to underline the importance of integrating in the constitution "the fact that Canada is a multicultural nation."[34] This request was then repeated by other groups before the joint parliamentary committee, and the minister for multiculturalism, James Fleming, insisted to Cabinet that it be included.

This pressure resulted in the reintroduction of the concept — not in the preamble this time, but in the charter itself. Eddie Goldenberg, former adviser to Jean Chrétien, would later say that the affair was "popular and unproblematic," even if in Quebec it raised a great deal of opposition. "Once it was there, very few people wanted to argue with us, I mean what could they say, that Canada isn't multicultural?"[35] Indeed, who could deny the fact that the country included citizens of various origins who dressed differently, had distinct culinary preferences, different skin pigmentation, and all the rest? Multiculturalism would be trivial if it settled for speaking such obvious facts. After all, who could deny that there were cowboys out West with country music, odd clothes, and bravery (or insanity, depending on the point of view), who would jump on a mustang or a bull's back during the Calgary Stampede? These observations made, does it become necessary

168 · The Battle of London

to include this reality in the constitution, without which cowboys would be victims of discrimination and suffer from having their rights flouted?

Words, evidently, have power. It was no coincidence that the term "multiculturalism" found its way into the constitution. For Trudeau, it had become the essence of the country: "Every ethnic group has the right to preserve and develop its own culture and values within the Canadian context," he said in 1971. "To say that we have two official languages is not to say that we have two official cultures, and no particular culture is more official than another."[36]

In short, the inclusion of multiculturalism in the constitution was part and parcel of the social re-engineering project aimed at transforming Canadian citizens into bilingual beings without cultural reference points. In the same way as language rights in education, which we have spoken of, Trudeau entrusted this mandate to judges instead of the lawfully elected representatives of the people, since the majority would likely reject such a project.

While the intention might be clear, a question remains. What is a right to culture? What shape should such a concept take in a constitution? As Roger Tassé, then deputy minister of justice, would later explain, no one in Ottawa seemed to clearly understand where all this would lead:

> We didn't even know what multiculturalism and indeed culture meant, how could we grant a right to it? Also how could someone enjoy their culture in the same way that they would in another country. They could do to a point but not fully. The implications for such a clause were so broad that they were inconceivable.[37]

Tassé wasn't the only one asking himself questions. John Ford was sharing his own concerns with London:

> To Trudeau and Liberal intellectuals who think all along Cartesian lines the solution has seemed obvious: a new constitution which will create a legal framework for unity, with courts to enforce it and a Federal Government strong enough to impose unifying policies ...
>
> This suits the bureaucrats of Ottawa, who have a vested interest in the aggrandisement of Federal power.

Nor is Trudeau's dream of Canada bilingual and bicultural from shore to shore ignoble. Such a meritocracy,
where the yardstick of merit would be bilingualism and
biculturalism, appeals to the minds of academia and
media, and, particularly, to the anglo-francophones of
Montreal, who see themselves as the real *élite*. But to
ordinary citizens throughout Canada decreasing numbers of whom are bilingual or bicultural, the realisation
of the Trudeau dream could become the creation of a
divisive and unacceptable procrustean bed to alienate
them still further from the Ottawa bureaucracy; and
multiculturalism rather than biculturalism has already
become a vogue word of the Government … if enacted,
Trudeau's constitution seems bound to lead to endless
and divisive litigation.[38]

This analysis was well-received in London, especially by minister of
defence Francis Pym, who was on the cusp of replacing St. John-Stevas as
parliamentary leader, and had thus received a front-row seat to patriation.
He read Ford's cable "with considerable interest," and found that it was the
"most useful account of events so far."[39]

Meanwhile, the federal government kept mentioning, with polls to back
up its claims, the extent to which the charter was popular, underlining of
course the testimony by the numerous groups who had intervened before
the joint committee. By dint of having endlessly heard the same message,
everyone ended up believing that there existed strong support for the federal
government. In this context, on December 10, 1980, Gallup published
a poll revealing that 58 percent of Canadians were opposed to Trudeau's
unilateral approach. As Emery Davies explained in a message to London,
this result "was a considerable surprise to the vast majority of observers …
this is at total variance with what the government has been saying about the
results of its enquiries in the polls and certainly what has been fed to us by
various reliable sources within the Federal government."[40]

A few weeks later, a new poll conducted for CBC by Carleton University's
School of Journalism confirmed the first number. This time, 65 percent of
respondents were opposed to unilateral patriation, with 26 percent approving.[41]

What meaning can we divine from such results? For Michael Kirby, Trudeau's counsellor, these numbers were explained by the fact that Canadians "inherently do not like conflict. Any time I have ever surveyed an issue in the Canadian public on anything, there was conflict; most of them want the problem to go away."[42] The opposing hypothesis would be that the country's population was opposed to what Trudeau was doing at the time. But how is it possible to reconcile this latter interpretation with the very large majority of Canadians who supported the charter?

Ottawa was describing the charter's dispositions, and judges were to consider them as a metronome that beat to an exact measure, functioning with the precision of a Swiss watch. With such a tool, there was to be a single possible result: the protection of human rights.[43] As a pamphlet distributed by the federal government explained, "Now these rights will be written into the constitution so that you will know exactly where you stand ...[44]

Nothing, however, could lead us to believe that the insertion of such rights in a charter would lead to these results. In the federal project, rights were described in a very general, almost vague fashion, and would thus be subject to wide interpretation by judges. Moreover, those who most hoped to see a charter included had the intention of pushing for a plethora of new rights, with uncertain results.

Everything seemed to indicate that the public at large didn't comprehend this aspect of the political fight. The population supported the charter in polls since it was not opposed to virtue; who could be against fundamental rights? Polling data would likely have been different if respondents had been asked whether they agreed to take responsibilities away from elected officials and hand them over to judges who were virtually nominated for life, and who would gain power over controversial political questions.[45]

On the other hand, opposition in Parliament against unilateral patriation had reached new levels. By 1980, Canadians had been living in a federal system for 113 years. One of the foundations of federal systems is the idea of double legitimacy: national and regional. Sharing of powers between provinces and Ottawa is one of its incarnations. As Peter Lougheed recalls, in constitutional matters, "the prime minister does not speak for Canada. That is why we have a constitution."[46] This angle can help us understand the reluctance facing Ottawa's unilateral approach; the objection was based on a manoeuvre that stood in opposition to the history and political traditions of the country.

THE FRENCH CONNECTION

The general outcry certainly satisfied John Ford, who chose this moment to begin a tour of Manitoba, then Quebec, warning Ottawa's allies, supplying ammo to the rebels — in short, adding fuel to the fire. In Quebec, on December 8, he met with Claude Morin, who wanted to talk shop. Quebec's contacts in London were suggesting that the position of the provinces would be reinforced if they could propose a plan to replace the federal one.[47] Ford confirmed the information. As he'd explain to his colleagues at the Foreign Office, Lévesque might even accept a provincial consensus in the knowledge that a firm declaration on patriation and an amendment formula by a majority of premiers would make it much more difficult for Trudeau to confuse the patriation and the bill of rights issues in a propaganda campaign against the premiers with the Canadian public."[48]

This possibility seemed so intriguing that, as soon as he returned to Ottawa, Ford spoke of it with the French ambassador, Pierre Maillard. Would it be possible for France to use its privileged relationship with Quebec to push Lévesque in this direction? French president Giscard d'Estaing was to meet with the PQ leader in the following days. Certainly, the Brit continued, Quebeckers should put aside their demands for a better sharing of powers in exchange for patriation. Ford believed, however, that the francophone province would be hedging its bets if it obtained an amendment formula similar to the one developed in Victoria while simultaneously blocking Trudeau.[49] Ford added that Lévesque was considering this option.

Maillard replied that his country would be quite distraught to see the British Parliament become Trudeau's accomplice. Moreover, he added, the federal government had recently threatened France with economic reprisals after it had refused to participate in a summit of the Francophonie — the French-speaking countries — after Ottawa had opposed Quebec having its own delegation. Ford left the meeting with the conviction that his counterpart would echo his own proposal.

We don't know whether Giscard d'Estaing did indeed speak to Lévesque about the subject. One thing is certain, in any case: the British government was now preparing itself for the worst-case scenario. As Ford wrote to the assistant deputy minister, Derek Day, "Controversy over the Canadian constitutional proposals continues to develop here, as it does with you. I fear that we may all be in for a fairly torrid time over this issue in the months ahead."[50]

The situation was so serious that by the end of November the Cabinet decided to send an emissary to Trudeau. The unlucky messenger was to share the following: "While the government is committed in principle to introducing in Westminster whatever measure is requested by the Canadian government and parliament, the passage of the bill at Westminster would be considerably eased if the request could be delayed until the Supreme Court of Canada had advised that it is *intra vires* (i.e. valid) in Canadian law."[51]

It remained to be seen who would be sent across the pond. Lord Carrington was seen as too well-known a figure, while Ian Gilmour, who had less experience, wasn't a big fan of Trudeau and was thus deemed to be the wrong man for the job.[52]

THATCHER ENDANGERS THE GOVERNMENT

The messenger was finally chosen: Francis Pym, minister of defence, whose functions aroused little interest. Ottawa was informed of the operation, and an artificial military component was tacked onto the program during his visit, in order to provide misinformation. One swallow does not a summer make: for once, no leaks occurred. Both on the British and the Canadian side backs were sore from self-congratulating for having kept the operation a secret. However, both governments would pay the piper for this confidential process; the whole affair would be brought to light a few weeks later.

Meanwhile, Thatcher prepared the ground on Trudeau's end in a letter she sent him in early December: "I should say at once that there has been no change in our policy since I saw you in June … there are, however, points bearing on timing at this end which can, I believe, be most usefully explained to you at first hand."[53] Trudeau agreed to meet with the British minister of defence, all the while telling Thatcher that he was happy that "your message made it clear that there has been no change in your government's position."[54]

On December 17, just before leaving for Ottawa, the prime minister met with her messenger. Pym was a centrist, a member of the old guard whom she'd inherited from her predecessor, Edward Heath. For her, he was a minister who lacked conviction. For him, she was a radical ideologue who was propelling the country toward a social and economic abyss. Pym was one of the leaders of the wets; he had numerous supporters and rarely missed an opportunity to criticize his leader.

The dossier of the Canadian constitution wouldn't be an exception. As he told John Ford while in Ottawa, "I can't see how Mrs. Thatcher could be allowed to endanger the government by attempting to force the issue."[55] Less direct when he met her before leaving, he nonetheless revealed his opinion: "In my view a bill for the patriation of the Canadian constitution will, if the Canadian government do not modify their request, get through neither the House of Commons nor the House of Lords. The more members of parliament go in the matter, the less they like it." As for the Opposition, it was adopting an attitude that was "unhelpful, if only because they see an opportunity to make timetable difficulties for the government."[56]

It followed, Pym thought, that Trudeau should be compelled to give up his charter. The British government had to be especially careful to avoid being beaten on this issue by opposition coming from its own ranks.

Thatcher replied that such remarks would constitute a considerable surprise for Trudeau: "If the message is conveyed too starkly, there will be a real risk of an explosion on the Canadian Prime Minister's part with all the consequences that this might have for Anglo-Canadian relations, for the Queen's position and for Canada's membership of the Commonwealth." She was steadfast: "You should not tell Mr. Trudeau that there is no hope of meeting his request." Instead, she insisted, Pym should express the potential difficulties, all the while explaining that these would be much less important if the Supreme Court judged the issue *intra vires*. Pym should also explain that the British government had no authority over Kershaw's Foreign Affairs Committee. Thatcher concluded by stating, "I continue to feel strongly that the U.K. cannot look through the Canadian Government's request. We have to do our best to meet it."

It was indeed important to spare the federal prime minister, Pym agreed, before adding, "It would be wrong to disguise from Mr. Trudeau that it is extremely unlikely that the legislation, if submitted as at present envisaged, will go through." Pym had his mind made up on the situation and, whatever Thatcher might think, he had no intention of deviating from his intention. This state of mind would certainly not contribute to a healthy Anglo-Canadian relationship.

Whatever the case may be, the British minister arrived in Ottawa on December 19. During a constructive and amicable discussion with

Trudeau, Pym described the difficulties that were emerging in the British Parliament. Unless Ottawa abandoned the charter, it would be impossible for the federal request to be approved in the current session.[57] Trudeau believed that the opposition to his project would not be diminished by his putting the charter aside. Moreover, he claimed that the situation was urgent and that he was determined to keep going forward.[58] Both men then discussed means of accelerating the process. If Manitoba's Court of Appeal rendered a decision favourable to the federal government, this would certainly change the situation, Pym explained.[59]

Remaining cordial, Trudeau was still determined to be very direct. As the English emissary reported in a message sent to Thatcher immediately following the meeting, "Trudeau was clearly unwilling to accept that delay would in fact lead to greater chances of acceptance ... he made it clear that in the event of rejection he would appeal to public opinion in both Britain and Canada against the obstruction of backbenchers at Westminster but left undisclosed what further action he would take."[60]

After having met with Mark MacGuigan, who more or less expressed the same thoughts as his prime minister, the minister of defence took stock of the situation with John Ford, the British High Commissioner. For the past few months, Ford had been champing at the bit. But this time, instead of attempting to convince his colleagues at the Foreign Office from afar, he had an opportunity to broach the topic with an important figure in the government. He wouldn't miss this opportunity. "We should prepare the ground beforehand," he stated, "and hope by our steeliness of purpose at best to deter Trudeau and at least to diminish his chances of profiting by it."[61]

Ford notably believed that London could take cover behind the issue of *sub judice*, which would give both time and ammunition to the rebellious provinces. Thanks to interventions in the House as well as other speeches, he continued, "we should also do all we can to underline that we are not colonialist and that parliamentary worries in the U.K. are about Trudeau's attempts to force us to be so by imposing on Canada what Canadians do not want to do for themselves." Moreover, Ford said, the British shouldn't be moved by eventual threats of independence as well as turmoil in the Commonwealth. He, for one, didn't let himself be influenced by these factors: "I am retiring in the early summer and this could be helpful. If I am to follow that course, some risk would be involved for me personally and it would be unfortunate if I were to be declared non grata; but this is a risk I will gladly shoulder if it would help."

"I approve but I hope it will never come to that,"[62] Pym replied, asking Ford to lay his ideas out on paper and send them back to London. The latter would do just that the next day, sending two cables in which he described the former polemicist of *Cité Libre* as "an intellectually arrogant bully who fights dirty and is not to be trusted." He received no answer to his cables. The diplomat understood that he would not be receiving instructions. Thus, if the whole affair soured, it would be possible to disavow him entirely and claim he overstepped his mandate. And since Pym was Thatcher's emissary and gave his okay, Ford concluded that he'd received a green light to go on the offensive.

When Pym returned to London, the constitutional dossier was once again discussed in Cabinet. Among other topics tabled, everyone seemed to agree that it would be essential to find a way to counter the accusation of colonialism that might be thrown in the face of the British government.[63] Solicitor General Michael Havers was also charged with enlightening the government on the judicial aspects of the affair, notably in terms of precedents. Precedents had been invoked, as we have seen, by London and Ottawa, to justify an automatic agreement to a federal request. But the more Havers dug into the topic, the more he began to have doubts. He soon shared his thoughts with the rest of his colleagues:

> So far as the precedents go at all they point in the opposite direction, in the sense of the federal government recognising (in their 1965 White Paper) and hitherto respecting an obligation to consult and carry the provinces with them before pressing a request for an amendment of the BNAA which vitally affects the federal/provincial relationship.
>
> The argument … just described is persuasive and may well commend itself … as establishing that precedent is on the side of the Provinces … whatever reasons we may assign, now or in the future, for accommodating the Federal Government, we should be on very shaky ground if we relied simply on precedent.[64]

And just like that, Havers destroyed the government's official position. While he wasn't a member of the wets, he'd nonetheless given Gilmour and Pym precious munitions to support their claim that the policy of a blank cheque given to Ottawa was a mistake. He also sowed doubt among ministers who had not yet developed a fixed opinion on the question. None of this, obviously, pleased Thatcher. Yet fortunately for her, Havers's note remained secret. It wouldn't provoke renewed controversy in a dossier already heavy with the weight of existing polemic. The catch was that the members of Kershaw's committee were beginning to come to the same conclusions. And they were just about ready to publish their report.

CHAPTER 11

THE EMPIRE STRIKES BACK

Every dirty political trick in the book was used as the Battle of London raged on. In the widening and deepening gulf of conflict and disagreements, there were the divisions within the British government itself, divisions that would lead to a series of misunderstandings between colleagues, between Ford and the Foreign Office, Pym and Thatcher, the Canadians and British. All the while, parliamentarians were choosing their camps: for Ottawa or against it, behind the wets or the dries, supporting or opposing the Iron Lady.

In early 1981, new fires needed tending to. In addition to the Foreign Affairs Select Committee, headed by Anthony Kershaw, a new ad hoc parliamentary committee was created, following an initiative by Conservative MP Jonathan Aitken and Labour MP Georges Foulkes. Meeting in mid-January to begin their work, they asked that the government come to explain its policy. Thatcher was unfortunately unable to send Carrington or Ridley, whose conviction and fidelity couldn't be doubted. Lord Privy Seal Ian Gilmour would be sent in their stead. He was a terrible choice: Gilmour was a wet, suspicious of his boss, with no affection for Trudeau, and lacking deep conviction for the cause. He was already beset with doubt by the time he made his way to appear before the fifty-five MPs, a sizeable contingent of parliamentarians considering the intensity of other parliamentary work early that year.[1]

Another surprise: no less than half the MPs present spoke, with a lone member supporting the government position according to which any federal request had to be satisfied to protect proper relations with Canada. The rest of the speakers rattled off a list of objections. Why should Westminster approve a request against which a majority of provinces stood opposed? Didn't the British have a duty toward the provinces? Wasn't forcing a charter on Canadians the ultimate act of colonialism? Why shouldn't they simply send the constitution to Canada, with no bells and whistles attached, no charter or amendment formula or anything else? This last idea, raised by a number of MPs, clearly roused the members of the committee.

Such a scenario, Gilmour replied, would be the worst of all, the equivalent of giving carte blanche to Trudeau. Gilmour reminded the members that the simple idea that the British Parliament had a role to play in this entire affair was "implicitly patronising and colonial."[2] Taking him at his word, an MP wondered which avenue should be taken in order not to appear colonialist: vote for, against, or abstain? Gilmour hesitated, stammering that he wasn't an expert on colonialism. He ended up saying that abstaining would likely be the best attitude to adopt.

On January 23, Francis Pym met with Jean Wadds to share his impressions on the evolution of the dossier. Not long before this meeting, Jean Wadds was still congratulating herself that Pym had replaced that blasted St. John-Stevas as parliamentary leader. Reality caught up with her at that very first meeting. Currently, Pym told her, parliamentarians believed that it wasn't up to them to adjudicate the debate between Ottawa and the provinces[3] — "British MPs are not elected to make decisions on Canadian political issues and the charter is not our business."

An unacceptable argument, Wadds replied. The federal government takes full responsibility for the constitutional request, she continued, which is, it should be added, very similar to other requests made in the past.

This first clarification made, the Canadian railed against Kershaw's committee, which was giving too good a deal to the recalcitrant provinces and their allies. Wadds and her colleagues had been forced to once again present the situation to MPs and lords and explain, among other things, that the provinces currently had so much power in the decision-making process that it prevented the federal government from properly managing the country's economy. If the British supported the provinces, the latter's position would only be reinforced, causing further economic and political turmoil. Quebec might be lost for good, and the British should expect a major confrontation between Canada and the United Kingdom.

Pym entirely agreed with this final point. A refusal by Westminster to support the federal request would lead to a very serious situation indeed. This is why Her Majesty's government was still hesitant to ask Parliament to vote on the measure, he added. Ideally, all parties should wait until Kershaw's committee tabled its report and the decision of Manitoba's Court of Appeal was handed down, since that province's tribunal would be the first to pronounce itself on the validity of the federal request.

HATFIELD VS. MCKIBBEN

As differences of opinion began to accumulate behind the scenes, there was quite the jostling on the main stage, as well. The premier of New Brunswick, Richard Hatfield, hopped across the pond in January to glad-hand and make speeches, with one notable speech coming before the Diplomatic and Commonwealth Writers Association of London, whose members included a number of journalists. A perfect crowd for his message, since Hatfield began his speech by denouncing the journalists themselves: they had made the mistake of writing that Canadians should settle their problem in Canada. Hatfield, who didn't appreciate this at all, called on them to stop writing such nonsense. He then moved on to the role of British parliamentarians in the whole affair. They certainly possessed the right to discuss the resolution that would be presented to them. But no more than that. Like postal workers mechanically stamping a letter, they must automatically approve the request, he stated. What would happen if this didn't occur? "This would be humiliation," he continued. "We would simply declare our independence and then the constitutional monarchy will have a short life."[4] Those who saw a threat in these words should be reassured, Hatfield continued, "I'm not threatening; I'm predicting what will happen."

At that moment, Alberta's agent general, who was in the room, exploded. "This is nonsense!"[5] McKibben called out to the premier as silence descended on the room. The Albertan weighed Hatfield for a few seconds, then decided to let him finish his speech, better to accuse him later on of being a blowhard. With his remaining time, Hatfield concluded by stating that only Trudeau had the capacity to fulfill the ambitions of Canadians, particularly that of Quebeckers.

Unfortunately for Hatfield, his intervention didn't have the desired effect on MPs and lords. He met a number of them during his time in London, and all of them were predicting that the federal request would be rejected. The visitor also had the opportunity to discuss this prediction with Robert Armstrong, cabinet secretary and highest civil servant in the U.K. The latter explained that the government pretty much thought that Ottawa's demand would be refused, adding that Trudeau was perfectly aware of the situation.[6]

Hatfield was so shaken by the lack of support that on returning to his own country, he scored a point against his own team by declaring to the press that "when Trudeau gets to England he may find a very unfriendly climate."[7] This comment completely contradicted the federal government's narrative, and the victim of this friendly fire, Trudeau, didn't have any other choice but to react during a press conference. With his usual flair, he began by comparing patriation to the abolition of slavery in the United States. "It wasn't easy, but it had to be done. This is peanuts compared to what had to be done there."[8] In any case, he explained, Thatcher would use "a three-line-whip," meaning that the utmost pressure would be applied to ensure that any dissidents voted in the right direction.

John Ford was furious. In his opinion, Trudeau had just spread disinformation. Organizing a media leak, he met Robert Sheppard of the *Globe and Mail* to reveal the content of the Thatcher-Trudeau discussion of June 25, 1980. Trudeau had never mentioned a charter of rights, Ford began. Moreover, Trudeau had also minimized the extent of provincial opposition, insisting that he'd attempt to garner as much support as possible. Relieved by the promise, Ford explained, Thatcher had offered her support to an operation that, in its spirit, was limited to patriation combined with an amendment formula. This is why she was so surprised to learn, when she met with MacGuigan and Roberts, that a charter of rights would be making the journey with it — a charter opposed by a majority of provinces.

Sir John barely had time to punctuate his last sentence before his comments were on the front page of the *Globe*. The paper ran the following:

"Contrary to assertions by the Trudeau Government, Margaret Thatcher's administration has never undertaken to support a Canadian constitutional package that included a charter of rights and freedoms — or any package that lacked broad provincial and public support."[9]

The effect of this front-page news was immediate ... and devastating. On one hand, television stations were looping the images of Trudeau leaving 10 Downing Street, maintaining that he hadn't discussed provincial opposition with Thatcher. On the other, the prime minister was shown in his present version, attempting to avoid the journalists' questions. "I honestly don't remember saying that," he'd stated. "If I said it, it must have been with tongue in cheek." Hounded all day by journalists and the opposition, Trudeau finally told the truth. He lied, he admitted, but it was for a good cause: "I recognized that when I talked to the press I was still putting on, perhaps, a show of hoping that against all hope and in spite of 53 years of failure to get unanimity, we would get it this summer ... I regret this lack of candor."[10]

This first sliver of an admission of guilt only increased the intensity of questions. Was it true that Minister Francis Pym had warned him during his visit? Had Thatcher really assured him that she'd pass his measure at any cost? Hounded from every side, the prime minister continued to unravel the thread of his story. Pym did indeed come to speak of the constitution. Trudeau told him that judicial procedures were nothing more than a tactic by the provinces to gain time. As for Thatcher, they'd had a long conversation on the constitution, he said, and not an exchange of only a few minutes, as he'd previously indicated. Moreover, Thatcher had only been given the details in October.

Trudeau was in a real bind. But those who believed that these revelations would put him down for the count were wrong: the Liberal leader was always at his best when his back was against the wall. He'd push back by claiming that he'd received guarantees: "Until Mrs. Thatcher is prepared to say the contrary, my word must stand. If she says she will not comment because she will not reveal a confidence, I hereby authorize her to say the contrary."[11] This statement temporarily shut up his detractors, especially since Thatcher kept herself from contradicting her Canadian counterpart.

John Ford was delighted by the turn of events. The whole affair, he cabled back to London, "is being adduced as further evidence that Mr. Trudeau has been less than honest in what he has reported here about Canadian discussions with Her Majesty's Government."[12]

Perhaps. But Thatcher didn't share Ford's vision; she saw this new controversy from an entirely different angle. Through her diplomatic adviser, Michael Alexander, she clarified her thoughts to the members of the diplomatic service, as recounted to us by Martin Berthoud:

> Mr. Alexander thought Mrs. Thatcher's specific commitment with regard to patriation carried with it the clear message that the Government would do their utmost to get the measure through parliament, including a three line whip if necessary. He implied, therefore, that it was irrelevant whether or not the Prime Minister had used these words. Mr. Alexander remarked in passing that he thought Mr. Pym was paddling his own canoe on patriation; he suggested that Mr. Pym had got rather out of hand.... In general, I got the strong impression from Mr. Alexander that in his eyes, and those of the Prime Minister, the all important point was that we were fully committed to the Federal Government and what Ministers said now to the Canadians and others should not be inconsistent with this.[13]

Despite Thatcher's attempt to set things right, her message was muddled by an unprecedented number of leaks. After the *Globe and Mail*, the CBC revealed the letter from Thatcher to Trudeau written in December 1980, in which the prime minister explained the true nature of Pym's visit. State television also reported that the Commonwealth's Secretary-General had attempted to influence the British government. These revelations had barely been digested when the *Globe and Mail* mounted a new charge, making public one after the other the summaries of meetings between St. John-Stevas and MacGuigan in November, as well as the Wadds-Pym meeting that had just occurred, insisting in the latter case on the request by the Briton that the charter be set aside. All of this seemed too good to be true for Ford. Commenting on these numerous leaks, he warned the Foreign Office that it was now important to "recognize that there is some mole in Canada House [the Canadian High Commission in London] and that the security of messages on this subject passed to the Canadians is virtually non-existent."[14]

A SPY AT THE HIGH COMMISSION

To explain these leaks, the Canadian diplomats had another theory — one that was itself revealed by a leak. They believed themselves victims of the British Secret Services, the CBC revealed. "We must take it for granted that phone conversations of this sort are all monitored and taped by suitably equipped countries, including certainly Britain, France, the U.S.A. and the Soviet Union,"[15] it was possible to read in a message that the CBC attributed to Jean Wadds. "Why give Britain notice of our strategy, concerns or judgments of some of its key players," she continued, inviting everyone to use the telex. It was a more secure means of communication, she stated, especially when it came to confidential tactics that shouldn't be revealed to the British — the most recent effort being the attempt to "snow" Jonathan Aitken in the hopes that he might switch sides.

These revelations were, of course, ripe for sensationalism. In the House of Lords, Carrington suffered an attack at the hands of the official critic, Lord Beswick.

> Beswick: "My Lords, would the noble Lord take this opportunity of denying an apparent allegation in the press that agents of Her Majesty's Government, in this context, have been tapping the telephone lines of the High Commissioner for Canada?"
>
> Carrington: "My Lords, it is the convention in parliament and outside that we never make comments on that kind of thing."[16]

In Ottawa, Mark MacGuigan was furious and refused to comment. More open to speaking his mind in his memoirs, he recalled that the affair was quite serious, since the documents were indeed authentic.[17] This is why he asked the RCMP to hunt down the mole who'd presumably infiltrated his ministry. The RCMP's sleuths soon put their hand on their man, a sovereignist who, it seemed, had been acting as a spy for years. MacGuigan wanted charges to be brought against the man, but Trudeau overruled him. That could have serious repercussions in Quebec, he believed, and what's more, the mole had likely been caught after falling prey to an operation in which illegal surveillance had been used. MacGuigan was perplexed, but forced to give in. The suspect got off with being fired and no more.

As this was occurring in Canada, the waltz of visits continued in the British capital. At the end of January, it was Sterling Lyon's turn to see the sights. He had the opportunity to make a speech at the prestigious Barber-Surgeons' Hall, an edifice that had been rebuilt twice and had served as a place for political rallies since the Middle Ages. In this setting of wood panel and portraits of Henry VIII, Lyon spoke before a crowd of MPs and businesspeople. Two things need to be done, he told them in substance. First, the British must vote against the constitutional request. As it ignored the will of the provinces, the request contradicted the spirit of federalism. The worst-case scenario is a federal proposition that would push Canada toward republicanism, he continued. Why? Because the charter forgoes the principle of the sovereignty of Parliament, Lyon explained, becoming increasingly heated. He certainly didn't lack superlatives to describe Trudeau's proposal: "A folly, reckless, senseless, embarrassing, illegal, unconstitutional, immoral, and a repudiation of consensus and civility!"[18] In the next few years, he predicted, Canadian courts would begin to use the charter in the same way as the Americans have been doing with their own documents. One verdict after another based on the new constitutional document would lead the courts to create law on whatever subject it might study — for example, school children's access to school buses for transportation.

This is why the British should rid themselves of the old Canadian constitution as quickly as possible, the Manitoban continued. How? After having said no to Trudeau, they should proceed, of their own initiative, to unilateral patriation combined with an amendment formula requiring the consent of all ten provinces to modify the Supreme Law. To act any other way would be colonialism in another form, since it would be equivalent to imposing a constitution on Canadians without their consent.[19]

No sooner had Lyon finished his speech than Kershaw's committee proved him almost entirely correct. On January 30, the group tabled a unanimous report after having listened to testimony by the best constitutionalists in the United Kingdom, jurists at the Foreign Office, Lord Carrington, and Nicholas Ridley, as well as having read written testimony by British Columbia, Newfoundland, Alberta, Prince Edward Island, and Quebec, and examined some of the federal government's documents. The essential portion of this reflection was to consider Ottawa's thesis according to which any request that came from the federal Parliament was to be automatically approved by Westminster:

> Since 1930 [the move] has been towards the more explicit recognition of a right of the provinces to be consulted about certain sorts of proposed amendment, and of a duty not to forward to the U.K. Parliament a request for any amendment of those sorts without provincial assent, perhaps even unanimous provincial assent.... If the U.K. Parliament were to proceed on the basis that it ought to accede to such requests automatically ... it would thus be treating the Canadian Government and Parliament as having, in constitutional reality, a substantially unilateral power of amending or abolishing Canada's federal system ... the U.K. Parliament's fundamental role in these matters is to decide whether or not a request conveys the clearly expressed wishes of Canada as a whole, bearing in mind the federal character of the Canadian constitutional system.[20]

This news was "a bombshell," the *Guardian*'s editorial stated.

"Music to my ears," Gilles Loiselle said.

"Marvellous," added his Albertan counterpart, James McKibben, specifying that it was one of the most important documents to have been written on the constitution: "I don't see how in the world Mr. Trudeau can ignore it."[21]

Sir Anthony summarized it this way: "It means we are free to reject the request and are indeed obliged to do it. I'm afraid it will upset Mr. Trudeau."[22]

The reasoning at the Foreign Office — where the document was obtained a few days before its official publication — was along these lines as well. It was decided that no comment should be made in the short term in order to analyze the entire document more deeply. Meanwhile, Martin Berthoud noted that there was "considerable danger of Mr. Trudeau or another Canadian minister giving some early and ill-considered response to the Foreign Affairs Committee report. It is important that we should warn the Canadians of the disastrous consequences which this could have with regard to opinion in this country."[23] Carrington agreed and quickly sent a message to John Ford, inviting him to tell the federal side that an angry response would only add fuel to the fire.[24]

HOLD YOUR NOSE

Trudeau seemed to get the message and did no more than minimize the entire affair. "I know that it is not the position of the British Parliament or the British Government," he stated in the House[25] — which did nothing to abate the political and media storm. After a few days, the prime minister finally cracked under the pressure and went on the offensive: he compared Kershaw's committee and its reports to George Lucas's film, *The Empire Strikes Back*,[26] before following it up with one of his most famous declarations. If the British parliamentarians didn't like his constitutional resolution, they could "hold their noses while voting it."[27] In private, he'd become even more vitriolic. When one of his advisers referred to the upcoming visit of a member of the royal family, he threw out: "Always remember, they shit, too."[28]

Nothing calming from that quarter; but Anthony Kershaw wasn't a man who retreated easily. Drawing his sword, the former cavalryman began a new charge. He crossed the Atlantic to travel through Canada, explaining his report in every city that would have him, as if he were a bestselling author touring his latest book. He created a media spectacle wherever he went, notably in Edmonton where he debated Mark MacGuigan, who seemed hard-pressed to defend his point of view in front of a hostile crowd.

Thankfully for the federal government, another foreign commentator spoke on the situation, this time in Ottawa's favour — none other than former Australian prime minister Gough Whitlam. With his usual aplomb, Whitlam declared that Great Britain had simply no other choice than to accede to the federal government's request. If not, there would not only be repercussions in Canada, but in Australia and other Commonwealth countries as well.[29]

Whitlam wasn't the only one predicting dire consequences. A report published by the federal government a few weeks after Kershaw's, construed as a sort of retaliatory report, claimed that Anglo-Canadian relations would undoubtedly suffer.[30] According to Ottawa's document, the British committee didn't understand the generosity of the federal government's proposal, an offer that would finally give a judicially recognized role to the provinces in the constitutional amendment process, and this without threatening provincial powers. The document also questioned the legitimacy of British parliamentarians in the affair. They certainly didn't have the mandate to be guarantors of federalism, contrary to MPs in Ottawa, who were elected by the Canadian population and were responsible solely to them.

This attack was poorly received by Kershaw and his colleagues. As John Finnis, the constitutionalist hired to research and write the report, recalls, "There was an atmosphere of gloom at first. Members thought they might have been shown up as having blundered."[31] But Finnis believed that the federal reply was lacklustre. He was then asked to prepare an answer to Ottawa, a task which the former Rhodes Scholar was happy to accept, even if "it was as hard as I've ever worked in my life."[32]

After two weeks of work, he emerged from the library, having prepared a new tome, which he presented to the members of the parliamentary commission. "They sort of laughed with relief, delight and relished the opportunity to vindicate themselves publicly as soon as possible," he explained.

Kershaw's reply was published two weeks after Ottawa's, and concentrated most notably on factual errors made in the federal document. According to the federal report, Westminster had always agreed with requests coming from the Senate and the House of Commons. Yet, "the paper ignores the Canadian Parliament's request of June 1920, which the U.K. government repeatedly declined to act upon."[33] In that case, Ottawa had made a request for constitutional modification in order to apply Canadian laws beyond the country's borders for transport by air — a request that was refused. Except for this omission, which was immediately picked up by the media, Kershaw's reply examined the question of the accountability of federal MPs, which would give the federal Parliament — as opposed to British parliamentarians — the legitimacy to intervene in the constitutional question. The committee members saw in this a sophism:

> If the U.K. parliament were to enact a constitutional package of the type proposed in the face of widespread provincial opposition, the Canadian electorate would not itself be able to reverse the effects of the unilateral request. The new constitution enacted by the U.K. parliament would stand unaffected by the election results, even if those results expressed the electorate's unequivocal disapproval of amendments for which, perhaps, they had not given the federal government and parliament any mandate. The contentious parts of the new constitution could not be altered by the new majority in the Canadian parliament.[34]

CANADA AND THE COMPACT THEORY

The British committee's reply was right on the nose. "Inherently unreasonable," wrote the *Times* on the federal position. "Ottawa gets a sharp rebuke," added the *Daily Telegraph*.[35] As Mark MacGuigan would later recall, Kershaw's report was "an unmitigated disaster for the federal government."[36]

This whole affair wasn't only a disaster because of the political turmoil it caused. It also pointedly affected Trudeau's proposed doctrine. In the report's wake, journalists questioned him once again. Why should Westminster automatically approve his proposal and refuse to hear the provinces' voices?

"Because there can only be surely one government spokesman for Canada. There cannot be eleven, or else we are not one state."[37] Years later, he still insisted on this aspect:

> There were only two ways to solve the conundrum. The government of Canada could accept the compact theory, recognizing that our country was nothing more than a

community of communities, in which fundamental powers (including the power to patriate the constitution)
flowed from the provinces that had freely united to form
a loose confederation. Or the government of Canada, as
the sole governing body empowered to act in the name of
all Canadians, could reject the compact theory, hold that
Canada was something more than and different from the
sum of its parts, and proceed to patriate the constitution
unilaterally. We chose the latter course.[38]

Patriation would, in short, represent a final rejection of the compact
theory that Trudeau so hated, and which has since been declared invalid
by a number of observers, political scientists, jurists, and other special-
ists.[39] This is the reason why 1982 would be the year of triumph of the
vision according to which the country could only be understood by a
strong federal government, the incarnation of a nation whose regional
diversity is a secondary characteristic. Bolstered by such legitimacy, the
central government could dispose of a much greater ability to spend,
intervene, and set norms in their fields of jurisdiction, as well as take
control of their natural resources, et cetera.

This logic can be quite attractive. The problem is that it does not
reflect the way events unfolded in 1980–81, but instead the way Trudeau
wanted us to remember the events *post facto*.[40] In fact, Canada as a compact was invoked numerous times in front of the British. The premier
of Nova Scotia and members of Newfoundland's government, among
others, brandished the concept before John Ford when he was touring the
Maritimes in the autumn of 1980. The compact was also mentioned in
British Columbia's memorandum presented to Kershaw's committee, the
memo reminding Kershaw what Trudeau had been saying before becoming prime minister: "Federalism is by its very essence a compromise and
a pact, it is a pact of quasi-treaty in the sense that compromise cannot be
changed unilaterally. That it not to say that the terms are fixed forever;
but only that in changing them every effort must be made not to destroy
the consensus on which the federated nation rests."[41]

Quoting Winston Churchill back when he was minister of colonies,
Quebec emphasized its position in an informative document it distributed

in the United Kingdom: "The British North America Act is the fundamental Act governing the Constitution of the Dominion of Canada, and the different Prime Ministers of Canada voluntarily entered into that union. Adherence to the union was something in the nature of a treaty."[42]

The idea of the compact was also defended by Prince Edward Island. As noted in the province's memorandum to the Kershaw committee, and contrary to what Trudeau claimed, this vision of the country couldn't be reduced to a federal government as puppet in the hands of the provinces: "The federal government is the paramount of the two levels of government of Canada and, to a large extent, the embodiment of the nation, particularly beyond the boundaries of Canada. But despite its paramountcy, it must not be overlooked that sovereign powers in specific areas of jurisdiction were also assigned to the provinces ... undiminished by any power of the federal government."[43]

Thus, any constitutional modification not receiving a strong support by the provinces should be rejected by Westminster.

The compact theory wasn't the only concept against which Trudeau rebelled. Alberta chose to put the accent on the right of provinces and customs. Saskatchewan developed the theory of so-called "substantial consent,"[44] according to which Ottawa cannot act without substantial support by the provinces, even unanimous consent according to Quebec.

Be it out West, in the Maritimes, or in Quebec, Westminster was seen as the guarantor of the contract that was represented by constitutional rule; these discussions were not without influence in London, as can be imagined. As John Finnis wrote, "MPs were aware that Canadians often conceptualized these rules in terms of a compact. To that extent they thought of the Canadian-British constitutional conventions as somehow containing the notion of a compact."[45] This situation certainly made an impression on Michael Kirby, who commented during a visit to the British capital: "Some people believe in the compact theory of confederation," Trudeau's adviser wrote in a secret memorandum. It thus became imperative to begin a new information campaign because, "if this theory is valid, what justification is there for proceeding with constitutional amendments without the support of the provinces?"[46]

The idea of Canada as the result of a compact wasn't a new one in Great Britain. It was already used back when the debate was on Confederation in

1867, when British politicians discussing the topic in the House designated the Canadian constitution as a compact.[47] This concept was still present in the minds of observers a century later; doubly so, since it fed into another vision of Canada, most notably defended by Roy Megarry, the publisher of the *Globe and Mail*. The daily led a merciless battle against Trudeau in its editorial pages, and Megarry decided to bring the fight to London in February 1981. Invited by the Royal Commonwealth Society, he began by reminding his audience that his newspaper, which strived to be Canada's national daily, was founded by George Brown, himself one the fathers of Confederation. "Without him, without his persistent political dedication, the colonies of British North America would never have come together." He continued with his vision of Canada:

> Our opposition leader, Joe Clark, recently described Canada as "a community of communities." This, as I have tried to demonstrate in my preceding remarks, is what we are. A community of communities. I do not celebrate this. I do not bemoan it. I simply accept it as a fact. My travels across our country and the interaction we have with our readers as a national newspaper, tells me we have to accept it as a fact. We are a community of communities.[48]

For Trudeau, this concept was entirely detestable, almost as much as that of the compact. Years after patriation, he was still railing against what he called the "community of shopping centers" — a disorganized collective entity without a soul that could never claim the status of a true nation. Once again, he attempted through these comments to rewrite history, forgetting what the past Trudeau really said and did. This selective amnesia notably excluded his solemn speech to the nation on the evening of the 1980 referendum:

> To live together as Canadians, is to first accept each other as we are, with our linguistic and cultural differences … to live together as Canadians, does not mean to leave our soil and our cultural originality behind. As Emmanuel Mounier wrote, we all have many small nations under the

greater one and, in this sense, one can be authentically
Quebecker, Newfoundlander or Albertan all the while
being Canadian.[49]

Written by André Burelle, this speech didn't invoke Mounier by chance.
With Jacques Maritain, he was one of the major figures of French personalism. This philosophy constituted one of the two great influences on
Trudeau's worldview, the other being the traditional liberalism of Thomas
Hill Green and Lord Acton. "Trudeau was an individualist anti-communi-
tarian through passion and a communitarian-personalist through reason,"
Burelle explains. "Mr. Trudeau lived this conflict between his emotional
preferences and his rational convictions with difficulty, sometimes going as
far as not admitting it to himself."[50]

In the early days of his political career, Trudeau had his antinational-
ism toned down by Jean Marchand and Gérard Pelletier. His personalist
tendencies still influenced his actions. In 1980, this was no longer the case.
Only André Burelle still pushed the prime minister in this direction, but
the former had knowingly placed him far from the constitutional dossier
and asked Jim Coutts, Michael Kirby, and Michael Pitfield to work on the
topic in his stead. If Trudeau still claimed to be influenced by Mounier in
his speeches, he almost always acted out of profound hatred for nationalism.

To truly understand his internal conflict, we should realize that liberalism and personalism are not easy to reconcile. For personalists, liberalism transformed the individual into an interchangeable and disincarnated
concept.[51] However, only the state of the incarnated self is suitable for a
human being, since he or she must spiritually exist in both knowledge
and love. Since he or she dominates by thought over space and time, since
the person shows himself or herself capable of love, liberty, and morality,
the individual is seen as a metaphysical being, constituting a universe
and evolving in a relationship with society that is both dependent and
transcendent. The individual is thus part of a social whole that is larger
than the person and whose common good must prevail over individual
good — an axiom that can lead to the sacrifice of one's life in the name
of the motherland and the values it represents.

Here is where liberalism commits its sin, according to Mounier. By
relegating the spiritual dimensions of a human being to the private sphere,

liberalism compels the public sphere to move toward latent individualist materialism. Society as perceived by this doctrine is reasonable, respectful of the rights of each and all; fundamentally, it isn't a human society, but a disincarnated one, thus inhuman. The individual living in the purely liberal society is only able to escape this trap by psychologically immolating himself on the pyre of an abstraction — that of universal man, in reality an ordinary man, who is a subject of law but deprived of substance, benefitting from a charter but separate from his points of reference, lost in the anonymous billions of his kin who enjoy liberties more or less identical to his own.[52]

As the Puritans conceived of man without flesh, the source of sin, Trudeau came to conceive of the individual without his community. The notion of common good was shrugged off, as if lovers were no more than the sum of two individuals.[53] In truth, he was the true apostle of the "community of shopping centers." Not Joe Clark or Roy Megarry, who refused to break from the past in the name of some abstraction. Not the members of Kershaw's committee, who, starting from a different perspective, refused to forget that the community of communities is partly incarnated by the provinces. And not the British High Commissioner, who, by endlessly opposing the prime minister, set off the ultimate diplomatic tempest.

JOHN FORD CALLED BACK TO LONDON

Since Francis Pym's visit, Ford openly sought by any means to block Trudeau. His attitude created some worry and nervousness in London. A diplomatic incident could happen at any moment. In early January 1981, Deputy Minister Michael Palliser formally called on the High Commissioner to be discreet and subtle, despite Trudeau, "who seems to be making life increasingly difficult for us."[54]

A problem remained: Ford was fundamentally in disagreement with this more discreet approach and he'd received Pym's encouragement to act as he saw fit. The diplomat was especially frustrated when he observed that, despite the leak he'd orchestrated, Trudeau continued to claim that Thatcher, along with her ministers, had given him guarantees. "If Mrs. Thatcher does not now say something quickly," Ford wrote to London, "I see a danger that wounding accusations may be launched against us, implying unworthy motives for our keeping mum and letting leaks dribble out the truth slowly."[55]

For Thatcher, the moment wasn't right to change course; that is, to stop supporting Ottawa. Lord Carrington was thus charged with transmitting a message to Ford with his boss's recommendations, which he did by explaining to the High Commissioner that "our central aim is to maintain good relations with the Federal government. At this stage I think this is best served by continuing to keep a low profile, and not responding hastily to remarks made by Mr. Trudeau under pressure in Canada."[56]

But this sentiment was too little too late. By the time this call to order was sent, a new crisis had arisen. A few days before, Ford had gone for a bit of a skate at Rideau Hall, followed by a reception hosted by the governor general. The table had been set so that the British representative found himself next to New Democratic MPs James Manly and Ian Waddel, who supported Trudeau, as did their party. Before the two men had understood whom exactly they were speaking to, the conversation veered onto the issue of the constitution.

> Ford: "It seems to me that the amendments sought by your party will not protect properly the resources of the Western provinces. Moreover this constitutional package is going to create a confrontation with the British parliament."

> Waddell: "Ed Broadbent told us that there was no problem with the British parliament, who are you to tell us that anyway?"

> Ford: "I am the British High Commissioner!"[57]

This reply left Waddell stunned. After nearly falling out of his chair, the MP got himself together. Cut to the quick, he bee-lined toward Trudeau's table, attracting the eyes of other diners as he stomped past. In front of the whole room, Waddell told the prime minister about the conversation he'd just had with Ford, throwing an accusatory look or two in the latter's direction, pointing at him with his index finger. The mood, which had been light a few moments before, suddenly became tense.

It seemed the episode would go no further until it was brought to light on February 5. At the same time as Ford was receiving the order to keep a low profile, Ed Broadbent relayed the British representative's words to Mark MacGuigan. Both men decided to raise the issue on the floor of the House, in the shape of a question asked by Broadbent. The leader of the New Democrats attacked Ford, saying of his attitude that it was an "intolerable interference in Canadian affairs. It is, to put it bluntly, none of his business."[58]

"Unacceptable,"[59] MacGuigan added, specifying that "there is simply no question, nor could there be a question, about the obligation of the British Government in this matter, nor about the position which the Canadian Government is taking."[60] Off the floor, Broadbent was still enraged. Seconded by Waddell, he continued to bad-mouth Ford for a number of minutes in a press conference.

The leader of the New Democrats had barely finished speaking when the phone line at the British High Commission exploded with calls from journalists looking for reactions. Ford called a press conference on the spot. He first attempted to lessen the importance of the affair by repeating over and over that it was normal for a foreign representative to lobby — an explanation no one believed. The ambassador was subjected to hostile questions spewed forth from a pack of journalists. *Do you deny having attempted to convince the NDP to vote against patriation?*[61] *Are there limits to the political interventions of an ambassador? Are there tensions between Thatcher and Trudeau? Is the NDP acting foolishly in supporting the latter? Do you call lobbying the criticism you've made about the energy policy of the government in Windsor?*

As the press conference went on, the exchanges between Ford and the journalists became more and more damaging to Anglo-Canadian relations. Ford defended himself as best he could, but only managed to mire himself further in controversy, as the journalists licked their chops with glee. Meanwhile, Trudeau claimed that any discussion on the substance of his project in Great Britain would be the equivalent of General de Gaulle's famous *"Vive le Québec Libre!"*[62]

Never one to back down from a fight, Jean Chrétien jumped in the ring to state that "we are not afraid of collision with the British Government … we don't have to receive any lessons by an envoy."[63]

Ford reported back to London the rumour according to which he would soon be declared *persona non grata* and kicked out of the country. "I have realised from the beginning that I am the meat in the sandwich," he wrote. "I hope that the Federal government will not PNG me and I am reverting to a low profile."[64] The incident was immediately discussed at the highest levels in London, where it was decided that Ford would be recalled for consultations. His replacement, Lord Moran, would simultaneously be announced for May, a move that had been planned for a while, but that just might help appease the federal government.

John Ford was reprimanded by his superiors and asked to explain himself. This decorated veteran of the Second World War had seen much worse, and didn't falter. He told those willing to listen that Pym had endorsed his conduct and that he'd received numerous encouraging comments following his interventions before the media. Back for a short hop in the Canadian capital in March, Ford indulged himself once more, speaking his mind on the whole affair: "Eventually the historians (if they ever bother with such events) will agree that we here in Ottawa acquitted ourselves to good effect."[65]

CHAPTER 12

THE FEDS STRIKE BACK

When Trudeau began his patriation project, he'd started strong in the summer and continued doing well in early autumn, receiving Thatcher's support, winning over Ontario and New Brunswick, and managing to keep
Saskatchewan and Nova Scotia isolated from the Group of Six. But now the
situation seemed more uncertain in Great Britain, while in Canada the consultations of the Joint Parliamentary Committee were dragging on, the courts
were considering the case, and the Opposition was relentless in the House of
Commons. Along with all that, Jean Chrétien fell ill. Months of constitutional
battles had taken their toll on him and he was hospitalized for exhaustion.[1]

The federal government had to rally its troops and counterattack.
Fortunately for them, on February 3, the Manitoba Court of Appeal rendered a verdict that would recharge the feds' batteries. In a three-to-two
split decision, the court declared that the central government didn't require
provincial consent to send a request for constitutional change to London.

The federal government celebrated the decision, which was a cold
shower for the provinces. "I am not disappointed," the attorney general
of Manitoba, Gerry Mercier, declared with a grim look. "It's one step in
attaining the objective of having the Supreme Court of Canada make a
final determination."

This explanation was echoed in Edmonton by his colleague Neil Crawford.[2] In Quebec, Claude Morin pointed out that the court was divided and doubts remained. He predicted that the affair would continue for months and in the end would need to be adjudicated by the Supreme Court.

Meanwhile, despite the optimistic statements offered by some provincial representatives, the situation was worrying enough for the rebellious provinces to organize an urgent high-level meeting. The event took place in Montreal, at the Ritz-Carlton Hotel, six days after the court's decision. The six premiers took the unusual step of speaking with one another without advisers or ministers present, and made a number of decisions.

First, they needed to find a new approach to rally Nova Scotia and Saskatchewan to the rebellion. In the case of Regina, the fruit seemed ripe for the picking. Over the previous weeks, Blakeney had attempted — in vain — to bring Trudeau to adopt a position more respectful of provincial powers, which would have convinced him to take the federal government's side.

Second, the premiers made the crucial decision to agree on an amendment formula, to have something to propose instead of being in a state of static opposition, for which they'd been amply criticized. John Ford, among others, had encouraged them to go in this direction.

They also agreed to continue their activities in other spheres: first in public opinion, through ad campaigns, as Newfoundland and Quebec had been doing; before the courts, as well, where there was still work to do; in London, where the six premiers were hoping to travel whenever the constitutional request made its way across the Atlantic.

They decided to coordinate their action in the British capital to ensure efficiency. Each province would adopt its respective resolutions condemning Ottawa and send it to the United Kingdom. As Sterling Lyon explained, "We are more determined than ever to continue the struggle on all fronts." He quoted Kershaw's report as supporting his position, while René Lévesque accused Ottawa of lying when it came to the actual content of discussions in London. The Quebecker, in fine form, promised that Westminster would undergo a "constitutional bombardment."[3]

A SOURCE NAMED *DEEP THROAT*

This political barrage didn't have the expected effect, as the Alberta agent general in Great Britain, James McKibben, learned a few days later. He was the one who'd managed to infiltrate Thatcher's inner circle after having converted Ian Gow, her parliamentary secretary, to the provinces' cause.

Gow had been one of the first to lend his support to Thatcher during the palace coup that had given her the party's mantle in 1975. Enjoying her trust, always on the same ideological wavelength, always by her side, acting as confidant, counsellor, major-domo, guide, baggage handler, and private secretary, he exercised great influence over the prime minister.

Gow was well-positioned to measure the extent of dissatisfaction caused by the patriation issue among backbenchers. This is why he spoke to James McKibben, whom he regularly met in seamy restaurants and other disreputable joints, most often late in the evening so their illicit contact might remain secret. When McKibben wrote his reports back to Edmonton, he gave Gow the codename Deep Throat. No one knew his identity in the Albertan capital.

Two weeks after the premiers' conference in Montreal, McKibben and Gow met up to take stock of the situation. The numerous documents and letters that the provinces had been sending to British MPs had begun to get on the nerves of a number of people, Gow informed him.[4] Moreover, he went on, the Iron Lady hadn't changed her mind and would present the constitutional request in the House when she received it. She'd take some time before doing so, however, since she feared complications if she rushed ahead, notably in terms of potential repercussions on the Commonwealth.

Deep Throat then described the opposition Labour Party's current approach to patriation. The problem stemmed from the fact that McKibben and his colleagues' lobbying efforts had been expended mostly on the Conservatives, he stated. Little effort had been made among Labour MPs, who were ideologically closer to the federal Liberals. The result was, inevitably, that the provinces were having trouble convincing the left.

The meeting ended on that note, and McKibben quickly understood the wisdom of Gow's advice. He bumped into Denis Healey, the deputy leader of the Labour Party, not long after. As soon as he saw him, the latter turned his back and walked away, declaring as he left, "You are a conservative and I do not pay attention to conservatives."

The Albertan was stupefied.[5]

Fortunately, there was good news on other fronts. At the end of February, during a new strategy meeting that brought together the ministers responsible for the constitutional dossier, the rebellious provinces officially welcomed two new additions to their camp. Claude Morin, host of the meeting being held in Montreal, wasn't just half-proud to announce that Saskatchewan and Nova Scotia had joined the rebel side. He saw in this a sign that public opinion had begun to turn against the federal government. "There is an increased awareness across Canada that the federal Government has lied to everyone and the British have realized they are being asked to put their finger between the bark and the tree,"[6] he declared. This supersized group would now be called the "Gang of Eight."

This situation didn't make a dent in the federal government's intention, which continued to expend a good part of its efforts to convince the British parliamentary leader, Francis Pym, to push things through in London according to Ottawa's will. This approach hadn't worked when Jean Wadds had contacted him the first time, but why not try a second time? A new meeting was organized between the Canadian High Commissioner and the British minister, a discussion in which Michael Kirby, who was then travelling in Great Britain, participated.

Despite the fact that he was somewhat less inflexible and friendlier than last time, Pym was neither content nor optimistic. He asked how their last conversation ended up on the front page of the newspapers,[7] clearly unhappy about the numerous leaks coming out of Ottawa. Wadds apologized, explaining that the mole had been found and that extreme precautions were now in place; leaks were no longer a problem. The Briton seemed far from convinced. During the entire meeting, he spoke less than usual, and carefully chose his words, as if he were speaking publicly. But that didn't mean he intended to spare the federal government, which was demonstrated by his second question, demanding whether it was true that there were no longer six, but eight provinces opposed to the federal government. "How unfortunate!" he exclaimed upon hearing the answer.

Wadds didn't particularly appreciate this last remark, but she lowered her head and pushed on, explaining that the constitutional request was to arrive in March or April. The Canadian government hoped that once the bill had been adopted, Thatcher and the Queen might come to Canada for the official celebration, scheduled for July 1. Pym couldn't believe what he was hearing and, in Wadds's words, he "disingenuously expressed surprise that the Queen had plans to visit Canada."

Surprised or not, the Briton became more sombre. Before cracking open the champagne, he warned, a few difficulties needed to be solved, both in substance and in timing, referring to the charter and the government's legislative program, always very full. "We are very sympathetic to potential problems on timing," Wadds replied, "but that issue now has its own momentum and the request will probably be delivered with some ceremony, including delivery to the Queen. The Canadian people would want quick action."

Pym didn't see it from this angle. "We cannot ignore parliamentary responsibility and inner functioning of Westminster!" he warned. "We cannot expect momentum to overcome their very real problems. If this is pushed, it will fall flat on its face!" The Canadian demands are "unrealistic," he continued, adding that the federal government had also been warned by his predecessor, St. John-Stevas.

At this stage, it was impossible to say how the government would pilot the resolution through once it arrived. Thatcher might want to move quickly, but she and Pym would need to talk it through. One thing was certain, however; it was "important that there should be no comment in Canada on the issue when the address [was] in the United Kingdom," Pym said, explaining that British ministers had abstained, on their end, from making controversial declarations.

Here, Wadds announced that Trudeau would be making an important speech about the constitution on March 23. He was intending to speak about the expectations Canada had regarding the United Kingdom. Pym jumped up from his chair. Such a speech would have serious consequences in Westminster, he growled, almost urging his interlocutors from preventing their prime minister from speaking.

There was some good news, nonetheless, the parliamentary leader admitted: the decision by the Manitoba Court of Appeal was favourable to Ottawa. But there was worry that the case would be appealed to the Supreme Court. According to Wadds, the provinces would most likely wait for the decision by Quebec's appellate court as well as Newfoundland's before proceeding. In any case, she continued, the issue at hand was political, not judicial. Pym was in perfect agreement. However, "arguments based on awaiting decision for courts could have considerable effect. Wouldn't it be nice if the court cases were finished before we have to vote on the resolution?"

The minister then referred to the ferocious parliamentary battle being led by the Conservatives against the Trudeau government in reaction to the patriation project. The debate was dragging on in Ottawa, he said, non-committal. Why should the British Parliament not have the right to consider the constitutional dossier as slowly as the Canadian Parliament did? Wadds didn't find this one very funny. She answered tit for tat that the best interest of both governments was to get this whole episode over with as quickly as possible, adding that Trudeau felt strongly that "if this could be dealt with as a matter of urgency it would not fester."

The conversation then moved to Kershaw's report. Pym explained that his government was preparing a written response to the arguments presented in the document. Their response would be ironclad. He was convinced that they'd be able to turn the tables on Kershaw's committee. These were the only positive words the Brit spoke during the entire meeting.

As for the rest, Pym was inflexible, promised nothing, and refused to budge. To what end? The Conservative government had lost control over the parliamentary program, if not its MPs. The man was sure of nothing and, consequently, couldn't promise anything.

Nonetheless, despite this fruitless meeting with the parliamentary leader, Michael Kirby continued to hope that the Thatcher government would accede to Trudeau's desires. But there was work to do still. As he'd write to the prime minister, "My personal assessment is that we will probably have to exert considerable pressure on the British government in order to get them to pass the measure before their summer recess."[8]

THE PERILS OF THE FRANCOPHONE BBC IN CANADA

Within the British government, the anxiety was palpable, and a new incident reinforced this siege mentality. Always ready to lend a hand to his old friend Trudeau, former British prime minister James Callaghan stood in the House to upbraid Conservative MPs. "You will make fools of yourselves if you throw the bill out," he declared, defiant. As a journalist following the debates noted, "The response to the former Labour prime minister was a bellow of rage from the Tory benches which clearly shook those ministers present."[9]

The constitutional question was so serious that, if we are to believe the *Daily Telegraph*, Thatcher decided to avoid the short hop to Canada during a trip to the United States in February and March 1981. Such a trip would have placed her in the heart of the turmoil.[10]

The same thinking guided her when she received an unusual request from Labour MP David Ginsburg. Bilingual, he was a former journalist of the BBC French service. He was sometimes interviewed by Radio-Canada about the constitution. With the turmoil surrounding patriation, he mentioned to the leader of the government that numerous English-speaking Canadians listened to the BBC for information direct from British sources. Unfortunately, no equivalent existed for French Canadians, despite the fact that the famous public radio network was already producing French content in France and Africa. Expanding this service to Canada would allow francophones to have a fairer summary of events in the United Kingdom.

The prime minister replied that with existing budget constraints, such a project might be quite difficult, not to mention that it would take time for the BBC to find its audience, and the constitutional issue would most likely be over by then. But the main reason for her refusal was entirely different: the potential reaction by the Trudeau government: "Ideally it is desirable that French-speaking Canadians should be able to hear BBC broadcasts relating to the Constitutional Question in French. But if a French Service to Canada were to be started at this time, however balanced and well intentioned, there is a very real risk that the Federal Government might see it as smacking of interference in Canada's internal affairs."[11]

Absolute caution was appropriate, since one couldn't foresee where the next threat might come from: Australia, perhaps? Labour MP Michael English had recently written to Australian prime minister Malcolm Fraser to learn about his government's policy vis-à-vis patriation. English was a pro-province troublemaker who was doing everything in his power to slow the process down. In the fall, he unsuccessfully presented a parliamentary motion enjoining Her Majesty to simply send the patriation request back to Canada as soon as she received it, without moving the process any further along. Clearly informed about English's intentions, Malcolm Fraser answered that since Australia wasn't concerned, he would make no comment on the question. Aware of the difficulties Thatcher was facing in this dossier, Fraser informed her of the new development. She immediately wrote back, answering that "if I may say so, the line you took was of course exactly right. Thanks for keeping me in touch."[12]

English didn't manage to light any new fires. This was fortunate for Trudeau and his allies, since with Saskatchewan now part and parcel of the rebellion, tensions risked being cranked up higher still. From the Western plains, where he followed the evolution of the situation, Roy Romanow, minister of inter-governmental affairs in Saskatchewan, believed London wasn't where the Eight should be putting their energy; the British would never dare prevent the federal team from moving forward on this issue. But he sent his deputy minister, Howard Leeson, to London anyway, in order to evaluate the situation.

Once in London, the emissary quickly went to work. He first spoke with Gilles Loiselle. The latter shared his convictions with Leeson. The federal resolution would be defeated if it was presented to Westminster.[13] Loiselle's analysis would quickly be contradicted by Saskatchewan's agent general, Merv Johnson.

A third opinion was needed. Leeson would get it from none other than Anthony Kershaw. The latter was crystal clear: despite Trudeau's insults, the report from his committee and the aversion of the British people for the charter, opponents to it added up to no more than a hundred or so MPs, a number of whom would likely not bother to vote.

Following this conversation, Leeson had a key meeting with Alberta's agent general. For McKibben, the arrival of a representative from Saskatchewan was a godsend, and he immediately referred to the Labour MPs. If a majority of them supported Trudeau, he said, it would entirely cancel the impact of pro-provincial dissidence within the Conservative Party.[14] Consequently, it was crucial to win votes on the left. Led by the only New Democratic government in Canada at the time, Saskatchewan was the only province able to make inroads with Labour. It was urgent for Minister Romanow, who was also vice-premier of the province, to visit London.

ROMANOW THE *INGÉNU* VISITS LONDON

Even if Romanow wasn't entirely convinced by the operation, he decided to make his way to London in mid-March. Above all, he was intending to meet with MPs, but also believed a meeting with a British minister would be appropriate. A request was made to Nicholas Ridley, and transmitted through the intermediary of the Canadian High Commission. It was exactly the sort of imitative taken by the provinces that the federal government hated. Romanow knew all about Ridley's opinions: he saw the provinces as tiresome. A man with a dry and cold demeanour, he would likely take advantage of the meeting to pass along his message. Ottawa decided not to object too strongly to the affair.

On his end, like Voltaire's *Ingénu*, Romanow landed in London, not suspecting what was lying in wait. Listening to him, one would think that everything would work out roundly. He even predicted to the press that his discussion with Ridley would constitute a turning point between Her Majesty's government and the rebellious provinces.

Poorly informed as to his hosts' disposition, Romanow was equally so in regards to Sonny Ramphal, the secretary of state of the Commonwealth, whom he met before speaking with Ridley. Romanow began by explaining his province's position. Saskatchewan wanted nothing to do with a referendum in the amendment formula, and also believed the charter of rights should be toned down, notably by respecting provincial powers to a greater extent. His government, he said, put forward truly reasonable positions, and it was reluctantly that he'd joined the rebellious provinces.[15]

Completely ignoring what Romanow had said, Ramphal went on the offensive. He underlined the extent to which he'd been impressed by Mark MacGuigan's recent presentation in Edmonton, adding that "whatever their reasons for lobbying in London and exerting pressures on the British government, provinces are in fact perceived as acting as colonies and as attempting to force British government to act as a colonial government." Ramphal concluded by telling his counterpart to stop acting in this manner once and for all.

En route to the Foreign Office, where he was to meet Ridley, the visitor shared his impression with Christian Hardy, number two at the High Commission. He felt that the discussion with Ramphal hadn't gone very well. He hadn't seen anything yet …

The day before, Thatcher had survived by the skin of her teeth the adoption of her austerity budget. No less than forty conservative MPs had voted against her or abstained, despite the fact that the measure was a vote of confidence. This illustrates to perfection the critical situation in which Thatcher found herself. Her loyal Ridley was in a terrible mood.

The British minister began the meeting by criticizing Romanow's declarations in the media concerning their meeting. He'd have preferred their discussion remain private, he declared, furious. Romanow was thrown off by this opening move. He stammered a few apologies, then laboriously attempted to explain his province's position.[16] Ridley cut him off and threw another punch: "Why are you making such a fuss, coming to London and putting the British government in an awkward position?"[17]

"It is Trudeau who is responsible for the position in which the British government found itself," Romanow replied, trying to get back on his horse.

"We don't want the provinces to lobby in London," Ridley interrupted.

The minister from Saskatchewan maintained that the provinces were making legitimate demands, mentioning Kershaw's report in support.

"Keep away from London, you cannot win!" Ridley hammered home by way of answer, continuing with a comprehensive criticism of the Foreign Affairs Committee. In any case, he indicated, "it is unthinkable that the British government would consider any alternative other than to accept at its face value any eventual joint resolution of Canadian national parliament. To think otherwise is not on."[18]

This wasn't what was agreed upon in the Statute of Westminster, Romanow stated; the British had a constitutional responsibility toward Canada.

"I don't know what Canadian negotiators then had in mind but the British did not regard themselves as having accepted such trusteeship," Ridley exclaimed.

Even if the conversation led nowhere, Romanow persisted, asking three questions that were "verging on rudeness ... that probably served to only upset the British hosts even further," according to Christian Hardy, who was attending the meeting.

First, the visitor began, asking whether the government intended to use its whips? Second, would it wait for an eventual decision by the Supreme Court? And finally, would it help the provinces to slow the process down so there might be a new constitutional conference, which was likely to lead to a compromise?

Ignoring this last question, Ridley said that the Supreme Court had no power over the British Parliament, even if he admitted in passing that some MPs were preoccupied by this aspect. As for whips, the Brit couldn't deny what all the evidence pointed to: they weren't particularly efficient. It would thus be possible to go no further than giving "the strongest possible indication of government position to backbenchers."

The meeting ended on that note. Romanow was completely dispirited. And as if this wasn't enough, only thirteen of the eighty MPs on the Aitken-Foulkes committee attended his address to the group. Worse still, he felt by the tone of their questions that many of them were tempted to join the federal government's side.

Romanow's meeting with Denis Healy, the Labour deputy leader, wasn't much of a success either, if we are to believe an article in the *Globe and Mail*. Not long before, Healey had received a visit from the secretary of the federal wing of the New Democrats, Robin Sears, who convinced him to support Ottawa, despite the fact that Labour hadn't yet come up with their official position on patriation. Romanow attempted to change Healy's mind, but failed miserably.[19]

The misfortunes of Saskatchewan's vice-premier didn't end there. The day after his meeting with Ridley, the *Globe and Mail* ran a front-page story saying that Romanow had hit a wall, and describing a meeting ending in resounding failure.[20] Who orchestrated this leak? Doubts fell on Christian Hardy, who barely concealed his glee at Romanow's hardships. But the federal diplomat was quick to deny such accusations and shared his claims of innocence with Romanow himself, the latter not believing a single word out of Hardy's mouth.

Furious, the visitor spoke with his heart on his sleeve at a press conference just before returning to Canada, claiming that the newspaper had placed him in a "tremendously awkward spot. The *Globe and Mail* matter is almost part of a deliberate campaign to undermine what I think has been, up to now, a very effective provincial position advocated here in London," he said, adding that it was false to claim that he'd been rattled.[21] The story was based on a "subjective comment apparently by some official in attendance at the meeting." As for his meeting with Denis Healey, he claimed there wasn't a sliver of truth in what the *Globe* was reporting.

REEVES HAGGAN'S AGAPES

Romanow returned to Canada, convinced that the provinces would never win in England. As well, his visit to London had sown concern within the ranks of the rebellious provinces, particularly Alberta, where the affair was closely followed. In addition, the federal machine was now putting on quite the production. The protagonists were Jean Wadds and her second-in-command, Christian Hardy, who participated in various public demonstrations. The artistic director, Reeves Haggan, also played the role of conductor, organizer, coach, hatchet man, and cheerleader. His great specialty was his bacchanalian prowess at every dinner party in town. Alone or with colleagues, he breakfasted, lunched, and supped each day with a multitude of stakeholders in the city's best houses, where he drank only the finest wines. The federal team was meeting on average between ten and twenty people a day, a rhythm that impressed the Albertan agent general to such an extent that he actually warned Edmonton of these goings-on. By the month of May, the federal government would have met each of the some six hundred MPs of the House of Commons at least once.[22]

While they weren't the only ones being invited out to eat, the MPs remained the principal beneficiaries of the "agapes" of Reeves Haggan and his colleagues, especially if they'd been identified as counting among the undecided. A group of MPs of the tiny Social Democratic Party noticed this pattern. They were firmly behind Ottawa and, consequently, hadn't been invited out to eat. One of them decided to contact Reeves Haggan. Listen, he told him, there are some issues that a few individuals among our parliamentary group don't understand. Clarifications would be necessary. Reading between the lines, the Canadian invited a delegation of Social Democrats to supper. After a few good bottles of wine and a few thousand dollars of public monies spent, they were thoroughly clarified: they'd certainly be behind Ottawa now.

If Haggan — a man with an impressive physique — enjoyed the hushed ambiance of the best lounges and restaurants, he also didn't hesitate when it came to twisting a few arms. When Wood Gundy invited Sterling Lyon to a lunch conference during a trip to London, Haggan warned: mind your own business and stop inviting the provinces to your activities.[23] Event organizers who allowed provincial politicians to exercise their right to free speech by speaking on the charter designed to protect just this right, were all subject to the same threats, be it the Commonwealth Parliamentary Association, the Canadian Club, or the Maple Leaf Club.

The federal government was attacking on every front, seconded by key actors, like the Commonwealth's Secretary-General, who'd regularly speak about the issue with the British government. He did this so often that Lord Carrington ended up putting Ramphal on his black list, refusing to acknowledge him. Never disheartened, the Secretary-General sent him a letter in which he offered his unsolicited advice: why bother with discretion when you're sure you hold the answer? According to the head of the Commonwealth, the solution was an amendment voted by Westminster that would give powers over constitutional modifications to the federal Parliament. The operation would have the advantage of entirely avoiding the debate about the charter in Great Britain, and it could then be adopted by MPs and senators in Ottawa. The fact that even Pierre Trudeau had never thought of attempting to ask for such powers didn't seem to deter the Secretary-General. As he explained to Carrington, "Provided this was done at the request of the Canadian parliament … this would amount to a full and perfect patriation."[24]

Ah, it was all so simple now!

Ramphal was so looking to distinguish himself in this affair that in February 1981 he made a suggestion to Allan Gotlieb that Trudeau write to the Commonwealth heads of state. As Wadds noted in a cable to Ottawa, "Brits would be most upset, need we say," adding that a certain unease was beginning to develop among the Commonwealth nations' representatives in London faced with the perspective of a confrontation between the British and the Canadians.[25]

These reservations didn't keep Ramphal from inviting himself to Canada a few weeks later to once again speak about the constitution. Even the federal government began to find this ally troublesome. As Mark MacGuigan wrote to Trudeau, "Mr. Ramphal has indicated that his primary interest in coming to Ottawa at this time is to discuss the constitution with you. Both the British government and British parliamentary opinion would certainly be highly sensitive to any public indication to this effect, and for our part we do not feel the need for Mr. Ramphal to come to Ottawa to discuss the constitution."[26]

Fortunately, Canadian diplomats had more than one trick up their sleeves for visiting international civil servants with time on their hands. External Affairs provided Ramphal with a program entirely geared toward North-South issues. He would be so busy meeting people and visiting places that he'd barely have enough breath left to say "constitution." The only flaw in the plan was a thirty-minute meeting with Trudeau. It would be Ramphal's best opportunity to speak to his favourite issue. The two men had already talked about this during a meeting in October 1980 in New York, a situation that hadn't advanced the federal government's side. As MacGuigan explained to Trudeau: "The Foreign Office is aware of that conversation and we must assume that they learned it either directly or indirectly from Mr. Ramphal … the British government will look very dimly on any attempt to pressure them now, when we are cooperating … no good purpose would be best served by bringing Ramphal into our thinking at present."[27]

Trudeau would remain aloof during the March 31 conversation. As motivated as usual, Ramphal began by announcing a few obvious facts. First, he said, it was important to counter provincial misinformation in London, as if Trudeau didn't know this. He went on to say that Thatcher could move forward and present the federal resolution in Westminster, and then blame her MPs if the motion failed. Very interesting; no one in Ottawa had thought of that!

Then the Secretary-General continued with more interesting information. He'd spoken to a number of Commonwealth leaders, figuring that it would have been awkward for Ottawa to do so at this stage. The leaders didn't share Kershaw's interpretation of the Statue of Westminster at all. Ramphal warned them that this question would likely make an appearance at the Commonwealth Summit scheduled for Melbourne in October 1981.

Trudeau answered that the time wasn't ripe to play the Commonwealth card, and on that conclusion, the men took leave of each other. The prime minister was careful not to go too deeply into details with Ramphal, but he was seriously considering calling on the other leaders of the former British Empire if things didn't go his way.

HOW JEAN CHRÉTIEN ENTERED ROYAL FOLKLORE

But let's not get ahead of ourselves. The plan was still to seduce Britannia rather than wage war on her. The man tasked with this was none other than Jean Chrétien, who made a notable visit to London at the end of March. First stop, first difficulty: the minister of justice began his visit with a speech at the prestigious Canada Club … a place reserved for men only. What to do about

High Commissioner Jean Wadds? In this gentlemen's club founded in 1810, many still seemed to regard tradition as sacrosanct. However, refusing entry to a representative of the Canadian government when the club was named after the country was a recipe for a diplomatic incident. Fortunately, the club's leaders came up with the idea of giving Wadds the status of "honorary man," the same way Saudi Arabia had done during the Queen's visit to the Arab kingdom.[28]

There was a real crowd at the meeting, including a number of ministers and former ministers. Jean Chrétien made quite the impression.[29] He began by saluting the dignitaries who had decided to come, including Denis Healey, the former Labour finance minister, whom Chrétien knew well. He had a lasting impression of Healey, who'd remarked after a speech he'd delivered in both official languages, "Denis thanked me by saying I understood neither your French nor your English!"

Discovering *le petit gars de Shawinigan*'s colourful and humorous side, the attendees drank in his every word. Chrétien recalled his years as minister of Indian Affairs in the early 1980s, and shared an anecdote. The Queen, accompanied by Prince Charles, was in the middle of a visit to the Great North, where she was to inaugurate a plaque commemorating the exploits of explorer Alexander Mackenzie. In front of three thousand people, the master of ceremonies came to see Chrétien. So filled by the emotion of the royal presence, he was much too shy to sing "O Canada." What to do? "When the time came, I went to the microphone and I began to sing. Unfortunately, I knew only the French words. Since no one else knew them, no one else joined in, and I had to sing the whole thing solo. My wife said she had never been so embarrassed in her entire life."

The minister's talents as a singer didn't go unnoticed. A few months later, Prince Charles recognized him during an official reception. "But how could I forget you?" he said, "Your singing of 'O Canada' in the North last summer has become part of the royal folklore."[30]

The circumstances were such that Chrétien met the Queen five times in two years, notably during a trip to London, where he was asked at the last minute to accompany veterans of the First World War to Buckingham Palace. "You again!" the Queen exclaimed, seeing him enter.

"Your Majesty, I am *the* royalist from Quebec!"

The crowd went wild for that one. Now that Chrétien had charmed the attendees with his anecdotes, it was time to get serious and deliver his message. During the referendum, Chrétien explained, "I told Quebeckers that if they decided to stay in the Confederation, we'd change the status quo and that the Constitution would protect both official languages. We need to create a charter of rights that will guarantee us the fundamental rights that we all Canadians care about.... It's in this way that we'll be able to ensure education in the mother tongue of the minority."

Neither Trudeau nor Chrétien described their promises made during the referendum this way, and they certainly did not emphasize a charter with so-called "linguistic rights." But no one would contradict the visitor who, contrary to the discourse he maintained in Canada, spoke of the charter not as tool to defend fundamental rights, but as an instrument whose purpose was to reinforce federal structures, the unity of the country, and multiculturalism. Canada "is not a melting pot," Chrétien explained, for each can keep his culture. "We have a very diverse society by the fact that many Canadians are originally from the British Isles, but a good number of French were there before them.... And then there are Russians, Hungarians, Germans, etc."

The orator finished his speech by entirely rejecting the possibility that the federal request might embarrass the British government. Yet this embarrassing parliamentary situation was the subject about which ministers Nicholas Ridley and Ian Gilmour wanted to speak to him. Chrétien would meet them on March 26.

The Canadian minister began by stating that the federal government wasn't looking to increase the breadth of its powers, contrary to what was being said. There was quite a lot of misinformation in this respect.[31] The problem was founded on the "ever expanding shopping list which is the hallmark of the provincial bargaining theme. The list became unacceptable and the federal government called the bluff." Perhaps, Ridley answered. But the problem in Great Britain wasn't linked to the warrants or faults of the federal project. He insisted on the fact that "people have been persuaded by the provinces that Westminster has the role of guardian or trustee and they are asking the question why is the government of Canada proceeding despite all this opposition?" Moreover, parliamentarians didn't understand why Ottawa couldn't be satisfied with simple patriation without the charter. "MPs don't like the thought that the prime minister, Trudeau, is pulling a fast one."

This comment cut Chrétien to the quick. He replied by underlining the importance that his government was putting on the whole affair, adding that if he was questioned on the role of Westminster, he'd frankly answer that "the federal government's decision to proceed is none of your business." As Martin Berthoud noted after the meeting, "Chrétien found it difficult to get away from the slightly tub-thumping manner which may be appropriate in the Canadian Parliament but does not necessarily go down too brilliantly with our Ministers."

In any case, the two Brits attempted to calm things down. Nobody was contesting the visitor's point of view: he was preaching to the choir, and the British couldn't ask for better than to get rid of this blasted constitutional affair. It's more a question of the way of presenting things, Ian Gilmour explained. And there was another problem: "While the British government can put the case publically in parliament, it cannot lead a campaign aimed at backbenchers."

Following these clarifications, Chrétien then met Francis Pym.[32] At this stage, the federal government was still hoping to announce the new constitutional law on July 1. The federal envoy insisted on this point, explaining that it was crucial that the Canadian resolution, which would arrive in Great Britain some twelve days later, be introduced in the House of Commons before Easter. "This would avoid all kinds of speculations," he said. The visitor also explained that his government wanted the second reading of the constitutional project to be entirely bypassed. After all, he reminded Pym, Thatcher had promised that she'd go forth "as expeditiously as possible."

"Time and preparation is the most tactful way of handling this request," Pym replied. If we attempt to "railroad the request through Westminster, I can guarantee it won't get through." The government, he continued, "is not in a position to lead a campaign to dissuade MPs that they are not to take into account a degree of provincial opposition or consider themselves trustees for Canadian federal structure."

THE CHIEF JUSTICE JUMPS IN THE FRAY

Pym was particularly interested in the potential involvement of the Supreme Court in the affair. Confident, he announced to Chrétien that the Supreme Court would hear Manitoba's appeal on April 28, and this before any announcement to this effect had been made. How can his confidence be explained?

The previous day, the Foreign Office had received a confidential message from John Ford, stating, "We have heard in confidence that the Supreme Court decided today that it will hear the Manitoba appeal on 28 April, considerably earlier than the Federal Government expected. The Chief Justice gave the impression (to a federal government source please protect) that he hoped to hand down the Court's views before the parliamentary process was complete in the U.K."[33]

This information was immediately shared with the solicitor general of Great Britain, Michael Havers. The latter confirmed what everyone feared: this development would "make it very difficult, if not impossible, to get the U.K. Parliament to act on the Canadian request in advance of the anticipated ruling of the Supreme Court of Canada." Those who wished to wait for the judges to speak on the matter would now have "very strong arguments available."[34]

These new difficulties stemmed from Bora Laskin, whom Trudeau had named judge to the Supreme Court, and later chief justice. Laskin, a great supporter of the charter, was obviously communicating with the executive branch, sharing information with a source within the federal government, a source that then transmitted this information to the British government. Why? Because, having clearly been informed of the British government's difficulties with the issue of *sub judice*, he was attempting to accelerate the judicial process.

What was happening, exactly? Toward the end of March, probably on the twenty-sixth, Laskin had summoned the federal government's lawyers, John Scollin and Barry Strayer, and Manitoba's lawyer, Kerr Twaddle. The latter wanted the Supreme Court to decide his government's case as quickly as possible, fearing that the case might not be studied before the federal government had time to vote the constitutional resolution through and send it to London.

Laskin turned toward the two federal lawyers to better upbraid them. "Surely the government does not plan to proceed with the adoption of the resolution before our hearing."[35] Somewhat uncomfortable, Strayer replied that, indeed, the government had no intention of waiting for the Supreme Court to hand in a decision. Laskin pulled a face and explained that he'd set a date so that the procedures might begin the following month. Strayer added that Newfoundland and Quebec's judicial actions wouldn't be over by then. Both those provinces wouldn't have the opportunity to be heard by the highest tribunal if things moved quickly. Laskin dismissed this argument entirely.[36]

Laskin wanted the Supreme Court to intervene as expeditiously as possible in the process, motivated by his desire to help Trudeau's charter see the light, even if he disagreed with the latter on the means to reach this objective. He believed the case could be closed within two months, thus paving the way for patriation in Westminster.

Beyond issues of timing, let's note here that the highest tribunal should never have intervened, as it was preparing itself to do, in questions relating to constitutional conventions. As Trudeau himself said, all of it was, fundamentally, a political question. From a legal standpoint, first and foremost, the highest tribunal couldn't prevent the federal Parliament from sending a request to the British Parliament. Second, its role isn't to give its opinion on non-justiciable constitutional conventions. As the constitutionalist Peter Hogg noted at the time, answering a question on conventions, the Supreme Court acted "outside of its legal function and [attempted] to facilitate a political outcome." R.S. Kay, another constitutionalist, would add on his part that the Supreme Court "intervened as another political actor, not as a court of law."[37]

Whatever the case may be, the information according to which the highest tribunal aimed at handing down its decision before the end of the parliamentary session in Westminster had an immediate effect on the politicking in London. The British certainly intended to use this new information to force the federal government's hand. During his conversation with Chrétien, Francis Pym put pressure on the former on the *sub judice* issue, but Chrétien simply pushed his objections aside. "You should look at this as a challenge," he said, jovial.

"I am dedicating my mind to that end," a somewhat perplexed Pym replied. "It may well take us longer than you expect or want, just as you took longer than we wanted," he added, specifying that the British government would also need to present its response to the Kershaw report, and that a debate on the floor was to be expected. After these steps, he said, "we will have a go."

The conversation ended with a warning. Clearly aiming a shot at Trudeau,

Pym stated that "the British should not be criticized in Canada," explaining that besides Ford, the British had kept from commenting on the way the federal government had been proceeding. "If feelings are aroused, it will only make the matter more difficult."

Despite these differences in perspective, everyone left the meeting satisfied. Be it with Gilmour and Ridley or Pym, the conversations had been relatively constructive and cordial. The federal government had been expecting much worse. But the debate raged on within the British government. At the end of March, the ministers most concerned by the Canadian constitution held an important meeting on the topic. Among the notables, we find Havers, Gilmour, Ridley, and, of course, Pym. The group reached the following conclusion:

> It was agreed to recommend to the Cabinet that the Government should await the outcome of the Supreme Court hearing of the Manitoba case before acting on any Canadian request. The Canadian Government had been warned when their emissaries saw the Prime Minister in October 1980 that the Parliamentary situation would be very difficult if a case was still pending before the Supreme Court at the time any request was received, and they could not fairly claim that the Prime Minister's commitment to facilitate the handling of the Federal Government's proposals at Westminster was unconditional, although they had since chosen publicly to present the undertakings which they had received in that sense.[38]

The Thatcher government was thus preparing to suspend parliamentary procedure because of the *sub judice* principle, even if that meant angering Trudeau. From the very start, Ottawa had maintained that the Supreme Court had no place in deciding a political question. Consequently, the federal government had refused, up until that point, to have the land's highest tribunal validate their efforts. But now, on March 31, Newfoundland's Court of Appeal decreed that Ottawa was acting unconstitutionally. The provinces, the court decided, were autonomous communities, and the federal government was putting Canadian federalism in peril by proceeding in a unilateral fashion.[39] Even if, a few weeks later, Quebec's Court of Appeal, as Manitoba's before it, decided in Ottawa's favour, the defeat in Newfoundland changed the situation by creating a fair degree of doubt on the legality of unilateral patriation.

Facing parliamentary obstruction by Joe Clark's Conservatives in the House on this issue, the federal government felt there was little choice left and changed its tune. It now decided to submit the question to the Supreme Court and suspend the debate in Parliament. As Mark MacGuigan explained to Lord Carrington, two things motivated the federal government's decision: first, their approach seemed illegitimate following the decision in Newfoundland; second, Ottawa accepted the British government's arguments.[40]

The consequences of this decision were immediately felt in the British capital, as testified by discussions that occurred in Cabinet in early April. Nicholas Ridley explained: "Mr. Trudeau's decision to hold up despatch of the resolution to London pending the decision of the Supreme Court had taken much of the heat out of the Opposition in Parliament." Thatcher also began to feel more serene about how the story would unfold. Like Ridley, she believed that the constitutional resolution could be introduced in the House at the end of July, after the Supreme Court's decision. The middle of summer would mean the end of the parliamentary session in Westminster; everyone would be eager to leave on vacation. Thatcher and Ridley believed the government would be able to maximize its chances to get rid of this damnable constitutional ball and chain.[41]

The impression that now dominated within the government was that the Supreme Court would decide in Ottawa's favour, as two of the three provincial courts had done. The federal government was projecting an aura of confidence that certainly reinforced this sentiment. Trudeau even went for a soothing statement: "If we should lose in the courts and in Britain, you know, I won't claim that I have been poisoned. I'll just say my political judgement was bad, or my legal judgement was bad, and then we'll go on to try and solve problems as before."[42]

The prime minister was indeed right to demonstrate such serenity. Throughout the month of April, his government was finally receiving encouraging news from London. This was particularly true on April 16, when Nicholas Ridley invited Christian Hardy over for supper in order to talk constitution.[43] The British minister was optimistic. For the past few weeks his government had been tallying MPs on both sides of the question. Despite Kershaw's report, Trudeau's sensational claims, the common front of eight provinces, and the lobbying by Loiselle, McKibben, and the rest of the gang, the federal government still held on to a small majority within the House, at least among the elected officials who'd demonstrated an interest in the constitution. Ridley was clear: the tide had shifted in Ottawa's favour. The war wasn't yet won, but the worst seemed to have passed.

CHAPTER 13

QUEBEC AND ITS ALLIES

If spring was a time of renewal for the federal government in London, it also heralded René Lévesque's resurrection. This new development surprised observers, but certainly not Lévesque himself. During a meeting with the consular corps the preceding winter, the highest ranked consul had asked the PQ's chief to evaluate his chances of winning the next election. The premier had just come out of a meeting with his main pollster, Michel Lepage, and the latter was clear: the PQ would win with 50 percent of votes and some eighty ridings.

Lévesque essentially repeated Lepage's analysis to the diplomats who were questioning him: "I believe we can count on the same number of seats as last time, at least seventy-two."[1] The consuls were somewhat perplexed by this prediction, as were the two journalists who'd sneaked into a closet to spy on the proceedings. When they heard Lévesque, they emerged from their hiding spot, cackling like geese at the idea of spreading this news. By the time Lévesque left the room, he was faced with a chorus of laughing journalists, waiting for him while "holding their sides." Though he was furious, Lévesque didn't let his frustration show. He repeated to the assembled media and his own troops that the PQ was far from dead; his objective was to counter any sort of defeatism that might spring up.[2]

Buoyed by an electoral budget in the spring and, as Lévesque himself would say, "our incredible luck" at facing a Claude Ryan possessed by some sort of "power trip of disconcerting intensity," the premier called the election.[3] Of the seven electoral campaigns that Lévesque would lead, this one would be his easiest, with Ryan perceived as arrogant, weak, pretentious, and untrustworthy.[4] What's more, the Liberal Party leader was treated as insignificant by Trudeau. As Robert Bourassa would remark, by refusing to wait for his federalist ally to be elected in Quebec before attempting patriation, Trudeau had given Ryan his walking papers.[5]

All this obviously pleased the PQ, which presented the constitution as one of the campaign's three main themes — the other two being the economy and family policy. Trudeau was accused of having betrayed his promise made during the referendum, of threatening Bill 101, and having destroyed the Canadian federal system.[6] Faced with this political incarnation of Beelzebub, the following question needed to be asked: "Who will be the stronger versus the government in Ottawa, [Lévesque or Ryan]?"[7]

"To ask the question is to answer it," the PQ's program replied.[8]

The answer would be laid out on April 13. With 49.3 percent, the PQ obtained its best result, never since repeated. The Liberals, on their end, obtained 46.1 percent of the vote. The electorate had never been so divided between the two major parties. The Liberals had managed to keep only 77 percent of the support garnered by the No camp on the night of May 20, 1980.

The respective results of the parties were important, since they contradicted the idea that Trudeau had long proposed, and would continue to promote until his death: a majority of Quebeckers supported his constitutional reform. This statement was refuted by the results of the election of 1981, in which patriation had been one of the most important issues. The PQ victory can be interpreted as real opposition to the Trudeau project, since an important number of No voters finally settled on voting for Lévesque. As for the 46 percent of support garnered by the Liberals, it certainly did not represent unconditional support for Trudeau, since Ryan himself opposed the prime minister's constitutional goals, albeit discreetly. Finally, Roch La Salle, the Union Nationale's new leader, who'd received 4 percent of the votes, was also a strong critic of Ottawa. The strongest data point — and the most concrete — indicating Quebeckers' support for patriation has to be the results of this spring election. And they demonstrate a repudiation of the prime minister.

This is one of the reasons why Trudeau minimized the vote's significance. As he would write to Lévesque, "The results of this election will only surprise those who ignore everything of [the] Quebecker's legendary prudence, who've always refused to put all their eggs in the same basket."[9] If he meant by this that Quebeckers prefer to vote red in Ottawa and blue in Quebec, he was in a good position to know that this theory didn't hold water. When Pearson was still prime minister, when Trudeau was an MP and then minister, the reds had "cohabited" in Quebec and Ottawa for three years; a majority of Quebeckers trusted Liberals both at the provincial and federal level. And from 1970 to 1976, the Quebec counterpart was as red as he was: Robert Bourassa. Thanks to his selective memory, Trudeau avoided any uncomfortable reassessment of the true level of support he had in the province of his birth.

Meanwhile, the eight rebellious provinces were continuing their fight. For the past few months, they'd been wrestling with a powerful argument from the other side: their seeming inability to come up with an alternative scenario to Trudeau's. At the end of 1980, British Columbia's premier, Bill Bennett, started promoting the fact that the anti-Trudeau contingent should come up with their own proposals.[10]

This process ended up being more difficult than it seemed, notably due to Nova Scotia and Saskatchewan's recent joining. The latter wanted nothing more than to return to the negotiating table, influencing other provinces in the same direction, notably British Columbia. To this we must add the conflict that inevitably appears when eight premiers and eight ministers of intergovernmental affairs — sixteen strong characters with sixteen different perspectives — gather in the same room. These pitfalls made it difficult to find common ground.

The exercise was made more complicated by the fact that Claude Morin, in early March, left the negotiations to run an electoral campaign. Quebec was represented at the table by Deputy Minister Robert Normand. On March 27, the latter participated in an important meeting in Winnipeg with a number of ministers and civil servants of the Gang of Eight. The discussions revolved around a patriation scenario that would put the charter of rights to one side — a requirement that came from Quebec City — in exchange for which the francophone province would agree to give up its request for better sharing of powers before the patriation of the constitution.

The group would propose to go no further than a supreme law with an amendment formula. To do so, they would look for inspiration in a proposal initially made by Alberta in January 1979, the "Vancouver formula."[11] This approach had its foundations in the principle that all provinces were equal. There would be no particular status or veto right for Quebec, Ontario, or any other province. Constitutional changes would be made following approval by the federal Parliament and seven provinces representing at least 50 percent of the population. In the case where a constitutional change could be perceived by a province as encroaching on its jurisdiction, a right of withdrawal could be exercised.

All well and good, Normand said. However, for him, financial compensation should be offered to a province that withdrew from an amendment. The idea wasn't popular at all among the other premiers, in particular with Allan Blakeney from Saskatchewan. The latter believed that such a disposition would give rich provinces a de facto veto right. If they took their marbles out of an amendment and asked for financial compensation, the amendment would be impossible to successfully implement due to the economic effects that would be caused by a withdrawal from a richer province.[12] This option also risked considerably displeasing Trudeau, who'd see it as piecemeal separatism. Blakeney, seconded by Buchanan and Bennett, opposed the idea. But he found resistance in Peckford, Lougheed, and Lyon, who were resolute in their desire for agreement and had considerable influence in the alliance. After long discussion, a compromise was found. Withdrawal could only occur if two-thirds of the legislative assembly of the withdrawing province agreed, thus making it much more difficult to achieve.

The agreement was supported by the eight premiers via two conference calls, the second of which occurred three days before the Quebec election. Lévesque was forced to remove himself from his campaign schedule for a few hours. But he had no choice. The public signing of the agreement was to occur on April 16, three days after the election. In his memoirs, written four years after the fact, he claimed to have formally warned his colleagues: "In all honesty, we [in Quebec] will have a few important objections to air out."[13]

His memory of events is contested by Peter Lougheed. According to him, Lévesque did say he was uncomfortable with the fact that withdrawal with compensation could only be exercised with a two-thirds majority in provincial assemblies, but hadn't made a meal of it. As his Albertan ally would remind him, "At no time during this call did you suggest that you had major reservations about the amending formula."[14] These words were pulled from a letter sent to Lévesque only a few weeks after patriation had occurred, and so offer a more credible version of the story.[15] As well, Lougheed's words are corroborated by Bill Bennett of British Columbia.[16]

FIRST MYTH: QUEBEC WAS BETRAYED BY ITS ALLIES

This correction of Lévesque's objection is important, since the whole affair would be brought back to the table during the Gang of Eight meeting on April 15, the night before the public signing ceremony. The heads of the rebellious provinces met in Sterling Lyon's suite at the Château Laurier Hotel in Ottawa; Lyon welcomed his guests with a suitcase full of alcoholic beverages brought in from his home province. But a suitcase full of alcohol wouldn't be enough to iron out the difficulties.

A combative René Lévesque, buoyed by his re-election, arrived in the capital, where he discussed the question of a two-thirds majority in the legislative assemblies with his colleagues in "relentless" fashion. "I was ready to spend the entire night at it," he wrote. "Fortunately, the seven others had made the mistake of calling a press conference for the next morning with the view of announcing the agreement."[17] And so the discussion would last until two in the morning. Lévesque reminded the group that his province had agreed to lose its veto right, as well as accept a certain level of equality among the provinces. The others thought he was exaggerating, but would eventually relent when they realized he wasn't backing down.

This nocturnal negotiation, bad-tempered and at the eleventh hour, was noticed by the journalists, who rushed to the following day's press conference. As Robert Sheppard and Michael Valpy, who were present at the conference, wrote, the ink on the agreement wasn't yet dry and already "the strains within the eight were readily apparent."[18]

But what was the true reach of this agreement that the seven anglophone provinces supposedly betrayed, according to a myth that Quebec would later spread? Did its signing mean that the Gang of Eight's position was now cast in stone? According to Lougheed, it was clearly understood that the document didn't constrain the signatories to an immutable common position.

Allan Blakeney believed the same thing, as well as other premiers. The agreement's only objective was to force Trudeau to return to the negotiation table in good faith. As the Albertan would write to the Quebecker, "There were no objections to this position."[19] This version was, however, contested by Lévesque and those who accompanied him at the time. Lévesque maintained that the agreement was, in a way, cast in stone, and that the anglophone provinces later altered their engagement, betraying Quebec.

To speak of betrayal is an exaggeration. We should understand that the Gang of Eight was an unnatural alliance in which, according to Roy Romanow, "opposition to Ottawa was the unifying factor that kept this shaky and mistrustful group together."[20] The forced marriage would give birth to a misunderstanding. As Louis Bernard, then secretary of the Executive Council of Quebec, explains, "It was understood among the Eight that the formula that had been the subject of this signed accord constituted a whole and shouldn't be subject to piecemeal negotiation. From this point of view, it was all or nothing. But it was also agreed that the formula should be discussed with Ottawa."[21]

However, Quebec and the seven anglophone provinces perceived the signing of this agreement very differently. Quebec saw a whole that could be exchanged for another agreement, a comprehensive and unanimous one, but nothing else. For the other seven provinces, it was a worthwhile strategic position to force Trudeau to abandon unilateral patriation. Such an objective must also leave the door open to other agreements, in whatever form, that would not necessarily be unanimous, according to some of the premiers. As Lougheed would tell Lévesque, "By no stretch of the imagination was a province placed in the position that if Mr. Trudeau reversed his position and accepted the position of a particular province on its constitutional goals, such a province would still be precluded from accepting Mr. Trudeau's new and different proposals or could do so only with the concurrence and consent of the other seven provinces in the Group of Eight."[22]

Members of the Quebec government were aware of these divergences in interpretation, which tend to contradict the betrayal hypothesis. In the months that followed the agreement's signing, the idea that it had limited scope was repeated a number of times, notably by Roy Romanow.[23] The question that needs to be asked is this: Why would Quebec be so keen to sign an agreement with the seven anglophone provinces?

Well, simply because it was the sole way to block Trudeau. As Claude Morin recalls, "We were convinced that the federal project would be rejected in London as long as Ottawa had only two provinces behind it, Ontario and New Brunswick."[24] If they went it alone, the Quebec government would be discredited in Great Britain and give credence to Ottawa's claims that the PQ was negotiating in bad faith. The strategy was to insist on the idea that the agreement had to be accepted in its entirety or rejected, all the while keeping the Gang of Eight together, even if these two objectives would become increasingly difficult to reconcile.

This line of reasoning was true for the anglophone provinces, as well, for which there was no solution outside of an alliance with Quebec. With 25 percent of the country's population, Quebec was by far the most populous province among the rebels and remained the heart of one of Canada's national communities. Its bureaucracy contributed strongly to the fight by producing anti-Trudeau arguments. In London, Quebeckers were leading the fight with panache; only the Albertans were able to contribute in a comparable manner. Of course, no one ever forgot that René Lévesque was a sovereignist and, because of this, Trudeau's project to judicialize Canada, as well as his push for bilingualism and multiculturalism in Quebec, was particularly unacceptable to him. But as Robert Sheppard and Michael Valpy noted, "The others used him as well, and it was not entirely a devil's bargain."[25] Some of the premiers, like Lyon, were also convinced that Quebec's concord was necessary for constitutional reform. The alliance of these eight provinces and the good relations it ensured with Lévesque were seen as a means to an end.

SECOND MYTH: QUEBEC NEVER CONSENTED TO PATRIATION

Lyon's appraisal of the situation — that Quebec's concord was indispensable for constitutional reform — also allows us to set aside a second untruth, according to which Quebec would have never consented to constitutional patriation. As Louis Bernard explains, "It is certain that Quebec would have signed a patriation agreement following the Group of Eight's formula. Lévesque himself had already signed it!"[26]

How can we imagine that if he had received what was laid out in the agreement signed with his colleagues, Quebec's premier would have gone back on his word and declared that, in the end, none of it was suitable? Such a scenario is hard to picture. Lévesque was in good faith, and working for an agreement that would protect Quebec's powers and identity. "If something positive had come out of these negotiations," Claude Morin explains, "and if that thing had kept our options open, we would have accepted it."[27]

Of course, with the inclusion of what Lévesque called in private "that damn charter,"[28] no positive outcome was possible. His very being and convictions forced him into a frontal collision with the prime minister's single-minded outlook on this issue. Canada, in the eyes of René Lévesque, is a country to which his ancestors consented through a pact; the charter made this pact meaningless by removing from Quebeckers their exclusive domain over education. Lévesque's Quebec was the homeland of the country's francophones, "the only part of the world where we can be fully ourselves"[29]; bilingualism and multiculturalism undermined the foundations of Québécois identity. Lévesque's Quebec had values grounded in democracy; the charter would give rise to a government of judges. There was no way to go along with any agreement as long as the charter wasn't taken off the table, or at least reduced to an unimportant declaration.

For Trudeau — the same Trudeau who'd put hundreds of people behind bars during the October Crisis without charges, trial, or access to a judge thanks to the War Measures Act — there was only one explanation for this refusal: René Lévesque was simply hostile to fundamental freedoms. He said just that of Quebec's premier and his partners on the day the Gang of Eight sealed its alliance. "What's surprising," he said, "is that the provinces didn't agree to protect the fundamental right of Canadians"[30] — as if democratic freedoms were under serious threat in the country.

But who cares about reality? According to Trudeau, the situation was even worse than it looked, since the amendment formula proposed by the Gang of Eight would allow provinces to withdraw from certain constitutional changes. Painting an Orwellian portrait of Canada, he maintained that "we could have, for example, the protection of women's rights in Quebec, but not in Ontario. We could have the protection of aboriginal rights in Manitoba, but not in Saskatchewan. We could have freedom of speech on Prince Edward Island, but not in Nova Scotia." The prime minister concluded by claiming that the Eight's proposal would turn the country into this famous "confederation of shopping centers," or even lead to its implosion.

THIRD MYTH: QUEBEC LOST ITS VETO BY ITS OWN FAULT

To this criticism, Trudeau would add another after the fact: the Eight's amendment formula led to Quebec's loss of its veto right. This is the third myth we will be considering. Lévesque supposedly imprudently exchanged his veto right for a right of withdrawal with compensation, which would, in the end, be set aside in the final agreement of November 1981. The PQ government was thus guilty of this loss for Quebec, while the head of the federal government was ready to recognize such a right in his own unilateral proposals. A few years after the fact, Trudeau would even confide to historian Ramsay Cook his hope that history would remember his regret at Quebec's loss of veto power.[31]

The problem with this reasoning springs from the fact that the idea that Quebec had a veto right was seen, until 1981, as a fundamental constitutional principle. In 1964, for example, Jean Lesage gave his support to patriation after negotiations led to the Fulton-Favreau formula. He ended up changing his mind and backing out of the agreement. At the time, everyone accepted that Quebec had exercised its veto right, and through it ended Diefenbaker and Pearson's attempts to patriate the constitution. The same situation occurred when Bourassa first accepted, than rejected, the Victoria formula in 1971. But now, in 1981, the Supreme Court would decide that unanimous consent by the provinces wasn't necessary for patriation, thus preventing any of them from exercising a veto. A year later, it more directly invalidated the notion that Quebec had such a right.

A judicial decision resulted in Quebec losing its veto right. If it had existed, the fact that Quebec exchanged it against a right of withdrawal in the context of a political agreement between eight provinces could not in itself have caused the loss of veto power, as the agreement had no judicial value.

Some would argue that the loss of veto can't be considered from a judicial as much as a political point of view. There existed a veto from this standpoint, and René Lévesque would have lost it by signing the agreement on April 16, 1981. Perhaps. But supposing that, politically speaking, such a right existed for Quebec, the necessary conclusion then is that Pierre Trudeau was the main reason for the loss of Quebec's veto, since he was the one who first pushed for patriation without the provinces' consent. To the extent that the agreement of the provinces was no longer necessary for this operation, it is obvious that the consent of a single province, Quebec or any other, is that much more unnecessary.

The prime minister was ready to give Quebec a veto right in the amendment formula he'd proposed in October 1980, but only after he had a chance to make fundamental changes to the constitution ... without the consent of Quebec and seven other provinces. Over the course of his reign, Trudeau more than once evoked the possibility of unilateral constitutional action, before finally acting on his words. The agitation and provocation over the course of months sapped the legitimacy and practice of unanimity, a custom at the foundation of Quebec's veto right. In Canada, as in Great Britain, this attitude made the idea of reform without provincial consent increasingly acceptable. In the end, this would be the conclusion of the Supreme Court, led by its chief justice, would reach.

CHAPTER 14

COUP AT THE COURT

Over the course of spring and summer 1981, London remained the theatre of unprecedented diplomatic activity for Canadians. The back-and-forth between the federal government and the British continued over the procedure for patriation and the date on which the process would finally come to an end. Trudeau dug in his heels for July 1. He even sent an invitation to the Queen for that date, to put pressure on the British. A conflagration was inevitable.

David Collenette, parliamentary secretary to House Leader Yvon Pinard, was one of those sent to the front lines. His adversary was none other than Francis Pym. Messenger for Trudeau, Collenette landed in London in mid-May. He explained to Pym that the federal leader was "adamant that the U.K. Parliament should pass the Canadians' measures through by 1 July." Certainly, he admitted, Canadians had been late in adopting the resolution itself, but the United Kingdom should act rapidly once the Supreme Court gave it the green light: "Until the British Parliament enacts the legislation, the government will be treading water in Canada and the healing process with the provinces cannot begin."[1]

The theme of reconciliation with the provinces, a new line from the federal government, didn't stir Pym. "It looks as though the right message about the British parliamentary situation is not getting across," he answered, reminding the visitor that Canadians had been warned on multiple occasions. "The House of Commons has never been a rubber stamp and I expect difficulty whatever the Supreme Court says. Barring a miracle I do not expect the legislation to go through by 1st July. Just as Mr. Trudeau has been unable to get his proposals through on the timescale he wanted in Canada, so it is likely to be difficult for us."

Collenette took note of this and reassured Pym that he'd pass the message along. The meeting ended on that note. The British weren't happy at all. Martin Berthoud, on his end, had serious doubts, which he shared with Emery Davies in Ottawa: "My own guess is it may get garbled on the way because of fears of Mr. Trudeau's reactions to Mr. Pym's exposition of the realities of the situation here. I therefore suggest that you take suitable opportunities to underline Mr. Pym's points to your senior and reliable contacts."[2]

Davies didn't need to search far and wide to find someone to speak to. Michael Kirby was on Elgin Street a few hours later. After having heard out Davies, the prime minister's adviser explained that, according to Collenette, Pym seemed "less bleak than previously." As London feared, Trudeau's inner circle was veering toward joviality to avoid displeasing the big cheese. Carrington, on hearing this, immediately sent new instructions to Davies: "It is important that the Canadians should be under no misapprehension about the chances of their legislation getting through Parliament by July 1st. You will no doubt therefore take an early opportunity of rubbing the message home with Kirby."[3]

Davies made sure the message was hammered in one more time, but it was no use, since the federal government further descended into its fantasy. And they weren't the only ones: the aboriginals were now refusing to understand anything at all. For the past month, they'd been told ad nauseam that the United Kingdom's responsibilities in regards to ancestral treaties had been transferred to Ottawa in 1867. "No matter," the First Nations seemed to be saying — notably Albertan aboriginals, who had sent a delegation of twenty-four to London. Their chief, Wallace Manyfingers, made an appearance at Buckingham Palace on May 7 to present a petition to the sovereign. You're out of luck, he was told; Her Majesty was on a trip abroad. In that case, the Prince of Wales would do well enough, the visitor replied in substance.[4] He was told that members of the royal family didn't receive petitions and that they should be sent to the governor general.

Unable to get past the gates of Buckingham Palace, the aboriginals settled for symbolically smoking the peace pipe on Westminster Square, in front of Parliament. This less than satisfactory result didn't curb their enthusiasm. The National Indian Brotherhood decided to establish an office in London and hired a constitutionalist to plead their case.

Meanwhile, British consul Murray Simons was beginning to get results in Quebec. On May 19, he was in Quebec City to attend the inaugural session of the National Assembly, during which Lévesque read a powerful speech repeating Quebec's opposition to Trudeau's project. The charisma of the PQ leader — his powerful language, and cavernous and solemn tone — worked once again, even among those who believed themselves immune. "The old pro was in great form and received a rousing reception from those on his side of the house," Simons reported back to London. "The Liberals were correspondingly subdued, and Mr. Ryan seemed like a burn-out case."[5]

Two days later, the consul would attend a meeting with Claude Morin and Robert Normand, who both assured him that Quebec wouldn't give up the constitutional fight — a choice made at a recent Cabinet meeting — even if the Supreme Court's decision was unfavourable to them. Moreover, whatever might happen, there would be no early elections on the theme of sovereignty.[6] The government would instead describe its raison d'être under the heading of Quebec autonomy, Morin continued, adding that his party had become Maurice Duplessis's successor.

Quebeckers indeed intended to continue fighting their battle on the other side of the Atlantic. With his colleagues from other provinces, Lévesque would travel to London, a city that had left an excellent impression on him when he had spent time there during the war. As Simons noted, Quebeckers had been galvanized since the publication of Kershaw's report, confident they could win the Battle of London. It was essential to discourage them.

Keeping himself from putting the cart before the horse, Morin nonetheless invoked the potential consequences of a loss in Great Britain. He used the word *rebellion* to describe the possible follow-up to patriation agreed on by London despite provincial opposition. "We may go as far and even beyond all legal means in pursuing the Quebec Government's aims," the PQ minister explained, a comment Simons believed to be "doubtless[ly] intentional … with the intention of making one's flesh creep."

If this was indeed Morin's objective, we can assert that his shot missed the mark entirely. Instead, it got Simons's poetic soul bubbling, he who embroidered his summary of events by citing King Lear, Shakespeare's unfortunate sovereign, who suffers every calamity under the sun after having shared his kingdom among his daughters: "I will do such things — what they are, yet I know not: but they shall be the terrors of the earth."

A CRUSADER FOR THE CHARTER

Stage left, a new character enters, preparing to play a surprising role in this story.

Born in 1912 to a family of Jewish immigrants, Bora Laskin, the future chief justice, studied at the University of Toronto in the 1930s and later became a professor there. He built himself a reputation of being a serious, dynamic, forthcoming man who knew how to remain simple.[7] With an abundant white mane, slicked back, and dark, penetrating eyes, he carried himself with natural authority. That served him well in the multiple arbitrages he oversaw in labour law cases.

Laskin the academic was particularly interested in the constitution and questions of human rights. At the time, his concept of the subject left little room for the place of the courts in the protection of fundamental freedoms. He even opposed the integration of a charter into the constitution.[8]

He made an about-face starting in 1965, the year he became an appellate court judge in Ontario. The moment he landed on the bench, the reservations he had regarding judicial interventionism no longer seemed relevant.

His nomination to the Supreme Court in 1970, and as chief justice in 1973, allowed him to move from theory to practice. He became a crusader for the power of judges.[9]

Trudeau counted on Laskin to ensure the triumph of his cause in the spring of 1981. Meanwhile, Quebeckers were under no illusion. As René Lévesque confided to Murray Simons, "The Chief Justice is a lost cause as far as Quebec's case is concerned."[10]

Lévesque wasn't the only one to believe that Laskin had no respect whatsoever for French Canadians. This opinion was shared by the chief justice of the Quebec Superior Court, Jules Deschênes, a magistrate who, in 1979, had been the first to invalidate Bill 101.

Despite the fact that Laskin prefaced a book by Deschênes on, of all things, judicial independence, the chief justice of the Superior Court never forgave Laskin's attitude during the centenary ceremony of the Supreme

Court in 1975. As he'd write in his memoirs, "The Right Honourable Bora Laskin — God keep his soul — didn't utter a single word in French."[11] Deschênes was so angered by this that he would still regret, years later, not having made a scandal of it in the middle of the ceremony.

On their end, the British were not concerned at all about the chief justice's anti-Quebec attitude. Instead, they simply concentrated on the information they were receiving thanks to him, information they'd use to put more pressure on Ottawa. The federal government could no longer realistically argue against intervention by the Supreme Court, since their fear that the process might be bogged down was no longer current; after all, the chief justice himself was claiming that the entire affair would be expedited.

Laskin confided only in the federal government and the British. He evidently had no intention of transmitting his game plan to Trudeau's opponents. This would give the opportunity to urgently prepare a plan, and deepen and strengthen their lobbying efforts in London to counter a decision by the Supreme Court that would be unfavourable to them. Better if his opponents were surprised; the federal government and the British would enjoy privileged information and be better prepared.

Laskin wasn't the only Supreme Court judge to speak to the British and the feds. In October 1980, his colleague Willard "Bud" Estey gave John Ford his impressions on patriation. The legality of the process would be questioned, he said, indicating that the Supreme Court would need two months to make a decision.

The political and legal situation also seemed to preoccupy him to a high degree:

> Judge Estey said that he had studied the Draft Bill attached to the Resolution and thought it defective in law. It seemed to him to have taken no account of the development of the U.K.'s constitutional practice of granting freedom to ex-colonies since the grant of independence to India…. The fact that the Indian constitutional instrument was defective had led to a lot of tiresome litigation afterwards and he feared that if the Canadian Bill was passed in its present form the Canadian courts would be in for a lot of trouble. He said that he had mentioned his fears to an official of the Department of Justice.

Judge Estey said that he had returned last week from a trip out West and had been much struck by the alienation of the population from the federal government. He had addressed a group of young lawyers and found them alarmingly indifferent to the concept of Canada and said that he had talked to premier Blakeney of Saskatchewan, who would like to exercise some positive role to solve the crisis but was fearful that he would lose the support of his electorate.[12]

It is quite striking to see a judge of the Supreme Court freely engaging in a political conversation with a representative of the executive branch — in constitutional matters, London remained the imperial government and, consequently, John Ford was a member of the executive branch. Yet Estey was indicating that the court was likely going to be seized with the case, thus warning Her Majesty's government.

In addition, it's important to note that the judge also engaged in a political conversation with a premier involved in the patriation process, and he did not have very flattering comments about the West; in his eyes, the population was indifferent to their own country. One might believe these words straight out of Trudeau's mouth. What's more, Estey shared these thoughts at a time when "it was obvious that an appeal to the Supreme Court of Canada was inevitable," as Roy Romanow later wrote.

But the most troubling aspect of his dubious behaviour is certainly that instead of acting like a judge he became a legal adviser for the federal government, warning Trudeau that his constitutional resolution would face legal problems. Coming from a sitting judge at the Supreme Court, this advice must have been taken very seriously at the Justice Department. No doubt this confidence was meant to help the government succeed in its attempt to patriate the constitution and impose something that Willard Estey was very much in favour of: the charter.

But should we be surprised by Estey's attitude? At the Supreme Court, the example came up from on high, from Bora Laskin. He was not afraid to jump into the political fray either, publicly no less! In 1976, as Trudeau was threatening for the first time to unilaterally patriate the constitution, the highest judge in the land spoke on the topic during a conference in Australia. Believing himself to be before a crowd that wouldn't repeat his words, far from the Canadian media, he expressed the view at the Australian National

University that "any attempt by the British Government or Parliament to go behind a resolution of the Federal Houses would be strongly resented and could lead to the departure of Canada from the Commonwealth."[13]

This is practically word for word one of the arguments that the federal government was using during the long years of the Battle of London, though even Trudeau never dared to publicly threaten to leave the Commonwealth. What's more, the federal government could have practically written the reprimands Bora Laskin made to the provinces in March of 1981. The chief justice claimed — in a speech in Toronto — that the provinces were completely wrongheaded in making demands for greater oversight of the Supreme Court:

> There seemed to be some sentiment by the ministers engaged in the constitutional discussions that the Court should be regionalized, that appointments to it should be made on that basis and that, moreover, it should be enlarged to accommodate regionalism.... It saddened me that there was so little understanding manifested … about the significance of the fidelity of its members to their oaths of office.
>
> What was dismaying to me as I watched and read about the constitutional proceedings that took place last year was the total misconception that so many ministers and first ministers had about the Supreme Court. They treated it in political terms and, fallaciously, regarded it as a federal institution on par with the Senate. Let me say, as forcibly as I can, that the Supreme Court of Canada is not a federal institution; it is a national institution and its members are under no federal allegiance merely because they are federally appointed. Just as there is no federal allegiance, there is no regional allegiance and no political allegiance.[14]

Whether impartial or not, one thing is certain: the British seemed well informed about what was going on at the Supreme Court. On May 21, as the constitutional question was being discussed in a Cabinet meeting, Francis Pym offered the following explanation to his colleagues: "The Supreme Court is now expected to deliver its judgment on the constitutional issues now before it at the end of May or early in June. The judgment is unlikely to be unanimous, though the general expectation seems to be for a majority for the view that the Federal Government's proposals are not unconstitutional."[15]

Two weeks later, Robert Armstrong received information from Clerk of the Privy Council Michael Pitfield, and informed Thatcher's diplomatic adviser, Michael Alexander:

> In the course of a meeting which I had yesterday with Mr. Pitfield, the Secretary to the Canadian Cabinet, the subject of the Canadian constitution came up. Mr. Pitfield said that it was now hoped that the Supreme Court would report very early next week, perhaps on Monday, 15th June. Mr. Trudeau was very confident that the Supreme Court would find in favour of the Federal Government's position, but Mr. Pitfield thought that this might well not be unanimous: the verdict might be on the basis of a six to three or seven to two majority.[16]

How could Pym on the British side and Pitfield-Trudeau on the Canadian side present themselves as being so well-informed on the evolution of the situation at the Supreme Court? It seems that new leaks were occurring in the highest court. On June 12, questioned by the press on the upcoming decision, Trudeau maintained that he hadn't spoken to a judge. Perhaps. But, as we will see, this certainly wasn't the case with his inner circle.

Among the potential sources in the tribunal, there is, of course, Bora Laskin, who at the time was just starting out on a trip to Great Britain, crossing the Atlantic on the *Queen Elizabeth II* from New York. It was near the end of June, and, as luck would have it, he arrived in London around the same time as Trudeau was visiting Mrs. Thatcher.

Just arrived in London, however, Laskin decided to interrupt his vacation and return to Ottawa for a few days. The decision surprised quite a few in the federal capital, and a number of people asked questions as to his motivations. Lord Moran, who wanted to know more, immediately cabled London with the following message:

> You may have heard from Canada House that the Chief Justice at present on holiday in Europe proposes to return to

Ottawa from 5 to 8 July to confer with his colleagues on the Supreme Court after which he will go back to Europe. At this stage the Federal government have no repeat no inside information as to the reason for Laskin's return to Ottawa.[17]

While the federal government knew nothing at the time, they would soon gain deeper insight, as would the British. On June 26, the same day the heads of government were meeting, Laskin called, as if by pure coincidence, Michael Pitfield, Clerk of the Privy Council, who was also in London. Pitfield then met his counterpart, Robert Armstrong, who reported the conversation in the following terms: "Mr. Pitfield said that he had had a call from the Chief Justice of the Supreme Court to say that he was cutting short his holiday in this country and returning to Canada at the beginning of July to meet with his colleagues on the Supreme Court for two or three days. The Chief Justice said to Mr. Pitfield: 'You know what that means,' and then rung off."[18]

Pitfield was able to decode this seemingly enigmatic message. He told Armstrong that it meant that the Supreme Court's decision was to fall on July 7. The date of July 1 was now clearly an impossibility, which didn't prevent Pitfield from insisting that the adoption of the constitutional resolution be made over the summer session, which ended in late July, instead of waiting until the fall session.

All that remained was for Trudeau to plead his case to Thatcher, which he did a few hours later; the two prime ministers spent two and a half hours together, officially to prepare for the G7 summit in Montebello in July. But of course the opportunity was too good not to speak about the constitution. Thatcher asked her visitor whether he had "any idea" when the court would decide.[19]

TRUDEAU'S EXTRAPOLATIONS

Trudeau hesitated before answering Mrs. Thatcher's question, but the temptation was too strong. The prime minister explained that Laskin was temporarily suspending his vacation in England to go and deal with the court's decision. What should be concluded from this? Trudeau then demonstrated an extraordinary capacity for extrapolation. The chief justice, he told her, came to the following conclusion: "It would damage the reputation of the Supreme Court if it became clear that they had been unable to make up their minds in two and half months while the provincial courts had reached [a] conclusion in a shorter period. I am very sore with the Supreme Court." He continued, saying, "Having taken on the case in the way they had, they should have pronounced much sooner." Laskin was likely feeling humiliated, "by the failure of the Court to make up its mind more rapidly," Trudeau believed, adding that Laskin's decision had probably been written weeks ago. But as he wasn't "in a position to force the other judges to write their own judgements, he has … created a very difficult problem for both heads of government."

In short, according to Trudeau, Laskin was returning to Ottawa to close the case once and for all. The Clerk of the Privy Council was aware of this, as was his boss. Why? Because, realistically, the chief justice had kept them in the loop of the tribunal's deliberations, be it with no more than hints and piecemeal information.

Let's consider for a moment how Trudeau explained the chief justice's actions. The latter was attempting to accelerate the process, thinking about the prestige of the institution he led. Instead of taking time to come up with the best possible decision, Laskin was behaving like a politician. His objective was no longer so much to judge as to position his tribunal, to ensure its prestige and authority in a process that strongly resembled the legalization of politics — a concept that became from then on the paradigm of the highest court.

The prime minister also warned his counterpart that action should be taken as quickly as possible once the decision came down, otherwise "the provinces will have time to hack around." Impossible, the Iron Lady replied in a velvety voice: "The legislative programme between now and the recess is absolutely full." The only solution would be to prolong the parliamentary session. However, "to add an extra week to the session at the beginning of August will be very bad. The most likely people to turn up will be those hostile to patriation. I fear that to force the house to resume after the Royal Wedding would cause ill feeling quite apart from the merits of the patriation questions." Trudeau understood these difficulties well. He then asked whether it might not be best "to put the resolution to the House of Commons for, say three days, and then if necessary, acknowledge that it would have to wait till the autumn."

"To try and fail would be the worst of all worlds, it would be uncertainty," Thatcher answered, refusing to give an inch. In that case, Trudeau predicted, "there might be criticism and indeed anger if the British government does not make the effort." Of course, he took the pains to add that he himself "would neither feel nor express anger." But then the provinces might organize referendums to counter Ottawa. The risk that they might succeed was indeed real, he maintained.

"I am extremely anxious to avoid any action which would damage relations between Britain and Canada," Thatcher specified, to explain her refusal to acknowledge Trudeau's request: "One has to recognise that the bill will not necessarily go through the House of Commons, and thereafter the House of Lords, as rapidly as one might like."

Discouraged, Trudeau gave up. The decision was up to them, he conceded: "We have fallen so far behind with our own timetable that we are in no position to put pressure on Her Majesty's Government."[20]

The conversation ended on this apparent concession. But if Trudeau stepped back, it was only to better leap forward when he met the media as he left the meeting. "I think Mrs. Thatcher will realize, as much as we do, the disadvantage of having a positive judgment come out of the court, having it dealt with in Canada and then having it hang around for that many months. I don't think it's an eventuality any British prime minister would be looking forward to," he concluded.[21]

Despite these statements, as Trudeau left London, the idea of patriation over the course of the summer ceased being an option. To understand why, it's best to return to Laskin. As he told Pitfield, the chief justice was preparing to return to Canada for a few days, but before doing so, he met British solicitor general Michael Havers. A few weeks before, Jean Wadds had informed Ottawa that Havers had been designated to answer, in the British House of Commons, all questions of a judicial nature in relation to the constitutional resolution that would be sent by Ottawa.[22] The solicitor general found himself at the heart of a political process on which the Supreme Court of Canada was to pronounce itself. A source at the Foreign Office, press secretary Ian McCrory, had also warned Ottawa that a tight decision, even favourable to Ottawa, would be seen in London as a draw, with all the complications this might entail.

At this stage, all information was confidential. It is impossible to know if Laskin was informed or not of Haver's crucial role, but he certainly took advantage of his trip to Great Britain to speak with him. The gist of their conversation is known to us thanks to a cable sent by Lord Carrington to Lord Moran in Ottawa. Exceptionally, the document was marked with the mention "please protect fully" and was classified secret, which means, in the British system, that if it were revealed, its content might represent "life-threatening, disruptive to public order or detrimental to diplomatic relations with friendly nations."[23] The message described the exchange between Laskin and Havers.

> The Chief Justice said there was a major disagreement among the members of the Supreme Court. He was returning shortly to Ottawa but clearly did not expect this would bring about the immediate resolution of their difficulties. If no quick solution was found, he did not expect judgement to appear until the end of August. We needed to bear in mind that the judgement needed to be carefully polished and produced in both languages. The Attorney General commented that he could well see that a historic verdict of this kind needed to be meticulously prepared and polished.
>
> In view of the confidentiality of the Chief Justice's conversation with the Attorney General, it would clearly be wrong for you to reveal at this stage that we now have a clear indication of further likely delay by the Supreme Court.[24]

Was the federal government aware of Laskin's confidences with Havers? One person, Henry Richardson of the Canadian High Commission, had sat through a portion of the conversation, but swore to speak not a word of it to anyone. Informed of Richardson's promise, Lord Moran replied to Carrington that "unless there are factors in this of which we are unaware, it seems unlikely in the extreme that Richardson will not have reported fully."[25]

What is without doubt is that Laskin, soon back in London, continued to share information. On July 15, he was invited to lunch at the Middle Temple. Formerly the property of the famous Templar order, this medieval church was now occupied by the English Bar. After the meal, the magistrate met with Ian Sinclair, one of the Foreign Office's jurists who worked on patriation. The Briton reported on the meeting in the following terms: "He said he had recently gone back to Ottawa 'to try to knock a few heads together' (to use his own words). He had not, however, been very successful in this task. The clear implication was the Supreme Court was still seriously divided."[26]

This new confidence must be studied side by side with other remarks made in another meeting, between the Clerk of the Privy Council and the highest-ranking civil servant in Canada, Michael Pitfield, and his counterpart,

Robert Armstrong. Their meeting occurred a few days earlier in Ottawa, when Laskin was still in the capital. The Brit reported on the conversation this way: "Pitfield said that the Supreme Court had reconvened, and he supposed that the object was for the Chief Justice to 'bang their heads together'; but he seemed resigned to the fact that they would not be handing down a judgement this week."[27] The Canadian spoke of the judge's actions using an almost identical expression as the one reported on by Sinclair, who heard it directly from Laskin himself. How are we not to think that Laskin had spoken to Pitfield once again?

On September 10, it was Lord Moran's turn to take part in a little informative session with the chief justice. According to the High Commissioner, Laskin declared that "unlike the Prime Minister, he could not dragoon his colleagues, who were highly independent in their view (this, I think, was an oblique way of saying that the court was divided."[28]

THE REVOLT OF THE ELITES AND THE BETRAYAL OF DEMOCRACY

The chief justice's actions need to be examined closer, first in terms of the motives that might explain his behaviour, but also in regards to the objectives he was pursuing. Let's begin with his objectives. With the series of new confidences he distributed over the summer, Laskin was attempting to correct the message he'd transmitted back in March to a federal source who'd then informed the British government. At the time, he said that the process would be a quick one, telling the British through a source not to lose patience with Trudeau's project, as well as not to concede an inch to the provinces; the highest court in the land was about to intervene to facilitate the process. Instead, the opposite situation now prevailed. The Supreme Court was moving at a glacial pace, in addition to being divided. It was essential to inform the imperial government of this development, which Laskin did thrice instead of once over the summer of 1981, notably by speaking with Michael Havers. This information isn't mundane, since the solicitor general, as well as the other ministers who had a stake in this issue, predicted that a close decision would make the constitutional project's adoption a more difficult proposition. Her Majesty's ministers understood quite well the message conveyed by Laskin and could prepare for the legislative battle to come. The more prepared they'd be, the more Laskin might see this charter's birth once and for all.

A few years after the charter was set in the constitution, Laskin's successor, Brian Dickson, would tell those unhappy with the charter to address their grievances to politicians. Judges never wanted the charter, he explained, they simply obeyed political power when a new role was bestowed on them.[29] Oft-repeated by supporters of judicial powers, this statement is entirely contradicted by Laskin and Estey's role.

This clarification made, let us turn to the worse offence. By revealing to politicians in real time information on the deliberations for a case in which they were stakeholders, or by giving legal advice to the government, Laskin committed an infraction of ethics, infringed rules, flouted his oath, and desecrated the constitution he was sworn to protect, since, let us not forget, the separation of powers is a fundamental constitutional principle in Canada. And this very serious infraction was committed by the judge in a one-of-a-kind cause. Indeed, as Trudeau himself would say, the patriation reference is the "most important decision the Supreme Court ever rendered or ever will render."[30]

Questioned about this affair years later by the author of the present work, some participants couldn't believe what they heard. "I would not have anticipated that the chief justice would do that," Peter Lougheed said. "His role is to be neutral at the outset."[31]

"It goes without saying we would have hit, and hard, had we known that," Claude Morin added. "This demonstrates absolutely unacceptable collusion since the Supreme Court becomes a consenting agent to the federal power play. It might have been determinant in the proceedings."[32]

However, Laskin seemed to see no wrong in what he'd done. In fact, he continued to preach to each and all. As we've seen, he had already lectured the provinces. He then asked Thomas Berger to apologize — Berger, the judge from British Columbia who had, in the *Globe and Mail*, denounced the lack of recognition of aboriginal rights in the charter. Laskin stated that a judge who "feels so strongly on political issues that he must speak out is best advised to resign from the bench."[33]

Berger would refuse to apologize, invoking a distinction between current political affairs and the protection of fundamental rights. Ironically, this is likely the reason Laskin gave himself to rationalize his behaviour. After all, the man was deeply convinced of the superiority of justice founded on the charter instead of common law and parliamentary sovereignty. As one of his biographers wrote, "Laskin the judge argued that the constitutional protection of fundamental rights and freedoms was not only consistent with democracy but the essential underpinning of democracy."[34] We should add to this that he firmly espoused, according to Roy McMurtry — then attorney general of Ontario — a particular vision of national unity: that of a strong central government and a country which, thanks to the power of the courts, would not suffer the odious fate of becoming a community of communities.[35]

In short, the chief justice confused it all, patriation with Confederation, Trudeau's charter with the birth of democracy. In some ways, he took himself for both Thomas Paine and John A. Macdonald. But he was held up by the limited means of legalized politics. He lacked any real political constituency and, of course, had no mandate to intervene when he saw his work as defending Canada and democracy. How can one not be disposed to break all sorts of rules to ensure the triumph of such a noble cause? As Ian Binnie, Supreme Court judge from 1998 to 2011, noted, Laskin possessed "the soul of a rebel ... and remained a radical thinker."[36] He was canonized by the Canadian judicial establishment for his radicalism. Prizes, grants — including one from the Social Sciences and Humanities Research Council of Canada — a prestigious speaker series, a debate tournament, as well as the law library at the University of Toronto all carry his name. As Binnie writes, "Bora Laskin was and continues to be a heroic figure."[37]

Beyond Laskin's preference for the charter and the power of judges, his motives need to be further studied. How can we explain that his convictions led him to commit such serious transgressions? The explanation might be found in what the American historian and essayist Christopher Lasch named "The Revolt of the Elites and the Betrayal of Democracy."[38] By elites, we are referring to the knowledge elite, a group consisting of individuals working in education, information, arts, bureaucracy, and, of course, law. For a number of these professionals, Western culture represents a system of domination that seeks to ensure the conformity to prevalent bourgeois and patriarchal values that keep minorities (women, ethnic minorities, homosexuals, et cetera) in a permanent state of subjugation.[39] According to Lasch, these elites have thrown themselves into an unending quest to make the collectivity more tolerant, egalitarian, inclusive, and politically correct.

The problem comes from the majority, which doesn't wish to participate in this large-scale social engineering and feels a profound need to sustain shared assumptions in order to maintain the community's cohesion.[40] Here is where the revolt of the elites turns into a betrayal. With the charter project, Laskin sought to advance the social project of a minority of the knowledgeable elite. Faced with the opposition of the provinces, his reaction was similar to that of the elites Lasch describes: "When confronted with resistance to their initiative they betray the venomous hatred that lies not far beneath the smiling face of their benevolence, that of the upper middle class. Opposition makes humanitarians forget the liberal virtue they claim to uphold. They become petulant, self-righteous, intolerant."[41]

In this manner, Laskin was the instigator of the theory of dialogue between the executive and judicial branches, which his admirers would later develop, and according to which it is legitimate for judges to impose their will by making political decisions. While it is never admitted by jurists, this approach is grounded on the belief that politics is a lesser phenomenon than law.[42] The first manifestation features political squabbles, while the second is the noble defence of fundamental rights. Judges are thus more apt to determine what constitutes a right and to define its limits. With a better capacity than elected officials to establish the principles on which rights are founded, they become the best interpreters of the law.

To reach this conclusion, Laskinians have disregarded a few historical lessons. In the nineteenth century, for example, the Supreme Court of the United States declared slavery legal, while an elected official, Abraham Lincoln, led a bloody war to abolish it. But examples like this do not shake their convictions. For Laskinians, law is what the courts say, end of story. Law is an absolute and authoritarian power that magistrates have assumed the right to, dressing it with the noble patronage of "constitutional supremacy." As the Supreme Court would write a few years later in the Vriend decision, the adoption of the charter gave rise to a "redefinition of our democracy."[43]

At the time of patriation, Lévesque kept repeating that the federal government was committing a coup d'état. The accusation seemed exaggerated, the product of a lively and fundamental debate between the PQ leader and his old enemy Trudeau. We can't say the same thing about John Ford. As his mission in Ottawa came to a close, he warned London one last time in a cable very well-received by his colleagues and some ministers. His analysis wasn't specifically geared toward the Supreme Court, which had just seized the case, but on the entire patriation operation as piloted by Trudeau. The prime minister's efforts to patriate the constitution was a "tour de force, as Mr. Lévesque described it — a veritable attempt at a coup d'état to change the balance of power in the federation."[44]

CHAPTER 15

NULL AND VOID

The summer of 1981 was one of expectation. The Supreme Court's decision was upcoming, but all was calm — the one before the proverbial storm. On both sides of the issue, troops were being mobilized without knowledge of what dawn would bring.

Within this context, the British High Commissioner in Canada was cutting his teeth on his new position. Lord Moran, known as John Wilson, had arrived in the federal capital in June. His father's reputation — he was Winston Churchill's doctor — preceded him wherever he went. He was also the author of a prize-winning biography of Sir Henry Campbell-Bannerman, prime minister under Edward VII. Moran was seen by External Affairs as intelligent and competent. He'd been preparing for months for his new mission.

Finally rid of John Ford, the federal government hoped that Moran's arrival would signal a new beginning. The first step was a meeting between the diplomat and Trudeau.[1] In a rare occurrence, the prime minister began by revealing his state of mind. "When I look at the press clippings and the letters to the editor, I am surprised at the extent to which I have become a scoundrel in the eyes of some of the public,"[2] he said, referring to his image overseas. "It is not like that, Prime Minister," Moran reassured him. Referring to opponents of the constitutional request, he stated that a number of them "think they know about Canada and that may be rather arrogant but they have been lobbied heavily."

Trudeau expressed doubts about the Supreme Court's decision. If it returned unfavourably, the best laid plans would turn to dust: "No one believes we are trying to establish a unitary state. If the bill passes, there will be grumbling but Canada will emerge stronger. If the court says this cannot be, what will the victory cry of the government's opponents be? That they have protected Canada from having its own constitution and charter? That there will be no aboriginal rights and no minority rights for school?" Before making a decision, the court would need to consider all these questions, the prime minister observed, without even mentioning that, if the constitutional project were to be rejected, it would also need to pronounce itself on an amendment formula.

His worries didn't end there. Trudeau continued by speaking of the British Parliament. At first, he said, he found it inconceivable that the British Parliament would refuse to agree to the charter. But now he saw that the Kershaw report recommended just that. How would Thatcher react to this development? Certainly she wouldn't contradict him, Trudeau worried aloud.

"I am sure not," the Brit immediately replied. Thatcher was particularly preoccupied by the practical aspects of the operation. He felt she would proceed "without rushing and without causing problems in parliament. The federal government having gone to the Supreme Court should make it easier with the uncommitted." A clear and favourable judicial decision in Ottawa would certainly help, he added.

THE NEW NORTHERN IRELAND

Lord Moran seemed quite satisfied at having contacted the political icon that was Pierre Trudeau. The High Commissioner hadn't realized it, but the prime minister had played for him the oldest song and dance in the world. To the prince, the role of protagonist; to his valet, antagonist. Indeed, the latter would be played by Michael Pitfield, who would have Moran over a few days later.

After the usual pleasantries, the Clerk of the Privy Council explained that Ottawa hoped for one thing only: to better Anglo-Canadian relations, notably thanks to increased trade. Trudeau still hoped for a quick adoption of his project by Westminster, without which there would be a risk of "wrecking activities by people like Claude Morin of Quebec."[3] Moran replied that, according to a recent conversation with Lord Privy Seal Ian Gilmour, such a scenario seemed impossible. He then referred to the meeting in June between both prime ministers, underlining that it would be ideal if the constitutional request wasn't sent to Great Britain before October.

But Pitfield wasn't listening. He insisted, as if Moran hadn't quite understood. You see, he continued, the government should be quite unpopular due to joblessness and inflation. Yet it isn't. Why? Thanks to "national popular support for its attitude on the constitution. We will play on it," he said, adding what Moran described as "flesh creeping remarks about the dire consequences of any failure on our part to comply with the Canadian government's wishes. At one point he said that if we did not comply we would have a transatlantic Ulster on our hands!"

The only way to avoid Canada becoming another Northern Ireland was to do what Pitfield described. "The British representative is more important than any other ambassador, including the American one. Your position is unique, with all the advantages and problems of an old family relationship, but equally the risks of misunderstanding and embarrassment are much greater with us than with anyone else."

Outraged by his comments, Moran defended himself. He, too, wished only for the flowering of relations between Canada and the United Kingdom. He had no intention whatsoever of taking part in the quarrel between Ottawa and the provinces, despite the fact that he intended to speak with everyone, including people like Lougheed and Lévesque. As he wrote to London after the meeting, "He is warning me that a liberal government in which the prime minister and many of his senior colleagues are French Canadians tend to see the British High Commission as naturally at home with the Progressive Conservatives, the business community of Toronto ... and the exclusively English-speaking world of Alberta and the West."

Pitfield had just defied Moran, but the latter wasn't the sort of man to back down in such circumstances. After all, the more he studied the Canadian problem, the stronger his aversion to Pierre Trudeau, his advisers, his ministers, his constitution, his philosophy, and his politics became — as testified to by a note he'd write at the end of his mission:

He has never shaken off his past as a well-to-do hippie and draft dodger.... Many of my colleagues here admire him. I cannot say I do. Mr. Trudeau has maintained that only by an increase in Ottawa's powers could Canada develop as a strong state. He treated provincial premiers with contempt and provincial governments as if they were town councils ... few Canadians share his extreme centralising stance. Most believe that Canada's diversity and geographical spread need a federal system and a division of powers, with each level treating the other, as seldom happened in Mr. Trudeau's time, with courtesy, respect and understanding.[4]

Moran also directed some of his ire toward Marc Lalonde and his "widely discredited National Energy Program, discriminating blatantly against non-Canadian companies ..." The policy, he felt, would worsen joblessness, ruin the energy sector, and deprive the country of foreign investments, notably British investments. A failure, across the board, would reflect the character of the federal ministers Trudeau surrounded himself with: the High Commissioner spoke of them as being "unimpressive and a few we have found frankly bizarre."

The British agent in Canada consoled himself, however, by turning his attention to Canadians. They are a reasonable people, who suffered nonetheless from an inferiority complex. "Anyone who is even moderately good at what they do," he wrote, "in literature, the theatre, skiing or whatever, tends to become a national figure." Moran found people from Alberta, Saskatchewan, and the Maritimes particularly kind, but he certainly didn't believe Canadians who worked in the federal government were anything like them. "The most difficult Canadians, the most prickly and unforthcoming are undoubtedly some of those who work for the Federal Government in Ottawa."

After the scolding he received at the hands of the Clerk of the Privy Council, the ambassador made a decision. He headed to the West, bastion of the rebellion, to meet the main figureheads of the opposition to Trudeauism and report their points of view back to London.

There was at least one piece of good news that came out of this part of the country, and it sparked hope that the conflict between the Western provinces and the central government might end. In early September, Edmonton and

Ottawa had concluded a truce of sorts in the energy wars that had divided them. The federal government had agreed to triple the price of crude oil, bringing it near global prices, in exchange for an increase in the revenues it would receive from oil production.[5] Lougheed essentially got what he wanted. By the time he met Moran, the Albertan assured him that the energy agreement represented a positive development that might just favour a constitutional peace,[6] words that were repeated by Allan Blakeney to the High Commissioner during a stop in Saskatoon.[7] In Winnipeg, Lyon took advantage of the Brit's visit to speak about the Quebec issue. Not enough people were listening to what Quebec's premier was saying, he explained. "Whatever the Federal Government and Parliament or the British Parliament might do, Lévesque would never accept the charter of rights." He added the following warning: "All Quebec would be with him [faced with] the distortion of the federal structure by an unrepresentative Federal Government." Manitoba would join the fight alongside Quebec, and the fight would be an epic one, he promised. Everything would be done to resist the charter, even if it meant being unjustly accused of civil disobedience.

EIGHT SEATS FOR LONDON

Like the rest of his rebellious colleagues, Manitoba's head didn't hide his intentions: he informed Moran that he would make his way to London to plead his case and wished to meet with Thatcher. Lyon didn't know it, but he was preaching to the choir. Moran was working hard behind the scenes so that the Eight might be received at the highest levels in the British capital. He wrote to London with the following note:

> My strong advice is that the provincial premiers should
> be received with the Canadian High Commissioner by
> the Prime Minister. It is Mrs. Thatcher they wish to see.
> They are the first ministers of large, wealthy and import-
> ant provinces like Quebec, Alberta, British Columbia and
> Saskatchewan; they are proud men, with electorates to
> whom they must speak on their return; and their provinces
> and governments are of great importance to us commer-

cially, especially Alberta and British Columbia.... I see no reason why the Federal authorities should object if their High Commissioner is present.[8]

This advice was received with some apprehension by the Foreign Office, especially since Moran had warned his colleagues that, if the Eight went to London, Hatfield and Davis would do the same. The High Commissioner's arguments were "persuasive," Martin Berthoud admitted in an internal note. But the person responsible for the North American division believed that "it would still probably be right for them not to be received at a level above Mr. Ridley."[9]

The decision made its way up to Lord Carrington, who took some time to consider it. He used the latest London visit by Mark MacGuigan to speak his mind on the topic. Aware of the rebellious premiers' plans, the federal minister hoped to convince his counterpart to stop this whole business before it went any farther. There'd be no issue if they decided to petition the government one by one, the head of the Foreign Office explained. "If, however, a large group of them asked to see the prime minister it might be tactically disastrous if she declined to see them," he continued. "Such a refusal would be criticised in Parliament and elsewhere."[10] The ultimate objective was to do nothing that might harm the chances of successful passage of the constitutional resolution, Carrington concluded.

The decision to set up a meeting with the Gang of Eight represented a victory for Moran, who, however, didn't stop there. He then attempted to influence British policy toward the charter in a note sent to London:

The proposition, that the British Parliament should be asked to pass a virtually unalterable but controversial Charter of Rights for another independent country, however much argued by Mr. Trudeau that such a Charter is desired by the people of Canada, seems essentially unreasonable. Hence the shrill line taken last October ... by the 2 Canadian ministers, "the British could not afford to get into the substance of the matter," (said by Mr. Roberts) though in a sense that is exactly what the Federal Government [is] forcing us to do ...

> Mr. Roberts seems to have tried to mislead our Ministers at the meeting saying "the Charter of Rights was essentially in response to the demand from Quebec." In fact, it is the recently re-elected Quebec Government which objects the most passionately to the Charter, as over-riding their cherished legislation giving French pre-eminence in the province …[11]

After asking himself whether it wouldn't have been better to refuse the charter in the first place, Moran reminded his readers that the rebellious provinces had agreed on an amendment formula, and that 90 percent of Canadians favoured a negotiated solution in Canada, according to a poll conducted over the summer. The charter, he continued, was a foreign body in the parliamentary system, associated with American republicanism or, worse yet, with the Soviet Union. Yet, except for Quebec, which was a unique case, "our friends here, the Canadians who believe in the Queen, the British connection, etc., are practically all in the anti-Trudeau camp, while those who support the Trudeau package are, generally speaking, no great friends of ours. The Federal Government is seeking to force us to side with them and have been pretty successful in achieving this objective."

The debate raged on in the Foreign Office, with Berthoud, with great fidelity of purpose, arguing in favour of Thatcher's line. "It is of course arguable that the British Government had a choice and could have not intervened," he wrote in a note destined for Deputy Minister Derek Day. "But … the choice was between going along with the Federal government with whom we have our relations or with the provinces with whom we do not. In other words, there was no real alternative but to accede to a federal request."[12]

In the end, Moran failed, despite the fact, as Berthoud himself high-lighted, that the British had obtained the federal government's concession to let the Supreme Court consider the question before they made a decision. If the Supreme Court's decision went against Trudeau, "the cup should pass from our lips. If it finds in favour of the Federal government, then the Parliamentary handling of the problem will be simplified."[13] The only risk, Berthoud conceded — and it was a considerable one — would be a split decision. This would without a doubt be the worst possible scenario.

Moran wasn't satisfied at all by this answer, and led another charge a few days later:

> I suspect that most Canadians have only a hazy idea of what it is and think generally that a document guaranteeing fundamental freedoms, democratic rights, non-discrimination, the use of the 2 official languages and minority language educational rights must obviously be a good thing. I think comparatively few Canadians (an exception is Mr. Sterling Lyon, Premier of Manitoba) grasp the very fundamental nature of the Charter, which, being entrenched, would override the Federal and all Provincial legislatures and be subject only to interpretation by the courts. It would be a complete departure from the British concept of a sovereign parliament (which makes it all the odder that the British Parliament should be asked to pass it) …
>
> On top of this, a good many lawyers think that the Charter may well have very unfortunate practical consequences. It could conceivably give a green light to criminals like drug pushers and pornographers and to the extreme demands of minorities. It remains extraordinary that we should be asked to pass it, something we would hardly be asked to do for India or France or the United States. I do not think many Canadians yet grasp just how bizarre such a request is.[14]

At the Foreign Office, which stood alongside 10 Downing Street, and was one of the ministries most favourable to Trudeau's government, this warning was ignored. The provinces were nonetheless actively preparing themselves for the Supreme Court's decision, expected to be handed down any day now. In mid-September, the Gang of Eight's deputy ministers for intergovernmental affairs met in London to prepare. It was decided that James McKibben would be the coordinator for all agents general. Additional personnel were hired, and lobbying firms contacted. Joint activities with First Nations were organized. The dissident provinces also armed themselves with an official emblem, the coat of arms of each of the eight provinces set in a circle around a red maple leaf; envelopes and letterheads were produced with the emblem apposed. The only thing missing was a flag.

The federal government was also actively preparing.[15] They expected to mobilize the various centres for Canadian studies in the United Kingdom. Canadian multinational corporations would also be called upon to play a role, and new preparatory documents were produced. New Brunswick and Ontario would be asked to help.

THE CONSTITUTION: LABOUR'S ULTIMATE WEAPON

The Labour Party convention was gearing up, scheduled for the end of September in Brighton. The night before the convention, the satirical magazine *Punch*, always well-informed, reported that Labour was giving increased attention to the constitution, even if it constituted "a tedious issue which bores even Canadians. Whole camps of lumberjacks fall asleep discussing it. The very thought of it virtually guarantees that a Mountie will fail to get his man."[16]

How to explain Labour's interest? Simply stated, a constitutional project would need to be extensively debated in the House. The government can't suspend debates and force a vote. As the magazine explained, Labour MPs were gleefully rubbing their hands in anticipation:

> What an endless, bottomless mine of time-wasting oppor-
> tunities that presents.... Commons' top time-wasters ...
> they can give you 2 hours on the Paper Clips Retention
> Order, or 90 minutes on the British Rail Catering
> (Improvement of Sandwiches) Bill without even thinking
> about it. Imagine what they will do with an entire consti-
> tution! Nobody in Britain ever gives a moment's thought
> to the Canadian constitution so that it is politically pure
> gain. With a little skill they can destroy the government's
> program for a year by the simple expedient of leaving no
> time to debate anything else ... and there is nothing at all
> Mrs. Thatcher can do about it.

This description terrified the federal government's diplomats, who immediately attempted to independently verify these claims. What they discovered only managed to confirm their fears:

> Information from our sources in Labour Party says that a group of MPs led by Ian Mikardo have identified 70 amendments which they will attempt to secure to Canada bill.... Labour party is gearing all its resources to oppose and stop at any cost government bills on 1) Trade unions 2) Municipal financing ... this last bill is nothing less than an attack against local government which no matter how justifiable in economic terms, will be greatly resented as an encroachment of central power on local government, a cornerstone of democracy in a unitary state. These bills ensure stormy session with labour prepared to use any means at its disposal to quote filibuster unquote. Canadian bill offers an opportunity for labour to burn up parliamentary time.[17]

The federal government understood quite well how serious the situation was. Little did they know that the reality of it was worse still. While they correctly anticipated the difficulties the more radical Labour members would make for them, they also greatly overestimated their support among the party's major figures, notably its new leader, Michael Foot, who was believed to support Trudeau thanks to their warm relationship. However, since Nova Scotia's premier, John Buchanan, had joined the Gang of Eight, the latter had been using one of the most effective cards at the rebels' disposal: Jeremy Akerman. Deputy minister of intergovernmental affairs for his province, this man of British origin was a singular character. The former head of Nova Scotia's NDP, he'd abandoned the party to pursue a career with the Conservatives. After patriation, he'd even launch an acting career in Hollywood. But Akerman, more than anything else, was a good friend of Labour's new leader. He'd even worked as a volunteer in his political cabinet back when Michael Foot was a minister, during the famous winter of discontent in 1978–79, a season of generalized strikes that had paralyzed the United Kingdom and led to Margaret Thatcher's rise to power.[18]

Their common cause during that singular time had bound the two men together. When they saw each other again eighteen months later, Foot was the leader of his party and Akerman the emissary of his province. As the latter recalls:

> We had a number of dinners and lunches over time. Mr. Foot also helped me organize meetings and took four MPs with him at one of them, at one of the London clubs, I think it was the Royal Automobile Club.
>
> He never actually said that he supported us, not in so many words, because at that point he was leader of the opposition. But he led me to believe that he supported the position of the gang of eight. I had every reason to believe that he supported us. Otherwise I don't know why he would have gone out of his way to steer towards other members of the house. He would say go and see this folk, go talk to this man and things like that.
>
> I think Michael was sympathetic to us because he was already thinking in terms of devolution, of devolved power to Scotland and Wales, because he represented a Welsh constituency and he did understand what a federal or devolved system was.[19]

NULL AND VOID

As the rebellious provinces took advantage of the Labour Party's convention to win over support, the Supreme Court finally handed down its decision on September 28, 1981, as a storm blew its way through the Ottawa Valley. The judges even asked the CBC to transmit a live feed of its decision — a first in the history of the court, albeit one that would be marred by technical problems. One of the microphones placed in front of Bora Laskin didn't work, so that viewers at home were unable to hear him speak. Jean Chrétien, who was holding down the fort in the capital in Trudeau's absence, watched the event from his office and barely understood the decision. Bill Bennett, the Gang of Eight's new spokesperson, was in the same situation, following the day's events from his offices in Ottawa.

As Laskin had previously announced to the British and the federal government, the court was divided, except on one question. All the judges recognized that the federal project encroached on provincial jurisdictions, contrary to what Ottawa had been stating from the start. On the issue of legality, seven of the nine judges maintained that the federal process was legal, pointing out that a tribunal didn't have the authority to prevent the federal Parliament from sending a constitutional resolution to the British Parliament; the two judges named under Diefenbaker were nonetheless in opposition to the majority. However, six of the nine magistrates maintained that the federal process was not according to constitutional conventions, which held that Ottawa move forward only with the support of a substantial number of provinces on a dossier as complex as constitutional patriation. The three other judges, including Laskin and Estey, of course, supported the federal government.

Trudeau was bitter, even if he didn't say so publicly at the time. "This was, in my view, a faulty judgement," he later wrote in his memoirs. "I believe the dissenting judges led by Chief Justice Bora Laskin were right when they said, in effect, 'It's a legal question, and we can't talk about conventions, which are agreements among politicians.'"[20] For Trudeau, the decision was more defeat than victory. Even if he obtained recognition of the legality of his process, he would be forced to pay a huge political price if he didn't obtain greater provincial consent before moving forward; this situation would quickly cause him almost insurmountable problems, as we'll get to later.

What must be highlighted, however, when considering what the British archives have revealed to us, was that this judgment was sullied by serious irregularities. As we've seen over the course of the past few chapters, Chief Justice Laskin, as well as Judge Estey, had intervened directly in the political process by secretly revealing information to both the British and Canadian governments.

We need to understand that the principle of separation of powers is as important in our system as that of ministerial responsibility, another constitutional convention according to which the government must call elections if it loses the confidence of the House. To violate such a convention represents a fundamental assault on the rules that sustain democracy.[21] In such circumstances, a single conclusion can be drawn: the decision of the Supreme Court should be considered null and void. If such a situation arose today, it would undoubtedly lead to a mistrial.

In our judicial system, the violation of a constitutional convention leads to a political sanction. Except that, in our case, for a political sanction to be given, the entire affair would have had to have been aired out. If the conduct of at least two of the nine judges had been revealed in the explosive atmosphere of the time, the Supreme Court would have been completely discredited, and so would have Trudeau's government. The affair would probably have led to a very legitimate refusal by the provinces to submit to the decisions of the highest tribunal, as well as provoking the fall of the Liberal government, the death of the charter, and a constitutional crisis without precedent. But since Trudeau's opponents didn't have access to all the facts, they couldn't mount a full and complete defence and weren't able to react the way they should have. As we write these lines, justice still hasn't been rendered.

Reading these revelations, some will likely seek to minimize or forgive Laskin's behaviour, under the pretext of it being ancient history. We need to move on, they might say, as if the Charter of Rights were no longer in effect. Some will say that the charter was a good thing and its adoption necessary, as if the end justified the means. Others still will certainly invoke the decision, mostly unfavourable to Trudeau, to say that the affair wasn't that serious. After all, the chief justice's manoeuvring failed. As if a bank robber who botched his crime suddenly became less guilty.

However, it isn't unreasonable to consider that without the behind-the-scenes manoeuvring by the chief justice and Judge Estey, the Supreme Court might have found the federal process illegal, as Newfoundland's Court of Appeal had done before it, which might have forced the federal government to retreat. But this is not what occurred. If the decision was a partial defeat for Ottawa, it also considerably weakened Quebec and Manitoba's position.

As the audiences were beginning, discerning observers had already noticed the direction in which the court, under Laskin's helmsmanship, was intending to lean. As John Ford noted, "The most telling intervention may have been that by the Chief Justice who apparently said he did not accept the argument of the Manitoba lawyer (Kerr Twaddle) that there was a constitutional convention now crystallised into law which required that all provinces must agree to constitutional changes that infringe [on] their rights."[22]

A few years later, Professor Michael Mandel would summarize the situation well: "Unanimity among the provinces and the federal government was simply not achievable so long as Trudeau and Lévesque had to sign the same document. The freedom from unanimity which the Supreme Court presumed to grant made possible the only conceivable agreement, one that would exclude Quebec."[23]

Isn't it legitimate to consider the constitutional patriation process led by Trudeau with the complicity of the chief justice of the Supreme Court, Judge Estey, and British authorities to be a coup d'état, as John Ford had written to Lord Carrington in the note quoted at the end of our previous chapter? Trudeau himself would come close to admitting that this word was a legitimate one to use when, a few years later, he claimed that what was needed was "almost a putsch, a *coup de force*"[24] to modify the Canadian constitution.

To understand this better, let's examine the concepts we're talking about here. A coup d'état is a notion that shouldn't be confused with that of a military putsch. As historian Maurice Agulhon, a specialist on the issue, explains, the latter concept is applied when a group "attempts to seize power through force" and "assaults the State from the exterior, without the complicity of institutions, but by causing violence unto them."[25] A coup d'état, on the other hand, "carries a supplementary characteristic, that of a power play led from within the institutional system, or by someone who already owns a large measure of power … or disposes of powerful accomplices."[26]

This is indeed the case with our situation, since Trudeau, helped by Laskin, attempted to reverse the existing constitutional order, even if it meant violating the rules that order prescribes, that is, the separation of powers. As Agulhon explains, "For us of the modern age, a coup d'état is a violation of Law. Yet respect for law is at the heart of liberal ethics and democracy."[27]

CHAPTER 16

THE LADY'S NOT FOR TURNING

While the Supreme Court's decision might have been expected, it still managed to take some by surprise. Peter Lougheed was in Munich, promoting Calgary as a destination for the 1988 Winter Olympics. Bill Davis was in Fiji. Ed Broadbent was flying back from Paris. Trudeau had just arrived in Seoul, en route to the Commonwealth Summit in Australia. As such, the prime minister received no more than the bare outline of the decision over the phone. Michael Pitfield, who was accompanying him, spent the entire night on the phone with Ottawa, trying to get his head around the decision's subtleties, despite the constant echo and distortion of the line that accompanied this transoceanic discussion.[1]

"We won!" Jean Chrétien exclaimed on hearing that the court had confirmed the federal government's process. "Yes!" his deputy minister Roger Tassé rejoiced.[2] Following Trudeau's indications, the message of the day would be quite clear: Ottawa had won. Chrétien stood before the press to explain that the question of legality was far more important than the one regarding respect for conventions. As an example, he used the simplest logic possible: in the past, television cameras weren't allowed into the Supreme Court. Given new circumstances, this practice had now been set aside.[3]

When asked whether the British might not be interested in the "convention" aspect of the decision, Chrétien replied that he was convinced Thatcher's government would pass the resolution. Later in the day, he specified that to act in any other way would be the equivalent of treating Canada as if it were a colony. The British surely wouldn't want that, as "they have already their hands full with Northern Ireland."[4]

On Elgin Street, these declarations roused Lord Moran's anger. He immediately produced a vitriolic analysis that, when it reached London, spread like wildfire. With such an unfavourable decision, he wrote, a reasonable person would have concluded that it was impossible to continue full speed ahead. "It therefore seemed strange that without any cabinet consideration and before there had been time even to study the document properly, the minister of justice, after the briefest consultation with Mr. Trudeau, should have come out flatly in favour of going ahead." The prime minister, Moran believed, must be quite disappointed.

> He may think that the project is doomed but, if that is so, it would be much better for it to be killed in the British Parliament than by his government, in which case he could lay the blame on us. If therefore the Prime Minister tells him in Melbourne that prospects for an easy passage in the British Parliament are now even more doubtful than before he may secretly be less concerned than he admits.
>
> Now that the Federal Government is taking the line that constitutional conventions do not matter, it can be argued that there is less compulsion on us to observe the conventions, that we do whatever we are asked to do by the Canadians on the constitution. If Mr. Trudeau is in fact contemplating ultimate defeat with the blame being laid on us, it may conceivably be less damaging for us simply to find a legal means if possible to divest ourselves of responsibility of the Canadian constitution and return it to Canada for them to deal with any changes in it.[5]

As Moran was attacking Trudeau behind the scenes, the eight dissident premiers were preparing their own response to the decision. As soon as it was announced, Bill Bennett began a round of phone calls that lasted two and a half hours. Some of his colleagues, like Lougheed, wanted to take a hard-line approach. Others believed a conciliatory tone was the way to go. Finally, British Columbia's premier declared that the Eight were quite happy with the decision, which demonstrated they'd been right all along — a statement, however, he made without conviction.[6] On his end, René Lévesque couldn't resist calling a press conference to explain Quebec's position. The Supreme Court's decision constituted a clear victory for the dissidents, he claimed.

Moreover, the NDP announced that it demanded a new federal-provincial summit without which it would withdraw its support.[7] This warning wasn't without consequence in Great Britain, where the Labour convention was still in full swing: a part of the discussions surrounded the decision. The federal New Democrats had sent as observer Robin Sears, the party's director. Federal diplomats were also in attendance, and a number of MPs offered their advice:

> Michael English's considered opinion is that the court's decision allows opponents to use word quote unconstitutional unquote and that this will be equivalent to kiss of death in Westminster given British parliamentarians' respect for constitutional propriety and quote conventions unquote.
> Right Honourable Roland Moyle and Nigel Spearing (member of Kershaw committee) provided following advice: Our cause would receive maximum benefit if Blakeney and Saskatchewan NDP could reach agreement with federal government and throw their support. Both acknowledged weight Saskatchewan NDP brings to lobby as a sister socialist party ... in general court decision has set back our efforts over last nine months to educate and impress British parliamentarians.[8]

On his end, Trudeau was still in South Korea, where everyone was waiting for him to react on the airwaves. The problem? The federal government was still considering the meaning that should be given to the decision, as well as what its potential consequences would be. Deputy Justice Minister Roger Tassé thought that the legal aspect was pre-eminent; it was time to push ahead.[9] Michael Kirby stated that it was necessary to put a new offer on the table, and then move ahead with a referendum if that option failed.

The problem was that if a new proposition — a more generous one — was refused, it would be well-nigh impossible to then return to the original offer. Ottawa would have discarded an option for no gains at all.

No clear conclusion emanated from these discussions, and a sombre Trudeau appeared before the cameras, offering a speech that was designed to avoid closing any options. After repeating that the legality of his process was no longer in question and that his government would go forward, he maintained that he hadn't "ruled out absolutely the possibility of listening to what the provinces have to say." However, he backed those words up by stating that he nonetheless had no intention of trading rights for powers: any negotiation with that in mind would be pointless.[10]

THATCHER AND THE LAST CHANCE

Even though he seemed determined not to give an inch when it came to the charter, Trudeau's difficulties were clear to those closely observing the affair. The cabinet secretary, Robert Armstrong, explained the situation to Thatcher:

> Though Mr. Trudeau is putting a brave face on the Supreme Court's ruling, I would judge that he is well aware that it has weakened his political position. He cannot now pretend that what he is about is other than a breach of constitutional convention; and he would, therefore, be a good deal less convincing, both in Canada and in Britain, if he complained that the British Parliament's failure to pass this bill was a breach of the constitutional convention that Westminster should pass without alteration any measure duly requested and approved by the Canadian Parliament.[11]

Armstrong came to this conclusion after having spoken with Michael Pitfield. As he explained to his boss, the latter "made it clear that Mr. Trudeau is counting on the British Government continuing to adhere to their commitment to introduce at Westminster whatever bill is duly approved by the Canadian Parliament. If there were any suggestion of weakening or qualifying that commitment, his position in Canada would be seriously undermined. He will, therefore, be seeking to find out from you whether that commitment still holds firm."

In a weakened position, Trudeau was more dependent than ever on his British counterpart. She was his last chance, and he had no intention of giving up. However, some believed that Thatcher had no reason to help him. Lord Moran's suggestions were becoming increasingly popular among the administration and the government, even among those who, up until that time, had been Ottawa's allies. The first among them to reverse his position was Martin Berthoud. He prepared scenarios in view of a meeting between the two heads of government. A first scenario would be that the prime minister act "as non-committal as possible. She might take the line that … we will do our best to pass legislation … but she must warn him that there is a considerable possibility of failure. She might also take the line that preliminary indications are that a request made under present circumstances would not be a proper one and could therefore not be entertained by Parliament here."[12]

Berthoud's defection, combined with Lord Moran's hostility, was not dramatic in itself for the federal government. After all, they were only civil servants. But their recommendations would soon rally the new Lord Privy Seal, Humphrey Atkins, as well as — and especially — Lord Carrington, who up until then had been an indefectible ally for Ottawa within the Cabinet. Since Trudeau seemed determined to go forward, Carrington suggested that the prime minister tell him that "the judgment adds a new dimension … which could greatly increase the difficulties in getting the Canada bill through Parliament. If Mr. Trudeau attempts to remind the Prime Minister of undertakings given to him, she might similarly take the line that there now appears to be a whole new situation."[13]

Along with the Foreign Secretary's own process, a special committee made up of six ministers, including Havers, Pym, and the chief whips of both houses, studied the affair. The group met two days after the decision to determine which recommendations to press. Humphrey Atkins, Lord Privy Seal, started them off. We should follow Lord Moran's prescribed course of action, he said. Thatcher "should commit herself as little as possible. She can even go further by saying that Mr. Trudeau should not send the legislation."[14] Lord Chancellor Quintin McGarel Hogg continued by stating that the decision would only further increase difficulties in Parliament, but that the government should nonetheless introduce the motion. After all, he said, Canada was an independent country.

It was then Michael Havers's turn to speak. It had been established that the federal government was violating conventions, he noted. But they were saying to whomever was willing to listen that they were going to continue full steam ahead. They felt that might open a door for them. The British government, in their mind, could do the same thing and "enact a short bill patriating the Canadian constitution without at the same time enacting the federal government's proposals for amendment."

This idea wasn't considered any farther, at least for the time being. However, every member of the committee agreed that the adoption of the Canadian resolution would be harder than previously believed. Especially since Jean Wadds and her colleagues had just committed a blunder: right after the decision, they distributed a pamphlet claiming Ottawa's victory because the federal process was deemed legal. The document made no mention of the part of the decision that touched upon conventions and was, incidentally, far more critical of Ottawa, as if the British MPs and Lords would simply never hear about it.

What's more, the provinces also prepared their own pamphlet. It mentioned that the federal process was legal, while underlining that it went against the weight of conventions. The Eight also sent to London a team of jurists led by Yves Pratte, whom the federal diplomats called "Big Gun." The former Supreme Court judge certainly didn't belie his reputation. With authority, he explained day after day to MPs and various other influential characters the meaning of the decision made by the Supreme Court, which, according to him, represented a firm condemnation of Ottawa's project. His shelling was devastating.

All the while, "the tendentious nature of the pamphlet recently circulated by the Canadian High Commission will only serve to make matters worse," as the British ministerial committee noted during their meeting. Consequently, "Trudeau should be asked to seek a measure of consensus before coming to London."

In the end, this would be the main gist of the message sent to Thatcher by the committee:

> The nature of the judgement of the Supreme Court, and particularly the qualifications about the constitutional conventions, raise major new issues which will greatly increase the difficulties we had in any case foreseen with parliament. We have always told Canadian ministers that opposition in

Canada is likely to be reflected in this country. Given the degree of Canadian opposition to Mr. Trudeau's present proposals in the current atmosphere we think there is a real possibility of a bill based on them not getting through.[15]

British ministers weren't the only ones reaching conclusions on the question. In Melbourne, Robert Armstrong was doing the same with his counterpart, Pitfield, while preparing the meeting between their bosses. The Canadian explained that the element judged to be of critical importance by Trudeau was the court recognizing Ottawa's legal right to continue its current trajectory. The prime minister knew from the start that his project violated conventions, Pitfield explained.[16] Certainly, conventions were of great importance, but they are not carved in stone, he claimed. It is for the government and Canadian Parliament to decide when they must be set aside for something new. Canadians would be able to cast judgment on Canadian politicians in the next election if they objected, something they wouldn't be able to do with the British.

Pitfield kept from mentioning that, in the hypothetical situation of the population disavowing the Liberal government during an election, it would in no way affect the changes that would have been introduced by Westminster, in particular the new charter. Set in constitutional stone, the charter would be shielded from a dissatisfied electorate, who would have no recourse to force the government to shed the document.

The Clerk of the Privy Council also didn't elaborate on the fact that the federal government wasn't elected with the mandate to impinge on the jurisdiction of its provincial counterparts. These respective governmental levels answered to their own separate (at least in part) electorates and didn't possess, in virtue of the constitution, either the mandate or the legitimacy to infringe on each other's jurisdictions. They held their own mandate from the people to act in their spheres of responsibility.

Of course, Armstrong wasn't duped by his counterpart's omissions. He replied by speaking about the central issue of the charter, which the judges had unanimously concluded would infringe on provincial jurisdictions. Wouldn't it be possible to simply give it up, as Brian Peckford proposed? Absolutely not, Pitfield answered, explaining the federal government's strategy in the upcoming fight. It was the moment of truth for Quebec, he said. Trudeau had the intention of pulling the more moderate provinces away from the Gang of Eight. However, as Armstrong reported to Thatcher, "Though he may be able to detach some of them, he cannot hope to get enough to satisfy any of the stock amending formulas, all of which require any change to be agreed [upon] by both Ontario and Quebec." In other words, the federal prime minister already knew that he would be unable to satisfy his home province. He would need to isolate it before then ignoring his own proposed amendment formula that gave Quebec a veto; the province's opposition would simply be disregarded. The Supreme Court's decision allowed him to move in this fashion. According to Armstrong: "Trudeau expects an early challenge from Quebec, and some kind of showdown with monsieur Lévesque; and he regards it as essential to have on the statute book those provisions in the Charter of Rights which assure French minority rights."

Meanwhile, Pitfield explained that Trudeau would certainly not blame the British government if his project were to be defeated in Westminster, even though he might find a few British parliamentarians to blame. Anglo-Canadian relations wouldn't be affected, he stated.

This promise was received with a healthy dose of skepticism on the British side, most notably by Lord Carrington. He certainly was right to have his doubts. A detailed economic and political retaliation plan had been produced by Ottawa and was all ready to go. But the time for an anti-British offensive was certainly far from ripe. Instead, Pitfield stated that the prime minister had a plan "which would, he hoped, ensure that the bill reached Westminster with a greater degree of Canadian provincial support, and with a good chance of being acceptable at Westminster."

What was Trudeau's plan? Realistically, he was considering the proposition for a double referendum, which he'd soon submit at the federal-provincial conference on November 4.

The conversation continued. Armstrong explained that, while it was still early to make a definitive assessment, everything seemed to indicate that the Supreme Court's decision would make the adoption of the constitutional project more difficult. What's more, "the government will have to regard to its domestic legislative priorities: there are several financial bills which have to be enacted by a certain date, including a major and highly controversial bill on local government finance."[17]

Whatever the case may be, the important thing at this stage was the position Thatcher would take when she met with Trudeau. On this point, Armstrong didn't share the opinion of the members of the ministerial committee:

It seems to me that nothing that has happened gives any reason for departing from the commitment you have given and repeated: that the British Government will introduce as government legislation at Westminster and invite parliament to pass any measure duly requested and approved by the Canadian Parliament. You could go on to confirm to Mr. Trudeau that the Supreme Court's ruling on the question of constitutional convention will certainly exacerbate the difficulties of getting the bill through Westminster, and that anything he can do to modify it so as to make it acceptable to more of the provincial governments would reduce the dangers of defeat, and improve the prospect of getting the bill through in reasonable time.

TRUDEAU MISLED THATCHER

Better than anyone else, Armstrong was always able to measure Thatcher's moods. For her, this whole patriation business was an anachronism, and it was essential to close the case as quickly as possible, all the while preserving good relations with the faithful ally that was Canada. It was from this perspective that she approached her meeting with Trudeau on October 5, at the residence of the British Consul in Melbourne.[18] The prime minister began by saying that she hadn't been able to read the decision itself, but she understood that Ottawa's project, while legal, was in opposition to constitutional conventions. "This is likely to encourage some of my supporters to persist in their opposition to what is proposed," she stated. Her government would nonetheless introduce any request that emanated from the Canadian Parliament, with the objective of getting "the measure through with the greatest possible degree of support."

Trudeau couldn't have asked for more. And he certainly understood the difficulties his counterpart faced. He promised to do everything in his power to make her end of the bargain as smooth as possible, adding that he would once again speak with the premiers to see whether a new federal-provincial meeting might be useful and an agreement possible. "But I have to say that there is not much chance of a compromise. The provincial premiers who are opposed to the government's proposals had always said that, even if they lost the legal issue, they will continue the political fight." All of this would lead to additional delays, harm both governments, and have repercussions on Anglo-Canadian relations, he warned.

The fact of the matter was that both governments were elected and responsible to their respective electorates, Thatcher answered. The key issue was to preserve warm relations between the two countries. The resolution's success would depend on progress on the Canadian front as well as the way in which the British government would be able to present the situation in Westminster, she added.

Trudeau certainly accepted Thatcher's evaluation on this front. He specified, however, that the longer Canadians waited, the greater the consequences would be on relations between Ottawa and London. Provincial lobbying would continue with renewed vigour, more premiers would make their way to London, MPs and Lords would come to Canada, and so on. If such a situation lasted any longer than necessary, Trudeau insisted, "I would have to tell Canadians not to listen to British backbenchers. At some stage you might need to say to provincial premiers that you cannot in law take cognizance of their arguments."

The prime minister then moved on to René Lévesque: "The premier of Quebec is intent on stirring up trouble," he said. "If there has to be a fight with Quebec, it is best to fight it now [rather] than later … when the majority of Canadians support the substance of the federal government's proposals, if not the method of putting them into effect." Trudeau went on to explain that even if a majority of Canadians didn't approve of the way he was proceeding, it didn't change the fact that 80 percent of them supported patriation and the inclusion of a charter in the constitution, according to various polls.

This last comment certainly surprised Martin Berthoud, who had been made aware of the substance of the conversation. "Mr. Trudeau referred to polls misleadingly in his discussion with the Prime Minister," he wrote in a note. "We will need to refute this as appropriate in our briefing of Mrs. Thatcher on her return."[19]

Moreover, Trudeau mentioned to Thatcher that his opponents had never dared denounce the principles of the charter itself, seeing how popular it was. They instead claimed it as theirs in their battle against federalism. However, the Eight, and not only René Lévesque, rejected the principle of the charter itself. Why such opposition? They had simply not understood that the charter would reduce the powers of the federal Parliament as much as those of provincial legislatures. That said, Trudeau stated he was ready to reduce the size of the charter, but was expecting Lévesque and most likely Lyon to maintain their opposition.

The head of the government also reminded his counterpart that on December 11, the Statute of Westminster would be celebrating its fiftieth birthday. What an excellent date that would make for the complete independence of Canada! At this point in the conversation, Armstrong intervened: this would require the project be presented in the House around mid-November, which makes it impossible. Thatcher was less categorical. It would be hard, "but I will keep the date at the back of my mind," she reassured Trudeau.

"When one is going to do something that is right, there is nothing to be gained by procrastination," Trudeau replied. "The fight cannot get worse and, therefore, it is better to be brought to a conclusion."

In their thirty-five-minute discussion, Thatcher demonstrated that she still supported Trudeau. Despite this, British officials had taken precautions this time so the Canadian wouldn't lend her any intentions before the media. First, it was agreed there'd be a joint press release. There would be no question of mentioning whips. The communiqué instead explained that the constitutional resolution would have to wait for the next parliamentary session before being introduced in Westminster, and mentioned the Canadian prime minister's acceptance of this.

Despite these nuances, the Iron Lady had pulled her ally out of a political no man's land into which he'd been cast by the Supreme Court decision — a precarious position where enemy fire could have ended his project entirely. A single hesitation by Thatcher, a detail or a nuance too far, could have killed it and led to the triumph of the Eight. Against her ministers' opinion, ignoring the Foreign Office and disregarding criticism from her own party, she saved his skin. She demonstrated, once again, that "The Lady's not for turning," as she so famously said.

LOUGHEED IN LONDON

The provinces were on the warpath, invigorated by the Supreme Court's decision. Four British parliamentarians visited Canada, invited by Quebec — all expenses paid, of course. As a federal diplomat noted sarcastically, "It is no great trick to get the British to accept all-expenses-paid trips."[20] Not too hard, indeed, but also quite efficient. This is what Lord Moran noticed: "I have observed that those members of both houses who have come here recently (the latest is Lord Limerick) appear to be impressed by the degree of opposition to the federal government's proposals and to return to London with their doubts reinforced."[21]

Among the quartet visiting Canada as the Supreme Court was presenting its decision was Tony Marlow, the colourful Conservative MP who'd joined the rebel camp and took the opportunity to reveal his preferences. "It is quite obvious we are being asked to change the balance of power between the federal government and the provincial governments," he stated during a press conference. "It is not the business of the British parliament ... that is something for Canadians to decide for themselves."[22]

"We in Parliament have a very high regard for the importance of constitutional conventions," Jonathan Aitken, also a member of the delegation, added. The main problem was the charter, he said, and Ottawa's chances had certainly decreased following the court's decision. The last two times a constitutional law project was presented in Westminster, he concluded, the government had lost its bet.

The British MP turned the affair into a crusade. He dedicated himself body and soul. His trip gave him the opportunity to debate the issue with a number of key personalities, including Jean Chrétien. Returning to London, no sooner had he disembarked from the plane than he met with Peter Lougheed, who was returning from Germany and took the opportunity to stop in London; the Alberta premier wanted to evaluate the situation himself. The meeting took place at the Dorchester Hotel, next to Hyde Park.[23]

Lougheed: "Are you serious about debating this issue?"

Aitken: "Absolutely. We will stick up for the provinces and examine the bill. I don't think we will win [in] the end but we will debate it properly and we may even win some clauses here and there."

Lougheed: "That is fine. That gives me a bit of extra leverage I need to get a deal out of Trudeau."

If he was comfortable in the face-to-face meetings and those with small groups that filled his time in London, Lougheed was just as comfortable with the press. He never hesitated to speak to journalists and share his interpretation of the Supreme Court's decision. "It's been a devastating blow to Mr. Trudeau's attempt to end-run the provinces and to change the character of Canada," he stated. Attacking the federal prime minister relentlessly, he found particular cause for ire in the fact that the latter had ignored the decision about conventions. "It's almost like a prime minister who is defeated at the polls saying I am not going to resign because there is nothing written down in the law that says I have to. That's unacceptable!"[24]

Convinced, convincing, and conservative, Lougheed was naturally taken quite seriously by British Tories, whose party convention in Blackpool was the event of the fall. Every dissident province sent its own representative, in addition to organizing cocktail parties and inviting civil servants to lunch. The operation hurt the federal government, as the High Commission in London noted:

> Provinces demonstrated at Blackpool willingness to take advantage of every opportunity and ability to mount and sustain intensive lobby determination to project … a unity in opposition and professionalism by making use of PR specialists to produce attractive court decision and leaving its readers with impression that court would have done something about legality if it could have but that decision now rests with U.K.[25]

While this operation to charm parliamentarians was a success, the most important goal was to demonstrate to the British government that the common front of the Eight was solid, despite a few splits and cracks. Worried by this situation, Claude Morin took it upon himself to play a game at which he excelled: liar's poker. His new opponent was Murray Simons, the British consul in Montreal, while deputy minister Robert Normand attended as the third wheel in this game of bluff that took place in early October.

Normand opened. He stated that "the only dissident premier who might be wavering is Mr. Blakeney; but his attorney general, Mr. Romanow, is sound on the matter, and could be relied on to keep his premier up to the mark."[26] Morin then explained that Trudeau would likely attempt to mount a charge against the Eight's unity, but all signs pointed to that strategy failing. "I have never known such unshakeable opposition, and in the light of the Supreme Court's judgment a split is unlikely." Moreover, both Quebeckers added, the battle in London would be unimaginably fierce if Trudeau didn't rein in his attacks.

Clearly, however, Morin and Normand weren't convincing enough. In his report, Simons claimed that the government of Quebec had accepted that a defeat in Westminster was likely and, moreover, that Lévesque was thinking of presenting candidates in the federal election. According to the PQ polls, Lévesque had a 51 percent approval rating to Trudeau's 25 percent.

It was then Simons's turn to speak. He began by referring to Quebec's latest advertising campaign. Called *"Minute Ottawa"* in French ("Hold on, Ottawa"), the ad featured a series of billboards. On it, a hand is crumpling a flag of Quebec while the British flag flies on the horizon. "We have not appreciated the use of the Union Jack," the consul stated. "This could be taken to imply that we are in some way conniving with the federal government."

Even if the provinces had good reason to complain about Her Majesty's government's attitude, Morin and Normand immediately backed off, apologizing. They blamed the ad's creative director: "He must have been unable to resist the chance to stir up some anti-anglophone feeling by implying that the British were involved in Mr. Trudeau's game plan," both men suggested.

Morin quickly attempted to change the subject. Quebeckers would never accept Trudeau's charter, he said. In the hypothetical situation where the British Parliament approved his proposition, the PQ government was currently considering ways "to make normal administration within Canada unworkable." As Simons noted in his report, "By outlining for me in such detail an alarming picture of what might follow British acceptance of Mr. Trudeau's proposals, the intention may have been to cause the British government to reflect on the desirability of the federal plan, instead of supporting the provincial position, simple patriation plus amending formula."

The day following this meeting, René Lévesque managed quite the coup at the National Assembly in Quebec City. On October 2, his government rallied a majority of provincial Liberals in favour of a parliamentary motion denouncing Ottawa's attitude, as well as requesting that constitutional talks resume. One hundred and eleven parliamentarians voted for the motion, while nine anglophone Liberal MLAs voted against. Far from seeing a disavowal of his policies, Trudeau — then in Melbourne — instead bragged that the federal Liberals now represented the only "real opposition" to Lévesque's government, a declaration that angered Claude Ryan: "If Mr. Trudeau wants to become head of the Quebec Liberals," he replied, "all he has to do is run against me in a leadership convention."[27] As Lord Moran wrote in a cable to London: "There is a clear break between the provincial and federal liberals on this issue."[28]

Eleven days later, Bill Bennett, the new spokesperson for the provinces, met Trudeau at his Ottawa residence. The discussion took place in the solarium. After having toured the provincial capitals, the Eight's spokesperson was now convinced that an agreement could be reached. It all depended on Trudeau. The latter had made an offer the night before, which, when one looked at it closely, was strikingly similar to the one he was already offering. Trudeau understood that it wasn't enough, but he was truly skeptical about the provinces being earnest in their desire to resume talks. He believed that Bennett was bluffing or that he wasn't really speaking in the Eight's name. But Bennett insisted: "They [i.e., the other premiers] are agreeable if you put something [on the table] that is reasonable."[29] In the end, however, the two men couldn't seem to find common ground. Trust was at an all-time low and nothing was agreed upon, not even a resumption of talks.

A few days later, the annual meeting of the ten provincial premiers took place at the Ritz-Carlton in Montreal. The atmosphere was peculiar. Bennett was both spokesperson for the eight dissident provinces as well as chairman of the annual conference of all ten, which now resembled a battle between the Hatfield-Davis duet and the rest of their colleagues. The New Brunswick native, the Ontarian, and their staffs had rooms apart from the rest of the delegations, one floor away, to make it difficult for them to learn any sensitive information. The Quebeckers chose a room from which they might spy on Bennett and the rest of the delegation from British Columbia, whom they suspected of playing a double game.[30]

As the conference's work began, Davis and Hatfield were invited to leave the room. Davis didn't take this expulsion to heart, but Hatfield, who'd gone to bed quite late the previous evening, grumbled as he left the conference room. The next day, he would give an emotional press conference, during which he accused "dark forces" of attempting to take over the country.

With the two wet blankets out of the room, the Eight began planning. They listened to a presentation by the deputy minister for intergovernmental affairs of Alberta, Peter Meekison. He reported to his colleagues on the coordination of agents general in London, an operation led by his province. The

representatives were asking the eight premiers to agree on the text of a petition that would eventually be transmitted to Westminster. The text should be
signed by every premier so that it might be ready to transmit whenever the
opportunity seemed ripe. Presenting such a petition to the British Parliament
was to follow a strict and time-consuming process: if the document wasn't
ready by the end of the meeting, it might be too late for it to be useful at a
later date. The Eight decided to follow the advice of their emissaries. They
agreed on a text, signed it, and it was immediately sent to London.[31]

The conference was also an opportunity for Bill Bennett to make a public
appeal to Trudeau. The latter needed to be ready to "compromise quite a
bit" or be forced to give up his project. Meanwhile, the Eight didn't adopt
a position of compromise.[32] The answer would come back quickly enough;
it had been pre-recorded two days earlier in the form of an interview with
Trudeau on CTV. The interview was broadcast the first day of the provincial
meeting, as the prime minister had requested. With a firm voice that left no
room for interpretation, Trudeau set out an ultimatum: the provinces had
two weeks to come to an agreement with him, or he'd go to London without
them. "If there is obviously no agreement or possibility of agreement," he
stated, "we will have to do the legal thing and give Canadians what they
want, a charter in the Canadian constitution. It is obvious that the premiers
are stalling in preventing us giving the people what they want."[33]

ROBERT ARMSTRONG'S ANXIETY

Trudeau's statement didn't exactly fly under the radar across the pond, and
it led to strong criticism, notably during a Cabinet meeting, which took
place on October 20. The common apprehension was that the head of the
Canadian government might arrive in London with his resolution, but
without general agreement from the provinces. Lord Carrington underlined
the extent to which the situation was critical. Thatcher would need to once
again warn Trudeau when she saw him in two days' time in Cancun for a
scheduled summit on North-South issues.[34]

The British prime minister wasn't opposed to Carrington's idea, but saw it as
a risky strategy nonetheless. A meeting with her Canadian counterpart would
undoubtedly arouse interest from the press. All eyes would be on the British

and Canadian leaders. An attempt by Lord Carrington to go through Mark MacGuigan would be more discreet, though the message might get diluted.

A decision was hard to come by. But time was running out. The Cabinet decided that Robert Armstrong would call Michael Pitfield that very day. The men knew each other well, had become friends over time, and each had the trust and ear of their respective prime ministers. During the Melbourne meeting, Trudeau had asked whether the British government had any advice to offer regarding the ways federal lobbying in London should proceed. This question could be the pretext for the call, the idea being that the secretary of the Cabinet could share his worries as to potential failure in the British Parliament.[35]

Armstrong didn't need to be drawn a picture. He immediately called Pitfield. After a few words on strategy, he went to the heart of the problem: "Since my return from Melbourne, I have been very impressed by the degree of opposition to the federal package in parliament," he offered. "This is giving me anxiety about the possibility of failure. A greater degree of provincial agreement in Canada could make a crucial difference," he continued. "Mr. Trudeau has spoken of compromise, any compromise which could bring the agreement of extra provinces would pay real dividends."[36]

In lieu of an answer, the Clerk of the Privy Council said he hoped that recent events were understood in the right light in London, especially the patience which Ottawa had shown toward the provinces since the Supreme Court's decision. Armstrong reassured him, stretching the truth somewhat. He added that Bennett's optimistic statements hadn't passed undetected either.

Bennett had actually recently asked Trudeau to organize a new federal-provincial meeting, Pitfield said. The prime minister would likely accept this offer. There was a real possibility of coming to an agreement with a substantial number of provinces, he added. That was for the best, Armstrong beamed, adding that an agreement would make a great impact when the resolution arrived in Westminster.

The day following this conversation, Trudeau announced that he was inviting the premiers to Ottawa: the last chance for an agreement. The meeting would take place on November 2. But this changed nothing about Thatcher's game plan, as she finally decided to let Carrington pass the British government's message on to Mark MacGuigan. The men briefly met under the Mexican sun. "The British government have reluctantly come to the conclusion that because of the Supreme Court judgement it cannot assure the passage of the joint address," Carrington opened. "Backbench opinion is just too intransigently opposed for even the whips to make the difference."[37]

MacGuigan was surprised. "My information is nothing like so gloomy," he said, adding that "a compromise is most unlikely." The Brit replied that "a bill without a compromise is very much harder. The chief whip is doubtful." Whatever might happen, the Canadian said, the resolution would arrive in the first week of November.

Behind his mask of incredulity, MacGuigan was worried. As he would explain years later, "Although I did not take this counsel of gloom as being necessarily the final British word on the matter, I realized that it had not been said lightly. I passed it on to the prime minister at once as a serious assessment."[38]

Meanwhile, Lord Moran continued his sabotage as he embarked on a new tour of dissident provinces. On October 21, he was in Halifax, where he met with John Buchanan. Nova Scotia's premier, who'd studied constitutional law at Queen's, simply couldn't believe that Trudeau was rejecting conventions out of hand. Trudeau would destroy the country's constitution, push Quebec into revolution, and the West to separate, he claimed. What he wanted was a republican, unified Canada, where the provinces were reduced to insignificance. "His dream of governing Canada from a single centralized government, [which] has been reflected in his writings and later in his political career, is unrealizable in a vast country. So we are coming close to the situation where Canada's only hopes for survival lie with the British Parliament. Having won massive support in a recent election, in which the constitution was [the] real issue, I am going to go to London for sure."[39] Buchannan concluded by repeating his opposition to the charter of rights, while claiming that he was ready to make concessions if it would lead to some sort of agreement.

There was a small opening for negotiation, which Moran also noticed in Brian Peckford, whom he met with the next day. The latter maintained that the simple fact that Trudeau had decided to wait a bit longer before going to London indicated that he understood that unilateral patriation posed a serious problem.[40] "A good deal of what was said on both sides was posturing to bring pressure on the other side," he explained. "An agreement is quite in the cards. The last time there had been a real negotiation everyone had been prepared to make real concessions, even Lévesque on language rights."

If Trudeau remained as stubborn, however, it would be a whole other story, he added. There would be an "all-out war." He insisted that "every possible legitimate initiative" would be taken and that he would "go to London." Moran then asked him what would happen if Westminster approved the federal project anyway. "I would take a rain check," Peckford answered, predicting that at least five provinces would refuse the measure if that were the case.

The Newfoundlander wasn't the only one open to negotiations. It was also the case with Bill Davis, who met with British consul Ray Holloway in the Ontario capital. It was a courtesy call that had been scheduled for some time but, as the Brit noted, "Davis wasted no time and started immediately to talk about the constitution."[41] It would be a real shame if the dissident premiers went to London instead of taking care of the dirty laundry at home, the Ontarian noted, specifying that he himself would make his way to the British capital with Hatfield to plead the federal government's case. "Nobody should be under any misapprehension," he said. "The Prime Minister means business and will take the matter to London whether or not there is an agreement. He can be very stubborn."

This warning made, Davis showed his hand. He was ready to alter his position to reach an agreement. He believed that at least four of the eight dissident premiers would also be ready to accept an amended charter of rights, according to their levels of flexibility. If they were open to negotiating, Trudeau should do the same, he concluded.

On his end, Lord Moran returned to Ottawa. He sought to understand the federal government's impression of its own chances of reaching an agreement. He used a meeting with Jean Chrétien to ask the question — and spoke with him in French, a gesture much appreciated.[42] The minister of justice opened by stating: "There might be room for an agreement but unanimity is certainly unattainable. Quebec is unlikely to agree to any deal; this would put Lévesque in an impossible situation vis-à-vis his own party. But the government must satisfy public opinion that an honest effort has been made."

Without consent by the largest number of provinces possible, parliamentary difficulties in Great Britain risked being insurmountable, Moran warned. The chief whip had run a few polls by Conservative MPs, and the results weren't very encouraging. The Brit repeated this warning a number of times throughout the discussion. But they fell on deaf ears, with Chrétien simply repeating that there'd be consequences for Great Britain, without offering up any details.

The problem, he said, going into a long diatribe, was that the federal government was determined to defend the rights of Canadians, especially those of the anglophone minority in Quebec. And Ottawa didn't want to trade powers for fundamental rights. "My children are growing up bilingual because they live in Ottawa. But my brother in Quebec is denied the freedom to give his children an education in English schools if he wanted. Only the Federal Government is defending the English speakers in Quebec. We are now their champion, even though there are no votes in it for us. If the project failed, there would be no future for English speakers in Quebec."

Moran listened politely; however, as he noted in a cable sent to London, "Mr. Chretien gives the impression of complete sincerity but he sees the problem entirely in terms of Quebec and of balancing the rights of English speakers in that province against French rights elsewhere...."

Meanwhile, things were heating up in London. Only a few days away from the moment of truth, the federal government's position was being demolished. This was notably the case within the Cabinet, where anti-Trudeauists were now in the majority, not to mention the fact that Ottawa could no longer depend on Thatcher. John Freeland, jurist with the Foreign Office, reported to Moran that Michael Havers, who was supposed to help House members understand the judicial question, was "still making difficulties. Obviously he would not speak against the resolution but his silence would be noted." Freeland suggested that the deputy minister of justice, Roger Tassé, speak with Henry Seal, Havers's deputy minister, in order to ensure that he did nothing that might comprise Ottawa's position.[43]

But it wasn't only Havers causing trouble. Kershaw's commission decided to write a third report following the Supreme Court decision.[44]

What's more, things were falling apart within the Labour Party. This is what Vivien Hughes, new with the North America division, observed. The only woman on the team, she was one of Ottawa's strongest backers. Hughes was so impassioned by the country that she accepted a job offer at the Canadian High Commission a few years later. For now, her objective was to ensure that patriation succeeded, and she made every effort to that end. Out of the blue, she received a call from a researcher with the Labour Party, David Lowe, who was looking to find out when the patriation request would be arriving in London. I have no idea, she answered, before inquiring about the situation in the Labour Party:

> He said the majority of the members approved in principle
> patriation but were totally opposed to any unilateral approach

by the Canadian Federal Government and to any measure which did not have the support of a reasonable number of provinces. In this they agreed with the Kershaw Report. Some felt they should only be asked to act on a request for patriation with an amending formula, and that the charter of rights was not for Westminster. There were a few politicians, such as Callaghan, who supported Mr. Trudeau, but apart from them the party in general supported the provinces. They attached a considerable degree of importance to the Supreme Court judgement and in particular to its attitude on conventions.[45]

If the situation was bad on the left, it became categorically catastrophic on the right. On October 29, twenty-one Conservative MPs wrote a letter to the *Times*, inviting their colleagues to reject the Canadian resolution. The federal government was flabbergasted. Reeves Haggan called Vivien Hughes to complain.

Haggan: "They [the twenty-one conservative MPs] are all extremely right wing. They favour hanging, are opposed to the European Economic Community, have empire links, support Enoch Powell on immigration, are widely varied in age, have interests in engineering and construction industries, but have no known specific Canadian connections!"

Hughes: "What conclusions do you reach from this?"

Haggan: "None. But I think they had all been got at by Alberta!"[46]

Reeves Haggan wasn't the only one to be surprised. Lord Carrington felt the same way, and he immediately wrote to Moran. "This letter is a worrying indication of the growth of the opposition to any resolution which does not have a substantial measure of agreement with the provinces. All the signatories are conservative. None has hitherto openly expressed opposition to the Canadian proposals. A number had been canvassed earlier this year by the Canadian High Commission and their views have ranged from neutral to 'almost certainly in favour.'"[47] Moran should "make appropriate use of the letter to reinforce the message which was conveyed to Mark MacGuigan at Cancun and that Sir Robert Armstrong made to Mr. Pitfield."

As the British government multiplied its warnings behind the scenes, the same information, as if by pure coincidence, was leaked to the press. An article by Julia Langdon was published in the *Guardian* four days before the last-chance federal-provincial conference. The title gave the punch line away: "Undemocratic Trudeau Move Faces Defeat in Commons." Supported by evidence, the author explained that a majority of British MPs would be voting against the federal request.

> One senior government official suggested yesterday that there was not a single conservative MP who considered the request to be justified in the light of the judgement of the supreme court in Canada
>
> This course would not cause much headache to the government whips who believe at least 30 Tory MPs would defy even a three line whip. Such a rebellious step would not upset most constituency associations. It would even find favour among some ministers, including members of the cabinet, who are understood to have grave doubts about the legislation ... contingency planning is underway.

On the day the article ran, employees of the British High Commission in Ottawa discovered graffiti on the walls of the Elgin Street office, referring to patriation. It was quickly removed before the press, occupied elsewhere getting reaction to the *Guardian*'s revelations, might learn of it. Always aching for a good fight, Jean Chrétien jumped into the ring when queried by the media. "Don't speak about groundswell. I've been there. Canada's constitutional battle is the last problem for them. They have a few problems that have a much higher priority than the Canadian constitution and 22 MPs who have been well wined and dined by the provinces." None of this impresses me, Chrétien continued. The British will need to weigh the consequences of a refusal. "They would not want Canada to become a complicating factor rather than an ally."[48]

The justice minister could put on a defiant face, but a federal defeat in London seemed all but assured. Alternatives were getting as rare as they were risky.

CHAPTER 17

PEACE THROUGH COMPROMISE

The provinces that opposed the federal plan had a considerable advantage in terms of their ground game. But paradoxically, this caused a host of problems for the Eight. First, some provinces simply didn't understand that they had the leg up on the federal government in London. If only the dissidents would stick together, Quebec was certain that Trudeau would be defeated overseas. Similar comments were heard from others in the provincial coalition, like a deputy minister from Nova Scotia, Jeremy Akerman.[1] Showing a bit less confidence, Alberta remained focused. "We felt we were gaining ground steadily with the British Parliament," Peter Lougheed explained. "That was the report we were getting with Jim McKibben."[2] Even Saskatchewan seemed to agree: "Victory seemed possible,"[3] Roy Romanow would say, despite the fact that his boss, Allan Blakeney, still had his doubts.[4]

Another issue was that a number of the premiers weren't actually hoping that Trudeau would lose, or at least wanted to avoid him suffering a humiliating loss. However, Quebec believed he should be forced to accept the April accord and patriate the constitution on that basis, end of story. If he refused, the federal leader would be beaten in London and have to abandon his project. Perhaps he might even retreat on the eve of the final battle.

But Quebec's perspective was far from being shared by the seven anglophone provinces. They'd never considered the April accord as an end in itself, but instead as a negotiation tactic. This was particularly true for British Columbia and Saskatchewan. Despite increasingly visible signals that victory in the British capital might be possible since the Supreme Court's decision, both these provinces were looking for compromise behind the scenes.

Bennett has established direct — and discreet — contacts with the federal government over the summer, and met with Trudeau in the fall. After the court had seized the case, it was Chrétien and Romanow's turn to get busy. The men made a bet with each other. If the federal process was in fact legal, Romanow would get a bottle of Scotch for Chrétien, and Chrétien would do the same if Ottawa's process was deemed illegal. They spoke on the phone the evening of September 28. "We won, you owe me a bottle of Scotch,"[5] Chrétien proudly told Romanow, who was, at the time, in the company of his Ontario counterpart, Roy McMurtry. A good sport, the federal minister invited both men to have a drink at his house. The pair arrived soon after, but without a bottle, since the liquor stores had closed for the night. After Aline Chrétien told her husband not to stay up too late, the trio spoke for about an hour. McMurtry stated that they should attempt to find an agreement, one way or another. The next day, a bottle of Scotch was sent to Chrétien's home, accompanied by a signed note by both provincial ministers.

Back in Regina, Romanow explained to Blakeney that Saskatchewan could either stay with the Eight or attempt to come to an agreement with the federal government, all the while attempting to convince other provinces to follow its lead. The premier was hesitant. He wasn't a fan of the charter, but believed that linguistic dispositions should be included in the constitution — not as fundamental rights, but as a constitutional comprise aimed at ensuring bilingualism. However, since Trudeau held the charter idea so close to his heart, "perhaps we could live with a minimal charter with an effective notwithstanding clause," he would later write. "And after decades of debate and a year or two of bargaining, I felt we owed it to the Canadian people to arrive at an agreement."[6]

In Winnipeg and in Quebec City, the Supreme Court's decision was seen as a victory. This certainly wasn't the time for compromise. Echoes of this were heard in Edmonton, as well, even if Lougheed, in private, seemed less categorical and attracted to the idea of a compromise. He opened up about this to Jonathan Aitken when he'd visited London. Evidently, he was keeping his cards close to his chest, observing Trudeau, watching Bennett, holding Lévesque in check, and continuing his bluff.

In mid-October, the annual conference of premiers took place in Montreal with the backdrop of this infighting; we have spoken of this conference in an earlier chapter. Despite the apparent solidarity and claims of working in good faith advanced by Saskatchewan and British Columbia, the secret manoeuvres were continuing unabated. The two provinces were trading working documents, with Ontario soon joining in the exchange.

This information-sharing was so delicate that precautions to keep them secret were doubled and tripled and multiplied again … in vain. On October 27, as the ministers of intergovernmental affairs of the Eight were meeting in Toronto, the *Globe and Mail* revealed the secret talks between these three provinces. Claude Morin accused his colleagues, Roy Romanow of Saskatchewan and Garde Gardom of British Columbia, of weakening the Gang of Eight. Supported by Dick Johnston of Alberta, he called on them to inform the Eight of their activities, especially if they had the intention of changing camps. Both men made amends, but Romanow nonetheless stated that his government would attempt to find a compromise with Ottawa during the last-chance meeting that would take place on November 2.

The Gang of Eight's cohesion was indeed tested — a situation that was noticed by the astute Lord Moran. "I very much doubt however whether Mr. Bennett does really share the Quebec government's views or that the other dissenting premiers will go along to with Quebec's totally uncompromising line," he wrote. "A number of them (Lougheed of Alberta, Buchanan of Nova Scotia, and Blakeney of Saskatchewan) seem to me to have kept their options open and to be seriously interested in a compromise solution, although this might require Mr. Trudeau to compromise on matters which I believe he regards as essential."[7] For Moran, negotiations could be successful, but not with Quebec.

THE REPUBLIC OF CANADA

The British representative wasn't the only one attempting to anticipate how the chips would fall. The federal government was preparing itself in case the affair went sour in London. Trudeau had a plan prepared by Michael Kirby a few months earlier, which consisted of various political and economic retaliatory actions to force the British to adopt the constitutional resolution. If this strategy was to be a success, the punitive measures had to be credible and the British needed to be convinced that Canada was "prepared to inflict and accept more punishment than HMG."[8] As the affair was of the highest importance for Ottawa, London had to have this impression, Kirby believed, adding that it was crucial to have public opinion on their side.

The federal government could mobilize Commonwealth countries against the United Kingdom. "The approach should focus on selected countries instead of the whole Commonwealth and then succeed with only 80%." The federal government believed it could obtain the support of prime ministers Lee (Singapore), Fraser (Australia), Williams (Trinidad), and perhaps Gandhi (India), as well as President Nyere (Tanzania). To coordinate the operation, the intention was to get Ramphal on their side; he was still chomping at the bit to jump into the fight. "We should request these governments to make their opinions known to the U.K. Our best support is likely from the Caribbean, Africa, Malaysia and Singapore." The countries of the G7 should be considered, as well, though "less easily mobilized around colonialism and their principal limitation might be damage limitation. The U.S.A. would be the most valuable ally if we could convince it that the issue needed to be settled quickly for Canada's unity and for harmony in the alliance. Your good relations with Schmidt … might encourage the Germans to speak quietly on our behalf."

Finally, money forms the sinews of war, as goes the Roman expression, and Kirby wasn't one to ignore his classics:

> A form of pressure the British would understand would be the quiet use of the Government's discretionary power to disfavour certain U.K. economic interests in Canada. A catalogue of possibilities in this regard is being prepared.
>
> This is, of course, a dangerous game in that the British can bring reprisals to bear as well. Economically they could affect not only our relations with them directly, but also use their leverage in the European Economic Community. Politically, they are a more important ally of most key powers than is Canada. Canada depends fairly heavily on the British for intelligence, diplomatic representation in some third world countries, and for military co-operation.

HMG's withdrawal of these would be more painful to Canada than to the U.K.[9]

However, Kirby concluded that if the federal government managed to get public opinion on its side, the operation had a good chance of success. Prepared in the spring of 1981, the plan was still topical in the fall. As Ottawa and the provinces were sharpening their swords in preparation for the final battle — all the while looking out the back door for a potential negotiated exit — the federal government was preparing a second set of plans to threaten the British and sending a sidekick on the offensive.

In this context, Murray Simons, British consul in Montreal, met with Jacques Olivier, the president of the federal Liberal caucus. The former union representative for the Confederation of National Trade Unions opened by stating that he never met with foreign representatives. But Simons was lucky; he decided to make an exception for him.[10] The MP told him that only 4 or 5 percent of Quebec's population had an interest in constitutional questions. The current brouhaha could be explained by the fact that "people could be roused by appeals to linguistic and other tribal totems and by real or imaginary threats to Quebec rights."

Above all else, it was important for the British to do what was expected of them, Olivier continued. If they didn't, they "would be obliged to unleash a campaign afterwards, blaming the English for their neo-colonialism." Quebeckers would then line up to support Trudeau against a resurrected British bogeyman refusing to grant Canada its independence, depriving Quebeckers of the rights they expected to receive under the charter's new regime. Such a perspective wouldn't necessarily inconvenience Olivier, who was slowly showing his teeth. "It would be a matter of some relief to us to be able to embark on a campaign, based on such a gut issue, after having for so long had the uphill task of defending Mr. Trudeau's proposals rationally. The PQ would have no alternative but to fall in behind the campaign. The federal government might follow up with a kind of unilateral declaration of independence." Relating Marc Lalonde's words, Olivier indicated that in such a case the Commonwealth would have to choose between Canada and Great Britain.

The British diplomat described the end of the discussion this way:

He said he hoped Trudeau would call a referendum on the constitutional issue and he was sure Trudeau would win it. He added that in external relations and internal, the federal [government] could bring sanctions to bear which were far more serious than those at the disposal of the provinces.

It was well known that in Quebec the position of the Queen or the Royal Family counted for nothing, and, in the circumstances he was describing, there was bound to be a release of Quebec national sentiment which was hostile to the concept of one Canada.

Murray was convinced that Jacques Olivier had received explicit instruction to speak in this manner. The latter had effectively described point by point the prime minister's backup plan if his project failed in London. The final stage would be Trudeau going all out by calling for a referendum on his proposal. If he won, he'd make a unilateral declaration of independence, and transform Canada into a republic.[11] In early October, Tom Axworthy, his adviser, was given the mandate of preparing a plan for this potential outcome.

UNILATERAL BRITISH PATRIATION

However, Trudeau wouldn't have the opportunity to use this nuclear option. After all, he wasn't the only one preparing himself for the worst: the British government was getting ready to introduce last gasp legislation to send the constitution back to Canada independently. Previously referred to by Ridley, Ford, Carrington, and Pym, this scenario was detailed by Robert Armstrong over the fall. The cabinet secretary of the government explained to Thatcher that two scenarios would be available to Westminster. In the first, the constitutional request would survive the second reading, but parliamentarians would decide to amend the proposal in committee, amputating the charter, despite the efforts deployed by the government. Some dissident MPs were, in fact, hoping to remove the charter from the proposal entirely. In the second scenario, the project would be rejected at its second reading.

If the Charter of Rights is deleted at committee stage, we

had better complete and pass the truncated bill with the patriation and amending formula provisions. If the bill fails at second reading, I believe we should then consider the immediate introduction, not on Canadian request but on our own initiative, of another bill containing only the patriation and amending formula provisions. Either of these courses would be in breach of the constitutional convention that the Westminster Parliament can act only on the request of the Canadian Parliament and cannot vary or modify the provisions requested; but the Canadian Government could hardly complain at our breaching that convention, when they themselves are in authoritatively confirmed breach of the constitutional convention....[12]

Over the month of October, this scenario, in a few different versions, was discussed a number of times in a feverish atmosphere in Whitehall, the main governmental district. Plans, from the tame to the wild, were considered in order to anticipate any and all potential repercussions. As Carrington indicated to Lord Moran, "It seems possible that following such consultations you will receive urgent instructions requiring action by you personally ... make sure you would be available in Ottawa."[13]

The High Commissioner was ready, but asked for additional information on the various plans that were circulating. Berthoud replied that the resolution would be introduced no matter what, even if it became evident that it would be defeated. "There might still be a first-class row: but the Canadians would not be able to fault the behaviour of Her Majesty's Government, in that we would have lived up to our commitments and done our best to fulfill them. We have repeatedly warned them of difficulties in Westminster."[14]

Moran took note of this. He did add, however, that if the British were to patriate the constitution unilaterally, both the charter and the amendment formula should be set aside. "Any formula we select is open to objection," he said. "The present one is strenuously opposed by the Western provinces. To select any other would be a gross interference in Canadian affairs. If Parliament rejects the Federal Government's package it would in my judgement simply be better to simply divest ourselves of legal responsibility. This would in the circumstances be widely understood here and would give us a neutral position in the internal political argument."[15] This line was well-received at the Foreign Office. "Here, we are inclined to agree with you," Berthoud replied. "If ministers decided to act unilaterally, it would be preferable overall to exclude an amending formula though such exclusion, of course, brings peculiar difficulties of its own."[16]

Every scenario was being considered, and Elgin Street's diplomats were asked to offer analyses of possible Canadian reactions in case of unilateral patriation by Her Majesty's government. In the absence of Lord Moran, who'd returned to London for consultations, Emery Davies, a political adviser, was on the case:

> Much would depend on the atmosphere generated by debate at Westminster and on the way in which unilateral action was presented to the Federal Government and publicly. If it had been clearly established that Westminster would not pass the federal package, it is arguable that Mr. Trudeau would welcome (if only in private) immediate unilateral patriation without an amending formula. It would enable him to go immediately to the country or, more probably, hold a referendum. In these circumstances he might not feel the need to play a strong anti-British card. Mr. Trudeau's worst-case scenario might well be: failure at Westminster and the responsibility left with him to undertake and justify further Federal Government action on the constitution. In this case an anti-British slant would seem evidently likely.
>
> In earlier discussion you felt that it would be inadvisable to consult Mr. Trudeau about unilateral action by HMG before the event. It might however be worth exploring this possible course of action. If Mr. Trudeau approved, fine. If he did not and was unable to offer any useful alternative, we would be able to say that we had done our best to find a way forward and that unilateral patriation seemed the least undesirable option, since the one thing that all the provincial governments and the Federal Government agreed upon was the need for patriation.[17]

THE LAST CHANCE SUMMIT

The British had reached this point in their questioning when last-ditch negotiations began in Ottawa. Sunday, November 1 was tenser than the night preceding a great battle. That afternoon, Trudeau's closest advisers met with Bill Davis's advisers in the Four Seasons Hotel. To find some sort of common ground, the Ontarians proposed that the charter include a disposition for derogation that would allow elected officials to prevail over judges if the latter invalidated laws while invoking the new charter. The federal government had, on its end, already prepared its proposal for a referendum on the charter, to be put forward if the negotiations failed. Bill Davis was aware of this tactic, and disliked it: "It will be like a free shot in a by-election," he believed.[18] He told Trudeau this face to face when the men met in the solarium of 24 Sussex around five in the afternoon. A referendum should only be used as a pressure tactic, and nothing more, Davis claimed. But Trudeau would have none of it.

The federal government had prepared a game plan for the conference. The first day, they would be flexible. The following day, they would offer to trade their amendment formula for that of the provinces, in exchange for consensus on the charter. The third day, they would reveal the double referendum scenario, one on the charter, the other on an amendment formula.

Meanwhile, the Gang of Eight was attempting to get its ducks in a row. This is what Peter Lougheed was told by his minister of intergovernmental affairs, Dick Johnston: British Columbia and Saskatchewan were looking for a deal; Claude Morin and he were forced to strong-arm a few provinces to get them to co-operate. Johnston expressed out loud what a number of people were thinking among the seven anglophone provinces: if an agreement was to occur, Quebec might not be part of it. Lougheed had to seriously begin considering that possibility. The premier nodded to show he'd understood.[19]

Lougheed then left for a meeting of the Eight in Bennett's suite at the Château Laurier. The idea, he told his colleagues, was to "smoke out" Trudeau, to force him to consider other positions to determine whether he was taking this round of negotiations seriously, or whether it was a purely cosmetic gesture.[20] Some of the provinces believed new proposals should be put on the table, just to see how the prime minister might react.

Lougheed then intervened a second time. Since no one could predict how the discussions would evolve, they should, out of respect for the rest of the Eight, always warn each other in advance of any change of position by their provinces during the negotiations.[21] Everyone agreed. As Lougheed would later tell Lévesque, defending himself against the accusation of betrayal, "Implicit in this understanding is the point I have reiterated throughout, that if and when Trudeau abandoned his unilateral process and got down to serious negotiations, then each of us was free to examine and review his position."[22]

Negotiations began the following day at the conference centre, divided into public sessions, private discussions, and a number of improvised confabulations here and there. Before the cameras, the prime minister stated that he preferred the Victoria amendment formula. But he was ready to accept another formula, he maintained. He was also adamant that recourse to referendum be part of the final amendment formula. On the charter, however, no concessions would be made. A charter had been under discussion in Canada since 1971, he underlined. So it was entirely untrue to say that it was a disposition "made in England," as the Eight maintained,[23] claiming that the charter had been the subject of failed talks in Canada, and that its only chance of survival was approval by Westminster.

Following a preordained scenario, Davis and Hatfield followed up with their own interventions. The former stated that he was ready to sacrifice Ontario's veto right, which had been provided for in Ottawa's amendment formula. Hatfield continued by proposing a charter on two levels: some rights, like linguistic and democratic rights, would be included in the project, while the rest would be negotiated later.

After this little performance, both the federal government and its two allies seemed like moderates, negotiating in good faith. Before them, the Eight were advancing, but without cohesion. Blakeney stated that he preferred the Eight's amendment formula over the referendum. Lévesque reminded his colleagues of the almost unanimous resolution of the National Assembly denouncing the federal project. He would be able to say yes to a charter, but only if it were quite limited. Lougheed continued by highlighting the importance of equality among the provinces. These principles having been reiterated in the public session, the first ministers continued their discussion behind closed doors, each accompanied by a minister and an adviser.

No one seemed willing to give an inch, and by the end of the day Trudeau had concluded that the exercise had not been fruitful.[24] The performance resumed on Day Two with the added feature of discussions having now given way to personal attacks.[25] This was particularly the case between Lévesque and Trudeau. The former accused the latter of having no mandate to patriate the constitution since he hadn't campaigned on that theme. The latter replied that Quebec's referendum had given the mandate to all levels of government to quickly act to solve the constitutional issue.[26] Lévesque stated that Trudeau had won thanks to money, fear-mongering, and misleading advertisement, to which Trudeau answered that, in the case of a federal referendum, "at least we won't manipulate the question."[27]

The exchange degenerated into a violent dispute over the linguistic propositions that Trudeau sought to include in the charter. If such dispositions didn't come to pass, the latter explained, the country would evolve toward two linguistic solitudes. According to Lévesque, attention should be paid to the future of French in Quebec. By taking away the right of provinces to determine who can go to French or English schools, supposedly to uphold fundamental rights, the prime minister was threatening the continued existence of Québécois culture. At one point, Trudeau became so outraged at being lectured to that he left the room. The Eight retired to Bennett's suite at the Château Laurier, on the other side of the street.

There, the provinces decided to send Bennett, Lougheed, and Buchanan to speak with Trudeau about a compromise to which Bill Davis had lent his support. The latter accompanied the three premiers to explain their proposal to the federal leader. The proposal itself consisted of returning to the agreement signed by the Eight in April, and adding to it a limited charter of rights as well as guarantees to the provinces in terms of transfer payments and natural resources. Trudeau wasn't interested at all; he accused the emissaries of playing the sovereignists' game.[28] You're letting yourselves be duped by René Lévesque, the prime minister threw out. I'm ready to negotiate, but if you think I've been mortally wounded by your attacks, you're wrong, he thundered.

Not impressed for a moment, Lougheed counter-attacked. He asked if Trudeau could illuminate them as to how his proposal was an answer to the promises that he'd made to Quebeckers.[29] Trudeau looked at the Albertan with daggers in his eyes … but didn't answer. Instead, he took leave of the delegation by stating that a truncated charter didn't interest him one iota. Bennett, Lougheed, and Buchanan returned to their colleagues. The Nova Scotian was beet red, to the point that his colleagues thought he was "shell-shocked."

On Wednesday morning, Trudeau announced to Davis and Hatfield that he would propose his referendum. Both men answered that he was making a mistake, but he was unwilling to listen to them. In the other camp, the Eight were having breakfast together, as they'd agreed to do every morning during the conference. Blakeney announced that he would be making a proposal that provided for a charter without linguistic rights as well as an amendment formula with a right of withdrawal but no financial compensation. Meanwhile, Bennett believed they should offer linguistic rights to Trudeau, knowing that this approach was even more unacceptable to Lévesque than what Blakeney had just offered. The atmosphere was poisonous. Lévesque and Lyon were furious. Both men accused the Saskatchewanian of weakening the alliance. Lougheed also rejected the proposal, but believed that, from a tactical point of view, it might be interesting to submit it to Trudeau in order to measure his reaction.

The conference continued, and Blakeney made his proposal. More than anything else, he was seeking to keep the discussion alive, fearing that the whole event might fizzle out.[30] The conference was going nowhere. The fears of Saskatchewan's premier seemed to be coming true. Lévesque announced that he'd leave later that afternoon, while Lyon, who was in the middle of his own electoral campaign, packed his bags and left for the airport, leaving the reins to his minister Gerry Mercier. Sizing up Trudeau one last time, he left with these words: "I will never agree to an entrenched charter."[31] John Buchanan left the conference, as well, but for other reasons. He had just learned his father-in-law had passed away.

At this stage, Trudeau played his trump card. He proposed a system that was composed of two referenda, which would be set into motion if, after two years, no agreement had been reached. The first referendum would determine whether Canadians wanted a charter. The proposal would need to receive approval by a majority on the national level, in Quebec and in Ontario, as well as in two regions, the West and the Maritimes. The second referendum would determine the constitutional amendment formula, between the Victoria formula (proposed by Ottawa) and the Vancouver one (put forward by the Eight). The British would vote on the legal framework that would permit such an exercise.

The federal government didn't give many details, but Lévesque seemed interested. Seeing new cracks appear in his makeshift alliance every day, he saw in this proposal an exit strategy, especially since he believed he'd be able to defeat Trudeau in a referendum on the charter. Lougheed wanted to know more. What would the nuts and bolts of the referendum be?[32] The session was adjourned for lunch with these questions pending. Seeing Lévesque's interest and the obvious reticence of the anglophone provinces, Trudeau laid it on thick before the press with the apparent goal of sowing discord in the alliance. He proudly announced a new Canada-Quebec agreement and added that "the cat is among the pigeons." On his end, Lévesque spoke of this double referendum as an honourable way of putting the crisis behind them and announced he would be remaining in Ottawa a little longer to discuss it.

Ontarians were frustrated by how the situation had evolved. We've been had, "that son of a bitch does not want a compromise," McMurtry told Davis, speaking of Trudeau.[33] As they were sitting down for lunch, Ontario's premier sent a message to his advisers to speak with their federal counterparts. The message was simple: "If you guys can't find a way to compromise, then don't count on us to be with you at Westminster." According to Hugh Segal, a close adviser to Davis, "the feds were stunned."[34]

Perhaps some were stunned, but not Chrétien, who took it upon himself to speak with the provincial delegations. The man who'd sworn to Roy Romanow that he'd never again fight in a referendum repeated the same message to each and all. "You know, guys, there's going to be a referendum. I don't want one and you don't want one. But I am telling you, I am going to go into your provinces, and I'm going to say you are opposed to freedom of religion and equality of women and all that, and I am going to clobber you."[35]

"We'll fight and we'll win," Lougheed declared in lieu of an answer.[36] He didn't like the idea of a referendum, but still believed he'd win it. Trudeau hadn't managed to get a single MP elected in his province since 1968, and the Liberal Party of Canada was at the bottom of the polls. The Victoria Charter would never fly in Alberta, he believed. Despite this, he wanted no part of the fight. The Eight talked it over during lunch. Peckford believed it was better to find a compromise than go for the referendum option. Lougheed repeated that Trudeau should submit everything by writing. "Let's pin him down," he said.[37]

Moving from words to action, Lougheed demanded that the prime minister — once everyone was back from lunch — demonstrate that his proposal for referenda truly took into account provinces besides Quebec and Ontario. He wanted to know what sort of majority would be necessary in the western part of the country. Wary, he wanted a written proposal; Trudeau agreed to do this. A break was taken, and the Eight once again got together. Lougheed explained that the referendum plan was idiotic. The provinces would be abandoning the moral and judicial authority that had been conferred by the

Supreme Court's decision.[38] Everyone agreed. The proposal was a trap, he continued, but if they held together, Trudeau would have to yield.

The break was over and Trudeau went around the table once again to sound out the provinces on his referendum. To the great surprise of the other premiers, Lévesque still seemed interested. The written text of the proposal was distributed. Trudeau explained that his charter and amendment formula would immediately be adopted by the British, contrary to what he'd insinuated that morning. Once patriated, the constitution would be discussed in Canada, and the two referenda would take place after two years to modify it. It all would follow an extremely complex system, which further worried the provinces. This is a plan to get patriation approved in London while bypassing the provinces, Blakeney and Lougheed thundered. Lévesque finally stated that he no longer supported the plan.[39]

Once again, the atmosphere turned poisonous. Criticism rained down on the prime minister, who simply shrugged it off. The linguistic issue was discussed once again. Trudeau and Lévesque were at each other's throats while the others looked on, powerless. Three hours later, the impasse still held. Peckford declared that he had a proposal to submit, but he preferred to discuss it the following day. Trudeau announced a last round of talks for the next day, starting at nine. After that, he would send his resolution to London.

The Eight met right after the conference. According to a popular interpretation, Lévesque, by briefly accepting the federal proposal for a double referendum, had broken the provincial alliance and was the impetus behind his own isolation. But the truth is more nuanced. Certainly, Lougheed and others rebuked Lévesque for having initially shown interest in the federal proposal. The actions of Quebec's premier and the recriminations he provoked were only one more manifestation of the Eight's lack of cohesion. That same morning, Saskatchewan and British Colombia had also gone off script with their own proposal, and of course the same two provinces had conducted secret meetings in the weeks preceding the final one. With each passing day of the conference, the Eight's solidarity slowly crumbled. Lévesque added to this dynamic, but he was neither the first, nor had he done it in secret. His attitude was far more loyal than that of other premiers. As Allan Blakeney noted: "I did not regard this as a breach of the understanding among the eight, except to the extent that he gave no advance notice to his colleagues."[40]

"I agree with Blakeney," stated Brian Peckford in this respect.[41]

What's more, by the time Lévesque intervened in the debate, some of the alliance's members had already written Quebec off. This was the case of Roy Romanow, convinced that it would be impossible to satisfy both Lévesque and Trudeau. On the afternoon of November 4, Romanow met with Chrétien and McMurtry in one of the kitchens of the conference centre in order to find a compromise. Ottawa would need to accept the Vancouver formula, but without financial compensation when a province withdrew from an amendment — a disposition dear to Quebeckers. In return, the provinces would accept the charter, which would be pared down thanks to an exemption clause.[42]

A few hours later, Trudeau met with his advisers and ministers after going for a swim. The atmosphere was electric; a number of them were simply looking for a fight. Chrétien insisted on his end that an agreement was possible, as he'd discussed earlier with McMurtry and Romanow. For one of his colleagues who preferred the referendum option, he had a scathing reply: "You put [on] your running shoes and sell it."[43] But the minister of justice could argue all he wanted; he was, for about an hour, the only one who believed an agreement was possible. Trudeau wanted none of it. Then the phone rang. Bill Davis was on the line and wanted to speak with Trudeau. "I think our people have worked out something pretty good. What do you think, Pierre?"[44] Trudeau grumbled that he didn't like the proposal discussed by McMurtry, Chrétien, and Romanow; there were too many compromises. Davis explained that he had spoken to Hatfield, and they were both in agreement that it was the way to go. "Rather than fight this thing to the bitter end, we have to tell you that we wouldn't go to London supporting you as we have until now if you don't accept some sort of compromise of this nature," Davis threatened. "We can argue details tomorrow, but we like the outline of the compromise."

A chastened Trudeau returned to the room where his advisers and ministers were waiting. "I think we may have to go for the compromise solution even though I don't like it — because otherwise … we'd be going to London alone."[45] Around the table, a few still believed they should go to England and stage the fight there. But Trudeau was all too aware of the difficulties that would await them if they committed themselves to such an adventure. Besides, the latest news from London was particularly worrying for Ottawa; it had made the rounds of the conference centre that day. James Callaghan, Trudeau's most solid supporter among the Labour Party, had changed sides. He'd informed Jean Wadds of his intentions, while a new batch of MPs were crossing the Rubicon with him.

Tom Wells, Ontario's minister of intergovernmental affairs, would tell — the following week — the British consul in Toronto that this development had been crucial, specifying that "the press had not got across the nearness of total disagreement."[46] Wells had followed developments very closely. He remained at Davis's side throughout the negotiations, except for a single hour.

The importance of events in London in Trudeau's decision to accept compromise was also corroborated by Mark MacGuigan. As he would write in his memoirs, "The situation in the British parliament was undoubtedly a significant factor in the prime minister's willingness to compromise."[47] Trudeau himself would write, "I was a sufficiently long-in-the-tooth politician by then to realize that sometimes you have to take second best."[48] On the night of November 4, 1981, the federal prime minister would give Chrétien instructions to work to find a compromise.

In the collective memory of Quebeckers, the events that followed became *La nuit des longs couteaux*, the "Night of the Long Knives," according to Claude Morin's interpretation.[49] In any case, Claude Morin's terminology, a reference to Hitler's assassination of his rivals within the Nazi Party in 1934, is, to say the least, totally excessive. If Quebec ended up isolated, the means through which this occurred wasn't the result of a plot, or a concerted desire by its seven allies to betray the francophone province. First, three other premiers in the Eight besides Lévesque were absent from the negotiations that night. Lyon had returned to Winnipeg. Lougheed decided to go to bed, as did his minister, Dick Johnston, and Bill Bennett of British Columbia. They strongly suspected that there would be further wheeling and dealing that night, but wished to evaluate the situation with a clear head the next morning.

Talks then began within the Gang of Eight and continued through the night of November 4–5. Newfoundland was the impetus behind the negotiations. Brian Peckford had concocted a compromise that he was unable to present that day. He asked his civil servants to discuss it with their counterparts from Saskatchewan, British Columbia, and Alberta. Newfoundland's premier asked them to wake him up if things were advancing in a positive direction.[50] This is what occurred, and Peckford arrived a little before midnight. The other premiers who joined the talks were Allan Blakeney (Saskatchewan), Angus MacLean (PEI), and John Buchanan (Nova Scotia). A few ministers responsible for the constitutional issue were also present. No representatives of Manitoba or Quebec were there.

The compromise that was being drawn up consisted essentially of Ottawa accepting the Eight's amendment formula, which would, however, be open to modification. A province would have the right of withdrawal without financial compensation. In return, the provinces would accept a modified charter of rights, not as forceful. A notwithstanding clause would allow a provincial legislature or the federal parliament to ignore a judicial decision based on certain dispositions of the charter. As for "linguistic rights" in education, Newfoundland's proposal provided for a province to be able to withdraw from obligations related to this clause if it obtained a majority in a referendum (Trudeau would object to this disposition the next day, and it would be scrapped). Representatives of the six provinces present that night hoped they had the foundations of a compromise, even if none of it was finalized.

The next step was to present the whole thing to the others. At this stage, Peckford believed it would still be possible to rally Quebec. He asked his minister of justice, Gerald Ottenheimer, who spoke fluent French, to contact the Quebec delegation.[51] The latter was unable to reach anyone in the delegation, but managed to speak with Ontario's delegations, which allowed Davis and Blakeney to discuss the proposal over the phone.

Attempts were also made to reach out to the Manitobans. Minister Gerry Mercier was finally reached on the phone, and told of the developments. This was important, since Lyon was as opposed as Lévesque to the charter of rights. Manitoba's delegation was informed in real time of the discussions, but this had very little effect. Indeed, the fact remains that over the course of the preceding weeks, six of the Eight's premiers had expressed, in varying degrees, a desire for compromise. Manitoba and Quebec would naturally be isolated from any solution.

This result was solidified the morning of November 5. Bennett and Lougheed, who'd slept through the night, examined the fruits of these talks and concluded that they could be satisfied with the results. Minimally, the exercise had demonstrated the provinces' good faith if the federal government refused to deal. Chrétien, on his end, was convinced that the eight provinces would support the compromise. He informed Trudeau, who, despite hesitating at first, relented and would in the end be delighted by the results. The minister of justice also spoke with Romanow. As an experienced politician, he asked the latter to ensure that Manitoba didn't sign the agreement, so that two provinces, and not just one, would be out of the loop.[52] His idea was to lessen the impression of Quebec's isolation — a surprising move, but one that was an avatar for the idea that, in the end, a more divided decision would be better for the country.

This was the situation when, at eight o'clock, the premiers of the Gang of Eight met for their daily breakfast. Six of the seven anglophones agreed with the proposal, with a few reservations. They especially wanted to see whether Trudeau would accept it as is. As was often the case, Lévesque was late, by twenty-five minutes this time. The meeting was practically over by the time he arrived. Realizing what was happening, he became furious. This compromise was unacceptable for Quebec, he stated, arguing that the best scenario was to bring the fight to London. The others believed that it was better to agree to this proposal, and perhaps attempt to ameliorate it. However, failure in Canada and renewed conflict in London would be bad for the country, they thought.[53] But according to Lévesque, the status quo would have been preferable, cancelling the consequences of a new failure. Seeing that the others wouldn't budge, he demanded that the right of withdrawal with financial compensation be reinstated. Lougheed seemed open to the idea and stayed on to speak with Lévesque one-to-one for another twenty minutes after the others left.

The Alberta premier then called Lyon, the other outcast in these negotiations, and counselled him to accept the charter. If he didn't, the Manitoban would have the unattractive task of explaining in the middle of an electoral campaign why he'd been the only premier to make common cause with Lévesque. Lyon was aware of this; his advisers had already alerted him to the potential consequences. He authorized his minister, Gerry Mercier, to sign the agreement, with one reservation: the agreement would need to be discussed and ratified by the legislature, particularly the question of fundamental rights to French schooling. Two weeks later, the Manitoba premier would lose the election to Howard Pawley's NDP, which quickly pushed through the November compromise.

Meanwhile, all eyes were on the last day of the conference, which began at 9:30 with a closed-door session. Lévesque was in a state of shock. He was wavering between rage and deep psychological distress, which he hid behind a proud air. Trudeau began the proceedings. Hiding his intentions, he opened with a scowl, keeping everyone on their toes — all the while giving a friendly conspiratorial kick under the table to his accomplice, Chrétien, sitting next to him. "Not bad, nice work. It makes a lot of sense,"[54] he finally said. Lévesque didn't share this outlook. He led another charge on the idea of a referendum. Trudeau replied that he regretted that this clause had disappeared, but, at least, a constitutional agreement was now quite possible.

The discussion turned to the charter and the reach of its notwithstanding clause — what would become Section 33. Lougheed wished to see this clause reinforced: it should be applied to dispositions on fundamental liberties and judicial guarantees, according to him. Trudeau consented, but required in return that when a clause was overridden, that override would need to be renewed every five years.

The prime minister refused that the "human right" to English schooling in Quebec and French schooling in other provinces be subject to the notwithstanding clause. It was essential for him that no province could pull out of the new regime of "minority language educational rights." Trudeau's requirement was directly aimed at invalidating Bill 101. Lougheed objected; he wanted no part of a manoeuvre whose purpose was to legislate by force, using the courts as intermediaries, within Quebec's jurisdiction. But the Albertan obtained almost everything he wanted — notably an amendment formula with a right of withdrawal, protecting his province's jurisdiction over natural resources, which were the object of an additional guarantee in the project currently on the table — and Trudeau now expected him to drop Lévesque and his language problem. Lougheed finally gave up. Quebec's former allies nodded in agreement.

The group then moved on to the amendment formula, so close to the Albertan's heart. Lévesque once again demanded a right of withdrawal with compensation, or a veto right. Trudeau replied that Quebec had given up that possibility, which the federal government had been ready to give him; of course, he once again forgot to mention that he would have accepted this option only after forcing Quebec to accept other unpalatable changes.

One by one, the premiers accepted what was being discussed. Trudeau made one last attempt to convince Lévesque in a dialogue that had never been so sterile. "Come on, surprise me. Make some kind of a gesture now that you've lost this inning. Come along we'll all do this together."[55] For Lévesque, it was out of the question. He hadn't obtained a right of withdrawal with financial compensation; instead of having its jurisdiction widened, Quebec saw responsibilities wrenched away from it in the area of education, thanks to the charter. Ontario wouldn't be bilingual, and a clause concerning the mobility of labour limited Quebec's capacity to legislate on the issue. The rout was complete. Morin had tears in his eyes, while Lévesque, in a last ditch attempt, called on Trudeau as a Quebecker not to allow such a thing to pass. Hope was futile. The session ended.

But the PQ leader wasn't done with his counterpart, addressing him sharply with these words: "You won't win this battle in the end! The people will decide!"

Trudeau replied, "The people have spoken, René. You've lost."[56]

On that note, Lévesque decided to leave Ottawa. Louis Bernard, the secretary of the executive council, believed that was a serious mistake, since a final session was to take place that afternoon, and it would be public. He asked Claude Charron, then parliamentary leader, to intervene. The latter pleaded with his boss to tell Quebeckers what was said that morning. Lévesque would relent, but wouldn't let his intentions be known to the other participants.

A PROMISE BETRAYED

The premiers were wary indeed: the idea of an empty chair where Lévesque should be seated, before an audience of millions in front of their TV sets, worried them. As each reflected on the consequences of their agreement, the federal government realized that the agreement hadn't been translated into French. That risked increasing the perception of Quebec's isolation. André Burelle was called in at the last minute to translate the document as quickly as possible. Years later, he would write:

> I left the conference center that day with the feeling of hav-
> ing been deceived alongside every other Quebecker to whom
> Mr. Trudeau had promised a renewed federalism inspired by
> the Pépin-Robarts report, Claude Ryan's beige paper, even
> by *A Time for Action*, in exchange for a majority NO vote
> to the sovereignty-association proposed by René Lévesque.[57]

Two weeks later, Burelle would write his letter of resignation.

Meanwhile, Lévesque made his way before his colleagues — to their apparent relief — for one last time. In front of the cameras, the nine other premiers congratulated each other on the agreement, and the spirit of compromise that, in the end, had overcome divisions. The leader of the Quebec government stated that the agreement was a betrayal, and that he would continue his fight. "What has just transpired will have immeasurable consequences for Quebec and Canada's future,"[58] he said, his voice breaking with emotion. In a later press conference, Lévesque let his feelings show, calling his counterparts "used car salesmen who wouldn't think twice before walking over their mothers for an ice cream cone."[59] He also referred to "a stabbing in the middle of the night."[60]

A few months after patriation, Lougheed would write a long letter to Lévesque, claiming that Quebec hadn't been betrayed by its allies. Citing a number of events in support of his thesis, he repeated that the April 1981 agreement had a strategic component, its purpose being to prevent unilateral patriation and force Trudeau back to the negotiation table. "I agree in principle with your account of the various events which led up to the agreement of November 5th 1981," Lévesque would answer, adding that only a few nuances separated his account from that of his colleague.[61]

With a calmer mind and far from the cameras, Quebec's premier had a more clear-headed view of events — and a less emotional one. But he still had blame to distribute, which he shared with Lougheed:

> The events in question cannot be correctly understood from Quebec's point of view without taking into consideration the fact that, in the May referendum, the advocates of federalism, including yourself, committed themselves to a renewal of our political system along lines satisfactory to the people of Quebec. However, you must admit, the constitutional agreement of November 5th is largely the opposite of that commitment. In fact, it has led to a reduction of Quebec's powers and to the negation of the existence here of a distinct society.[62]

Indeed, how would it be possible to forget promises made by the premiers who, following Trudeau's lead, had clearly given Quebeckers the impression that their aspirations could be satisfied within Canada? Bennett, Lougheed, Blakeney, and especially Hatfield and Davis came to Quebec to participate in the campaign and deliver this message.[63] Both the Ontarian and the New Brunswicker have a particular responsibility, since they became Ottawa's closest allies. Davis would go as far as taking pity on Quebec's premier, criticizing the attitude of its seven allies: "The saddest part is that Lévesque was never told. I will never

302 · The Battle of London

understand that. He had been working with the others. He was hurt."[64]

The seven premiers could at least take pride in having made an effort to find a solution compatible with Quebec's demands, before abandoning that avenue when faced with the following choice: a potential compromise with Ottawa, or a battle in London which frightened them. But most among them played the part of Pontius Pilate. In a conversation with Trudeau about Quebec's isolation, on November 5, Blakeney told him, "All right but be it on your head."[65] Years later, Lougheed would also throw the blame on the prime minister: "Why wasn't it Mr. Trudeau's responsibility to assure that the ultimate package had enough in it to meet the impossible promises he made during the referendum?"[66] Of course, Trudeau remains responsible, but we cannot ignore that Lougheed and Blakeney lent their names to the promises of change made by the federal leader during the referendum, as did some of their colleagues. To some extent, the promise made on May 14, 1980, was also theirs. Trudeau's credibility when he made that speech sprung from the fact that a number of premiers held the same line.

In this whole affair, Brian Peckford likely was the most coherent. Like his neighbours, Angus MacLean and John Buchanan, he kept himself from campaigning in Quebec and made no promises whatsoever. While he spoke of constitutional renewal, it was mostly to highlight the interest of his own province.[67]

These three premiers, along with Sterling Lyon, were free of Lévesque's blame, except for their legitimate reticence in recognizing Quebeckers as one of the country's founding peoples. At least they hadn't implied the opposite. As for Manitoba, Lyon's back had been against a wall, in the middle of an electoral campaign; even in this situation, he'd retained the option of rejecting the proposal if he was re-elected. The most conservative of provincial premiers never abandoned his nationalist colleague from Quebec. Faced with the charter proposed by Trudeau and the new country it sought to create, bilingual and multicultural, Lyon wished to preserve the British heritage of English Canada and Lévesque the French identity of Quebec.

But when it comes down to brass tacks, there's no way around the fact that only Quebec ended up isolated. As early as November 5, the most clairvoyant observers, like Gordon Robertson, former Clerk of the Privy Council, had foreseen what would occur, a situation that would once again threaten to tear the country apart: "It would be optimistic in the extreme," he wrote, "to think that we can avoid a new crisis on the question of separation in a very few years."[68]

CHAPTER 18

GOD BLESS
MARGARET THATCHER

The last day of the constitutional convention had barely come to a close when Trudeau flew off to New York to receive the Family Man Award for International Excellence.[1] Once he landed in the Big Apple, he used his first free moment to write a thank-you letter to Thatcher. He owed her what would be perceived, over time, as the great legacy of his career:

> My dear Margaret, while we are still in the first flush of our success after our recent federal-provincial conference on the constitution, I wanted to write you to express my enormous gratitude to you for your support over the last year and a half. It meant a great deal to me, both in my official functions and personally, that during the trying times of the last several months, I was able to count on the support and friendship of the Prime Minister of the United Kingdom. We shared common view of what would be the proper course of action by the British Government following a request from the Canadian Parliament, however controversial it may be, but I know that your holding to this view required courage and commitment. Certainly

your actions both before and after the Supreme Court decision were important in maintaining the credibility of the
Federal Government's strategy and, eventually, in producing the consensus which emerged on November 5th....[2]

A few years later, in a speech before the Senate, Trudeau would unchain
his lyrical soul: "Margaret Thatcher, God bless her!"[3] The prime minister's
gratitude was immense, and with reason. But it was also premature at that
point. Despite the fact that Trudeau believed the constitution was a done deal,
new complications would arise. These complications would move Thatcher to
suspend debate on the constitutional resolution to Trudeau's great displeasure.

The business had its problems in Canada, too. First there was the question
of Quebec's exclusion, which left a bad taste in the mouth of a number of
participants. The nine provincial premiers who had signed the agreement
asked Ottawa to see whether it would be possible to find some sort of common ground with Quebec.

But Lévesque wouldn't budge. The federal government turned to the
leader of the Opposition, Claude Ryan, to determine what sort of additions
could make the project easier to swallow. Ottawa was hoping to win over less
dogmatic nationalists. After a few days, Trudeau agreed to partially restore
the financial compensation that was supposed to accompany the right of
withdrawal in virtue of the April 1981 agreement. This mechanism could
be applied to language and culture. And he decided to moderate his attacks
against Bill 101 by including a mechanism for voluntary limited adhesion
to "linguistic rights." The fundamental right to study in English in Quebec
wouldn't be granted to the children of immigrants having studied in English
in a foreign country, except if Quebec consented to it. This disposition
meant that Bill 101 would have effect over anglophone immigrants.

FEMINISTS UNBOUND

As these modifications were being made, women's groups rose up against
the fact that the new notwithstanding clause could be applied to Section
28, which guaranteed the application of the charter to both sexes. Feminist
groups wanted this to be corrected. The controversy that followed is worth

looking into here. We should first question why it was deemed necessary to specify that the charter be applied to certain categories of citizens, for example, to both sexes. If we hadn't included this point, would we have concluded that the charter was applicable only to men? Was Canada in 1981 a country so sexist that it was necessary to specify that the charter was valid for both men and women? Of course not.

Be that as it may, demonstrations organized by the feminist lobby took place across Canada. The federal government openly encouraged them to mobilize, underlining that only the nine provincial governments could follow up on their demands. Beyond that, the federal government threw its own weight around. The minister responsible for the Status of Women, Judy Erola, offered space in her Ottawa offices for the movement as it was being organized.[4] For many observers, including journalists Robert Sheppard and Michael Valpy, this dynamic was the illustration of the victory of the people: "The constitution, for the first time, belonged to the people of Canada."[5]

Is this assessment true? First, we should ask how these demonstrations organized with the help of taxpayers' dollars and orchestrated by the federal government constituted a movement by the people of Canada demanding that its government return their rights to them. It might be fairer to see in this movement a bureaucracy and its feminist clientele mobilizing so that the government and the courts might intervene more in the life of all citizens, under the cover of the equality of the sexes.

In any case, the feminists were unbound and were ready to drag the provincial premiers through the muck; these nine white men were the target of all sorts of accusations. Blakeney was compelled to change his position under pressure. Ironically, the latter believed that women's rights would be curtailed if the premiers yielded to the feminist groups, who were asking that the notwithstanding clause not be applied to clauses regarding the equality of the sexes. Saskatchewan's premier had always thought of this disposition of the charter as allowing legislatures to put affirmative action programs in place for women. He couldn't understand this outcry.[6]

For the time being, he had something else on his mind. He had just met with an aboriginal delegation that was hoping that specific changes might be made in the final agreement. Sympathetic to their cause, he told them that the pact was sealed, but that he would be attentive to further circumstances that might allow for modifications. The feminist movement, and Ottawa's subsequent desire to ensure that Section 28 not be affected by the notwith-standing clause, gave him this opportunity. Blakeney announced that he was ready to accept such a change, provided that additional changes be made that would favour the aboriginal petitioners he had met.

Meanwhile, Ottawa was pressuring the other premiers. Political correctness made it so the premiers quickly understood that, no matter the soundness of their arguments, they would be perceived as a bunch of chauvinists if they remained opposed to the feminist lobby. All of them bowed to the pressure.

Next, it was time to find a way to bring satisfaction to First Nations. They were angered by the fact that the final agreement no longer included a clause that recognized their ancestral rights or treaty rights. Trudeau wasn't interested in any such disposition, which had been added following con-sultations led by the House and Senate joint committee in an earlier draft. He hadn't been opposed when a few anglophone provinces insisted it be removed from the November 5 agreement. British Columbia had a number of qualms about the disposition, since the majority of territorial claims by First Nations were over parts of its territory. The level of aboriginal mobili-zation was strong, particularly out West. As he was making his way into the legislative assembly in Edmonton, premier Peter Lougheed was taken to task by four thousand aboriginal demonstrators. He ended up supporting them and writing the clause specifying that their existent rights be protected.[7] On their end, Jean Chrétien and Ed Broadbent pushed Trudeau to include such a disposition in the agreement. They saw it as an important step in making Westminster's approval easier to obtain.[8]

In the end, the First Nations would obtain a clause, but one they per-ceived as incomplete. Feminist groups, meanwhile, were entirely satisfied, contrary to other groups lobbying over the charter. Helped by Senator Eugene Forsey, some groups were pushing for the abolition — pure and simple — of the notwithstanding clause.[9] Others were demanding the inclusion of rights for the unborn in the charter. After all, the charter didn't only open the doors for a plethora of left-wing groups; it did the same for pro-lifers, Christian fundamentalists, and other right-wing associations. No less enlightened than their left-wing counterparts, these groups also considered that their political objectives were akin to fundamental human rights, rights that should be imposed on society as a whole through the intermediary of the courts.

Despite this agitation, the constitutional resolution was finally adopted in the House of Commons on December 2, 1981. Only seventeen Conservatives, five Liberals, and two New Democrats voted against it. Six days later, the Senate followed suit. Trudeau hoped the process would be as smooth in London. After all, he'd made compromises, and, as he himself said, "Between the British parliamentarians holding their noses and me holding mine, I chose the latter."[10]

FINALLY, IN LONDON

The day following the vote in Commons, the prime minister spoke with Lord Moran to prepare for the upcoming days and weeks. The conversation was also a prelude to a phone call with Margaret Thatcher, which was to occur later that day.[11] The prime minister opened the conversation by expressing, once again, his "enormous gratitude" for the support he had received from Thatcher. "Her statement in Melbourne," he said, "which was so forthright, was a key factor in maintaining the federal government's bargaining tactics. The provinces knew they had some of the British MPs on the run and it mattered a great deal that they saw they did not have the British government on the run. Another British prime minister might have done the same as Mrs. Thatcher, but might have been also much more cautious. It had meant a good deal to count on her support."

Trudeau then discussed the schedule for the next steps. One question preoccupied him: the British government intended to vote on the constitutional question around the middle of February, but Trudeau would have liked the whole business to be done by Christmas. Moran explained that the first reading and the introduction of the project in the House would occur before the holidays, but that it was impossible for all these legislative steps to be concluded in such a short period of time. The High Commissioner specified that any sort of pressure, especially a public declaration, wouldn't help Ottawa's cause.

Trudeau didn't stop there. "This would have the advantage of completing the process before the Indians and Quebec become organized, because this would open up the possibility of further mischief." The head of the federal government was notably worried about the judicial action that Quebec had just begun, hoping to have the courts recognize its veto right.

Moran attempted to reassure Trudeau. Quebec's actions before Canadian courts would have no effect at this stage. As for Kershaw's committee, which Trudeau was equally worried about, it would no longer cause any problems, now that the motion had the support of nine provinces. The prime minister then asked whether unanimous consent by the provinces might equal patriation before Christmas. Moran avoided answering the question directly, but ensured that the final decision in Westminster was now a forgone conclusion. Would February 15, the anniversary of the Canadian flag, be a more realistic objective? Trudeau asked. The High Commissioner replied in the negative.

At this point, Michael Kirby intervened: "Would British parliamentarians be more likely to respond to a deadline if they knew the Palace was planning it?" Moran's answer was clear cut: "The Palace cannot be put in that position, it is not acceptable." In that case, Trudeau added, "we may have to proceed without the Queen. If we cannot make plans, we should just proclaim the day after."

"You should be clear," Moran replied. "If the Canadian government wants the Queen, this is entirely your matter. There will be no difficulty about discussing timing with the palace and the British government."

The High Commissioner continued by asking what the prime minister thought the course of action with Quebec should be. Trudeau answered that Lévesque had been lying from the start. He should never have signed anything, and now reality had caught up with him, especially on the economic front. No less than three hundred thousand people were leaving Quebec a year, he claimed, ten times more than before the PQ came to power. "They have probably concluded that the economic decline in Quebec is irreversible and they will not change any of their policies, like the language law, which are its cause. Thus they will make things worse hoping to drive their opponents out of the province and build on a base of resentment. This is why I am keen to fight Lévesque now, on my ground, on patriation and giving rights to French Canadians."

Moran was struck by this last comment and by his attitude over the past few days. The night before, the prime minister had barely participated in the final debate on the adoption of the constitutional resolution, letting Jean Chrétien speak in his stead. He'd even left the House without answering any questions.

This suggests to me that despite the general praise for his achievement, Mr. Trudeau is not happy with the outcome. At luncheon today he was the reverse of jubilant. All his life he dreamed of a framework of national unity coast to coast in which Quebec rest content but now flags in the province are flying half-mast. All the Quebeckers that I have met are sad that things have turned out in the way they have and Mr. Trudeau is of course a Quebecker. He put all the blame on Lévesque, not unreasonably, and made it clear that he is about to embark on major battle with Lévesque for the soul of Quebec, a battle he believes he can win.[12]

Sad or not, Trudeau called Thatcher to inform her of the incoming constitutional reform, slated to arrive in Great Britain on December 9. After warm thanks, the prime minister once again spoke about getting it passed before Christmas.[13] The parliamentary agenda was full before the holidays, the Iron Lady replied. Trudeau answered that he would trust her judgment, but feared potential actions by Quebec and the First Nations. "I am aware of that but I will not rush it. To apply pressure and to deny those interested in the bill a proper opportunity to express their views would simply create trouble. After all, it had taken the Canadian Government much longer than originally expected." The prime minister also reassured Trudeau as to Quebec's judicial action: it would have no impact.

Trudeau then moved on the mid-February date and the Queen's visit. Thatcher replied that it would all depend on the parliamentary process. "I hope that I am wrong but there could be difficulties about meeting such a deadline and getting it through before a possible visit of Queen in February. This would be cutting it fine." Sure, but Canadians might be irritated, Trudeau said. "I doubt such irritation would be justified," Thatcher replied. "After all, at an earlier stage we had been expecting to receive the Canadian request nearly a year ago."

Meanwhile, Trudeau continued his cutting exchanges with Lévesque, letter after letter, public declaration after public declaration. Following the advice of his minister, Jacques-Yvan Morin, Quebec's premier had announced to his federal counterpart that he intended to exercise his veto right by decree. At first the gesture was purely political, and Trudeau answered that the government of Quebec had given up its veto right in April 1981. By acting in this way, Lévesque found a powerful pretext to ask the court's opinion on the existence of a Quebec veto right, a process that would come to a close a year after at the Supreme Court. In an entirely foreseeable decision, Laskin and his colleagues affirmed that Quebec never had such a prerogative.

A BROKEN MAN

The veto by decree raised Jean Chrétien's ire. "Lévesque can pass a decree saying that there will be no snow over Quebec this winter. It will have the same effect."[14] The decree would pass on November 25 and be sent to London six days later. The province continued its battle in Great Britain, with its remaining allies, the First Nations coalitions. The events of the month of November had devastated Gilles Loiselle, who still attempted, with mixed results, to continue his work. But he'd lost faith. According to Jean Wadds, who had met him on November 6, the man was broken. The Canadian diplomat reported seeing Loiselle to Vivien Hughes. "He had always been most urbane and friendly, no matter what the state of negotiations. But I met him on Friday and he could hardly bring himself to utter a mono-syllable. Several of the other agents received the same response."[15]

Among the other agents general, satisfaction with the results was hardly an option. James McKibben was one of those less than satisfied, as he described in a letter sent to Jacques Frémont, Quebec's adviser on constitutional matters, who had just resigned from his post. After having underlined the extent to which he'd appreciated working with Quebec's delegation, he explained that his "pleasure at reaching federal-provincial agreement is tempered by the exclusion of Quebec, and my worry for our future."[16] Alberta's agent general also attempted to comfort Loiselle when he met him after the November 5 agreement. His state of mind reflected the general atmosphere in the British capital, as his adviser, Chris Watts, explained in a cable sent to Edmonton:

> Reaction in London to patriation agreement has been mixed. On one hand there is relief by government and politicians active in our cause that they will not be faced by difficult situation resolution would have placed them.

On the other hand consciousness exists that Quebec and native peoples ("2 of the 3 founding races" are excluded from agreement). Feeling exists that the first exclusion may have serious long-term implications for Canada (i.e. separation of Quebec much more likely). An official from the Labour Party, David Lowe, told him there is a sense of uneasiness on both sides and inquired if Alberta would pressure federal government to change this situation.[17]

The unease was genuine, and the aboriginals, or at least some among them, were determined to exploit this feeling by intensifying their lobbying in the British capital. This agitation didn't worry Jean Wadds. As she wrote in a note to Ottawa: "There is sympathy for natives and for Quebec, but this will most likely translate into expression of concerns rather than an attempt to block passage."[18]

"Aboriginals were quite divided," Labour MP Bruce George explained, he who was their champion in London. "Some among them were demanding for control over reservations, others, total independence. In the end, their coalition failed."[19]

If the aboriginal lobby seemed impotent, it was causing trouble nonetheless. In early December, Wadds was forced to attend a traditional ceremony in which some forty representatives of Alberta nations were participating, a sort of pow-wow for the press. They began with a long indictment accusing Ottawa of having lied and sold their rights to the "greedy provinces." The First Nations were asking the Queen to intervene. This demand was followed by five interminable incantations, prayers recited by chiefs and elders, according to Jean Wadds. After two and a half hours of this spectacle, Wadds had other fish to fry, and left the meeting without smoking the ceremonial peace pipe. Aboriginals, angered, accused her of lacking respect.[20]

THATCHER SUSPENDS THE DEBATE

Despite this mobilization, the British government introduced the constitutional resolution in the House on December 22. The same day, however, the Court of Appeal of England and Wales decided to hear the aboriginal case in early February. "This isn't the sort of thing that we ought to rush through,'" the chief justice, Lord Denning, declared, adding that "obviously it's of very grave importance to the Indians."[21] The First Nations would be able to contest the interpretation that the British government made of its obligations toward them.

In London, as in Ottawa, this development was like a thunderclap. Pym, worried, sounded out Conservative MPs. He then had an important meeting with Denis Healey, Labour's parliamentary leader. The latter warned him: "I may not be able to deliver my backbenchers on this. They will use the pending court decision as a means of delaying the bill for essentially domestic reasons. The merits of the case are not at issue but it would be imprudent to continue."[22]

That same night, Pym attended a meeting with Lord Privy Seal Humphrey Atkins and Chief Whip Michael Jopling. The latter was particularly preoccupied by the situation on the other side of the aisle, which greatly increased the risk of derailing the government's parliamentary program. The three men came to the same conclusion: these new developments had to be ground to a halt as quickly as possible. Once informed, the prime minister immediately saw the wisdom of this conclusion.[23] Thatcher and Francis Pym saw eye-to-eye: delaying the patriation process unduly would open a Pandora's Box. However, they were betting on a quick and favourable decision by the courts, which would allow them to return to the debate in a more serene context. If other judicial actions were brought before the tribunals, the government could claim to have already waited once, and that it was now time to move forward.

This new development created chaos in Ottawa, almost panic, especially since the federal government learned about it through the newspapers. The feds set out to exercise maximum pressure; there was a real fear that any new delays would derail patriation completely. Jean Wadds and Reeves Haggan received the less than enviable task of once again meeting with Francis Pym in early January.[24]

Haggan began by underlining the importance of March 15 as a new deadline — before the Quebec Court of Appeal began considering the Government of Quebec's claim to the existence of a veto right for the provinces. Pym ignored the comment. With the attitude of a Zen master, he counselled them on patience and fair play. "We wouldn't be any more advanced if there were problems before Westminster instead of the courts," he said. The Briton also explained that the process had to be suspended "because to have proceeded would have excited controversy and ensured the opposition would have used the issue to delay [the] legislature program. Confrontation at this stage could have been an expensive decision." He also added that he hoped, as did everybody, to see patriation signed, sealed, and delivered as quickly as possible.

In that case, the Canadians replied, it was essential to move quickly once the appellate court had come to a decision. Pym shook his head again. He sought to keep his room to manoeuvre intact and analyze the decision once it came down the pike. "If the verdict is split, or if the decision is such that there is a good deal in it to comfort the Indians, we will want to wait for second reading until after the case is heard by the House of Lords."

This would inevitably prolong the process by at least another two weeks. Wadds and Haggan took that like a slap in the face. What's more, the parliamentary leader refused to promise that he wouldn't also wait for the results of the procedures at Chancery Division by the West Coast Natives. The only good piece of news was that Pym consented to consult with the federal government; they would no longer be reduced to learning about developments in the press.

As Michael Kirby explained to Prime Minister Trudeau at the end of this conversation, "the meeting was not very satisfactory. It is clear that Pym intends to proceed at his own pace and when it suits him. He appears to have no sense of urgency."[25] There was only one thing left to do for Trudeau: go over everyone's head straight to the Iron Lady. "I realize this is elevating the disagreement with the U.K. government to the prime ministerial level very quickly. But I think it is essential that we do so if we are to avoid being caught in an ongoing series of delays which could stretch well past March 15th."

On January 13, Trudeau wrote a letter:

> My concern is that the decision to delay the start of second reading after the Court of Appeal rules on the Alberta Indian case provides a basis for demands for further delays in second reading. Opportunities before the courts abound: the Alberta case may be appealed to the Lords; as you know, British Columbia Indians have started proceedings in the Chancery Division; we anticipate that action of some kind

will be initiated by Saskatchewan Indians; other Indian groups, including the Cree in Northern Quebec, may also institute proceedings. Indeed, there is no technical limit to the number of cases that could be brought in both Canada and the United Kingdom …

In Canada, the government of Quebec will bring a reference to the Quebec Appeal Court on March 15th seeking a ruling on Quebec's claim to have a constitutional veto, a subject on which I understand Mr. Lévesque has written to you. This case will surely be appealed to the Supreme Court of Canada with proceedings likely to drag on into the fall of this year.

These proceedings, regardless of their outcome, will, unless the issue is settled expeditiously at Westminster, prolong and intensify the political problems in Quebec and throughout Canada. On the other hand, if royal assent could be given to the Canada bill before the Quebec Court proceedings commence on March 15th, it is virtually certain that the Quebec Court would find the issue hypothetical and therefore not one requiring a ruling on their part.[26]

The answer arrived twelve days later. Thatcher explained that she understood the situation quite well. "However, the Indian cause has attracted some support at Westminster and I have no doubt that, had we proceeded with second reading before the courts had considered the Alberta case, we would have aroused substantial opposition to the bill. We expect to know the decision of the Court of Appeal in the very near future and in the light of that we shall be considering urgently how best to proceed in parliament."

WHAT SORT OF ANSWER FOR LÉVESQUE?

As such, Thatcher promised nothing to Trudeau. But the latter could console himself; he was treated much better than René Lévesque. A few days before Christmas, Quebec's premier had also written to Thatcher:

In our estimation this agreement goes entirely against the alliance of Francophones and Anglophones that made the creation of the Canadian Confederation possible in 1867. Never before, in our history, had the British Parliament been asked to restrict, without their consent, the right and powers of the legislature of the government of Quebec. This constitutional change is an offensive — without precedent — against the powers allowing the only French-speaking society in North America to defend and promote its language and culture.[27]

At first, Thatcher wanted to reply rapidly, before December 25. But complications arose with the federal government. The latter wanted the British government to ignore Lévesque's missive and, like simple postmen, return it to Ottawa. They'd even prepared a draft letter that the British prime minister might use:

I have received your letter of December 19. The position of HMG in the U.K. in this matter is to be found in the observations by the Secretary of State for FCO upon the report of the Foreign Affairs Committee, dated December 1981 of which I note you have a copy. As you are aware in all matters concerning Canada the Queen is advised solely by the government and parliament of Canada. Accordingly, I have referred your letter to the Canadian authorities with a copy of this reply.

The draft letter was accompanied by note explaining to the British the reason behind this strategy.

A) Acknowledgement of letter. Simple statement that we have taken note of Quebec's position. Draft avoids any mention of government of Quebec and/or any phraseology which indicates that reply is a personalized one from Mrs. Thatcher.

B) It is for Canadian government to decide what is acceptable in Canada with regard to Canadian constitution.
HMG position is to act as expeditiously as possible on
request of Canadian parliament.

C) Copies of this reply and original correspondence have
been provided to Canadian authorities.[28]

From Ottawa, Lord Moran got wind of this draft letter. He immediately
reacted. If the press learned that External Affairs Canada had written Thatcher's
letter to René Lévesque, he said, it would create a scandal. Such a situation
would be seen as an insult to all French Canadians.[29] Carrington reassured
him: the federal government's draft letter had been ignored. However, the
Foreign Office was consulting with the federal government about its own draft
reply, and the text of the British letter would end up being rather similar to the
original Canadian document. Carrington's instructions were straightforward:
"The reply should be fairly uncompromising, leaving Mr. Lévesque no grounds
for hope that he will be able to hold up the process here and in no doubt
that his problems are an internal Canadian matter."[30] As Deputy Minister
De Montigny Marchand reported to Mark MacGuigan, "The Foreign Office
is reasonably confident that this advice will be followed." When Lévesque's
letter was transferred to the Canadians, the deputy minister added, Michael
Kirby's office would prepare a second answer, the definitive one, by Trudeau.[31]

But this scenario would never come to pass. On December 24, Thatcher
refused the draft letter submitted to her by her staff.[32] First, she wanted to
avoid any potential recriminations from Lévesque. He could accuse her of
suspending the parliamentary debate due to the judicial process begun by
the First Nations coalition, while simultaneously refusing to do the same for
Quebec's own judicial process before its Court of Appeal. The letter needed
to provide an argument to justify this differential treatment.

The Iron Lady also found that the message to Quebec's premier lacked
tact. She seemed to believe that it was disgraceful to kick a man while he was
down. The Foreign Office's diplomats were asked to return to their desks.
A few days later they gave her "a somewhat more sympathetic draft."[33] This
version would be handed to Lévesque on January 14 by Murray Simons,
who added that Lévesque could make it public if he so desired.

My dear Prime Minister,

Thank you for your letter of 19 December in which you
asked that the British government should take no action
on the federal resolution until Quebec had consented to
it or until the opinion of the Canadian Courts was known
on the question of Quebec's right of veto.

I have studied your request carefully. I was sorry to
learn that the province of Quebec was unable to agree
with the federal government and the governments of
the other nine provinces of Canada on 5 November. A
joint address from both Houses of the federal parliament
has now been submitted to Her Majesty. In accordance
with established procedure the British government are
now asking parliament here to pass a bill which will give
legal effect to the address from the Canadian Parliament.
Given the terms of the judgment of the Supreme Court
of Canada on 28 September 1981 and the fact that an
address has been submitted to Her Majesty I am satisfied
that the existence of further legal proceedings in Canada
of the kind to which you refer is entirely a Canadian
matter. I therefore do not think that it would be appropriate to suspend action on the Canada bill in the way
that your letter requests.[34]

A few years later, Claude Morin would complain of the "polite response"
served to his boss. "*The Canadian Way* was also being practiced in Great
Britain,"[35] he would write with resentment, unaware that without the intervention by the British prime minister, Trudeau would have committed a real
affront to Lévesque.

The Quebec premier, from that point forward, became an impotent
witness to the end of the patriation process. Gilles Loiselle sent a memorandum to both houses of Parliament, attempting to activate his contacts,
but to no avail. The First Nations action didn't manage any resounding
success. Four leaders, including Chief Charlie Girek, dressed in traditional
garb, managed to obtain an audience with the Pope thanks to the help of

London's *pro nuncio*, but that fizzled out as well. On January 28, England's Court of Appeal decided in favour of the federal government — only it had authority over aboriginal issues.

The last obstacle was the fact that the constitutional law of 1982 was bilingual, which meant that the Parliament of Westminster needed to also adopt it in French. A handful of MPs were riled up by this possibility. The last time such a thing had happened was in 1454, when the Norman Conquest's effects were still being felt by the English aristocracy. By now, this was water — oceans, even! — under the bridge. In the end, however, in an irony of history, the French version would be transformed into an annex of the English version. The adoption of the constitutional motion in the language of Molière would not take place.

On February 17, the debate on the constitutional project could begin again: Jean Chrétien was sent to Westminster to witness the proceedings. The resolution was sent to the parliamentary commission the next day with forty-four draft amendments, touching on a number of topics from the rights of the fetus to aboriginal rights. Every single amendment was rejected, save a few technical modifications. The constitutional law was finally adopted in the House of Commons on March 9, 177 votes to 33.

On March 25, the House of Lords adopted it in turn, unanimously. The only false note of the day was a Canadian who was viewing the proceedings from the visitors' gallery, and who began hollering and had to be escorted from the premises. The constitution was patriated.

THE BATTLE OF CANADA

As Lord Moran noted in November 1981:

> Trudeau achieved agreement with the other provinces
> only by giving up a great deal that he considered import-
> ant. He has not managed to increase the powers of the
> federal government at the expense of the provinces.
> On the contrary, people like Lougheed of Alberta have
> achieved all their objectives and maintained provincial
> powers substantially intact. Mr. Trudeau clearly thought
> it best to get the constitution back even on relatively
> unsatisfactory terms but he shows no signs of being very
> happy about it, and there are manifest difficulties in the
> present package.[1]

While the prime minister managed to impose his dearly held linguistic
rights despite Quebec's opposition, we can still assert that his centralizing vision of a Canada under the influence of his all-powerful charter was
somewhat diminished over the course of the eighteen decisive months that
marked the Battle of London.

This situation was reflected in the final result, which Pierre Trudeau would bitterly regret.[2] Ultimately, the winner would be the seven anglophone provinces that had stood in opposition to Ottawa. Thanks to the notwithstanding clause, they managed to hold onto a large portion of their prerogatives that might go against the letter of the charter or the authority of federal judges. It was the keystone of the November 1981 compromise: without it, the Charter would have never seen the light of day. This disposition not only embodies the principle of parliamentary sovereignty, but also that of a Canada founded on a community of communities, since it protects the provinces from decisions made by judges named by Ottawa. If the anglophone provinces emerged victors from the Battle of London, they were the great losers of the Battle of Canada.

This new contest was a result of the fact that "Trudeau made an effort to create, *a posteriori*, a mythology surrounding the Charter of Rights and Freedoms,"[3] according to André Burelle, and the notwithstanding clause was at the centre of this effort. The ink on the final agreement wasn't yet dry, and already every lawyer in Canada was rushing to attack the cursed disposition. Law students were circulating petitions demanding its abrogation, supported by the Canadian Bar Association.[4] The offensive was also supported by universities, notably by law faculties, which took a resolutely post-modern turn by sacralizing the Charter while damning Section 33. As Morton and Knopff observed, "The distinction between education and political action is dissolved completely in the charter litigation project of some law schools."[5]

In 1986, this dynamic certainly influenced the way events were perceived when, for the first time — and the only time to date, up to this point — the notwithstanding clause was used in English Canada, by Saskatchewan. The province's Conservative government imposed a special law to put an end to a strike of its twelve thousand civil servants. According to the constitutional law of 1982, the premier, Grant Devine, used Section 33 to prevent the courts from invalidating his new piece of legislation.

This decision was immediately followed by a deluge of criticism, notably a virulent attack by the *Globe and Mail*. In an editorial titled "Freedom on Hold," the prestigious daily claimed that this action constituted "a disturbing precedent for the casual suspension of guarantees of fundamental liberties." Saskatchewan was "treat[ing] the charter without respect,"[6] the newspaper concluded, a denunciation which didn't stop voters from giving a strong electoral majority to Grant Devine nine months later.

Meanwhile, Robert Bourassa's Liberals came to power in Quebec. In Ottawa, the Liberals were replaced by Mulroney's Conservatives. This situation led, in 1987, to the signing of the Meech Lake Accord, an agreement between the ten provinces and the federal government that was supposed to allow Quebec to officially adhere to the constitutional law of 1982. Among other things, the agreement contained a clause recognizing Quebec as a distinct society due to it having a francophone majority. This disposition was to also be used to interpret the constitution. Meech immediately raised controversy, fed in great part by Pierre Elliott Trudeau. The distinct society clause weakened the Charter, resuscitated dualism, and threatened the unity of the country, Trudeau asserted.

The former prime minister wasn't the only malcontent. The Supreme Court seethed just as much. As during the Battle of London, the judges threw themselves into the political debate to shoot down Brian Mulroney's efforts. While it is impossible to prove this hypothesis based on written documentation, contrary to the evidence we uncovered about the role of the Supreme Court in 1980–81, this interpretation is supported by convincing circumstantial evidence.

Let's start at the beginning. The magistrates were angered by the Meech Lake Accord because the provinces had finally obtained a right of review of Supreme Court nominations, which indisposed the judges to the highest degree. We have seen how Bora Laskin opposed this principle. In April 1988, Willard Estey followed suit. Contrary to what he had done seven years before, the judge didn't stop solely at behind-the-scenes manoeuvres. He issued a public warning, taking advantage of the fact that he was retiring from the bench. The involvement of provinces in judge selection would lead to terrible consequences for Canada, he claimed. "You could ruin confederation, there is no question about it. My instinct is that the accord is decentralizing, and should therefore be viewed by Canadian citizens with some suspicion."[7]

Everything points to the impression that this was the dominant opinion within the Supreme Court. Fortunately for the magistrates, a new challenge against Bill 101 would allow them to greatly influence the course of events. Anglophones were contesting the legal disposition that forced unilingual displays in Quebec. The Ford affair made its way to the Supreme Court, which decided the case in December 1988. Unsurprisingly, the five judges, all named by Trudeau, decreed that Bill 101 was contrary to freedom of expression as guaranteed by the Charter.

However, a very curious aspect of this case, and one that wasn't much noticed at the time, was how the court also annulled the limits to the use of the notwithstanding clause imposed in a separate judgment by the Quebec Court of Appeal, *Alliance des professeurs catholiques de Montréal.* The five judges of the Supreme Court declared that, contrary to what the lower court said, the invocation of this disposition was not subject to judicial limits. In other words, its use depends solely on the discretion of elected officials, and no court could impose any limits other than the ones specifically described in the constitution.

The Government of Quebec was waiting for the judicial opinion on Bill 101 before calling on the Supreme Court in this other case. However, the court jumped the gun on this second case in the *Ford* judgment by, to a certain extent, linking two separate decisions.[8]

How can we explain such a course of action? Realistically, the judges were attempting to rouse hostility toward the Meech Lake Accord. We should understand that even if there is no mention of the notwithstanding clause in the accord, it would quickly become the subject of debate. Trudeau accused Mulroney of having obtained nothing at all from the provinces in exchange for the great decentralization included in the accord. Among other things, the Conservative prime minister could have ensured that the notwithstanding clause be removed from the constitution entirely.[9] Mulroney replied that he was a saviour of rights and freedoms. By getting Quebec to join the constitution, he said, he greatly reinforced the legitimacy of the Charter. The francophone province would then be less likely to call upon the notwithstanding clause in the future.

How does all this connect with the decision handed down in *Ford*? The judges knew they would raise a clamour of indignation from Quebec nationalists when they invalidated Bill 101. They were thus simultaneously offering an exit strategy to the Bourassa government: the notwithstanding clause. Indeed, the court had validated its unlimited use. This solution had a price, however. Supporters of the Charter would undoubtedly lead a smear campaign against those using the notwithstanding clause, even if all Quebec was doing was simply using a disposition obtained by the anglophone provinces in the context of a constitutional agreement that was forced on it.

There is no doubt, moreover, that the magistrates were preoccupied to the highest degree by the constitutional negotiations, to the extent that they were ready once again to violate the principle of the separation of powers. In the midst of the Charlottetown Accord negotiations, one of the Supreme Court justices bumped into James Ross Hurley, a high-ranking civil servant on the Privy Council working closely with the dossier, at the Byward Market in Ottawa. The magistrate interrogated Hurley insistently. *Is it true that you will include this clause in the agreement? What about that one?* The civil servant, uncomfortable, dug in his heels and refused to answer the judge's questions. The judge then stated that he'd get the information from someone else. "Do you realize what you've just said?"[10] Hurley replied, astounded.

Before this seeming lack of misgivings, how can we not believe that the Supreme Court, in December 1988, undertook political manoeuvres to sabotage the Meech Lake Accord? No other explanation seems to better elucidate the strange coincidence of the two decisions made in the *Ford* judgment. If this was their intention, the magistrates got exactly what they wanted. The decision had just been handed down, and a huge outcry in Quebec forced Robert Bourassa to invoke the notwithstanding clause and pass Bill 178, which imposed unilingual displays in public places. This law created its own virulent reaction in English Canada, notably in Manitoba, where the accord would ultimately be terminated. As reprisal for Bill 178, Gary Filmon, the premier of that province, drove the first nail into the coffin by suspending debate on the adoption of the accord.

In the wake of the growing controversy, the Manitoba Women's Advisory Council publicly attacked the distinct society clause. The notwithstanding clause, the group claimed, would allow the Quebec government to force an increase in the francophone population by denying abortion rights or giving money to women who have large families.[11] Ontario feminists had the same sort of doubts. As Queen's Park was adopting the accord, some women chained themselves to the visitors' gallery to protest the fact that the right of women in Quebec was being sacrificed on the altar of Québécois nationalism.[12]

In this symphony of reprobation, Trudeau's thoughts on the use of Section 33 certainly remains one of the most striking. "All the malignancy of this clause came glaringly to light late in December 1988 when Bourassa invoked it to validate Bill 178 ... and bragged about having trampled one of the country's fundamental freedoms."[13] However, he himself used an entirely different tack in November 1981, promising to use the notwithstanding clause if the courts challenged the clauses surrounding the legality of abortion. "We reserve the right to say: notwithstanding this decision, notwithstanding the charter of rights as interpreted by this judge, the house legislates in such and such manner on the abortion issue."[14] However, at the time of the Meech Lake Accord, and after the Supreme Court had interpreted the Charter to make abortion more accessible, Section 33 became a satanic verse in the eyes of the former prime minister. He launched a political fatwa against those who used it, even if that meant denying what had been agreed on in the constitution.

This political manoeuvre worked better than he expected. With the failure of Meech Lake, and thanks to the Supreme Court, Trudeau won the Battle of Canada. In the end, he managed to impose, fully and completely, his vision of Canada.

THE BATTLE FOR TRUTH

I heard tell of the Battle of London for the first time in 1995, when I was employed at Quebec's Ministry of International Relations. One day at noon, as a group of us were walking toward a restaurant on the Grande Allée, my colleague Roger Langlois mentioned that he'd been working at Quebec House in London in 1980–82, explaining that the first version of Trudeau's project, supported by only two provinces, would have been rejected by the British Parliament if Ottawa had attempted to push its project through. This claim piqued my curiosity, since I'd been interested by the constitutional question for quite some time.

Ten years later, after a doctorate and two books on the theme of the triangular relationship between Paris, Quebec City, and Ottawa, I recalled that conversation and decided to tackle this decisive event in Canadian history. It took me a long time, almost eight years, and the research was sometimes frustrating, especially on the federal side of things. While the Canadian Department of Foreign Affairs agreed to unclassify almost all its documents, the Privy Council acted in an entirely different manner. After three years of effort, I was given documents so redacted they were unusable. Fortunately for the Canadian public concerned with knowing its own history, things went much better in Great Britain. The British documents, obtained following dozens of freedom of information requests, allowed me, among other concerned people, to reveal the Supreme Court's underhanded role in this affair. I discovered this aspect of the story at the end of the summer of 2010. I immediately understood I had explosive documents in my possession, and that it was absolutely crucial to keep the secret until the book's publication.

For two and a half years, I lived with Bora Laskin and Willard Estey's secrets. I anticipated there would be controversy when the book was finally published. I got it and then some. D-day would be April 8, 2013; the book would be launched at a press conference. That morning, as I was driving my youngest son to daycare, the radio announced Margaret Thatcher's passing. I had rubbed shoulders with the Iron Lady, albeit at a distance, during my consultation of the archives. I had read her biography and interviewed several of her ministers, colleagues, and MPs. I was in such a state of shock when I heard the news that I almost ran a red light. When I made it home, I realized I should keep away from my car that day. I am an admirer of the Iron Lady. Her death saddened me, even if I knew that this coincidence could only have a positive impact on my book.

This would be only one of the many events that would mark the book launch. The next day, the PQ government, through its minister Alexandre Cloutier, demanded that the Supreme Court settle the matter. Clearly surprised, the latter announced it would be conducting an internal investigation, something never before seen. I was surprised, encouraged, and overwhelmed by events. Interview requests from across the country were coming in. My work was being taken seriously.

The highest court would, however, soon disappoint. On Friday, April 26, in a two-sentence communiqué published in the late afternoon, it announced it had found nothing out of the ordinary and would terminate the investigation. The institution had not given a single detail regarding the documents it had examined, so it is impossible to judge the validity of its investigation. Far from settling the debate, this intervention only shrouded it in further confusion. As the Leader of the Opposition, Thomas Mulcair, noted, "What they seem to have said from [the Supreme Court's] cryptic, one-paragraph statement, is: 'We looked in our filing cabinet and we don't have them.' It's a clear indication that the Supreme Court had no intention of ever dealing with this issue seriously." [1]

Political reactions weren't limited to the Supreme Court's role. Far from it. In Quebec City, the PQ government hoped to discover the whole truth, and had the Opposition's support. A unanimous motion was soon adopted by the National Assembly demanding that the federal government publish the archives on the subject, following the Quebec Bar and former Premier Lucien Bouchard's lead.

In Ottawa, the Bloc Québécois and the NDP were echoing Quebec's message. Unfortunately, the Liberal Party didn't have the same attitude, and the government was even more at odds. The Conservatives were in no hurry to accelerate declassification. Their priority was the economy, and not "old quibbles." The National Assembly's motion was asking only to make public archives older than thirty years accessible; that work could have been easily and quickly accomplished by the government's archivists. How would that have harmed the economy?

Ottawa's refusal led the Government of Quebec to make freedom of information requests. In November 2013, new documents were made public, but the government censors had redacted an important amount of information. The federal government continues to prevent Canadians from learning about one of the most important episodes of our history.

We would have expected more from the Conservative Party, they who are always claiming they want to encourage knowledge of Canadian history among citizens. They spend $35 million to commemorate the War of 1812 according to *La Presse*, but it was impossible, despite several requests, to get this information from Heritage Canada despite numerous emails and phone calls?[2]

This armed conflict wasn't an old quibble for Stephen Harper, who has invited all Canadians "to share in our history and commemorate our proud and brave ancestors who fought and won against enormous odds."[3] After this important sum, in June 2013 the government announced the creation of a program aimed at promoting Canada's history for another $12 million. As these lines are written, a flurry of events has been organized or will be organized in order to commemorate various events in Canadian history. Among them, the twentieth anniversary of the Battle of Medak Pocket in 2013; the bicentennial of the birth of Sir George-Étienne Cartier and the seventy-fifth anniversary of the start of the Second World War in 2014; the bicentennial of the birth of Sir John A. Macdonald and the fiftieth anniversary of the Flag of Canada in 2015; the 175th anniversary of the election of Baldwin and

Lafontaine in 2016; and the 150th anniversary of the Fenian raids, the 125th anniversary of the Stanley Cup, the fiftieth anniversary of the Canada Games, and the centennial of the Battles of Vimy and Passchendaele, all in 2017.

It is legitimate for Ottawa to commemorate certain episodes of Canada's political and military history, aspects that are practically unknown in our schools and universities, where military history has been practically eradicated. From this perspective, however, it is unacceptable that the government censure the patriation archives under the pretext that it's an old quibble, or that the economy is the priority.

This attitude better fits the former Soviet Union, not Canada, and is a worrying tendency. It could lead to, for example, the government encouraging discussion over the Battle of Vimy, but not the conscription crisis. We could have access to documents about hockey and Canadian military victories. We'll be able to study John A. Macdonald and the creation of Confederation, but not archives concerning the violation of the constitutional rights of Franco-Manitobans during the nineteenth century, and those involved with the patriation of 1982, as the government is currently doing.

The situation in the United States is very different indeed. A few years ago, Bill Clinton, at the end of his presidency, decided to declassify some sixteen thousand documents about Washington's participation in the coup that overthrew democratically elected president Salvador Allende in Chile in 1973, in order to bring Augusto Pinochet to power. Despite this far-from-flattering past, American authorities did not try to deny the facts or censor historians.

And let's not forget that our country is the only one among Western democracies where there is no prescribed limit after which archives are automatically opened. Ours is also one of the worst countries in the world in terms of access to information — behind Angola, Niger, and Colombia, among others — according to Halifax's Centre for Law and Democracy, and Access Info, an organization based in Madrid.[4] Elsewhere, government archives are opened after twenty-five or thirty years, sometimes a bit more; here, documents can remained closed forever. This comment from some two dozen historians from every horizon who intervened in the debate says it all: "So that the public might have a more just idea of constitutional patriation, and Canadian history in general, so that historians might confirm, bring nuances to or deny Frédéric Bastien's claims, they would certainly need real access to documents."[5]

The more curious aspect of this affair was the Liberal Party's reaction. On one hand, the Liberals supported the 2013 program aimed at promoting history. Justin Trudeau had rare positive words for the Conservatives in this regard. "As a former teacher," he declared, "each time we get more resources to teach, it's a good thing. Especially when it's something as important as our history."[6] No one is against virtue, certainly, but when it comes time to act, as in the case of the patriation archives, Trudeau suddenly lost his affection for our history. "As for me, I'm not going to spend my time, my political capital, to reopen old wounds."[7]

Yet Justin Trudeau and Stephen Harper well know how important access to documentation is to the work of historians. The prime minister is well-positioned to speak on the topic, since he published a book about the history of hockey in 2014. He had access to all sorts of documents, but now hides behind civil servants to justify the fact that he is preventing other historians from doing their work. During the controversy surrounding the Battle of London, we shouldn't, he stated, politicize access to information nor should politicians intervene in the work of public administration in this matter.

This argument is a smokescreen. In our system, Parliament is sovereign. It voted in the Access to Information Act and remains free to modify it if it so desires. Civil servants follow the criteria established by politicians who have described these criteria through legislation. Modifying this law would be all it takes to allow them to act differently.

The Liberal Party of Canada, through Stéphane Dion, unfortunately sang the same tune as the government. The father of the Clarity Act claimed he wanted to let civil servants do their jobs, adding in the same breath that the issue of patriation should be left to historians, while his party was acting as an accomplice to a process whose objective was to prevent them from doing their work.

The former political scientist also decreed what was good and bad history by accusing the NDP of being irresponsible by asking for declassification of information. According to Dion, the act would sully the Supreme Court's reputation and the Charter of Rights itself. Apparently, there are taboo subjects of which historians should not speak, especially if it comes out that a fundamental principle of democracy — the separation of powers — was violated.

Besides the debate about access to archives, there were a number of comments about the content and logic of my book. While some were full of praise, others were quite critical, even defamatory. Peter Russell, the renowned political scientist, pointed out that Bora Laskin was Jewish, and that made my criticism of him anti-Semitic, of all things! If Bora Laskin had been black, Russell would have probably accused me of being racist, and if Laskin had been gay, Russell would have said that I was a homophobe.

Fortunately, most of my detractors stayed on the level of intellectual debate, instead of throwing around accusations that are as serious as they are unfounded. One of the *Globe*'s star columnists, Jeffrey Simpson, attempted to diminish my book's revelations. Based on his experience in London as correspondent at the time of patriation, he claimed that it was a non-event in the British capital. Patriation had set off nothing more than heartfelt yawns.

Like many others, Simpson attacked the credibility of my sources, notably John Ford. For many today, it seems that only a man in bad faith could have had reservations about Trudeau and his Charter project. Having known Ford himself, the columnist described him as being: "very full of himself ... possessed of a certainty that he, as Britain's high commissioner to Ottawa, had the responsibility to alert London to the perfidious plans of Mr. Trudeau. He not so cordially detested Mr. Trudeau, and the feeling was reciprocated without the cordiality."[8]

The former interim chief of the Liberal Party of Canada, Bob Rae, agreed. He, too, knew John Ford and claimed that he was "as opinionated as he was ill informed. It is Ford's accounts of alleged conversations with Laskin and Estey that form the basis of yet another argument that the judges were part of some nefarious federal plot."[9] Bob Rae added a comment about my book that, just like Jeffrey Simpson, he clearly hadn't read. "Bud Estey was one of the most brilliant legal minds of his day ... we remain a country deeply committed to both the rule of law and constitutional convention. Facile attempts to prove conspiracies, or to attack the integrity of two distinguished jurists who can't tell their side of conversations, hardly adds to our understanding."

These claims do not stand up to scrutiny. As we've seen, Lord Moran, Ford's successor, also became a fierce adversary of the leader of the federal government and his charter project. As for the actions of the judges of the Supreme Court, we were able to see that the facts were attested to in a number of different documents written by different people, not only Ford.

For many jurists, however, like Sébastien Grammond, dean of the civil law section at the University of Ottawa, and also Gil Rémillard, professor of constitutional law and intergovernmental affairs minister at the time of the Meech Lake Accord, the British documents raise a number of questions, as does the fact that the protagonists have passed away, just as Rae pointed out. As for the archives, they contain records of discussions between individuals that took place in a second-hand manner, and so represent hearsay. We should note that on three separate occasions, British diplomats summarized conversations that they had directly with Willard Estey and Bora Laskin. More importantly, claiming that facts are untrue because some of the sources are indirect or the individuals have died is tantamount to denying any relevance to history as a discipline. It would be like saying that nothing proved that Jesus Christ existed because no one today was a first-hand observer of his life and because all the sources that were kept of him, like the Gospel, for example, are all secondary documents. Jesus never wrote anything himself; neither did anyone who knew him. Those who did write never met him. Should we conclude that Christianity is based on hearsay?

This same argument was used, in another form, by law professor Philip Girard, Bora Laskin's biographer, who worked with Judge Estey in 1979–80. For Girard, who wrote no less than four articles on my book, the Foreign Office archives are no Watergate tapes. The absence of a verbatim transcript makes it difficult to really understand what people said and meant. According to this standard, the writing of history would be almost completely impossible because, 99.9 percent of the time, verbatim transcripts are not available.

Documents written by diplomats were also problematic because their content might be exaggerated. Diplomats want to make a good impression, and so tend to heighten revelatory content that, for example, a judge might make to them. They want to please their superiors, demonstrate their aptitude, get a promotion, et cetera. Consequently, we should be careful using information arising from diplomatic archives, at least according to some critics.

Besides the fact that this criticism is pure speculation and second-guessing, it is inadmissible for other reasons. Let's take John Ford and Lord Moran, two of those who gathered Estey and Laskin's words. These decorated veterans of the Second World War had nothing to prove. They owed nothing to anyone, and didn't hope for advancement. Their mission in Canada was the last of their careers, as they both took retirement after. Why would they have sought to exaggerate the confidences made to them?

The same thing goes for Lord Carrington and Robert Armstrong, both of whom also put pen to paper to report on the chief justice's words, the first to enlighten Moran in Ottawa, and the second to inform Michael Alexander, Margaret Thatcher's diplomatic adviser. Why would members of a government friendly to Canada and allied with Trudeau in his effort to patriate the constitution have exaggerated such comments?

Philip Girard seems ready to do anything to defend the man he wrote a biography about, and another man for whom he worked in the past, Willard Estey. He even claimed that if the latter was alive today, he could have sued me for libel. If the search for truth truly interests him, he should stop his swaggering and attempt to enlighten us about the jurists whom Etsey knew at the Department of Justice. We might then discover who the magistrate's source in the executive branch was.

Philip Girard, a man who defines himself as a law historian, would certainly be helpful if he joined his voice to others demanding that the federal government declassify the archives of the Privy Council and the Department of Justice. This comment also stands for those who have accused me of making a tempest in a teacup, of falling prey to conspiracy theories, paranoia, or to "draw historical conclusions from slight evidence," to use William Johnson's expression in the *National Post*.[10] If I've veered so off the mark, the opening of the federal archives should prove without a doubt that I've grossly exaggerated facts, twisted evidence, played with words, sinned by omission, et cetera. Girard, Johnson, Rae, Dion, and others should be first in line to push for openness and prove me wrong. Why has this facet of the debate been entirely omitted?

A last argument often brought against my book highlights the fact that these two judges were on the minority side of the decision. Whatever they said or did, this changes nothing. I predicted in the French version that this reasoning, completely speculative, would be used to discredit me. I said from the start that this explanation was erroneous. I add here only that this argument is without importance. The fact remains that Laskin and Estey should never have spoken to anyone. Their actions were serious in regards to Supreme Court jurisprudence itself. Simply following what the highest court ruled is not sufficient for judges to be impartial. Justice requires there to also be the appearance of impartiality. For this second condition to be attained, we must ask if a reasonable and well-informed observer could think that judicial independence was compromised. After considering the breadth of information revealed by the British archives about the Supreme Court in 1981, the answer is a clear yes. Whatever the number of judges actually implicated, the final decision, or the nature of the revelations made to policy-makers, the principle of judicial independence must be protected as a whole. One cannot respect it partially.

————

This version of the history of patriation remains incomplete. Not only due to federal government censorship, but also because I did not explore the archives of the numerous provinces. Despite the importance of this subject, an excellent record in terms of publications, a doctorate and the importance of my new research, I never obtained a research grant from SSHRC, despite five requests. I was systematically told that my project had a weak theoretical basis. Perhaps I should have proceeded in the manner of a sociologist or political scientist, creating a theoretical framework that would have provided the answer to my questions before I'd even opened my first box of archival material! For the historians at SSHRC, history is written by coming to a conclusion through following a theoretical framework. A conclusion always confirmed by the researcher, who, buoyed by his original bias, concentrates on the documents that support his theoretical premise, all the while ignoring materials that don't fit in with his framework.

In any case, we reproduced in the appendix a certain number of documents for the benefit of our readers. I invite people to examine the evidence and come to their own conclusion.

My project illustrates our national political history, and describes our country's leaders during momentous events. Unfortunately, this sort of history doesn't fit the themes that are currently in fashion, that is, the trilogy of *gender, race, and class*, subjects that currently receive hundreds of thousands of dollars each year.[11] And when SSHRC finances a project on national political history, it's for a predictably complacent biography of Pierre Trudeau.[12]

All of this slowed the completion of my project, and made it smaller in scope than I would have hoped. Only when I became a full-time professor at Dawson College, after several years spent in professional wilderness, was I able to seriously concentrate on my work. I am deeply grateful to my employer who helped me in this process. I am also grateful to the Canada

Council of the Arts that provided me with a writing grant during the years I worked on this project, as well as the Prêt d'honneur de la Société St-Jean Baptiste that helped finance my research trip to London in 2009.

I am also indebted to the many people who helped me with this project, and accompanied me in my personal life. Heartfelt thanks to my wife, Marie-Ève, my mother, Yvette, as well as my step-parents, Raymond and Louise. Thanks to my researchers, Samy Mesli and Howard Cohen, and law professor Pierre Thibault for his attentive proofreading, to André Braën, also a law professor, who shared his expertise with me for the English version, and to Robert Comeau for his encouragements. Thanks to my friend François-Philippe Champagne, who, in his absence, lent me his magnificent London apartment. Thanks to Chris Collins of the Margaret Thatcher Foundation, who gave me precious advice about my research in the British archives. I also want to thank all of the actors of the Battle of London still alive today who lent me their stories. I am also indebted to Philippe Burrin, my former thesis director, who taught me the profession of historian. Thanks also to Jack Granatstein for writing *Who Killed Canadian History?* Reading his work, which denounces the fate of political history in the academic world, gave me the courage to pursue my own work when doors were closing one by one. Finally, thank you to my friend Éric Bédard. Our exchanges about Clio enriched the formation of this story.

APPENDIX: DOCUMENTS

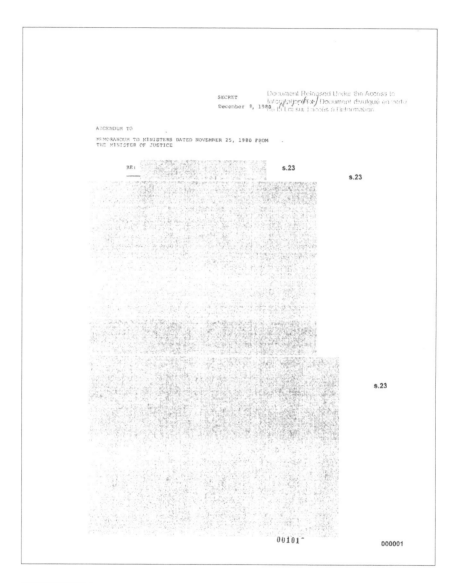

DOCUMENT 1:

After almost three years of unsuccessful attempts, I was able to get a pile of Privy Council documents on constitutional patriation. This is a representative example of what I was given.

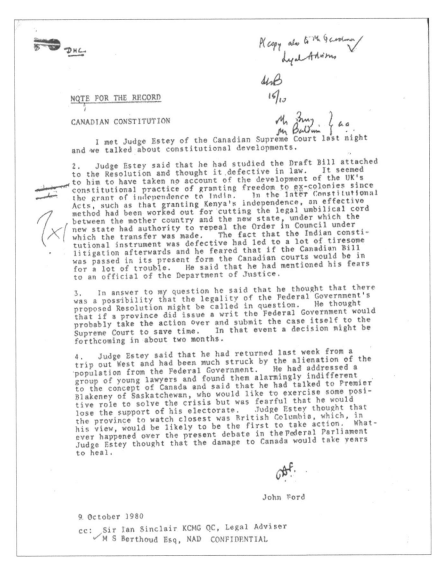

NOTE FOR THE RECORD

CANADIAN CONSTITUTION

I met Judge Estey of the Canadian Supreme Court last night and we talked about constitutional developments.

2.   Judge Estey said that he had studied the Draft Bill attached to the Resolution and thought it defective in law.   It seemed to him to have taken no account of the development of the UK's constitutional practice of granting freedom to ex-colonies since the grant of independence to India.   In the later Constitutional Acts, such as that granting Kenya's independence, an effective method had been worked out for cutting the legal umbilical cord between the mother country and the new state, under which the new state had authority to repeal the Order in Council under which the transfer was made.   The fact that the Indian constitutional instrument was defective had led to a lot of tiresome litigation afterwards and he feared that if the Canadian Bill was passed in its present form the Canadian courts would be in for a lot of trouble.   He said that he had mentioned his fears to an official of the Department of Justice.

3.   In answer to my question he said that he thought that there was a possibility that the legality of the Federal Government's proposed Resolution might be called in question.   He thought that if a province did issue a writ the Federal Government would probably take the action over and submit the case itself to the Supreme Court to save time.   In that event a decision might be forthcoming in about two months.

4.   Judge Estey said that he had returned last week from a trip out West and had been much struck by the alienation of the population from the Federal Government.   He had addressed a group of young lawyers and found them alarmingly indifferent to the concept of Canada and said that he had talked to Premier Blakeney of Saskatchewan, who would like to exercise some positive role to solve the crisis but was fearful that he would lose the support of his electorate.   Judge Estey thought that the province to watch closest was British Columbia, which, in his view, would be likely to be the first to take action.   Whatever happened over the present debate in the Federal Parliament Judge Estey thought that the damage to Canada would take years to heal.

John Ford

9 October 1980

cc: Sir Ian Sinclair KCMG QC, Legal Adviser
      M S Berthoud Esq, NAD CONFIDENTIAL

DOCUMENT 2:

This note, cited on page 233–34, was sent by British High Commissioner John Ford to the Foreign Office. It shows that Judge Willard Estey made a political intervention by giving his advice to the federal government on how to proceed with constitutional patriation. The extent to which Justice Estey was willing to share his political opinions with officials involved in the patriation process is also revealed here through his exchanges with the premier of Saskatchewan, Allan Blakeney, and John Ford.

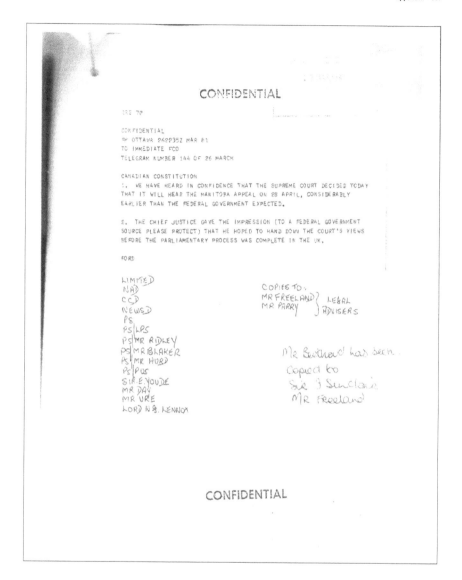

CONFIDENTIAL

CONFIDENTIAL
GY OTTAWA 2622352 MAR 81
TO IMMEDIATE FCO
TELEGRAM NUMBER 144 OF 26 MARCH

CANADIAN CONSTITUTION
1. WE HAVE HEARD IN CONFIDENCE THAT THE SUPREME COURT DECIDED TODAY THAT IT WILL HEAR THE MANITOBA APPEAL ON 28 APRIL, CONSIDERABLY EARLIER THAN THE FEDERAL GOVERNMENT EXPECTED.

2. THE CHIEF JUSTICE GAVE THE IMPRESSION (TO A FEDERAL GOVERNMENT SOURCE PLEASE PROTECT) THAT HE HOPED TO HAND DOWN THE COURT'S VIEWS BEFORE THE PARLIAMENTARY PROCESS WAS COMPLETE IN THE UK.

FORD

LIMITED
NAD
CCD
NEWSD
PS
PS/LPS
PS/MR RIDLEY
PS/MR BLAKER
PS/MR HURD
PS/PUS
SIR E YOUDE
MR DAY
MR URE
LORD N.G. LENNOX

COPIES TO:
MR FREELAND } LEGAL
MR PARRY } ADVISERS

Mr Bullard has seen.
Copied to
Sir J Sinclair
Mr Freeland

CONFIDENTIAL

DOCUMENT 3:

This document, cited on page 214, shows that Bora Laskin let it known to the federal government, and then to the British, that he was hoping to hand down the Supreme Court's judgment on patriation before Westminster would go into recess at the end of July. The British were pressing the Canadians to put patriation on hold until the court's view was known, which Ottawa refused out of fear that the process would be endless. Thanks to Laskin's information, the British were able to press Ottawa, saying the process was not going to be a long one.

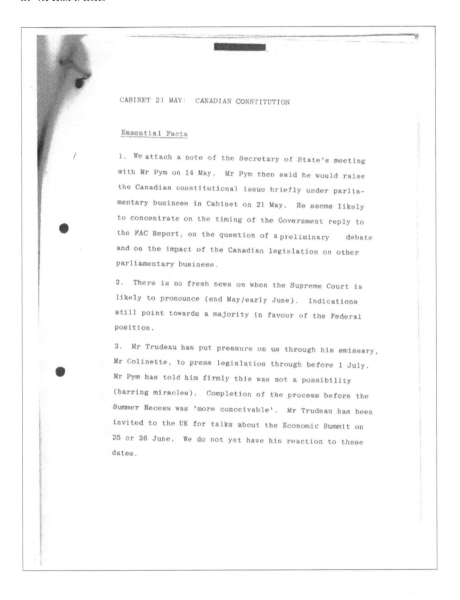

CABINET 21 MAY: CANADIAN CONSTITUTION

Essential Facts

1. We attach a note of the Secretary of State's meeting with Mr Pym on 14 May. Mr Pym then said he would raise the Canadian constitutional issue briefly under parliamentary business in Cabinet on 21 May. He seems likely to concentrate on the timing of the Government reply to the FAC Report, on the question of a preliminary debate and on the impact of the Canadian legislation on other parliamentary business.

2. There is no fresh news on when the Supreme Court is likely to pronounce (end May/early June). Indications still point towards a majority in favour of the Federal position.

3. Mr Trudeau has put pressure on us through his emissary, Mr Colinette, to press legislation through before 1 July. Mr Pym has told him firmly this was not a possibility (barring miracles). Completion of the process before the Summer Recess was 'more conceivable'. Mr Trudeau has been invited to the UK for talks about the Economic Summit on 25 or 26 June. We do not yet have his reaction to these dates.

DOCUMENT 4:

This document, not cited in the book, was used to brief the British Cabinet on the Canadian constitution. The second paragraph suggests that the British were hoping to get fresh news on the Supreme Court and when it was going to pronounce. Somehow the British had gotten indication that the judgment would be 6–3 in favour of Ottawa. See page 236.

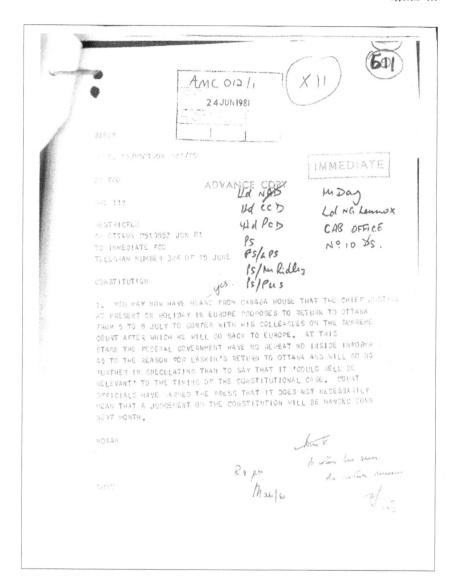

DOCUMENT 5:

This message, cited on page 236–37, from British High Commissioner Lord Moran was sent to FCO after it was learned that Chief Justice Bora Laskin was going back to Ottawa from London. It shows that the feds were hoping to get some inside information from the Supreme Court as to why the chief justice was cutting short his holiday in the U.K.

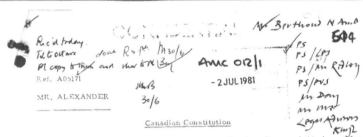

Ref. A05171

- 2 JUL 1981

MR. ALEXANDER

Canadian Constitution

I know that the Prime Minister and Mr. Trudeau discussed this issue before lunch, and that the Chief Whip and Mr. Pitfield discussed it over lunch; but I should nonetheless record the discussion which Mr. Pitfield and I had on the matter after lunch.

2.   Mr. Pitfield said that he had had a call from the Chief Justice of the Supreme Court to say that he was cutting short his holiday in this country and returning to Canada at the beginning of July to meet with his colleagues on the Supreme Court for two or three days.   The Chief Justice had said to Mr. Pitfield: "You know what that means", and had then rung off. Mr. Pitfield took it to mean that the Supreme Court could be expected to hand down its judgment on the Canadian Constitutional question about 7th July.

3.   Mr. Pitfield then represented to me the disadvantages which would accrue, to us as well as to the Canadian Government, if the matter hung around until the autumn without a decision at Westminster.   The Provincial Governments would use the interval for intense lobbying; referenda would be conducted in the Provinces; and the whole issue would become thoroughly muddied.   There would be great advantage in completing the process as quickly as possible, before the summer holiday.

4.   Mr. Pitfield said that the Canadian Parliament had had to extend its Session in order to deal with the estimates, which had been set back in some way.   Assuming - as he still did - that the Supreme Court's judgment was by a majority in favour of the Federal Government, the matter would come back to the Canadian Parliament as soon as the judgment was handed down, and could be taken through by, say, 10th or 11th July.   He thought that it would still be in the interests of us as well as of them that it should be taken through Parliament at Westminster before the Summer Recess.   He said that the Chief Whip had indicated to him at lunch that that could be very difficult indeed.

-1-

DOCUMENT 6:

This note written by Cabinet Secretary Robert Armstrong, cited on page 237, shows that Bora Laskin and Michael Pitfield, Clerk of the Privy Council, spoke on the phone. The conversation was brief. This suggests that Laskin knew what he was doing was wrong and thus did not want to take long. Despite the chief justice's cryptic message, Pitfield concluded that the court's decision would be handed down on July 7. The only sensible

CONFIDENTIAL

5.   I said that I thought that that was indeed the case. He could be assured that we were not less alive than they were to the advantages of dealing with the issue quickly, once the judgment was received.   Until today, however, we had been assuming that, since the Supreme Court had risen for its vacation without having handed down a judgment, we should not now see it until the autumn.   It was hoped that the House of Commons would rise for the Summer Recess before the Royal Wedding.   The programme had in any case been made more congested by the need to deal with the Representation of the People Bill which had just completed its progress through the House of Commons.   While it might in theory be possible for the House of Commons to sit again after the Royal Wedding, there would be great reluctance to do that; and, if the Canadian Bill was thought to be the reason for it, that would not provide a good climate in which to try to get the Bill through.   If the Canadian Bill was to be taken before 29th July, some other business would now have to be postponed until the "spillover" session in October. The alternative would be to take the Canadian Bill in the spillover; the House of Commons would not resume before 19th October, because of the Party Conferences in the earlier part of the month.   In these circumstances I did not know what the Parliamentary managers would think was the best thing to do, if the Supreme Court judgment was handed down early in July, and the Bill became available to Westminster about the middle of July.

6.   Mr. Pitfield and I agreed to keep in close touch.   I shall in fact be in Canada from 6th to 8th July for a meeting of Personal Representatives, and shall see Mr. Pitfield then.   He will let me know by telephone early, if there is anything new to report.

7.   I am sending copies of this minute to Mr. Fall, Mr. Heyhoe and Mr. MacLean.

ROBERT ARMSTRONG

26th June, 1981

-2-

DOCUMENT 6 (PAGE 2):

way he could come to such a precise conclusion was if he had had prior contact with the chief justice.

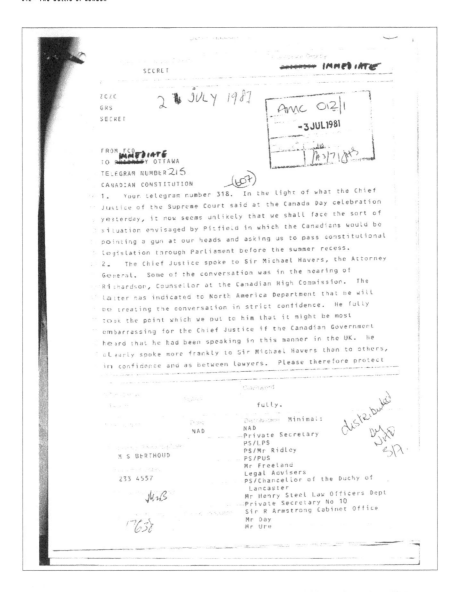

DOCUMENT 7:

This secret telegram from Lord Carrington, the foreign secretary, to Lord Moran, British High Commissioner, proves that Bora Laskin shared information with the British government and a Canadian diplomat. The extreme precautions taken to protect Laskin as a source shows how sensitive the whole affair was.

OUT TELEGRAM (CONT)

SECRET

2

<<<<
fully.

3.   The Chief Justice said there was a major disagreement among
the members of the Supreme Court. He was returning shortly to
Ottawa but clearly did not expect this would bring about the
immediate resolution of their difficulties. If no quick solution
was found, he did not expect judgement to appear until the end
of August. We needed to bear in mind that the judgement needed
to be carefully polished and produced in both languages. The
Attorney General commented that he could well see that a historic
verdict of this kind needed to be meticulously prepared and
polished.

4.   In view of the confidentiality of the Chief Justice's
conversation with the Attorney General, it would clearly be
wrong for you to reveal at this stage that we now have a clear
indication of further likely delay by the Supreme Court. You
will therefore want to respond to Pitfield's queries which were
put on the basis of a possible judgement in early July. On his
question whether there was any hope of early action here in the
event of a clear line from the Supreme Court, I see no need for
you to go beyond the language you have already used, quoting
the Prime Minister and Lord Privy Seal.

5.   On the Government reply to the FAC, you should say that
our position remains that this will not issue until the
Parliamentary proceedings in Canada are at an end and until we
know that the FAC themselves will not be producing a further
report. In this connection, you might ask Pitfield whether he
believes that Parliament is likely to reconvene early if the
Supreme Court judgement is given after the beginning of their
summer recess. (The Canadian High Commission here believe they
are at present likely to reconvene on 13 or 14 October).

CARRINGTON
NNNN

DOCUMENT 7 (PAGE 2)

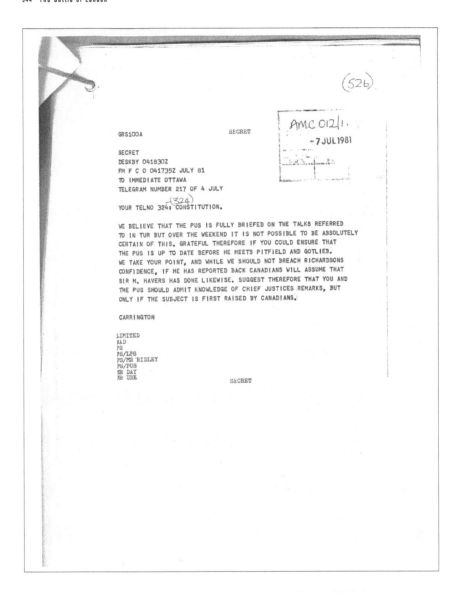

(52b)

```
GRS100A                    SECRET        AMC 012|1.
                                          - 7 JUL 1981
SECRET
DESKBY 041830Z
FM F C O 041735Z JULY 81
TO IMMEDIATE OTTAWA
TELEGRAM NUMBER 217 OF 4 JULY
                    (324)
YOUR TELNO 324: CONSTITUTION.

WE BELIEVE THAT THE PUS IS FULLY BRIEFED ON THE TALKS REFERRED
TO IN TUR BUT OVER THE WEEKEND IT IS NOT POSSIBLE TO BE ABSOLUTELY
CERTAIN OF THIS. GRATEFUL THEREFORE IF YOU COULD ENSURE THAT
THE PUS IS UP TO DATE BEFORE HE MEETS PITFIELD AND GOTLIEB.
WE TAKE YOUR POINT, AND WHILE WE SHOULD NOT BREACH RICHARDSONS
CONFIDENCE, IF HE HAS REPORTED BACK CANADIANS WILL ASSUME THAT
SIR M. HAVERS HAS DONE LIKEWISE. SUGGEST THEREFORE THAT YOU AND
THE PUS SHOULD ADMIT KNOWLEDGE OF CHIEF JUSTICES REMARKS, BUT
ONLY IF THE SUBJECT IS FIRST RAISED BY CANADIANS.

CARRINGTON

LIMITED
MAD
PS
PS/LPS
PS/MR RIDLEY
PS/PUS
MR DAY
MR URE                          SECRET
```

DOCUMENT 8:

This secret telegram, not cited in the book, was sent from Lord Carrington, the foreign secretary, to Lord Moran, British High Commissioner. The former orders the latter to fully brief the permanent undersecretary (deputy minister) at the Foreign Office about Bora Laskin. Again, all the precautions taken show how important Laskin's information was and that it was crucial that it should not become public.

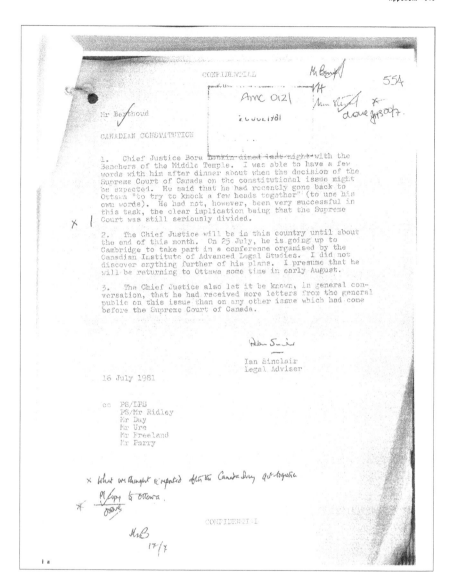

CONFIDENTIAL

AMC 012/

20 JUL 1981

Mr Berthoud

CANADIAN CONSTITUTION

1.   Chief Justice Bora Laskin dined last night with the Benchers of the Middle Temple. I was able to have a few words with him after dinner about when the decision of the Supreme Court of Canada on the constitutional issue might be expected. He said that he had recently gone back to Ottawa "to try to knock a few heads together" (to use his own words). He had not, however, been very successful in this task, the clear implication being that the Supreme Court was still seriously divided.

2.   The Chief Justice will be in this country until about the end of this month. On 25 July, he is going up to Cambridge to take part in a conference organised by the Canadian Institute of Advanced Legal Studies. I did not discover anything further of his plans. I presume that he will be returning to Ottawa some time in early August.

3.   The Chief Justice also let it be known, in general conversation, that he had received more letters from the general public on this issue than on any other issue which had come before the Supreme Court of Canada.

Ian Sinclair
Legal Adviser

16 July 1981

cc   PS/LPS
     PS/Mr Ridley
     Mr Day
     Mr Ure
     Mr Freeland
     Mr Parry

X What we thought expected after the Canada Day get-together
Pl copy to Ottawa.

CONFIDENTIAL

17/7

DOCUMENT 9:

This document, cited on page 240, written by Ian Sinclair, an official at the Foreign Office, shows that Laskin again shared information with the British government, informing them that the Supreme Court was still divided.

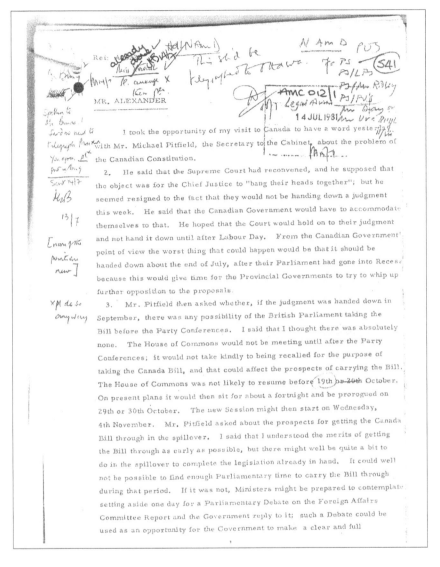

I took the opportunity of my visit to Canada to have a word yesterday with Mr. Michael Pitfield, the Secretary to the Cabinet, about the problem of the Canadian Constitution.

2. He said that the Supreme Court had reconvened, and he supposed that the object was for the Chief Justice to "bang their heads together"; but he seemed resigned to the fact that they would not be handing down a judgment this week. He said that the Canadian Government would have to accommodate themselves to that. He hoped that the Court would hold on to their judgment and not hand it down until after Labour Day. From the Canadian Government's point of view the worst thing that could happen would be that it should be handed down about the end of July, after their Parliament had gone into Recess because this would give time for the Provincial Governments to try to whip up further opposition to the proposals.

3. Mr. Pitfield then asked whether, if the judgment was handed down in September, there was any possibility of the British Parliament taking the Bill before the Party Conferences. I said that I thought there was absolutely none. The House of Commons would not be meeting until after the Party Conferences; it would not take kindly to being recalled for the purpose of taking the Canada Bill, and that could affect the prospects of carrying the Bill. The House of Commons was not likely to resume before 19th or 20th October. On present plans it would then sit for about a fortnight and be prorogued on 29th or 30th October. The new Session might then start on Wednesday, 4th November. Mr. Pitfield asked about the prospects for getting the Canada Bill through in the spillover. I said that I understood the merits of getting the Bill through as early as possible, but there might well be quite a bit to do in the spillover to complete the legislation already in hand. It could well not be possible to find enough Parliamentary time to carry the Bill through during that period. If it was not, Ministers might be prepared to contemplate setting aside one day for a Parliamentary Debate on the Foreign Affairs Committee Report and the Government reply to it; such a Debate could be used as an opportunity for the Government to make a clear and full

DOCUMENT 10:

This document, cited on page 241, written by Cabinet Secretary Robert Armstrong, shows that Michael Pitfield, while trying to guess what was going on at the Supreme Court, said the chief justice was trying to "bang their heads together." It bears a striking resemblance to an expression used by Bora Laskin when he spoke with Ian Sinclair, saying he had tried to "knock a few heads together" (see Document 9). This suggests that Bora Laskin spoke again with Michael Pitfield, using a similar expression he used with Sinclair.

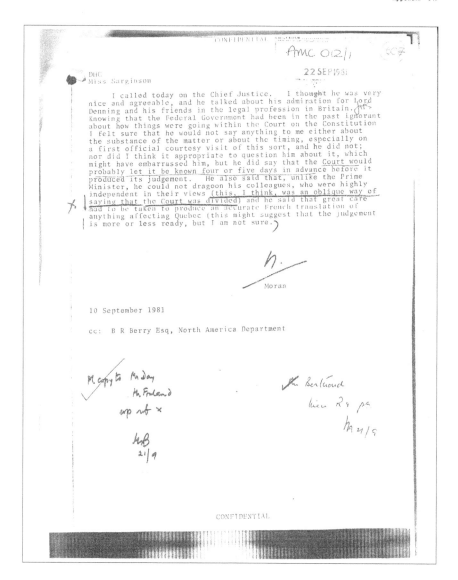

AMC 012/1

DHC
Miss Sarginson

22 SEP 1981

I called today on the Chief Justice. I thought he was very nice and agreeable, and he talked about his admiration for Lord Denning and his friends in the legal profession in Britain. Knowing that the Federal Government had been in the past ignorant about how things were going within the Court on the Constitution I felt sure that he would not say anything to me either about the substance of the matter or about the timing, especially on a first official courtesy visit of this sort, and he did not; nor did I think it appropriate to question him about it, which might have embarrassed him, but he did say that the Court would probably let it be known four or five days in advance before it produced its judgement. He also said that, unlike the Prime Minister, he could not dragoon his colleagues, who were highly independent in their views (this, I think, was an oblique way of saying that the Court was divided) and he said that great care had to be taken to produce an accurate French translation of anything affecting Quebec (this might suggest that the judgement is more or less ready, but I am not sure.)

Moran

10 September 1981

cc: B R Berry Esq, North America Department

DOCUMENT 11:

This document shows that Bora Laskin indicated to Lord Moran, British High Commissioner in Ottawa, that the Supreme Court was still divided, eighteen days before the tribunal rendered its decision. This document is cited on page 241.

NOTES

INTRODUCTION

1. *Globe and Mail*, April 19, 1982.
2. Ibid.
3. Note by John Ford to Lord Carrington, dated April 30, 1981. Document obtained from the Foreign Office following a freedom of information request.
4. Robert Sheppard and Michael Valpy, *The National Deal: The Fight for a Canadian Constitution* (Toronto: Macmillan, 1982), 304.
5. Archives of the Ministry of Foreign Affairs Canada, RG 25-A-3-C 25-6, 20-CDA- 16-1-4, vol. 11478, part 34.
6. Gordon Robertson, *Memoirs of a Very Civil Servant: Mackenzie King to Trudeau* (Toronto: University of Toronto Press, 2000), 269.
7. Interview with Michael Kirby, May 14, 2010.
8. *Globe and Mail*, April 19, 1982.
9. John English, *The Life of Pierre Elliott Trudeau, Vol. 2: Just Watch Me, 1968–2000* (Toronto: Knopf Canada, 2009), 527.
10. Pierre Elliott Trudeau, *Mémoires politiques* (Montreal: Éditions Le Jour, 1993), 297.
11. Sheppard and Valpy, *The National Deal*, 304.

12. *Globe and Mail*, April 19, 1982.

13. André Burelle, *Pierre Elliott Trudeau: L'intellectuel et le politique* (Montreal: Fides, 2005), 370.

14. Ibid.

15. Ibid., 81.

16. Archives of Foreign Affairs Canada, RG 25-A- 3-C 25-6, 20-CDA-16-1-4, vol. 11478, part 34.

17. Burelle, *Pierre Elliott Trudeau*, 377.

18. Sheppard and Valpy, *The National Deal*, 304.

19. Ibid., 305.

20. Translated from a French recording of the speech, played on Radio-Canada on April 17, 2012.

21. Michael Mandel, *The Charter of Rights and the Legalization of Politics in Canada* (Toronto: Thompson Educational Publishing, 1994), 357.

22. *Globe and Mail*, April 19, 1982.

23. A document written by Dick Johnston, minister of intergovernmental affairs, for Peter Lougheed, premier of Alberta, dated May 11, 1981; obtained from the Ministry of Intergovernmental Affairs of Manitoba following a freedom of information request.

24. Roy Romanow, John Whyte, and Howard Leeson, *Canada ... Notwithstanding: The Making of the Constitution, 1976–1982* (Agincourt, ON: Carswell/Methuen, 1984), 134.

25. Ibid.

26. Trudeau, *Mémoires politiques*, 281.

27. Diplomatic cable from the High Commissioner of Canada to London, sent to Ottawa, dated March 15, 1982. Archives of Foreign Affairs Canada, RG 25-A-3-C 25-6, 20-CDA-16-1-4, vol. 11478, part 33.

28. Sheppard and Valpy, *The National Deal*, 204.

29. Edward McWhinney, *Canada and the Constitution, 1979–1982* (Toronto: University of Toronto Press, 1982), 135.

30. Ibid.

31. Note dated March 26, 1982. Document obtained from the Cabinet Office following a freedom of information request.

32. Interview with James McKibben, October 13, 2009.

33. Interview with Daniel Gagnier, April 14, 2008.

34. Correspondence with Martin Berthoud, February 22, 2007.

35. Confidential letter by Martin Berthoud to Emery Davis, at the High Commission of Great Britain in Ottawa, dated February 3, 1981. Document obtained from the Cabinet Office following a freedom of information request.

CHAPTER 1: OPENING VOLLEYS

1. In 1907, the constitution was modified to change a disposition guaranteeing British Columbia certain subsidies from Ottawa. Victoria was vehemently opposed, but thanks to the approval of the eight other provinces, Ottawa asked for and obtained a modification to the clause.
2. Mandel, *The Charter of Rights and the Legalization of Politics in Canada*, 87.
3. Peter H. Russell, *Constitutional Odyssey: Can Canadians Become a Sovereign People?* 3rd edition (Toronto: University of Toronto Press, 2004), 55.
4. Jean-Louis Roy, *Le Choix d'un pays. Le débat constitutionnel Québec-Canada, 1960–1976* (Montreal: Leméac, 1978), 63–66, 70–71.
5. Michael D. Behiels, *Prelude to Quebec's Quiet Revolution: Liberalism versus Neo-Nationalism, 1945–1960* (Montreal/Kingston: McGill-Queen's University Press, 2003), 38.
6. John English, *The Life of Pierre Elliott Trudeau, Vol. 1: Citizen of the World, 1919–1968* (Toronto: Knopf Canada, 2006), 34–35.
7. *Globe and Mail*, July 5, 1976.
8. Note by the British High Commission in Ottawa, sent to the Foreign Office, dated May 8, 1976, Archives of the Foreign Office, FCO 82/501.
9. Document dated May 17, 1976. Archives of the Foreign Office, FCO 82/816.
10. As explained by Johnston to a diplomat from the Foreign Office in a note, dated May 17, 1976, Archives of the Foreign Office, FCO 82/816.
11. Romanow, Whyte, and Leeson, *Canada ... Notwithstanding*, 1984), 4.
12. Note by the private secretary of the prime minister, dated September 15, 1976. Archives of the Foreign Office, FCO 82/814.
13. J.L. Granatstein and Robert Bothwell, *Pirouette: Pierre Trudeau and Canadian Foreign Policy* (Toronto: University of Toronto Press, 1991), 341.
14. Note from a counsellor to the prime minister, dated September 15, 1976. Archives of the Foreign Office, FCO 82/814.
15. English, *The Life of Pierre Elliott Trudeau, Vol. 2*, 301.
16. Pierre Godin, *René Lévesque: L'espoir et le chagrin* (Montreal: Boréal, 2001), 15.
17. Ibid., 16.

18. Ibid., 17.

19. Ibid., 30–31.

20. Ibid., 56.

21. Ibid., 61.

22. Ibid., 75.

23. Ibid.

24. English, *The Life of Pierre Elliott Trudeau, Vol. 2*, 308.

25. Note by Bertram Anthony Flack, political counsellor at the British High Commission in Ottawa, to the Foreign Office. Document obtained from the Foreign Office following a freedom of information request.

26. "The Parti québécois Victory: A Personal View," a note from Simon Dawbarn dated December 8, 1976. Document obtained from the Foreign Office following a freedom of information request.

27. Ibid.

28. "The Separatists Take Power in Quebec," a note by Bertram Anthony Flack to Anthony Crosland, dated December 16, 1976. Document obtained from the Foreign Office following a freedom of information request.

29. Note by Ramsay Melhuish, in London, to Bertram Anthony of the British High Commission in Ottawa, dated December 23, 1976. Document obtained from the Foreign Office following a freedom of information request.

30. Godin, *René Lévesque: L'espoir et le chagrin*, 116.

31. Note by John Johnston, dated January 10, 1977. Archives of the Foreign Office, FCO 82/689.

32. Ibid.

33. Ibid.

34. Confidential note by John Johnston, dated January 21, 1977. Archives of the Foreign Office, FCO 82/689.

35. Summary of meeting, dated March 21, 1977. Archives of the Foreign Office, FCO 82/689.

36. Confidential note by John Johnston, dated March 28, 1977. Archives of the Foreign Office, FCO 82/689.

CHAPTER 2: ALL HANDS ON DECK

1. "Quebec: A Final Outlook," confidential note by Denis Symington, dated August 8, 1977. Document obtained from the Foreign Office following a freedom of information request.

2. Godin, *René Lévesque: L'espoir et le chagrin*, 167.

3. Ibid.

4. Ibid., 169.

5. Ibid., 190.

6. "Reactions to the Quebec Language Bill," confidential document by B. Austin to David Lyscom of the British High Commission in Ottawa, dated May 9, 1977. Document obtained from the Foreign Office following a freedom of information request.

7. Account by Gérald Pelletier in *The Champions*, a documentary produced by the National Film Board of Canada, 1986.

8. Pierre Godin, *René Lévesque: L'homme brisé* (Montreal: Boréal, 2005), 183.

9. "Quebec Language White Paper," confidential document by David Lyscom, dated April 27, 1977. Document obtained from the Foreign Office following a freedom of information request.

10. Godin, *René Lévesque: L'espoir et le chagrin*, 216.

11. Mandel, *The Charter of Rights and the Legalization of Politics in Canada*, 144.

12. Godin, *René Lévesque: L'espoir et le chagrin*, 143.

13. Note by David Lyscom, dated July 28, 1977. Document obtained from the Foreign Office following a freedom of information request.

14. Godin, *René Lévesque: L'espoir et le chagrin*, 217.

15. Ibid., 350.

16. Romanow, Whyte, and Leeson, *Canada ... Notwithstanding*, 14.

17. Godin, *René Lévesque: L'espoir et le chagrin*, 352.

18. Ibid., 13.

19. Note by Terry Empson sent to Ramsay Melhuish, dated September 21, 1978. Archives of the Foreign Office, FCO 82/814.

20. Telegram by John Ford, British High Commissioner in Ottawa, dated November 2, 1978. Archives of the Foreign Office.

21. English, *The Life of Pierre Elliott Trudeau, Vol. 2*, 384.

22. Godin, *René Lévesque: L'espoir et le chagrin*, 357.

23. As quoted in Romanow, Whyte, and Leeson, *Canada ... Notwithstanding*, 53.

24. Godin, *René Lévesque: L'espoir et le chagrin*, 357.

25. Romanow, Whyte, and Leeson, *Canada ... Notwithstanding*, 53.

26. Confidential note by John Ford sent to the Secretary of Foreign Affairs and of the Commonwealth, dated February 13, 1979. Archives of the Foreign Office, FCO 82/816.

27. English, *The Life of Pierre Elliott Trudeau, Vol. 2*, 385.

28. *Globe and Mail*, May 10, 1979.

29. Ibid., May 12, 1979.

30. Ibid.

31. John Campbell, *Margaret Thatcher, Vol. 1: The Grocer's Daughter* (London: Vintage Books, 2000), 163.

32. Granatstein and Bothwell, *Pirouette*, 352.

33. Ibid.

34. Campbell, *Margaret Thatcher, Vol. 1*, 331.

35. John Campbell, *Margaret Thatcher, Vol. 2: The Iron Lady* (London: Vintage Books, 2007), 5.

36. Note by K.D. Temple to Ramsay Melhuish of the North America branch of the Foreign Office, dated May 14, 1979. Archives of the Foreign Office, FCO 82/816.

37. Mandel, *The Charter of Rights and the Legalization of Politics in Canada*, 354.

38. Olive Patricia Dickason, *Les Premières Nations du Canada: Depuis les temps les plus lointains jusqu'à nos jours* (Quebec: Septentrion, 1996), 388.

39. Letter by Clive Linklater, national coordinator, sent to Margaret Thatcher, dated June 26, 1979. Archives of the Foreign Office, FCO 82/817.

40. Interview with Bruce George, January 4, 2013.

41. *Globe and Mail*, July 6, 1979.

42. Note by the Archbishop of Canterbury, Donald Coggan, to Lord Carrington, dated August 13, 1979. Archives of the Foreign Office, FCO 82/818.

43. Note by Martin Berthoud to Lord N. Gordon Lennox, British diplomat, dated October 1, 1979. Archives of the Foreign Office, FCO 82/818.

44. Note by K.D. Temple to Martin Berthoud, dated October 10, 1979. Archives of the Foreign Office, FCO 82/818.

CHAPTER 3: THE REFERENDUM FIGHT

1. English, *The Life of Pierre Elliott Trudeau, Vol. 2*, 428.

2. Ibid., 432.

3. Ibid., 457.

4. Ibid., 439.

5. Ibid., 443.

6. Note by John Ford to Lord Carrington, Foreign Secretary, dated March 27, 1980. Document obtained from the Foreign Office following a freedom of information request.

7. Godin, *René Lévesque: L'espoir et le chagrin*, 527.

8. Note from John Ford to Lord Carrington, dated March 27, 1980. Document obtained from the Foreign Office following a freedom of information request.

9. Sheppard and Valpy, *The National Deal*, 25.

10. Godin, *René Lévesque: L'espoir et le chagrin*, 532.

11. *Le Devoir*, April 23, 1980.

12. Godin, *René Lévesque: L'espoir et le chagrin*, 533.

13. Ibid., 451.

14. Ibid.

15. Note by John R. Rich, called "Reflections After Eighteen Months in French Canada," dated March 11, 1980. Document obtained from the Foreign Office following a freedom of information request.

16. Note by Martin Berthoud to John Ford, dated April 3, 1980. Document obtained from the Foreign Office following a freedom of information request. A copy of this note was sent to each of the heads of mission, including John R. Rich.

17. Note by John R. Rich, called "Reflections After Eighteen Months in French Canada," dated March 11 1980. Document obtained from the Foreign Office following a freedom of information request.

18. Ibid. Underline appears in original.

19. Ibid.

20. Note by John Ford to Lord Carrington, dated March 27, 1980. Document obtained from the Foreign Office following a freedom of information request.

21. Correspondence with Ken Curtis, between January 17 and 20, 2010.

22. Note by Martin Berthoud to John Ford, dated April 3, 1980. Document obtained from the Foreign Office following a freedom of information request. A copy of this note was sent to each of the heads of mission, including John R. Rich.

23. Correspondence with Martin Berthoud, February 22, 2007.

24. Correspondence with Malcolm Rifkind, January 20, 2008.

25. Note by John Ford to Martin Berthoud, dated April 29, 1980, entitled "The Situation in Quebec." Document obtained from the Foreign Office following a freedom of information request.

26. Interview with Robert Normand, December 14, 2006.

27. Note by John Ford to Martin Berthoud, dated April 29, 1980. Document obtained from the Foreign Office following a freedom of information request.

28. Sheppard and Valpy, *The National Deal*, 34.

29. Note by John Ford to Martin Berthoud, dated April 29, 1980. Document obtained from the Foreign Office following a freedom of information request.

30. Sheppard and Valpy, *The National Deal*, 33.

31. Notably during a debate in the House on May 9, 1980, and during a press conference on that same day.

32. Commentary by Brian Perry on a telegram sent by Alan Montgomery, diplomat at the British High Commission in Ottawa, dated May 13, 1980. Archives of the Foreign Office, FCO 82/819.

33. Taken from the documentary *Le Choix d'un peuple*, by Hugues Migneault, Les films de la rive, 1985.

34. Sheppard and Valpy, *The National Deal*, 14.

35. Pierre Elliott Trudeau, *Memoirs* (Toronto: McClelland & Stewart, 1993), 283.

36. Mark MacGuigan, *An Inside Look at External Affairs During the Trudeau Years* (Calgary: University of Calgary Press, 2002), 90.

37. I borrow this turn of phrase from Peter H. Russell, *Constitutional Odyssey*, 109.

38. English, *The Life of Pierre Elliott Trudeau, Vol. 2*, 446.

39. Burelle, *Pierre Elliott Trudeau*, 424.

40. "The Quebec Referendum," note by Alan Montgomery, diplomat at the British High Commission in Ottawa, to Martin Berthoud. Document obtained from the Foreign Office following a freedom of information request.

41. Godin, *René Lévesque: L'espoir et le chagrin*, 552.

42. Ibid., 542.

43. Burelle, *Pierre Elliott Trudeau*, 209.

44. Ibid., 206.

45. Note by Emery Davies to Lord Carrington, entitled "The Quebec Problem: The Penultimate Chapter?" dated May 26, 1980. Document obtained from the Foreign Office following a freedom of information request.

CHAPTER 4: THATCHER'S GREEN LIGHT

1. Claude Morin, *Lendemains piégés: Du référendum à la nuit des longs couteaux* (Montreal: Boréal, 1988), 14–15.

2. Ibid.

3. Jean Chrétien, *Dans la fosse aux lions* (Montreal: Les Éditions de l'Homme, 1985), 166.

4. Ibid., 167.

5. Ibid., 169.

6. Archives of the Executive Council, Quebec, E5 2005-10-003/289.

7. Godin, *René Lévesque: L'homme brisé*, 58.

8. Romanow, Whyte, and Leeson, *Canada ... Notwithstanding*, 64.

9. Ibid.

10. Theodore Roosevelt Association, "In His Own Words," *www.theodore-roosevelt.org/life/quotes.htm*. Accessed July 25, 2014.

11. Romanow, Whyte, and Leeson, *Canada .... Notwithstanding*, 139.

12. Ibid.

13. Interview with Michael Kirby, May 14, 2010.

14. Note by De Montigny Marchand to Pierre Trudeau, dated October 16, 1980. Archives of Foreign Affairs Canada, RG 25-A-3-C 25-6, 20-CDA-16-1-4, vol. 11478, part 3.

15. Archives of Foreign Affairs Canada, RG 25-A- 3-C, 20-CDA-16-1-4, vol. 8722, part 1.

16. Minutes of meeting between Nicholas Ridley and Allan Gotlieb in Ottawa, June 17, 1980. Archives of the Foreign Office, FCO 82/820.

17. Minutes of meeting between Nicholas Ridley and Jean Chrétien in Ottawa, June 18, 1980. Archives of the Foreign Office, FCO 82/820.

18. Ibid.

19. Ibid.

20. Ibid.

21. Ibid.

22. Ibid.

23. Interview with Michael Kirby, September 7, 2007.

24. Nicholas Wapshott, *Ronald Reagan and Margaret Thatcher: A Political Marriage* (London: Penguin, 2007), 148.

25. Margaret Thatcher, *The Downing Street Years* (New York: HarperCollins, 1993), 321.

26. Campbell, *Margaret Thatcher, Vol. 1*, 41.

27. The reconstruction of this meeting is based on the minutes of the archives of the Ministry of Foreign Affairs of Canada (RG 25-A-3-C, 20-CDA-16-1-4, vol. 8723, part 8), as well as the archives of the Cabinet Office. Document obtained from the Foreign Office following a freedom of information request.

28. *Globe and Mail*, June 26, 1980.

29. As cited in a note by John Ford sent to London, dated January 31, 1981. Document obtained from the Foreign Office following a freedom of information request.

30. *Globe and Mail*, June 26, 1980.

31. Note by Wayne Clifford to Oryssia J. Lennie, dated June 27, 1980. Document obtained from the Foreign Office following a freedom of information request.

32. Summary of discussion between Mark MacGuigan and Lord Carrington, dated July 8, 1980. Archives of the Foreign Office, FCO 82/820.

33. Note by Emery Davies to the Foreign Office, date July 15, 1980. Archives of the Foreign Office, FCO 82/820.

34. Cited in a preparatory document for a meeting between Margaret Thatcher, Mark MacGuigan, and John Roberts, dated October 3, 1980. Archives of the Foreign Office.

35. Sheppard and Valpy, *The National Deal*, 40.

36. Interview with John Ford, February 8, 2007.

37. Ibid.

38. Romanow, Whyte, and Leeson, *Canada .... Notwithstanding*, 67.

39. Ibid.

40. Ibid., 73.

41. Ibid., 86–87.

42. Cited by Varun Uberoi, "Multiculturalism and the Canadian Charter of Rights and Freedoms," *Political Studies* 57 (2009), 808.

43. Ibid., 809.

44. Cited by Burelle, *Pierre Elliott Trudeau*, 262.

45. Ibid.

46. Romanow, Whyte, and Leeson, *Canada .... Notwithstanding*, 85.

47. Cited by Burelle, *Pierre Elliot Trudeau*, 287–88.

48. Summary of a lunch between John Ford and Michael Kirby, sent to Martin Berthoud, dated August 13, 1980. Document obtained from the Foreign Office following a freedom of information request.

49. Sheppard and Valpy, *The National Deal*, 42.

50. Ibid., 46.

51. Ibid., 52.

52. Interview with Michael Kirby, October 2, 2007.

53. Quoted by Ron Graham, *The Last Act: Pierre Trudeau, the Gang of Eight, and the Fight for Canada* (Toronto: Penguin, 2011), 68.

54. Sheppard and Valpy, *The National Deal*, 52.
55. Ibid., 42.
56. Ibid., 44.

CHAPTER 5: JUSTICE VS. THE PROVINCES

1. Romanow, Whyte, and Leeson, *Canada …. Notwithstanding*, 76.
2. Sheppard and Valpy, *The National Deal*, 68.
3. Ibid., 68.
4. Romanow, Whyte and Leeson, *Canada …. Notwithstanding*, 67.
5. Mandel, *The Charter of Rights and the Legalization of Politics in Canada*, 91.
6. Quoted in James Kelly, *Governing with the Charter: Legislative and Judicial Activism and Framer's Intent* (Vancouver: UBC Press, 2005), 60.
7. C.S. Bradley, "The Language of Rights and the Crisis of the Liberal Imagination," in Anthony A. Peacock, ed., *Rethinking the Constitution: Perspectives on Canadian Constitutional Reform, Interpretation, and Theory* (Oxford: Oxford University Press, 1996), 88.
8. Alexander Hamilton, "The Federalist No. 84," in Federalist Papers, *www.foundingfathers.info/federalistpapers/fed84.htm*. Accessed July 25, 2014.
9. Bradley, "The Language of Rights …," 88.
10. *Globe and Mail*, July 5, 1980.
11. Quoted by F.L. Morton and Rainer Knopff, *The Charter Revolution and the Court Party* (Toronto: University of Toronto Press, 2000), 155.
12. Quoted by Janet Ajzenstat, "Reconciling Parliament and Rights: A.V. Dicey Reads the Canadian Charter of Rights and Freedoms," *Revue canadienne de science politique* 30, no. 4 (December 1997), 651.
13. Ibid., 656.
14. Quoted in Thomas Sowell, *A Conflict of Visions: Ideological Origins of Political Struggles* (New York: Basic Books, 2007), 13.
15. Allan Blakeney, *An Honourable Calling: Political Memoirs* (Toronto: University of Toronto Press, 2008), 179.
16. Bradley, "The Language of Rights …," 92.
17. Ajzenstat, "Reconciling Parliament and Rights," 657.
18. Ibid.
19. Ibid., 658.
20. Karen Selick, "Rights and Wrongs in the Canadian Charter," in Anthony A. Peacock, ed., *Rethinking the Constitution: Perspectives on Canadian*

Constitutional Reform, Interpretation, and Theory (Oxford: Oxford University Press, 1996), 104.

21. Ibid.

22. Hugh Donald Forbes, "Trudeau's Moral Vision," in Anthony A. Peacock, ed., *Rethinking the Constitution: Perspectives on Canadian Constitutional Reform, Interpretation, and Theory* (Oxford: Oxford University Press, 1996), 19.

23. Ibid., 26.

24 Mandel, *The Charter of Rights and the Legalization of Politics in Canada*, 140–41.

25. Pierre Elliott Trudeau, *Le Fédéralisme et la société canadienne-française* (Montreal: Éditions HMH, 1967), 165, 168.

26. Ibid., 31.

27. Blakeney, *An Honourable Calling*, 176.

CHAPTER 6: UNILATERALLY

1. Romanow, Whyte, and Leeson, *Canada … Notwithstanding*, 89.

2. Ibid., 91.

3. Note by John Ford, addressed to the Foreign Office, dated August 28, 1980. Archives of the Foreign Office, FCO 82/820.

4. Note by Lord Carrington to John Ford, dated September 1, 1980. Archives of the Foreign Office, FCO 82/820.

5. Interview with John Ford, February 8, 2007.

6. Note by John Ford to the Foreign Office entitled "The Canadian Mosaic: Its Glue and Its Weakness," dated May 7, 1980. Document obtained from the Foreign Office following a freedom of information request.

7. Sheppard and Valpy, *The National Deal*, 1.

8. Ibid., 3.

9. Ibid.

10. Ibid., 4.

11. Ibid.

12. Ron Graham, *The Last Act: Pierre Trudeau, the Gang of Eight, and the Fight for Canada* (Toronto: Penguin, 2011), 62.

13. Allan Blakeney, *An Honourable Calling: Political Memoirs* (Toronto: University of Toronto Press, 2008), 174.

14. Ibid., 5.

15. Interview with Robert Normand, December 14, 2006.

16. Marianopolis College, "Documents sur le rapatriement de la Constitution, 1980–1982," Quebec History, *faculty.marianopolis.edu/c.belanger/quebechistory/docs/1982/17.htm*; and Romanow, Whyte, and Leeson, *Canada … Notwithstanding*, 95.

17. Romanow, Whyte, and Leeson, *Canada … Notwithstanding*, 95.

18. Ibid., 216–17.

19. Quoted by Ron Graham, *The Last Act*, 83.

20. Ibid.

21. Romanow, Whyte, and Leeson, *Canada … Notwithstanding*, 96.

22. Ron Graham, *The Last Act*, 65.

23. Ibid., 83.

24. Note by John Ford to the Foreign Office, dated September 11, 1980. Archives of the Foreign Office, FCO 82/820.

25. Interview with Robert Normand, December 14, 2006.

26. Claude Morin, *Lendemains piégés. Du référendum à la nuit des longs couteaux* (Montreal: Boréal, 1988), 120.

27. Interview with Robert Normand, December 14, 2006.

28. Ron Graham, *The Last Act*, 64.

29. Summary of meeting between Emery Davies, Fred Gibson (director for Western Europe), and Michael Kirby, May 7, 1981. Document obtained from the Foreign Office following a freedom of information request.

30. Note by Emery Davies to Martin Berthoud called "The Leaked Pitfield Document of August 30th 1980 and Court Action," dated September 12, 1980. Archives of the Foreign Office, FCO 82/821.

31. Summary of meeting between John Ford and Allan MacEachen, sent to the Foreign Office, dated September 12, 1980. Archives of the Foreign Office, FCO 82/820.

32. Ron Graham, *The Last Act*, 66.

33. Claude Morin, *Lendemains piégés*, 133.

34. Romanow, Whyte, and Leeson, *Canada … Notwithstanding*, 98–99.

35. Note by John Ford to the Foreign Office, entitled "Failure of the Conference," dated September 13, 1980. Archives of the Foreign Office, FCO 82/820.

36. Note by Martin Berthoud to Derek Day, dated September 12, 1980. Archives of the Foreign Office, FCO 82/820.

37. Note by Emery Davies to Martin Berthoud, entitled "Canadian Retaliation," dated September 30, 1980. Archives of the Foreign Office, FCO 82/821.

38. Note by Lord Carrington to John Ford, dated September 17, 1980. Archives of the Foreign Office, FCO 82/820.

39. Note by Martin Berthoud to Christian Hardy, dated September 12, 1980. Archives of the Foreign Office, FCO 82/820.

40. Note by Martin Berthoud to a certain Baldwin, on the topic of Christian Hardy, dated September 11, 1980. Archives of the Foreign Office, FCO 82/820.

41. According to two documents dated September 12 and 22, 1980. Archives of the Foreign Office, FCO 82/820.

42. Sheppard and Valpy, *The National Deal*, 65.

43. Ibid.

44. English, *The Life of Pierre Elliott Trudeau, Vol. 2*, 47.

CHAPTER 7: THATCHER DISCOVERS THE CHARTER

1. Speech by Pierre Elliott Trudeau, October 2, 1980. Archives of the Foreign Office, FCO 82/831. See also Morin, *Lendemains piégés*, 136.

2. James Ross Hurley, *Amending Canada's Constitution: History, Processes, Problems and Prospects* (Ottawa: Ministry of Supply and Services, 1996), 55.

3. The reconstruction of this discussion is based on the archives of the Ministry of Foreign Affairs Canada (RG 25-A-3-C 25-6, 20-CDA-16- 1-4, vol. 8723, part 5, undated), and on two passages of Mark MacGuigan's book, *An Inside Look at External Affairs During the Trudeau Years* (Calgary: University of Calgary Press, 2002), 45, 92–93.

4. Note by Robert Armstrong to M. Alexander, dated September 29, 1980. Archives of the Foreign Office, FCO 82/821.

5. Note by John Ford to Martin Berthoud, dated August 7, 1980. Archives of the Foreign Office, FCO 82/820.

6. Note by Jane Ann Sarginson, of the British High Commission, to Vivien Hughes, of the Foreign Office, dated October 22, 1981. Document obtained from the Foreign Office following a freedom of information request.

7. Ibid.

8. Summary of meeting by Robert de Burlet, sent to Murray Simons, in Montreal, dated October 7, 1980. Archives of the Foreign Office, FCO 82/822.

9. Note by Emery Davies to Martin Berthoud, dated October 16, 1980, Archives of the Foreign Office, FCO 82/822

10. Note by Gilles Loiselle to Margaret Thatcher, dated October 3 1980. Archives of the Foreign Office.

11. Preparatory document for a meeting between Margaret Thatcher, Mark MacGuigan, and John Roberts, dated October 3, 1980. Obtained from the Cabinet Office following a freedom of information request.

12. Ibid.

13. Interview with John Ford, February 8, 2007.

14. MacGuigan, *An Inside Look at External Affairs*, 93.

15. Preparatory document for the meeting between Margaret Thatcher, Mark MacGuigan, and John Roberts, dated October 3, 1980. Obtained from the Cabinet Office following a freedom of information request.

16. The reconstruction of this conversation is based on the British summary (obtained from the Cabinet Office following a freedom of information request) and on the Canadian summary (Archives of the Ministry of Foreign Affairs Canada, RG 25-A-3-C 25-6, 20-CDA-16-1-4, vol. 8723, part 5, undated).

17. Note by adviser Michael Alexander, entitled "Prime Minister's Visit to Bonn," dated November 18, 1980. Document obtained from the Foreign Office following a freedom of information request.

18. *The Economist*, October 11, 1980. Archives of the Foreign Office, FCO 82/822.

19. MacGuigan, *An Inside Look at External Affairs*, 92.

20. YouTube, *www.youtube.com/watch?v=bcM38teBfu8*. Accessed June 13, 2014.

21. Matthew Lippman, "The Debate Over a Bill of Rights in Great Britain: The View from Parliament," *Universal Human Rights* 2, no. 4 (October–December 1980), 26.

22. Francesca Klug, *Values for a Godless Age: The Story of the United Kingdom's New Bill of Rights* (London: Penguin, 2000), 155.

23. Quoted in Glenn Abernathy, "Should the United Kingdom Adopt a Bill of Rights?" *The American Journal of Comparative Law* 31, no 3 (1983), 456.

24. Sheppard and Valpy, *The National Deal*, 208.

25. MacGuigan, *An Inside Look at External Affairs*, 96.

26. Archives of Foreign Affairs Canada, RG 25-A-3-C, 20-CDA-16-1-4, vol. 8722, part 3.

27. Archives of Foreign Affairs Canada, RG 25-A-3-C, 20-CDA-16-1-4, vol. 8722b, part 3.

28. Archives of Foreign Affairs Canada, RG 25-A-3-C, 20-CDA-16-1-4, vol. 8723, part 4. Note: Marchand's underline in the original.

29. Archives of Foreign Affairs Canada, RG 25-A-3-C, 20-CDA-16-1-4, vol. 8722, part 2.

30. Trudeau made this comment over dinner at 10 Downing Street, on June 26, 1981. Summary of meeting obtained from the Foreign Office following a freedom of information request.

31. Interview with Daniel Gagnier, April 14, 2008.

32. Interview with Jonathan Aitken, December 20, 2006.

33. Campbell, *Margaret Thatcher, Vol. 2*, 107.

34. Archives of the Ministry of Foreign Affairs Canada, RG 25-A-3-C, 20-CDA-16-1-4, vol. 8722, part 3.

35. Note by A.W. Sullivan to Mark MacGuigan, following a message sent to Jean Wadds in Ottawa, dated October 31, 1980. Archives of Foreign Affairs Canada, RG 25-A-3-C, 20-CDA-16-1-4, vol. 8722, part 3.

36. *Globe and Mail*, January 29, 1981.

37. Note by Mark MacGuigan to Pierre Elliott Trudeau, dated October 16, 1980. Archives of Foreign Affairs Canada, RG 25-A-3-C, 20-CDA-16-1-4, vol. 8722, part 3.

38. Note by Mark MacGuigan to Pierre Elliott Trudeau, dated October 28, 1980. Archives of Foreign Affairs Canada, RG 25-A-3-C, 20-CDA-16-1-4, vol. 8722, part 4.

CHAPTER 8: THE BATTLE BEGINS

1. Sheppard and Valpy, *The National Deal*, 178.

2. Ibid.

3. Ibid., 179.

4. Ron Graham, *The Last Act: Pierre Trudeau, the Gang of Eight, and the Fight for Canada* (Toronto: Penguin, 2011), 132.

5. Sheppard and Valpy, *The National Deal*, 8.

6. Ibid., 180.

7. Jean Chrétien, *Straight from the Heart* (Toronto: McClelland & Stewart, 1986), 144.

8. *Globe and Mail*, October 20, 1980.

9. René Lévesque, *Attendez que je me rappelle ...* (Montreal: Québec Amérique, 1986), 430.

10. Ibid., 430–31.
11. Sheppard and Valpy, *The National Deal*, 184.
12. Archives of the Executive Council, Quebec, E5 2008-11-004/205
13. Sheppard and Valpy, *The National Deal*, 184.
14. *Globe and Mail*, December 8, 1980.
15. Correspondence with Claude Morin, July 5, 2006.
16. Michael Pitfield's Report, quoted in the House by Conservative MP Perrin Beatty, Archives of Foreign Affairs Canada, RG 25-A-3-C 25-6, 20-CDA-16-1-4, vol. 8723, part 4.
17. Ibid.
18. Mark MacGuigan, *An Inside Look at External Affairs During the Trudeau Years* (Calgary: University of Calgary Press, 2002), 100.
19. For an explanation of the terms *wets* and *dries*, see Chapter 10, page 157.
20. Wikipedia, "Ian Gilmour, Baron Gilmour of Craigmillar," *wikipedia.org/wiki/Ian_Gilmour,_Baron_Gilmour_of_Craigmillar*.
21. Summary of meeting between Ian Gilmour, Lord Carrington, and Mark MacGuigan, dated November 10, 1980. Archives of the Foreign Office, FCO 82/823.
22. Ibid.
23. Note by Lord Carrington to John Ford, dated November 10, 1980. Archives of the Foreign Office, FCO 82/823.
24. Summary of meeting between Norman St. John-Stevas and Mark MacGuigan, dated November 10, 1980. Archives of the Foreign Office, FCO 82/823.
25. Note by the Canadian High Commission, dated November 10, 1980. Archives of Foreign Affairs of Canada. RG 25-A-3-C, 20-CDA-16-1-4, vol. 8722, part 4.
26. Note by Henry Steel to Michael Havers, dated November 11, 1980. Archives of the Foreign Office, FCO 82/823. See also, note addressed to Michael Alexander, diplomatic adviser to Margaret Thatcher, dated November 3, 1980. Archives of the Foreign Office, FCO 82/822.
27. Note by H. Steel to Michael Havers, dated November 11, 1980. Archives of the Foreign Office, FCO 82/823.
28. Sheppard and Valpy, *The National Deal*, 187.
29. Ibid., 189.
30. Note by Martin Berthoud to Mr. Parry, copied to Emery Davies, in Ottawa, dated September 19, 1980. Archives of the Foreign Office, FCO 82/820.

31. Interview with Gilles Loiselle, November 29, 2005.

32. Ibid., December 14, 2006.

33. The *Times* (London), February 15, 1981.

34. Note by Martin Berthoud to Mr. Parry, copied to Emery Davies, in Ottawa, dated September 19, 1980: summary of a lunch with Gilles Loiselle. Archives of the Foreign Office, FCO 82/820.

35. Note by Martin Berthoud to Gilles Loiselle, dated February 20, 1981. Document obtained from the Foreign Office following a freedom of information request.

36. Interview with Gilles Loiselle, December 14, 2006.

37. Romanow, Whyte, and Leeson, *Canada ... Notwithstanding*, 141.

38. Interview with Gilles Loiselle, December 14, 2006.

39. Note by Martin Berthoud, dated November 21, 1980. Archives of the Foreign Office, FCO 82/823.

40. Interview with Gilles Loiselle, December 14, 2006.

41. Mandel, *The Charter of Rights and the Legalization of Politics in Canada*, 354.

42. Ibid., 355.

43. Sheppard and Valpy, *The National Deal*, 167.

44. Note by Lord Carrington, dated November 11, 1980. Archives of the Foreign Office, FCO 82/830.

45. Note by Lord Carrington, Archives of the Foreign Office, FCO 82/830.

CHAPTER 9: THE WRATH OF THE WEST

1. *Globe and Mail*, November 1, 1980.

2. English, *The Life of Pierre Elliott Trudeau, Vol. 2*, 491.

3. G. Bruce Doern, *The Politics of Energy: The Development and Implementation of the NEP* (Toronto: Methuen, 1985), 33.

4. Romanow, Whyte, and Leeson, *Canada ... Notwithstanding*, 116.

5. Note by John Ford sent to London, dated September 29, 1980, Archives of the Foreign Office, 82/821.

6. Note by John Ford sent to London, dated October 27, 1980. Archives of the Foreign Office, FCO 82/822.

7. Summary of meeting with Pierre Maillard, sent to London by John Ford, dated November 18, 1980. Archives of the Foreign Office, FCO 82/823.

8. Note. Archives of Foreign Affairs Canada, RG 25-A-3-C 25-6, 20-CDA-16-1-4, vol. 11478, part 6.

9. Mark MacGuigan, *An Inside Look at External Affairs During the Trudeau Years* (Calgary: University of Calgary Press, 2002), 97.

10. Note by John Ford sent to London, dated May 7, 1981. Document obtained from the Foreign Office following a freedom of information request.

11. Note. Archives of Foreign Affairs Canada, RG 25-A-3-C 25-6, 20-CDA-16-1-4, vol. 11478, part 6.

12. Note by Martin Berthoud to John Ford, dated September 30, 1980. Archives of the Foreign Office, FCO 82/821.

13. Note. Archives of Foreign Affairs Canada, RG 25-A-3-C 25-6, 20-CDA-16-1-4, vol. 11478, part 3.

14. Note. Archives of the Foreign Office, FCO 82/826.

15. Note. Archives of Foreign Affairs Canada, RG 25-A-3-C 25-6, 20-CDA-16-1-4, vol. 11478, part 7.

16. Note. Archives of the Foreign Office, FCO 82/826.

17. Ibid.

18. *The Independent*, January 20, 1999: *www.independent.co.uk/arts-entertainment/jonathan-aitken-a-broken-man-1074975.html.* Accessed June 16, 2014.

19. Interview with Gilles Loiselle, December 14 2006.

20. The *Times* (London), October 31, 1980.

21. Interview with Jonathan Aitken, December 20, 2006.

22. Interview with James McKibben, October 29, 2009.

23. Note by Peter Meekison to Dick Johnston, dated November 7, 1980. Document obtained from the Ministry of Intergovernmental and International Relations of Alberta following a freedom of information request.

24. Campbell, *Margaret Thatcher, Vol. 2*, 37.

25. *Edmonton Journal*, November 25, 1980.

26. Note. Archives of the Foreign Office, FCO 82/824.

27. *Edmonton Journal*, November 26, 1980.

28. Ibid., November 28, 1980.

29. Ibid., November 26, 1980.

30. *Globe and Mail*, November 27, 1980.

31. Summary of a meeting between Sonny Ramphal and Lord Carrington, dated November 10, 1980. Archives of the Foreign Office, FCO 82/823.

32. Campbell, *Margaret Thatcher, Vol. 2*, 320.

33. Speech by Sonny Ramphal, December 11, 1980. Document obtained from the Foreign Office following a freedom of information request.

34. Note addressed to the Cabinet by Lord Carrington, dated November 10, 1980. Archives of the Foreign Office, FCO 82/824.

35. Ibid.

CHAPTER 10: THATCHER LOSES CONTROL

1. Campbell, *Margaret Thatcher, Vol. 2*, 78–79.

2. Ibid., 107.

3. See the analysis by John B. Johnson, a doctor in political science at the London School of Economics, who wrote to the *Globe and Mail* on the topic on February 25, 1981.

4. Interview with Jonathan Aitken, December 20, 2006.

5. Campbell, *Margaret Thatcher, Vol. 2*, 458.

6. Sheppard and Valpy, *The National Deal*, 197.

7. Note by Martin Berthoud to Harding, permanent secretary, and to Nicholas Ridley, undated. Archives of the Foreign Office, FCO 82/823.

8. Note by Gordon Lennox to a certain Blaker and to the permanent secretary, dated October 29, 1980. Archives of the Foreign Office, FCO 82/823.

9. Note by Lord Carrington to John Ford, dated October 30, 1980. Archives of the Foreign Office, FCO 82/823.

10. The *Times* (London), November 1, 1980.

11. The *Gazette* (London), October 30, 1980.

12. Note by John Ford to the Foreign Office, dated November 3, 1980. Archives of the Foreign Office, FCO 82/823.

13. Note by the Foreign Office to the British High Commission in Ottawa, dated November 3, 1980. Archives of the Foreign Office, FCO 82/823.

14. Note by Martin Berthoud to Anthony Parry, dated November 5, 1980. Archives of the Foreign Office, FCO 82/823.

15. Ibid.

16. Note by Martin Berthoud, dated November 6, 1980. Archives of the Foreign Office, FCO 82/823.

17. Internal note of the Foreign Office, dated November 6, 1980, summarizing Nicholas Ridley's position as well as his meeting with Anthony Kershaw. Archives of the Foreign Office, FCO 82/823.

18. Ibid.

19. Note. Archives of Foreign Affairs Canada, RG 25-A-3-C 25-6, 20-CDA-16-1-4, vol. 8723, part 4. Underlined by Jean Wadds.

20. Declaration by Pierre Elliott Trudeau on the House, note dated November 6, 1980. Archives of the Foreign Office, FCO 82/823.

21. Press conference by Pierre Elliott Trudeau, November 7, 1980. Archives of the Foreign Office, FCO 82/823.

22. Note. Archives of Foreign Affairs Canada, RG 25-A-3-C 25-6, 20-CDA-16-1-4, vol. 8723, part 5.

23. *Globe and Mail*, November 27, 1980.

24. Ibid.

25. Romanow, Whyte, and Leeson, *Canada … Notwithstanding*, 248.

26. Sheppard and Valpy, *The National Deal*, 137.

27. Mandel, *The Charter of Rights and the Legalization of Politics in Canada*, 182.

28. Sheppard and Valpy, *The National Deal*, 137.

29. Note. Archives of Foreign Affairs Canada, RG 25-A-3-C 25-6, 20-CDA-16-1-4, vol. 8723, part 7.

30. Tom Darby and Peter C. Emberley, "Political Correctness and the Constitution: Nature and Convention Re-Examined," in Anthony A. Peacock, ed., *Rethinking the Constitution: Perspectives on Canadian Constitutional Reform, Interpretation, and Theory* (Don Mills, ON: Oxford University Press, 1996), 245.

31. Romanow, Whyte, and Leeson, *Canada … Notwithstanding*, 248.

32. F. Morton and R. Knopff, *The Charter Revolution and the Court Party* (Toronto: University of Toronto Press, 2000), 67.

33. Russell, *Constitutional Odyssey*, 114.

34. Quoted, Varun Uberoi, "Multiculturalism and the Canadian Charter of Rights and Freedoms," *Political Studies* 57 (2009), 814.

35. Ibid., 821.

36. Ibid., 828.

37. Ibid., 818.

38. Note by John Ford to the Foreign Office, dated May 7, 1981. Document obtained from the Foreign Office following a freedom of information request.

39. Note by the Foreign Office to John Ford, dated May 12, 1981. Document obtained from the Foreign Office following a freedom of information request.

40. Note by Emery Davies to the Foreign Office, dated December 12, 1980. Archives of the Foreign Office, FCO 82/825.

41. The results were reported by John Ford in a note addressed to the Foreign Office, dated January 6, 1981. Document obtained from the Foreign Office following a freedom of information request.

42. Interview with Michael Kirby, May 14, 2010.

43. Mandel, *The Charter of Rights and the Legalization of Politics in Canada*, 39.

44. Ibid., 39–40.

45. Ibid., 39.

46. Interview with Peter Lougheed, April 12, 2011.

47. Morin, *Lendemains piégés*, 203.

48. Note by John Ford to the Foreign Office, dated December 9, 1980. Archives of the Foreign Office, FCO 82/825.

49. Note by John Ford to the Foreign Office, dated December 16, 1980. Archives of the Foreign Office, FCO 82/825.

50. Note by Derek Day to John Ford, dated November 21, 1980. Archives of the Foreign Office, FCO 82/824.

51. Summary of meeting between Lord Carrington and Margaret Thatcher, dated November 28, 1980. Document obtained from the Foreign Office following a freedom of information request.

52. Note by M. Whitmore to Robert Armstrong, general secretary of the government, dated November 28, 1980. Document obtained from the Foreign Office following a freedom of information request.

53. Letter by Margaret Thatcher to Pierre Elliott Trudeau, undated. Document obtained from the Cabinet Office following a freedom of information request.

54. Letter by Pierre Elliott Trudeau to Margaret Thatcher, dated December 11, 1980. Document obtained following a freedom of information request.

55. Note by John Ford to Michael Palliser, dated March 11, 1981. Declassified document.

56. Summary of a meeting between Margaret Thatcher and Francis Pym, dated December 17, 1980. Document obtained from the Foreign Office following a freedom of information request.

57. Summary of meeting. Archives of Foreign Affairs Canada, RG 25-A-3-C, 20-CDA-16-1-4, vol. 11418, part 9.

58. Summary of meeting between Pierre Trudeau and Francis Pym, dated December 17, 1980. Document obtained from the Foreign Office following a freedom of information request.

59. Summary of meeting. Archives of Foreign Affairs Canada, RG 25-A-3-C, 20-CDA-16-1-4, vol. 11418, part 9.

60. Summary of meeting between Pierre Trudeau and Francis Pym, dated December 17, 1980. Document obtained from the Foreign Office following

a freedom of information request.

61. Note by John Ford to the Foreign Office, dated December 20, 1980, summarizing the propositions made to Francis Pym during his visit. Document, classified "secret," obtained from the Foreign Office following a freedom of information request.

62. Note by John Ford to Deputy Minister Michael Palliser, dated March 11, 1980, summarizing proposition made to Francis Pym during his visit. Document obtained from the Foreign Office following a freedom of information request.

63. Summary of meeting between Margaret Thatcher, Francis Pym, and Lord Carrington, dated December 23, 1980. Document obtained from the Foreign Office following a freedom of information request.

64. Note by H. Steel to Michael Alexander, dated December 23, 1980. A copy of the letter was sent to John Freeland. Archives of the Foreign Office, FCO 82/825.

CHAPTER 11: THE EMPIRE STRIKES BACK

1. The *Times* (London), January 15, 1981.

2. Internal note, Foreign Office, dated January 28, 1981, unsigned. Document obtained from the Foreign Office following a freedom of information request.

3. The conversation between Francis Pym and Jean Wadds was re-created thanks to the Canadian summary (Archives of Foreign Affairs Canada, RG 25-A-3-C 25-6, 20-CDA-16-1-4, vol. 11077, part 11) and of the British summary. (Document obtained from the Foreign Office following a freedom of information request).

4. *Globe and Mail*, January 14, 1981.

5. Interview with James McKibben, October 13, 2009.

6. Note by Robert Armstrong, dated January 16, 1981. Document obtained from the Foreign Office following a freedom of information request.

7. *Globe and Mail*, January 22, 1981.

8. *Globe and Mail*, January 23, 1981.

9. *Globe and Mail*, January 31, 1981.

10. *Globe and Mail*, February 3, 1981.

11. Ibid.

12. Note by John Ford to the Foreign Office, dated January 31, 1981. Document obtained from the Foreign Office following a freedom of information request.

13. Note by Martin Berthoud, dated January 27, 1981. Document obtained from the Foreign Office following a freedom of information request.

14. Note by John Ford to the Foreign Office, dated February 8, 1981. Document obtained from the Foreign Office following a freedom of information request.

15. *Globe and Mail*, February 10, 1981.

16. Note. Archives of Foreign Affairs Canada, RG 25-A-3-C 25-6, 20-CDA-16-1-4, vol. 11077, part 16.

17. Mark MacGuigan, *An Inside Look at External Affairs During the Trudeau Years* (Calgary: University of Calgary Press, 2002), 99.

18. *Globe and Mail*, January 30, 1981.

19. Ibid.

20. House of Commons, *First Report from Foreign Affairs Committee, Session 1980–1981, Vol. 1: British North America Acts, the Role of Parliament*, 37 and 111.

21. *Globe and Mail*, January 31, 1981.

22. *Globe and Mail*, January 30, 1981.

23. Note by Martin Berthoud, dated January 29, 1981. Document obtained from the Foreign Office following a freedom of information request.

24. Note by Lord Carrington to John Ford, dated January 30, 1981. Document obtained from the Foreign Office following a freedom of information request.

25. *Globe and Mail*, February 30, 1981.

26. Russell, *Constitutional Odyssey*, 118.

27. Interview with Kevin McNamara, November 22, 2005. McNamara was an MP who sat on Kershaw's committee.

28. English, *The Life of Pierre Elliott Trudeau, Vol. 2*, 51.

29. Ibid.

30. *Globe and Mail*, March 26, 1981.

31. Correspondence with John Finnis, January 9, 2009.

32. Ibid.

33. House of Commons, *Foreign Affairs Committee, Supplementary Report*, April 15, 1981, xviii.

34. Ibid., xxi.

35. The *Times* (London), April 27, 1981; *Daily Telegraph*, April 27, 1981.

36. Mark MacGuigan, *An Inside Look at External Affairs*, 95.

37. *Globe and Mail*, January 23, 1981.

38. Quoted by James Kelly, *Governing with the Charter: Legislative and Judicial Activism and Framer's Intent* (Vancouver: UBC Press, 2005), 60.

39. In *Charter versus Federalism: The Dilemmas of Constitutional Reform* (Montreal: McGill University Press, 1992). Alan C. Cairns completely rejects the idea of federalism as a product of a compact between colonies having become provinces. See Robert Vipond ("Whatever Became of the Compact Theory? Meech Lake and the New Politics of Constitutional Amendment in Canada," *Queen's Quarterly* 96, no. 4, 793–811) underlines, mistakenly, that the notion of compact had been absent in the debates surrounding patriation.

40. This phenomenon of collective amnesia on the constitution was well analyzed by Paul Romney in "Provincial Equality, Special Status and the Compact Theory of Canadian Confederation," *Canadian Journal of Political Science* 32, no. 1 (March 1999), 34.

41. House of Commons, *First Report from the Foreign Affairs Committee, Session 1980–1981, Vol. 2: Minutes of Evidence and Appendices*, 203.

42. Quote in a note. Archives of the Foreign Office, FCO 82/827.

43. House of Commons, *First Report from the Foreign Affairs Committee, Session 1980–1981, Vol. 2: Minutes of Evidence and Appendices*, 180.

44. Romanow, Whyte, and Leeson, *Canada ... Notwithstanding*, 264.

45. Correspondence with John Finnis, January 9, 2009.

46. Note. Archives of Foreign Affairs Canada, RG 25-A-3-C 25-6, 20-CDA-16-1-4, vol. 8723, part 5.

47. Ramsay Cook, *Provincial Autonomy, Minority Rights and the Compact Theory, 1867–1921*, Studies of the Royal Commission on Bilingualism and Biculturalism (Ottawa: Queen's Printer for Canada, 1969), 9.

48. Speech by Roy Megarry before the Royal Commonwealth Society in London, February 3, 1981. Document obtained from the Foreign Office following a freedom of information request.

49. Speech by Pierre Elliott Trudeau on the night of the referendum. Archives of Radio-Canada. Originally in French.

50. Burelle, *Pierre Elliott Trudeau*, 68.

51. Ibid., 25.

52. Ibid., 26.

53. Ibid., 72.

54. Note by Michael Palliser to John Ford, dated January 7, 1981. Document obtained from the Foreign Office following a freedom of information request.

55. Note by John Ford to the Foreign Office, dated February 3, 1981. Document obtained from the Foreign Office following a freedom of information request.

56. Note by Lord Carrington to John Ford, dated February 5, 1981. Document obtained from the Foreign Office following a freedom of information request.

57. Interview with John Ford, February 8, 2007.

58. *Globe and Mail*, February 6, 1981.

59. MacGuigan, *An Inside Look at External Affairs*, 98.

60. *Globe and Mail*, February 6, 1981.

61. Note. Archives of Foreign Affairs Canada. RG 25-A-3-C 25-6, 20-CDA-16-1-4, vol. 11077, part 14.

62. *Long live free Quebec!* is the usual translation of de Gaulle's phrase.

63. *Globe and Mail*, February 7, 1981.

64. Note by John Ford to the Foreign Office, dated February 6, 1981. Document obtained from the Foreign Office following a freedom of information request.

65. Note by John Ford to the Foreign Office, dated March 10, 1981. Document obtained from the Foreign Office following a freedom of information request.

CHAPTER 12: THE FEDS STRIKE BACK

1. Jean Chrétien, *Dans la fosse aux lions* (Montreal: Les Éditions de l'Homme, 1985), 183.

2. *Globe and Mail*, February 4, 1981.

3. *Globe and Mail*, February 10, 1981.

4. Note by Deputy Minister Peter Meekison to Minister Dick Johnston, dated February 24, 1981. Document obtained from the Ministry of International and Intergovernmental Relations of Alberta following a freedom of information request.

5. Interview with James McKibben, October 13, 2009.

6. *Globe and Mail*, February 27, 1981.

7. The reconstruction of this meeting between Jean Wadds and Francis Pym is based on two Canadian documents: a summary of a meeting, dated March 13, 1981, and a note by Michael Kirby to Pierre Elliott Trudeau, also dated March 13, 1981. Archives of Foreign Affairs Canada, RG 25-A-3-C 25-6, 20-CDA-16-1-4, vol. 11078, part 20.

8. Note by Michael Kirby to Pierre Elliott Trudeau, dated March 13, 1981. Archives of Foreign Affairs Canada, RG 25-A-3-C 25-6, 20-CDA-16-1-4, vol. 11078, part 20.

9. *Daily Telegraph*, March 30, 1981.

10. *Globe and Mail*, February 9, 1981.

11. Draft letter by Margaret Thatcher to David Ginsburg, dated April 13, 1981. Document obtained from the Foreign Office following a freedom of information request.

12. Note by Margaret Thatcher to Malcolm Fraser, dated April 7, 1981. Document obtained from the Foreign Office following a freedom of information request.

13. Romanow, Whyte, and Leeson, *Canada ... Notwithstanding*, 148.

14. Ibid.

15. Summary of meeting prepared by Christian Hardy, dated March 19, 1981. Archives of Foreign Affairs Canada, RG 25-A-3-C 25-6, 20-CDA-16-1-4, vol. 11078, part 19.

16. Ibid.

17. Romanow, Whyte, and Leeson, *Canada ... Notwithstanding*, 149.

18. Summary of meeting prepared by Christian Hardy, dated March 19, 1981. Archives of Foreign Affairs Canada, RG 25-A-3-C 25-6, 20-CDA-16-1-4, vol. 11078, part 19.

19. *Globe and Mail*, March 19, 1981.

20. Ibid.

21. *Globe and Mail*, March 21, 1981.

22. Note by James McKibben to Minister Dick Johnston, dated March 31, 1981. Document obtained from the Foreign Office following a freedom of information request.

23. Ibid.

24. Note by Sonny Ramphal to Lord Carrington, dated February 8, 1981. Document obtained from the Foreign Office following a freedom of information request.

25. Note by Jean Wadds sent to Ottawa, dated March 20, 1981. Archives of Foreign Affairs Canada, RG 25-A-3-C 25-6, 20-CDA-16-1-4, vol. 11078, part 21.

26. Note by Mark MacGuigan to Pierre Elliott Trudeau, undated. Archives of Foreign Affairs Canada, RG 25-A-3-C 25-6, 20-CDA-16-1-4, vol. 11078, part 19.

27. Ibid.

28. *Globe and Mail*, March 28, 1981.

29. Note. Archives of Foreign Affairs Canada, RG 25-A-3-C 25-6, 20-CDA-16-1-4, vol. 11078, part 21.

30. Jean Chrétien, *Straight from the Heart* (Toronto: Key Porter Books, 1985), 189.

31. The reconstitution of this discussion is based on the British summary produced by Martin Berthoud, dated March 31, 1981 (document obtained from the Foreign Office following a freedom of information request), and the Canadian summary (Archives of Foreign Affairs Canada, RG 25-A-3-C 25-6, 20-CDA-16-1-4, vol. 11078, part 21).

32. Ibid.

33. Note by John Ford to the Foreign Office, dated March 26, 1981. Document obtained from the Foreign Office following a freedom of information request.

34. This comment was written directly on John Ford's note, dated March 26, 1981.

35. Barry Strayer, *Canada's Constitutional Revolution* (Edmonton: University of Alberta Press, 2013), 173.

36. Ibid.

37. Quoted in Michael Mandel, *The Charter of Rights and the Legalization of Politics in Canada*, 28.

38. Summary of meeting obtained from the Foreign Office following a freedom of information request.

39. Sheppard and Valpy, *The National Deal*, 232.

40. Summary of a meeting between Mark MacGuigan and Lord Carrington, dated May 5, 1981. Archives of Foreign Affairs Canada, RG 25-A-3-C 25-6, 20-CDA-16-1-4, vol. 11078, part 24.

41. Note by Vivien Hughes, dated April 9, 1981. Document obtained from the Foreign Office following a freedom of information request.

42. Note by John Ford to the Foreign Office, dated April 27, 1981. Document obtained from the Foreign Office following a freedom of information request.

43. The reconstitution of this conversation is based on the British summary, dated April 16, 1981 (document obtained from the Foreign Office following a freedom of information request) and on the Canadian summary (Archives of Foreign Affairs Canada, RG 25-A- 3-C 25-6, 20-CDA-16-1-4, vol. 11079, part 29).

CHAPTER 13: QUEBEC AND ITS ALLIES

1. René Lévesque, *Attendez que je me rappelle ...* (Montreal: Québec Amérique, 1986), 425.
2. Ibid., 58.
3. Ibid., 428
4. Godin, *René Lévesque. L'homme brisé*, 112.
5. Ibid., 119.
6. Sheppard and Valpy, *The National Deal*, 191.
7. Godin, *René Lévesque: L'homme brisé*, 119.
8. Ibid., 431.
9. Quoted in Martine Tremblay, *Derrière les portes closes: René Lévesque et l'exercice du pouvoir (1976–1985)* (Montreal: Québec Amérique, 2006), 710.
10. Sheppard and Valpy, *The National Deal*, 190.
11. James Ross Hurley, *Amending Canada's Constitution: History, Processes, Problems and Prospects* (Ottawa: Ministry of Supply and Services, 1996), 50.
12. Sheppard and Valpy, *The National Deal*, 193.
13. Ibid.
14. Institute of Intergovernmental Relations, *Constitutional Patriation: The Lougheed-Lévesque Correspondence* (Kingston: Queen's University, 1999), 19.
15. Ibid., 29. In his answer to Lougheed's letter, Lévesque didn't contest his counterpart's version of events, admitting that he agreed "in principle" with it, "though certain nuances could be drawn."
16. Sheppard and Valpy, *The National Deal*, 192.
17. René Lévesque, *Attendez que je me rappelle ...*, 438–39.
18. Sheppard and Valpy, *The National Deal*, 194.
19. Institute of Intergovernmental Relations, *Constitutional Patriation*, 20.
20. Romanow, Whyte, and Leeson, *Canada ... Notwithstanding*, 132.
21. Correspondence with Louis Bernard, December 6, 2011.
22. Institute of Intergovernmental Relations, *Constitutional Patriation*, 20.
23. Morin, *Lendemains piégés*, 366.
24. Correspondence with Claude Morin, December 11, 2011.
25. Sheppard and Valpy, *The National Deal*, 195.
26. Correspondence with Louis Bernard, December 6, 2011.
27. Correspondence with Claude Morin, December 6, 2011.
28. Correspondence with Claude Morin, December 16, 2011.

29. René Lévesque, *Option Québec* (Montreal: Les Éditions de l'Homme, 1968), 19–20.

30. Interview by Pierre Elliott Trudeau with Luc Lavoie (TVA), April 16, 1981.

31. English, *The Life of Pierre Elliott Trudeau, Vol. 2*, 534.

CHAPTER 14: COUP AT THE COURT

1. Note by Martin Berthoud to Emery Davies, following the conversation between Francis Pym and David Collenette, dated May 15, 1981. Document obtained from the Foreign Office following a freedom of information request.

2. Ibid.

3. Note by Lord Carrington to Emery Davies, dated May 18, 1981. Document obtained from the Foreign Office following a freedom of information request.

4. Note. Archives of Foreign Affairs Canada. RG 25-A-3-C 25-6, 20-CDA-16-1-4, vol. 11078, part 26.

5. Summary of meeting between Murray Simons, Claude Morin, and Robert Normand, dated May 21, 1981. Document obtained from the Foreign Office following a freedom of information request.

6. Ibid.

7. Faculty of Law of the University of Toronto, *www.law. utoronto.ca/prosp_stdn_content.asp?itemPath=3/4/15/0/0&contentId =1299*.

8. Robert Sharpe, "Laskin and the Constitutional Protection of Rights and Freedoms," in Neil Finkelstein and Constance Backhouse, ed., *The Laskin Legacy: Essays in Commemoration of Chief Justice Bora Laskin* (Toronto: Irwin Law Inc., 2007), 116.

9. Mandel, *The Charter of Rights and the Legalization of Politics in Canada*, 26.

10. Ibid.

11. Jules Deschênes, *Sur la ligne de feu: autobiographie d'un juge en chef* (Montreal: Stanké, 1988), 481–82.

12. Summary of meeting between Judge Estey and John Ford, dated October 9, 1980. Archives of the Foreign Office, FCO 82/822.

13. Leslie Zines, *Constitutional Changes in the Commonwealth* (New York, Port Chester, Melbourne, and Sydney: Cambridge University Press, 1991), 13.

14. Speech by Bora Laskin before the Empire Club of Toronto, March 12, 1981. Document obtained from the Foreign Office following a freedom of information request.

15. Summary of discussion of the British Cabinet on the constitution,

obtained following a freedom of information request.

16. Note by Robert Armstrong to Michael Alexander, dated June 10, 1981. Document obtained following a freedom of information request.

17. Note by Lord Moran to the Foreign Office, dated June 25, 1981.

18. Note by Robert Armstrong, dated June 26, 1981. Document obtained from the Foreign Office following a freedom of information request.

19. Summary of meeting between Pierre Elliott Trudeau and Margaret Thatcher, dated June 26, 1981. Document obtained from the Foreign Office following a freedom of information request.

20. Ibid.

21. *Globe and Mail*, June 27 1981.

22. Note to Ottawa by the Canadian High Commission in London. Archives of Foreign Affairs Canada. RG 25-A-3-C 25-6, 20-CDA-16-1-4, vol. 11078, part 24.

23. Wikipedia, "Classified information in the United Kingdom," *en.wikipedia.org/wiki/Classified_information_in_the_United_Kingdom*.

24. Note by Lord Carrington to the British High Commission in Ottawa, dated July 2, 1981. Document obtained from the Foreign Office following a freedom of information request.

25. Note by Lord Moran to Lord Carrington, dated July 2, 1981. Document obtained from the Foreign Office following a freedom of information request.

26. Note by Ian Sinclair to Martin Berthoud, dated July 16, 1981. Document obtained from the Foreign Office following a freedom of information request.

27. Note by Robert Armstrong to Michael Alexander, dated July 9, 1981. Document obtained from the Foreign Office following a freedom of information request.

28. Note by Lord Moran to the Foreign Office, September 10, 1981. Document obtained from the Foreign Office following a freedom of information request.

29. Mandel, *The Charter of Rights and the Legalization of Politics in Canada*, 36.

30. Philip Girard, *Bora Laskin: Bringing Law to Life* (Toronto: University of Toronto Press, 2005), 504.

31. Interview with Peter Lougheed, April 12, 2011.

32. Correspondence with Claude Morin, September 2, 2011.

33. Thomas R. Berger, *One's Man Justice: A Life in the Law* (Seattle: University of Washington Press, 2002), 150.

34. Robert Sharpe, "Laskin and the Constitutional Protection of Rights and Freedoms," 126.

35. Roy McMurtry, "Laskin's Legacy to National Unity and Patriation," 89.

36. Ian Binnie, "Laskin's Legacy to the Supreme Court," in Neil Finkelstein and Constance Backhouse, eds., *The Laskin Legacy: Essays in Commemoration of Chief Justice Bora Laskin* (Toronto: Irwin Law Inc., 2007), 51, 57.

37. Ibid., 53.

38. Christopher Lasch, *The Revolt of the Elites and the Betrayal of Democracy* (New York/London: W.W. Norton & Co., 1995), 276.

39. Ibid., 26.

40. Ibid., 28.

41. Ibid.

42. Bradley Watson, "The Language of Rights and the Crisis of the Liberal Imagination," in Anthony A. Peacock, ed., *Rethinking the Constitution: Perspectives on Canadian Constitutional Reform, Interpretation, and Theory* (Don Mills, ON: Oxford University Press, 1996), 92.

43. Quote in Stéphane Bernatchez and Marc-André Russell, "Grandeur et misère de la théorie du dialogue en droit constitutionnel canadien," *Le droit public existe-t-il?*, 8, *dev.ulb.ac.be/droitpublic/index.php?id=26.*

44. Note by John Ford to Lord Carrington, dated April 30, 1981. Document obtained from the Foreign Office following a freedom of information request.

CHAPTER 15: NULL AND VOID

1. Note to Pierre Trudeau, dated June 16, 1981. Archives of Foreign Affairs Canada, RG 25-A-3-C 25-6, 20-CDA- 16-1-4, vol. 11078, part 26.

2. Summary of meeting between Lord Moran and Pierre Elliott Trudeau, dated June 16, 1981. Archives of Foreign Affairs Canada, RG 25-A-3-C 25-6, 20-CDA-16-1-4, vol. 11078, part 26.

3. Note by Lord Moran to London, dated July 1, 1981. Document obtained from the Foreign Office following a freedom of information request.

4. Note by Lord Moran, dated June 12, 1984. Document obtained from the Foreign Office following a freedom of information request.

5. *Globe and Mail*, September 1981.

6. Note by Lord Moran to London, dated September 18, 1981. Document obtained from the Foreign Office following a freedom of information request.

7. Note by Lord Moran to London, dated September 8, 1981. Document obtained from the Foreign Office following a freedom of information request.

8. Note by Lord Moran to the Foreign Office, dated July 6, 1981. Document obtained from the Foreign Office following a freedom of information request.

9. Note by Martin Berthoud to Derek Day, dated July 15, 1981. Document obtained from the Foreign Office following a freedom of information request.

10. Summary of meeting between Lord Carrington and Mark MacGuigan, dated September 18, 1981. Document obtained from the Foreign Office following a freedom of information request.

11. Note by Lord Moran to London, dated September 14, 1981. Document obtained from the Foreign Office following a freedom of information request.

12. Note by Martin Berthoud to Derek Day, dated September 23, 1981. Document obtained from the Foreign Office following a freedom of information request.

13. Note by Martin Berthoud to Lord Moran, dated September 25, 1981. Document obtained from the Foreign Office following a freedom of information request.

14. Note by Lord Moran to London, dated October 5, 1981. Document obtained from the Foreign Office following a freedom of information request.

15. Note. Archives of Foreign Affairs Canada, RG 25-A-3-C 25-6, 20-CDA-16-1-4, vol. 11078, part 27.

16. Article reprinted in a note sent to Ottawa by the Canadian High Commission in London, dated September 14, 1981. Archives of Foreign Affairs Canada, RG 25-A-3-C 25-6, 20-CDA-16-1-4, vol. 11078, part 27.

17. Information contained in two notes by the Canadian High Commission in London, sent to the Canadian delegation at the Commonwealth Summit in London, dated September 30, 1981, and October 2, 1981, bearing the mention "secret." Archives of Foreign Affairs Canada, RG 25-A-3-C 25-6, 20-CDA-16-1-4, vol. 11078, parts 27 and 28.

18. Interview with Jeremy Akerman, January 11, 2010.

19. Ibid.

20. Pierre Elliott Trudeau, *Memoirs* (Toronto: McClelland & Stewart, 1994), 316.

21. Some jurists, like Henri Brun, argue that the separation of power is a rule of law, not a convention.

22. Note by John Ford to the Foreign Office, dated May 7, 1981. Document obtained following a freedom of information request.

23. Mandel, *The Charter of Rights and the Legalization of Politics in Canada*, 35.

24. Stephen Clarkson and Christina McCall, *Trudeau and Our Times,* 2 vols. (Toronto: McClelland & Stewart, 1990), 281.

25. Maurice Agulhon, *Coup d'État et République* (Paris: Presses de la Fondation nationale des sciences politiques, 1997), 10.

26. Ibid.

27. Ibid, 9.

CHAPTER 16: THE LADY'S NOT FOR TURNING

1. Sheppard and Valpy, *The National Deal,* 250.

2. Ibid.

3. Romanow, Whyte, and Leeson, *Canada ... Notwithstanding,* 185.

4. Note by Lord Moran to the Foreign Office, dated September 29, 1981. Document obtained from the Foreign Office following a freedom of information request.

5. Note by Lord Moran to the Foreign Office, dated September 28, 1981. Document obtained from the Foreign Office following a freedom of information request.

6. Sheppard and Valpy, *The National Deal,* 250.

7. Mandel, *The Charter of Rights and the Legalization of Politics in Canada*, 33.

8. Note by Canadian High Commission in London, sent to the Canadian delegation at the Commonwealth Summit in Melbourne, dated October 2, 1981. Archives of Foreign Affairs, RG 25-A-3-C 25-6, 20-CDA-16-1-4, vol. 11078, part 28.

9. Sheppard and Valpy, *The National Deal,* 256.

10. Transcript of Trudeau's press conference. Document obtained from the Foreign Office following a freedom of information request.

11. Note by Robert Armstrong to Margaret Thatcher, dated October 4, 1981. Document obtained from the Foreign Office following a freedom of information request.

12. Note by Martin Berthoud, dated September 28, 1981. Document obtained from the Foreign Office following a freedom of information request.

13. Note by Lord Carrington to the British delegation at the Melbourne Commonwealth Summit, dated September 29, 1981.

14. The discussions were recreated thanks to a note by Lord Carrington sent to Melbourne on September 30, 1981, as well as a summary of meeting made the same day. Both documents were obtained from the Foreign Office following a freedom of information request.

15. Note by Lord Carrington sent to Melbourne on September 30, 1981. Document obtained from the Foreign Office following a freedom of information request.

16. This conversation was recreated thanks to a note by Robert Armstrong to Margaret Thatcher, dated October 4, 1981. Document obtained from the Foreign Office following a freedom of information request.

17. This part of the conversation was reported in a note by Robert Armstrong to Derek Days, dated October 19, 1981. Document obtained from the Foreign Office following a freedom of information request.

18. The meeting was re-created thanks to a summary dated October 5, 1981. Document obtained from the Foreign Office following a freedom of information request.

19. Note by Martin Berthoud, dated October 7, 1981. Document obtained from the Foreign Office following a freedom of information request.

20. Note by the Canadian High Commission sent to Ottawa, dated October 28, 1981. Archives of Foreign Affairs Canada, RG 25-A-3-C 25-6, 20-CDA-16-1-4, vol. 11478, part 29.

21. Note by Lord Moran sent to London, dated October 16, 1981. Document obtained by the Foreign Office following a freedom of information request.

22. Statement made to the press on October 2, 1981, quoted in a note by Lord Moran to the Foreign Office, dated the same day. Document obtained from the Foreign Office following a freedom of information request.

23. Interview with Jonathan Aitken, December 20, 2006.

24. Statement made on British television, transcribed in a note by the Foreign Office, dated October 19, 1981. Document obtained from the Foreign Office following a freedom of information request.

25. Note by the Canadian High Commission sent to Ottawa, dated October 19, 1981. Archives of Foreign Affairs Canada, RG 25-A-3-C 25-6, 20-CDA-16-1-4, vol. 11478, part 29.

26. Note by consul Murray Simons sent to London, dated October 1, 1981. Document obtained from the Foreign Office following a freedom of information request.

27. *New York Times*, October 3, 1981.

28. Note by Lord Moran to London, dated October 2, 1981. Document obtained from the Foreign Office following a freedom of information request.

29. Sheppard and Valpy, *The National Deal*, 257.

30. Ibid., 258.

31. Romanow, Whyte, and Leeson, *Canada … Notwithstanding*, 152.

32. *Globe and Mail*, October 19, 1981.

33. Ibid.

34. Note by Roderic Lyne, secretary to Lord Carrington, to Michael Alexander, diplomatic adviser to Margaret Thatcher, dated October 20, 1981. Document obtained from the Foreign Office following a freedom of information request.

35. Note by Stephen Gomersall, secretary to the Lord Privy Seal, to David Wright, secretary to Robert Armstrong, dated October 20, 1980. Document obtained from the Foreign Office following a freedom of information request.

36. Summary of conversation between Robert Armstrong and Michael Pitfield, dated January 20, 1981. Document obtained from the Foreign Office following a freedom of information request.

37. This conversation was reconstituted from the British summary, dated October 22, 1981 (Document obtained from the Foreign Office following a freedom of information request) and from Mark MacGuigan's memoirs, *An Inside Look at External Affairs During the Trudeau Years* (Calgary: University of Calgary Press, 2002), 101.

38. McGuigan, *An Inside Look at External Affairs*, 101–02.

39. Note by Lord Moran sent to London, dated October 21, 1981. Document obtained from the Foreign Office following a freedom of information request.

40. Note by Lord Moran sent to London, dated October 22, 1981. Document obtained from the Foreign Office following a freedom of information request.

41. Note by Ray Holloway sent to London, dated October 20, 1981. Document obtained from the Foreign Office following a freedom of information request.

42. This conversation was reconstituted thanks to the British summary, dated October 28, 1981 (Document obtained from the Foreign Office following a freedom of information request) and the Canadian summary (Archives of Foreign Affairs Canada, RG 25-A-3-C 25-6, 20-CDA-16-1-4, vol. 11478, part 28).

43. Note by the Canadian High Commission sent to Ottawa, dated October 27, 1981. Archives of Foreign Affairs Canada, RG 25-A-3-C 25-6, 20-CDA-16-1-4, vol. 11478, part 28.

44. Correspondence with John Finnis, January 9, 2009.

45. Note by Vivien Hughes to Martin Berthoud and Berry, dated October 30, 1981. Document obtained from the Foreign Office following a freedom of information request.

46. This conversation was reconstructed thanks to a note by Vivien Hughes to Martin Berthoud, dated October 29, 1981. Document obtained from the Foreign Office following a freedom of information request.

47. Note by Lord Carrington to Lord Moran, dated October 29, 1981. Document obtained from the Foreign Office following a freedom of information request.

48. Note by Lord Moran sent to London, dated October 30, 1981. Document obtained from the Foreign Office following a freedom of information request.

CHAPTER 17: PEACE THROUGH COMPROMISE

1. Interview with Jeremy Akerman, January 11, 2010.

2. Interview with Peter Lougheed, April 12, 2011.

3. Romanow, Whyte, and Leeson, *Canada ... Notwithstanding*, 152.

4. Allan Blakeney, *An Honourable Calling: Political Memoirs* (Toronto: University of Toronto Press, 2008), 182.

5. Ibid., 252.

6. Ibid., 177.

7. Note by Lord Moran to London, dated October 2, 1981. Document obtained from the Foreign Office following a freedom of information request.

8. Note by Michael Kirby to Pierre Elliott Trudeau, entitled "Pressure for Patriation: Carrots and Sticks," dated March 13, 1981. Archives of Foreign Affairs Canada, RG 25-A-3-C 25-6, 20-CDA-16- 1-4, vol. 11478, part 19.

9. Ibid.

10. Note by Murray Simons to the Foreign Office, dated October 9, 1981. Document obtained from the Foreign Office following a freedom of information request.

11. Pierre Elliott Trudeau, *Mémoires politiques* (Montreal: Éditions Le Jour, 1993), 286.

12. Note by Robert Armstrong to Margaret Thatcher, dated October 4, 1981. Document obtained from the Foreign Office following a freedom of information request.

13. Note by Lord Carrington to Lord Moran, dated October 7, 1981. Document obtained from the Foreign Office following a freedom of information request.

14. Note by Martin Berthoud to Lord Moran, dated October 23, 1981. Document obtained from the Foreign Office following a freedom of information request.
15. Note by Lord Moran to Martin Berthoud, dated October 29, 1981. Document obtained from the Foreign Office following a freedom of information request.
16. Note by Martin Berthoud to Lord Moran, dated November 3, 1981. Document obtained from the Foreign Office following a freedom of information request.
17. Note by Emery Davies to Lord Moran, who'd returned to London, dated November 4, 1981. Document obtained from the Foreign Office following a freedom of information request.
18. Sheppard and Valpy, *The National Deal*, 265.
19. Ibid., 266.
20. Institute of Intergovernmental Relations, *Constitutional Patriation: The Lougheed-Lévesque Correspondence* (Kingston: Queen's University, 1999), 22.
21. Ibid., 23.
22. Ibid.
23. Romanow, Whyte, and Leeson, *Canada ... Notwithstanding*, 194.
24. Ibid., 195.
25. Graham, *The Last Act*, 41.
26. Romanow, Whyte, and Leeson, *Canada ... Notwithstanding*, 199.
27. Sheppard and Valpy, *The National Deal*, 273.
28. Institute of Intergovernmental Relations, *Constitutional Patriation*, 23.
29. Sheppard and Valpy, *The National Deal*, 276.
30. Blakeney, *An Honourable Calling*, 187.
31. Graham, *The Last Act*, 83.
32. Romanow, Whyte, and Leeson, *Canada ... Notwithstanding*, 205.
33. Graham, *The Last Act*, 141.
34. Ibid., 163.
35. Ibid., 190.
36. Ibid., 119.
37. Sheppard and Valpy, *The National Deal*, 285–86.
38. Ibid., 287.
39. Ibid., 286.
40. Blakeney, *An Honourable Calling*, 187.
41. Correspondence with Brian Peckford, February 24, 2013.
42. Graham, *The Last Act*, 192.
43. Terence McKenna, *The Deal*, CBC documentary broadcast in 1990.

44. Trudeau, *Memoirs*, 324.

45. Ibid

46. Note by Emery Davies to Martin Berthoud, dated November 17, 1981. Document obtained from the Foreign Office following a freedom of information request. The importance of Callaghan's change of heart was also attested to, with a few nuances, by George Anderson, of Foreign Affairs Canada, in a conversation with Davies.

47. Mark MacGuigan, *An Inside Look at External Affairs During the Trudeau Years* (Calgary: University of Calgary Press, 2002), 101.

48. Trudeau, *Memoirs*, 324.

49. Godin, *René Lévesque: L'homme brisé*, 171.

50. Correspondence with Brian Peckford, February 24, 2013.

51. Ibid.

52. Sheppard and Valpy, *The National Deal*, 214.

53. Romanow, Whyte, and Leeson, *Canada … Notwithstanding*, 210.

54. Graham, *The Last Act*, 217.

55. Trudeau, *Memoirs*, 325.

56. Godin, *René Lévesque: L'homme brisé*, 183.

57. Burelle, *Pierre Elliott Trudeau*, 361.

58. Godin, *René Lévesque: L'homme brisé*,-186.

59. Ibid.

60. Ibid., 171.

61. Institute of Intergovernmental Relations, *Constitutional Patriation*, 29.

62. Ibid.

63. Sheppard and Valpy, *The National Deal*, 33.

64. Ibid., 211.

65. Blakeney, *An Honourable Calling*, 189.

66. Terence McKenna, *The Deal*, documentary.

67. Comment by Brian Peckford made at the Conference Board de Toronto, *Globe and Mail*, May 7, 1980.

68. Sheppard and Valpy, *The National Deal*, 318.

CHAPTER 18: GOD BLESS MARGARET THATCHER

1. English, *The Life of Pierre Elliott Trudeau, Vol. 2*, 509.

2. Note. Archives of Foreign Affairs Canada, RG 25-A-3-C 25-6, 20-CDA-16-1-4, vol. 11478, part 30.

3. Pierre Elliott Trudeau, *Lac Meech: Trudeau parle ...*, texts collated and presented by Donald Johnston (Montreal: HMH, 1989), 59.

4. Sheppard and Valpy, *The National Deal*, 307.

5. Ibid., 305.

6. Allan Blakeney, *An Honourable Calling: Political Memoirs* (Toronto: University of Toronto Press, 2008), 192.

7. Sheppard and Valpy, *The National Deal*, 307.

8. Ron Graham, *The Last Act: Pierre Trudeau, the Gang of Eight and the Fight for Canada* (Toronto: Penguin, 2011), 219.

9. Ibid., 307.

10. Sheppard and Valpy, *The National Deal*, 303.

11. This conversation was reconstructed thanks to a summary of the meeting (Archives of Foreign Affairs Canada, RG 25-A-3-C 25-6, 20-CDA-16-1-4, vol. 11478, part 30) and a British summary of meeting (document obtained from the Foreign Office following a freedom of information request), both dated December 3, 1981.

12. Note by Lord Moran sent to London, dated December 3, 1981. Document obtained from the Foreign Office following a freedom of information request.

13. The conversation was reconstructed thanks to a British summary of meeting, dated December 3, 1981. Document obtained from the Foreign Office following a freedom of information request.

14. Sheppard and Valpy, *The National Deal*, 310.

15. Note by Vivien Hughes to Martin Berthoud, dated November 9, 1981. Document obtained from the Foreign Office following a freedom of information request.

16. Note by James McKibben to Jacques Frémont, dated November 19, 1981. Archives of Jacques Frémont.

17. Note by Chris Watts sent to the Secretariat of Federal and Intergovernmental Affairs of Canada, dated November 11, 1981. Document obtained from the Foreign Office following a freedom of information request.

18. Note by the Canadian High Commission in London sent to Foreign Affairs in Ottawa, dated November 18, 1981. Archives of Foreign Affairs Canada, RG 25-A-3-C 25-6, 20-CDA-16-1-4, vol. 11478, part 30.

19. Interview with Bruce George, January 4, 2013.

20. Note. Canadian High Commission in London sent to Foreign Affairs Canada, dated December 4 1981. Archives of Foreign Affairs Canada, RG 25-A-3-C 25-6, 20-CDA-16-1-4, vol. 11478, part 31.

21. *Globe and Mail*, December 22, 1981.

22. This information was contained in a note by Michael Kirby to Pierre Elliott Trudeau, dated December 30, 1981. Archives of Foreign Affairs Canada, RG 25-A-3-C 25-6, 20-CDA- 16-1-4, vol. 11478, part 31.

23. This information was contained in a note by the Canadian High Commission in London sent to Ottawa, dated December 23, 1981. Archives of Foreign Affairs Canada, RG 25-A-3-C 25-6, 20-CDA- 16-1-4, vol. 11478, part 31.

24. Note by Michael Kirby to Pierre Elliott Trudeau, dated January 11, 1982. Archives of Foreign Affairs Canada, RG 25-A-3-C 25-6, 20-CDA-16-1-4, vol. 11478, part 32. The meeting between Jean Wadds and Francis Pym was reconstructed thanks to a note by the Canadian High Commission, also dated January 11, 1982.

25. Note by Michael Kirby to Pierre Elliott Trudeau, dated December 30, 1981. Archives of Foreign Affairs Canada, RG 25-A-3-C 25-6, 20-CDA-16-1-4, vol. 11478, part 31.

26. Note by Pierre Elliott Trudeau to Margaret Thatcher, dated January 13, 1982. Archives of Foreign Affairs Canada, RG 25-A-3-C 25-6, 20-CDA-16-1-4, vol. 11478, part 32.

27. Document (originally in French) reproduced in Claude Morin, *Lendemains piégés: Du référendum à la nuit des longs couteaux* (Montreal: Boréal, 1988), 360.

28. This draft letter was contained in a note by the Canadian High Commission in London sent to Foreign Affairs Canada, dated December 22, 1981. Archives of Foreign Affairs Canada, RG 25-A-3-C 25-6, 20-CDA-16-1-4, vol. 11478, part 31.

29. Note by Lord Moran to the Foreign Office, dated December 29, 1981. Document obtained from the Foreign Office following a freedom of information request.

30. Internal Foreign Office note, dated December 21, 1981. Document obtained from the Foreign Office following a freedom of information request.

31. Note by De Montigny Marchand to Mark MacGuigan, dated December 22, 1981. Archives of Foreign Affairs Canada, RG 25-A-3-C 25-6, 20-CDA-16-1-4, vol. 11478, part 31.

32. The author did not recover the first draft note by the Foreign Office submitted to Thatcher.

33. Note by Roderic Lyne to 10 Downing Street, dated December 30, 1981. Document obtained from the Foreign Office following a freedom of information request.

34. Note by Margaret Thatcher to René Lévesque, dated January 13, 1982. Archives of Foreign Affairs Canada, RG 25-A-3-C 25-6, 20-CDA-16-1-4, vol. 11478, part 32.

35. Morin, *Lendemains piégés*, 318.

EPILOGUE: THE BATTLE OF CANADA

1. Note by Lord Moran to London, dated December 3, 1981. Document obtained from the Foreign Office following a freedom of information request.

2. He would confide this to Roy Romanow, according to the former deputy minister of Saskatchewan John Whyte, *Toronto Star*, November 10, 2011.

3. Burelle, *Pierre Elliott Trudeau*, 89.

4. Mandel, *The Charter of Rights and the Legalization of Politics in Canada*, 88.

5. F.L. Morton and Rainer Knopff, *The Charter Revolution and the Court Party* (Peterborough, ON: University of Toronto Press, 2000), 134.

6. *Globe and Mail*, February 15, 1986.

7. *Globe and Mail*, April 27, 1988.

8. Mandel, *The Charter of Rights and the Legalization of Politics in Canada*, 93.

9. Ibid., 94.

10. James Ross Hurley confided this to the author in two phone interviews, one of which was on February 14, 2012.

11. *The Gazette*, April 26, 1990.

12. Mandel, *The Charter of Rights and the Legalization of Politics in Canada*, 98.

13. Thomas S. Axworthy and Pierre Elliott Trudeau, *Towards a Just Society: The Trudeau Years* (Markham, ON: Penguin, 1992), 416.

14. Mandel, *The Charter of Rights and the Legalization of Politics in Canada*, 407.

AFTERWORD: THE BATTLE FOR TRUTH

1. *http://fullcomment.nationalpost.com/2013/04/29/thomas-mulcair-latch-es-onto-an-alleged-conspiracy-going-back-decades/*. Accessed July 25, 2014.

2. *www.lapresse.ca/actualites/politique/politique-canadienne/201309/24/ 01-4692847-les-conservateurs-veulent-creer-un-nouvel-elan-patriotique. php*. Accessed July 25, 2014.

3. *http://1812.gc.ca/eng/1305654894724/1305655293741*. Accessed July 25, 2014.

4. *www.ledevoir.com/politique/canada/353216/le-canada-fait-pietre-figure*. Accessed July 25, 2014.

5. *www.ledevoir.com/politique/canada/380560/appel-des-historiens-rapatriement-de-la-constitution-l-acces-aux-archives-est-essentiel*. Accessed July 25, 2014.

6. *www.lapresse.ca/actualites/politique/politique-canadienne/201306/11/01-4660102-ottawa-veut-promouvoir-lhistoire-canadienne.php* [original in French].

7. *http://quebec.huffingtonpost.ca/2013/04/11/constitution-opinion-justin-trudeau_n_3064262.html* [original in French].

8. *www.theglobeandmail.com/globe-debate/canadas-constitutional-dramas-cracked-jaws-in-london-from-yawning/article11417293/*.

9. *www.huffingtonpost.ca/bob-rae/patriating-the-constitution_b_3306744.html*.

10. *http://fullcomment.nationalpost.com/2013/05/09/william-johnson-on-quebec/*.

11. The SSHRC gave $59,000 for a project on this topic to historian Donica Belisle of Athabasca University in Alberta.

12. Historian and former Liberal MP John English received $72,000 for such a project.

BIBLIOGRAPHY

PRIMARY SOURCES

Archives of the Foreign Office (Ministry of Foreign Affairs of the United Kingdom)

Archives of the Cabinet Office (British Privy Council)

Archives of the Ministry of Foreign Affairs Canada

Archives of the Executive Council of Quebec

Archives of the Ministry of International and Intergovernmental Relations of Alberta

Jacques Frémont's personal archives

Correspondence between Peter Lougheed and René Lévesque published by the Institute of Intergovernmental Relations at Queen's University, 1999, 39.

INTERVIEWS AND CORRESPONDENCE WITH FIRST-HAND WITNESSES

Jonathan Aitken

Jeremy Akerman

Robert Armstrong

Louis Bernard

Martin Berthoud

André Burelle

Ken Curtis

John Finnis
John Ford
Jacques Frémont
Daniel Gagnier
Bruce George
Eddie Goldenberg
James Hurley Ross
Michael Kirby
Gilles Loiselle
Peter Lougheed
James McKibben
Kevin McNamara
Claude Morin
Robert Normand
Brian Peckford
Norman Spector

MEMOIRS

Blakeney, Allan. *An Honourable Calling: A Political Memoirs*. Toronto: University of Toronto Press, 2008.

Lévesque, René. *Attendez que je me rappelle*. Montreal: Québec Amérique, 1986.

MacGuigan, Mark. *An Inside Look at External Affairs During the Trudeau Years*. Calgary: University of Calgary Press, 2002.

Morin, Claude. *Lendemains piégés: Du référendum à la nuit des longs couteaux*. Montreal: Boréal, 1988.

——————. *Mes premiers ministres*. Montreal: Boréal, 1991.

Robertson, Gordon. *Memoirs of a Very Civil Servant: Mackenzie King to Trudeau*. Toronto: University of Toronto Press, 2000.

Romanow, Roy, John Whyte, and Howard Leeson. *Canada ... Notwithstanding: The Making of the Constitution, 1976–1982*. Agincourt, ON: Carswell/Methuan, 1984.

Thatcher, Margaret. *The Downing Street Years*. New York: HarperCollins, 1993.

Trudeau, Pierre Elliott. *Memoirs*. Toronto: McClelland & Stewart, 1994.

Trudeau, Pierre Elliott, and Thomas S. Axworthy. *Towards a Just Society: The Trudeau Years*. Toronto: Markham Penguin Books, 1992.

MONOGRAPHS

Agulhon, Maurice. *Coup d'État et République.* Paris: Presses de la Fondation nationale des sciences politiques, 1997.

Behiels, M. *Prelude to Quebec's Quiet Revolution: Liberalism Versus Neo-Nationalism, 1945–1960.* Montreal/Kingston: McGill-Queen's University Press, 2003.

Berger, Thomas R. *One's Man Justice: A Life in the Law.* Seattle: University of Washington Press, 2002.

Bernard, André, and Bernard Descôteaux. *Québec: Élections 1981.* Montreal: HMH, 1981.

Burelle, André. *Pierre Elliott Trudeau: L'intellectuel et le politique.* Montreal: Fides, 2005.

Cairns, Alan C. *Charter Versus Federalism: The Dilemmas of Constitutional Reform.* Montreal/Kingston: McGill-Queen's University Press, 1992.

Campbell, John. *Margaret Thatcher, Vol. 1: The Grocer's Daughter.* London: Vintage Books, 2007.

——————. *Margaret Thatcher, Vol. 2: The Iron Lady.* London: Vintage Books, 2007.

Cook, R. "Provincial Autonomy, Minority Rights and the Compact Theory, 1867–1921." *Studies of the Royal Commission on Bilinguism and Biculturalism.* Ottawa, 1969.

Dickason, Olive Patricia. *Les Premières Nations du Canada: Depuis les temps les plus lointains jusqu'à nos jours.* Quebec: Septentrion, 1996.

Doern, G. Bruce. *The Politics of Energy: The Development and Implementation of the National Energy Policy.* Toronto: Methuen, 1985.

English, John. *The Life of Pierre Elliott Trudeau, Vol. 1: Citizen of the World, 1919–1968.* Toronto: Knopf Canada, 2006.

——————. *The Life of Pierre Elliott Trudeau, Vol. 2: Just Watch Me, 1968–2000.* Toronto: Knopf Canada, 2009.

Girard, Philip, and Bora Laskin. *Bringing Law to Life.* Toronto: University of Toronto Press, 2005.

Godin, Pierre. *René Lévesque: L'espoir et le chagrin.* Montreal: Boréal, 2001.

——————. *René Lévesque: L'homme brisé.* Montreal: Boréal, 2005.

Graham, Ron. *The Last Act: Pierre Trudeau, the Gang of Eight, and the Fight for Canada.* Toronto: Penguin, 2011.

Granatstein, J.L., and Robert Bothwell. *Pirouette: Pierre Trudeau and Canadian Foreign Policy.* Toronto: University of Toronto Press, 1991.

Hillmer, Norman, and J.L. Granatstein. *Empire to Umpire: Canada and the World to the 1990s*. Toronto: Copp Clark Longman, 1990.

Hurley Ross, James. *Amending Canada's Constitution: History, Processes, Problems and Prospects*. Ottawa: Minister of Supply and Services, 1996.

Kelly, J. *Governing with the Charter: Legislative and Judicial Activism and Framer's Intent*. Vancouver: UBC Press, 2005.

Lasch, Christopher. *The Revolt of the Elites and the Betrayal of Democracy*. New York/London: W.W. Norton & Company, 1995.

Mandel, Michael. *The Charter of Rights and the Legalization of Politics in Canada*. Toronto: Thompson Educational Publishing, 1994.

McRoberts, K. *Misconceiving Canada: The Struggle for National Unity*. Don Mills, ON: Oxford University Press, 1997.

McWhinney, Edward. *Canada and the Constitution*. Toronto: University of Toronto Press, 1982.

Morton, F., and R. Knopff. *The Charter Revolution and the Court Party*. Toronto: University of Toronto Press, 2000.

Peacock, Anthony A., ed. *Rethinking the Constitution: Perspectives on Canadian Constitutional Reform, Interpretation, and Theory*. Don Mills, ON: Oxford University Press, 1996.

Roy, Jean-Louis. *Le Choix d'un pays: Le débat constitutionnel Québec Canada, 1960–1976*. Montreal: Leméac, 1978.

Russell, Peter H. *Constitutional Odyssey: Can Canadians Become a Sovereign People?* Toronto: University of Toronto Press, 2004.

Sheppard, Robert, and Michael Valpy. *The National Deal: The Fight for a Canadian Constitution*. Toronto: Macmillan, 1982.

Sowell, Thomas. *A Conflict of Visions: Ideological Origins of Political Struggles*. New York: Basic Books, 2007.

Tierney, Stephen, ed. *Multiculturalism and the Canadian Constitution*. Vancouver: UBC Press, 2007.

Trudeau, Pierre Elliott. *Lac Meech. Trudeau parle ... Texts collated and presented by Donald Johnston*. Montreal: HMH, 1989.

Wapshot, Nicolas. *Ronald Reagan and Margaret Thatcher: A Political Marriage*. New York: Markham Penguin Books, 2007.

JOURNAL ARTICLES

Abernathy, G. "Should the United Kingdom Adopt a Bill of Rights." *The American Journal of Comparative Law* 31, no. 3 (1983): 431–79.

Ajzenstat, Janet. "Reconciling Parliament and Rights: A.V. Dicey Reads the Canadian Charter of Rights and Freedoms." *Canadian Journal of Political Science/Revue canadienne de science politique* 30, no. 4 (December 1997): 645–62.

Bernatchez, Stéphane, and Marc-André Russell. "Grandeur et misère de la théorie du dialogue en droit constitutionnel canadien." Article taken from *Le droit public existe-t-il*, page 62 (*dev.ulb.ac.be/droit public/index.php?id=26*).

Lippman, M. "The Debate Over a Bill of Rights in Great Britain: The View from Parliament." *Universal Human Rights* 2, no. 4 (1980): 25–42.

Romney, P. "Provincial Equality, Special Status, and the Compact Theory of Canadian Confederation." *Canadian Journal of Political Science/ Revue canadienne de science politique* 32, no. 1 (March 1999): 21–39.

Uberoi, Varun. "Multiculturalism and the Canadian Charter of Rights and Freedoms." *Political Studies* 57 (2009): 805–27.

Vipond, R. "Whatever Became of the Compact Theory? Meech Lake and the New Politics of Constitutional Amendment in Canada." *Queen's Quarterly* 96, no. 4 (1989): 793–811.

INDEX